Semantic
Anthropology

Association of Social Anthropologists
A Series of Monographs

A. S. A. MONOGRAPH 22

Semantic Anthropology

Edited by

DAVID PARKIN

School of Oriental and African Studies
University of London, UK

ACADEMIC PRESS, INC.

(Harcourt Brace Jovanovich, Publishers)

London   Orlando   San Diego   New York
Toronto   Montreal   Sydney   Tokyo

ACADEMIC PRESS INC. (LONDON) LTD.
24/28 Oval Road,
London NW1

United States Edition published by
ACADEMIC PRESS, INC.
Orlando, Florida 32887

$c\,c$

312020

British Library Cataloguing in Publication Data
Semantic anthropology.—(Association of Social
Anthropologists monographs; 22)
1. Semantics—Congresses
I. Parkin, David   II. Series
412   P325

ISBN 0-12-545180-6

PRINTED IN THE UNITED STATES OF AMERICA

84 85 86 87   9 8 7 6 5 4 3 2

PREFACE

The previous ASA conference dedicated to the problems of language use and interpretation was held at Sussex University in 1969, the proceedings being published as *Social Anthropology and Language*, edited by Edwin Ardener, 1971. A general feature of that volume may be contrasted with the situation today. A high proportion of the contributors were linguists or anthropologists who saw themselves as "linguistic". The study of language and the study of society by anthropologists were regarded as separate endeavours, and it was primarily left to the editor to consider the implications of the movement from a) the anthropological use of language as a tool either of fieldwork or of understanding the apparent exotica of the "other", to b) the idea that theories about language might tell us something about theories of society; and that theories about language and about society were paradigmatically the same.

This preparedness to take Lévi-Strauss and his Saussurian values at his inspirational roots, shaped much of the most interesting developments of the seventies. Crick's book in 1976, *Explorations in Language and Meaning*, carried this further, raising, both implicitly and explicitly, many of the themes pursued in the chapters of the present volume: how our explanations are as semantically engulfing as are those of the people we seek to explain; how unwittingly we impose semantic shapes on the ethnographic data we claim to extract from other societies; and how, if we could only recognize this, we might exploit this common feature of "us" and "them" as self-defining meaning-makers.

From these and other sources, anthropological but also linguistic and philosophical, other concerns flowed. For example, if our own semantic webs shape the way we explain others, then how do we ever translate? Do we assume some areas of cultural behaviour as in some way premissed on universalistic principles, and some as purely relativistic, and if so in which proportions, and how do we recognize them? What credence do we in fact give to verbal statements by the people themselves as against our often intuitive insistence on what we perceive to be their "real" truths? How critical are we of our own supposedly authoritarian pronouncements on other societies? Anthropology may be intended as a mirror for mankind but how much do the person categories that we describe for other societies really mirror, in a sadly unidimensional way, our own categories? How, in view of this, do we continue to justify the dichotomy of subject and object?

While these questions arose out of a concern with language use and with theories about society taken from linguistics, they are now being answered in a manner that no longer requires such disciplinary distinctions. Semantic anthropology, the title of the ASA conference held at Durham from March 30 to April 2 1982 on which this volume is based, *is* social anthropology. It does seek for ideas in other disciplines, but confidently turns to its own body of accumulating ideas, its ethnography, for its major inspirations.

A major implication is that certain seemingly safe structuralist premises have come under scrutiny: the relation between signifier and signified appears too self-sealed a system for a discipline that now lets its informants speak for themselves rather than see the meaning by which their behaviour is guided as being generated by a cultural semiotic of underlying rules and classifications; this "new" arbitrariness of the relationship between signifier and signified, even if this distinction can continue to be sustained, suggests that we may, after all, have to concede some intentionality in the way people give meaning to objects, events, and emotions; intentionality obliges us to take seriously the view of person as self-defining, a problem which takes us back to many earlier pre-functionalist concerns of the kind dealt with by Dilthey and even Kirkegaard. From a view of interpretation which, so to speak, had objects out there waiting for their meanings to be revealed, we have moved to a view of interpretation as a creative process rather than one of discovery of the static.

"Creativity" is, admittedly, a very slippery concept, and has caused, and will continue to cause, us a great deal of trouble, much as the notion of "meaning" has over the generations. But we cannot run away from its implications as a motivating factor in social anthropology, just because we cannot agree on how to define it.

This is not to suggest that we fall into the ghastly trap of advocating an anthropology of free-for-all, anything-goes creativity, in which ethnographers, authors, and the people they study are happily portrayed as knowing no bounds in their euphoric quest for self-determination. Such boundless self-determination has its less happy corollary of the bounded determination of others. It is unlikely, in other words, that we can ignore the role of rules in social life. Rather, it is that we should re-assess, perhaps, what it is *we mean* when we talk of rule-governed behaviour — what kinds of rules, what autonomy can rules have, since they are, in the end, ideas (theirs and ours) which are transacted, sought after, and sometimes imposed? In other words, considerations of "power" and of "materiality", perhaps re-defined, remain central concerns.

The study of language may draw relevance from three general areas which are covered by the chapters in this volume: language as an entrée into our own and other cultural epistemologies and metaphysics; language as inseparably constituted *with* and not independently *by* action; and the uncovering, through a self-critical look at anthropological language, of our own assumptions, presuppositions, and even prejudices.

An especially deep debt of gratitude is due to Dr Bill Wilder, of Durham University, for organizing the conference at Collingwood College, and to Dr Ralph Grillo, the secretary of the ASA, for providing so much help in more general organization. Of the seventeen paper-givers at the conference no less than ten were from overseas universities, principally North American. This high proportion is unprecedented in ASA conferences but may be taken as a healthy reflection of the fact that the issues discussed can no longer be said to stem solely from a distinctively British social anthropology. Only one contributor, Dr W. M. O'Barr, preferred to place his paper elsewhere, feeling, quite rightly, that it did not address itself to the main concerns of the conference, interesting though it was. The chairpersons of individual sessions were Edwin Ardener, Nigel Barley, John Blacking, Joanna Overing Kaplan, and Andrew Strathern. These were joined by Sir Raymond Firth in a final, and most fruitful, summing-up session, chaired by the conference convenor, who thanks them and the paper-givers for their enthusiasm and support. Finally, thanks are due to the British Academy for a contribution towards the transportation costs of one of the paper-givers, to Sarah Matthews for commenting on the Introduction, and to the staff of Academic Press.

September 1982   David Parkin

CONTENTS

INTRODUCTION

DAVID PARKIN

Society and Language: Analogy or Essence?

The much-celebrated shift in social anthropology from a concern with "function" to an interest in "meaning" is spoken of in various ways. They hardly need to be repeated here. There are, however, a number of muddles remaining. In rejecting the idea of society as a body or machine, amenable in its workings to the investigative tenets of a positivistic science, scholars have brought in two broad but complementary assumptions which they have not yet disentangled: society is *like* language; society *is* language. Though rarely, if ever, identified in these terms, the two assumptions are implicit, often within the same analysis.

Lévi-Stauss's early claim that society could be seen to operate like a linguistic system did not in fact repulse the positivistic view of society as an object to be studied nor of social anthropology as, in some way, a science. But he reminded us that "science" could refer to systematic comparison and thence to systematic interpretation and need not deal, as if in a chemist's laboratory, with the application of laws to unresponsive phenomena. In applying our minds to the analysis of culture, itself a product of mind, we were at least bringing ourselves into focus, even if, as so-called post-structuralist critics have argued, we were not reflexive enough.

More generally, it is for his analogy of society with language that Lévi-Strauss inspired and continues to inspire a vast array of often detailed ethnographic studies which view cultures as communicating at various levels of intelligibility. However, as the stock of purely linguistic concepts failed quite to fit the ethnographic common-sense explanation, or as concepts in linguistics themselves changed, so the analogy weakened. As if in desperation the analogy gave way to the essence: society-like-language became society as a communication model (i.e. society *as* language). With "generative model" and "systems", with computers and cybernetics, we were almost back to machines. The dissatisfactions with the structuralist method became expressed tentatively and not always whole-heartedly, as if to betray the one might be to bring back the other.

The dissatisfactions overlap and can be summarised as follows: an over-emphasis on determining structures denies man's central role as a self-defining species; the view that meaning results from relations between signs limits our recognition of the human capacity to initiate interpretation; the distancing of the investigator as subject from the rules of signification as object lessons our willingness consciously to include ourselves as objects; the quest is premissed on fundamental structures of the human mind which presupposes a degree of cognitive universalism that is more presumed than demonstrated; and the special emphasis placed on the unconsciousness of mental creativity, (i.e. on our "uninvited guest"), artificially separates thought from bodily emotion in the act of creation.

One cannot blame a whole method for these alleged shortcomings any more than one can blame Lévi-Strauss, in whose works there is scattered recognition of these problems. Rather, this is what the various kinds of structuralism came to represent. The very term "structuralism" created its own epistemological impasse. The expressed dissatisfactions may well be unfair to a degree. But they have found backers in the humanities and have already coalesced as the critical assumptions of a range of alternative approaches which are supposed to differ from each other but which do so only in procedural minutiae and never in their grander claims. Thus, as well as post-structuralism, we now have (resurrected) hermeneutics, deconstructivism, criticial theory, phenomenology, interpretivism, and, in social anthropology itself, semantic anthropology.

Of course, the proponents of these approaches will protest their differences, which are, indeed, often brilliantly illuminating. Even within a supposedly single approach, as Hobart shows with reference to hermeneutics, the ferocity of debate makes the notion of a single approach more akin to personal idiosyncrasy than collective enterprise (*infra*: 47). But at the level of the grander claim, the not always explicit intention is to deny that an "essence" determines behaviour and thought and even to deny altogether the validity of such dichotomies as "essence" and "appearance". The persuasiveness of such explanatory dichotomies is illustrated in this volume by Gudeman and Penn (*infra*: 91), in their discussion of Universal and Local models. Many dichotomies parallel that of essence and appearance, including that discussed by Gudeman and Penn, and those between deep and surface structure, linguistic competence and performance, rules and behaviour, paradigm and syntagm, and, most notably, that of Saussure between *langue* and *parole*. Ardener was able over a decade ago to refer to this latter as the master exemplar of a whole range of such dichotomies in the social sciences and humanities 1971b: xxxii). And there is no doubt as to the intellectual force it has exerted on us. It made structuralism possible, and now it is under attack. By implication, all explanation premissed on the analysis of relational opposition is questioned also.

Are the deconstructivists, then, really ushering in a new era of post-binary bliss, to adapt Sturrock's whimsical expression (1982: 734)? Have we begun to withdraw the privileged place once given to underlying rules in governing conduct? How far do we now view "meaning" not as given us by systems of signs but as placed by ourselves on and through the objects and acts we see and experience?

Insofar as a concern with binary oppositions, rules, and systems, etc., has epistemologically been bound up with explanations of how society works its effects on us, it is true that anthropologists have been much engaged in reversing this priority. Alongside the concern in semantic anthropology with man as active meaning-maker more than as passive recipient, there have been a number of studies recently on the anthropology of selfhood and on personal identity, including the way in which names do more than reflect and classify but also create experiences (Ardener 1975a; Burridge 1978; Epstein 1978; Gell 1979; Beattie 1980; Lienhardt 1980; Rosaldo 1980; Tonkin 1980; Heelas and Lock 1981; and Barnes, Hastrup and Willis (*infra*)).

A recent critical shift has been from explanation to description. While this is a matter of degree, the movement away from functionalism has lessened our preparedness to explain how the "other" works in favour of describing it. Ethnographically sensitive monographs are deemed to be those which do not impose theoretical models to the extent of distorting the way people "really" think and act. This leads easily into a defence of cultural relativism and a refutation of the relevance of seeking universals. It also encourages the idea of extending the ethnographical sensitivity to include the anthropologist him/herself (e.g. Rabinow 1977; Cesara 1982). Reflexivity comes to refer not just to the ethnographer reflecting on his fieldwork and the manner in which field "data" are eventually turned into books (Crick *infra*: 16), but also to the fieldworker reflecting upon himself in the midst of the members of the society he is supposed to be studying, who in turn reflect both upon themselves and the anthropologist, and possibly upon the books he writes about them, and so on. This ontological hall of mirrors hardly requires scientific explanation, we tell ourselves. It requires the fine art of latticed description. The weaving of the descriptive pattern may become the aesthetic end rather than the analytical means. Some may question whether this stylistic quest, so readily associated with the interpretative elegance of Geertz (1973), is enough.

For instance, are we to ignore the fact that "they" (the "other") *do* sometimes wish to explain to themselves how things work and have causes, often by pointing out correct rules of behaviour, as Sansom demonstrates among an Australian Aborigine group (*infra*). It may well be true that, through our fixations on Zande granaries and the like, anthropologists have exaggerated the explanatory proclivities of others and even of ourselves (for, except when we are being anthropologists or scientists, we are usually content not to explain but simply to describe). But that other people do sometimes adopt mechanistic as well as ontological explanations of phenomena should remain an important concern for us.

Can we, then, describe "their" explanations without converting our descriptions into explanations? Even when we report their explanation in indirect speech, e.g. "They say/claim that twins are birds; that envy causes witchcraft; that men do not have a physiological role in procreation; etc.", we imply a possible alternative explanation. It is, therefore, impossible to report other peoples' explanations as neutral description, unless we accept at face value all that they say and simply reproduce the statement; twins are birds among Nuer; envy causes witchcraft among Azande; etc.

Does this matter? It may not if we can show that the distinction between description and explanation is here false. For a novelist to open his book with a description of a rapid gathering of heavy, black clouds, is to imply that these are some of the conditions that explain the occurrence of storms. Such description is always implicit explanation. Explicit explanation, by corollary, is that description which openly links cause and effect: heavy clouds indicate a late stage in the process of transpiration which causes storms. Hobart's example (*infra*: 41), "Those black clouds *mean* rain" combines both types: explicit and implicit explanation, i.e. clouds *cause* rain, or, clouds *signify* rain.

Here then, "meaning" is both description and explanation as conventionally understood. It is this ambivalence in the English usage of "meaning", implying both explanation and description, which made it the fashionable catch-word in the so-called transition in social anthropology from functionalism to structuralism and post-structuralism. First, institutions had functions which enabled society to work. This was the meaning (i.e. intention) of social institutions, and people believed in them. Then, meaning became not what society gives people, but rather what people create to make sense of society, i.e. to describe society meaningfully and therefore satisfactorily.

The first is explanatory meaning and the second descriptive meaning. Phrased differently the first is meaning used as part of explicit explanation, while the second is meaning existing as a source of intellectual and aesthetic satisfaction in its own right, and only implicitly illuminating how what is described is put together or works (e.g. myth).

If "meaning" has always had this ambivalence (and Hobart's other examples show more senses of the term), it is difficult to say that there was a discrete moment when descriptive meaning took over from explanatory meaning in the analysis of society. If there was no such discrete moment, then how can we talk of the transition from functionalism to structuralism (and post-structuralism) as an epistemological break (Ardener 1971a: 450; Crick 1976: 1)? Rather, it seems to have been less a sharp break and more a slide recognized after its occurrence.

This is more than a play with words. We see the slipperiness and hesitancy of the transition in the analytical transformations surrounding the word "function" itself. From the beginning the term carried its own ambivalence: in the teleological sense used by Malinowski and Radcliffe-Brown, it referred to the institutional satisfaction of the needs of society and/or culture; in the mathematical sense later used by Leach (1961: 6-7) and Southall (1965: 131-3) and others, it denoted possibilities emanating from societies seen as systems of logical relations. Merton's distinction between manifest and latent functions of institutions was an attempt to resolve the teleological confusion of the first usage (1957: 66). The term "unintended consequences" (of institutions) reduced still more the teleology and so gained favour in social anthropology (e.g. Cohen 1969: 4, 80). More recently Hanson has suggested that we can think of institutions, like propositions, as variously presupposing or implying each other. He calls this the implicational meaning of an institution, which is thus derived from its logical relations with other institutions (1975: 21, 51-2), a point of view which I have found useful in my own work (Parkin 1978: 13ff.). Hanson himself notes how "the concepts of unintended consequence and implicational meaning emerge as remarkably similar, for both concern logical relations among institutions and social conditions which are not, or not necessarily, recognized by natives" (1975: 72).

So, from an early linking of the concept of function with an organic or mechanistic analogy of society, we have come to a connection between meaning and society thought of as a logical system. The route has in fact been unbroken and is embraced by a single epistemology. Function as purposive behaviour is the sense of meaning as intended causation ("He means well"); society as a logical system is meaning in the sense of signification, with institutions, norms, roles, or whatever, only having meaning in oppositional and homologous relationship to each other. The epistemology is meaning itself, consisting of its two main parts: meaning as causation, and meaning as signification (i.e. semiology). All we have done is move imperceptibly from the first to the second.

If semantic anthropology just concerns meaning, then it has clearly been with us all the time. But an epistemology eventually raises questions about itself. It is this increased self-awareness or reflexivity in the practice of social anthropology that has sought the new label. The conference on which this volume is based began with the title of semantic anthropology. But it became clear during discussion that the key issues were those of self-awareness and even self-criticism in the cultural translation of ethnographic experience. Reflexive anthropology or critical anthropology could have been equally relevant titles.

Inevitably the place of language is central in this, not simply as a problem of how to understand and interpret the speech and concepts of the other, but also as one of how to recognize the part played by our own ordinary and analytical language in shaping our interpretation of other cultures. And, since we are ourselves professionally and intellectually no less members of a "tribe" than the peoples we study (see Holy and Stuchlik 1981: 25; and Crick and Hobart, *infra*), this latter problem becomes extended to the general one of how people's speaking and interacting with each other within a culture become fused as non-separable social facts, only partially translatable between cultures (see Ardener, Kendall, and Tonkin *infra*).

Reflexivity notes its own creativity. Anthropologists have therefore begun to question the structuralist premise that signs interrelate and affect us, yet can be little more than interpreted by us. They have wished to understand better the very process by which the sign-systems were created and the intentions of their authors. This is acknowledged as likely to lead us to indeterminate methodology and away from the rule-based security of sign-systems as determining structures. It leads rather to a view of language use as a form of social play, for the ethnographer and informant alike. It therefore necessarily dissolves any hard or fixed distinction between observing subject and observed object, while retaining the powerful concept of objectification as referring to what happens when persons permanently become how others define them (see Sansom *infra*: 190-191). It also renders false the separation of language and human interaction as isolable and independent systems (Ardener 1975b)

These and related issues will be dealt with below. This section began with the question of whether society is like language or is a language. If social events are meaningless without language either to carry them out, judge, comment on them, or convey them to future generations, society is indeed natural language, consisting not only of words, however, but also of gestures. The mistake has been to jump from this to the conclusion that linguistic concepts can be applied in its analysis. To do so is to convert society into nothing more than a metaphor for the socially decontextualised languages of grammarians and certain theoretical linguists.

Rules of Indeterminacy

Chapman observes that empirical material always gets taken up by theory (*infra*: 125). As Bourdieu states, there are three removes at which this may occur. There are native rules and theory, the anthropologist's rules and theory, and those governing the discipline, methodology, and theories of anthropology as a whole (1977: 3-9). The movement is increasingly away from the practical knowledge in any society of how to carry out everyday tasks. This practical knowledge, or habitus, stands pitted against the idea of rule-governed behaviour. It is innovative and situational and so negates the Durkheimian presupposition of social compulsion. We recognize this. Yet, in studying habitus, we still turn to the notion of rules as guiding and even prescribing behaviour. The term "rule" is used in at least eight of the chapters of this volume.

To some extent this is an honest recognition of the question of scale: we, or our informants, abstract patterns at one level and see them as constraining or encompassing variations at a more intensive level. But the use of the term covers various senses, which we must examine before deciding what motivates this hierarchical usage and whether it is legitimate.

Anthropological rules of method would be Bourdieu's third mode. But, by viewing anthropologists as a "tribe", we conflate all three.

The rules of method become our native prescriptions about how to make predictions and arrive at explanations of the peoples we study. Crick makes two sets of distinctions. First, there are rules for field-work and rules for writing anthropological books. A second distinction is between "scientific" anthropologists who argue that fieldwork and research must follow rules and 'humanists' who counter-argue that research designs obscure the ethnographer's and informant's motives and temperaments which give meaning to the relationship (*infra*: 23-28). To this we can add the impression that the humanists figure largely among those who also worry about how we portray our informants, to the extent even of suggesting how we should write our books about them. The same humanistic concern that rejects methodological distance between us and our informants, curiously becomes quite rule-conscious about publication.

In other words, as a tribe, anthropologists have rules of method about how to deal with other tribes, but also have rules of conduct towards them and each other. The first are seen as technical and the second moral rules. The moral become possible through reflection on the technical: to treat people in the way that scientists measure particles is to convert humanity into mute and therefore dominated objects.

Lest we be carried away by such grand thoughts of charity, however, we must recognize that there is also a professional self-interest in opposing rules of method. This is the realization that any such belief in methods assumes that it is good to standardize techniques, a development that would surely stifle the interpretive latitude that is the hallmark of many distinguished ethnographers.

Here, two reasons are sometimes given in defence of rules of method. First, we need them to assess an ethnographer's accuracy. But can they really help, since even the interpretation and description of any "social fact" is a personal creation as much dependent on the disposition and biography of the ethnographer as on who in the society he happens to observe and speak to? That two ethnographers disagree in their views of the same society normally owes more to this than to one of them perceiving more clearly some objective reality. Certainly, some ethnographers mis-interpret and so "get things wrong" more than others, but this is only ever a matter of degree, and it is doubtful that rules of method will rectify this more than discussion, advice, and greater sensitivity.

A more valid epistemological task is to detect and account for inconsistencies in what an ethnographer says, *not* in order to uncover falsehoods (though these may also surface), but in order to understand his "meaning", i.e. to ponder, no doubt inconclusively, the author's conscious and unconscious intentions behind apparent discrepancies of fact and interpretation. Pocock, in a celebrated but still unpublished paper (1973), calls this personal anthropology. Rules of method are, then, really questions of accountability: who writes what for whom, and why?

Another reason given for justifying rules of method is that, without them, we cannot claim that our students must be "trained", before, during, and after their fieldwork. The word "training", much beloved of such grant-awarding bodies as the SSRC, certainly has a technological ring about it. But there is no reason why our endeavours should be framed by the dominant sense of the word. We can as well argue that our training can never consist of supplying methods that anticipate comparable fieldwork conditions, for such comparability can never be measured; and that our training involves listening to the unashamedly idiosyncratic, interpretive, and personal problems of individual anthropologists. We thus turn on its head the assumption that a collectivist, standardized approach is desirable, but stress instead an infinite possible range. Apparent similarities of experience may emerge but need not be presumed beforehand nor codified afterwards as rules of method. I shall suggest at the end of this section why this apparent invitation to indeterminacy discomforts many anthropologists.

In the practice of many anthropologists the distinction between rules of method and rules of conduct parallels that of Searle between constitutive and regulative rules (1969: 33-42). The former are held to be part of the essence of the discipline without which it could not exist. The latter are seen as variable and therefore negotiable: what was a sanction then may not be now. A change in the constitutive rules of chess transforms it into another game. But an epistemology is not like a game in this dramatic Saussurian sense. It can undergo more gentle metamorphosis. The epistemology can be transformed through a gradual and overlapping re-naming of fundamental assumptions, as I have suggested has been the case in the switch from functionalism to structuralism. Gudeman and Penn argue a similar point in viewing the approaches of Radcliffe-Brown and Lévi-Strauss as both premissed on the universal Western model of a generative essence yet differing in their starting points and in the language they use to uncover that essence (*infra*: 93). One can switch from one approach to the other without dislodging that fundamental premiss. It would seem from this that constitutive rules, too, have their "derived" elements (the alternative and therefore negotiable approaches) as well as their "core" ones (the fundamental premisses).

As a tribe, we may appear to be exceptionally aware of our different senses of the term "rule". But we are far from clear about them. We are even less clear when we try to discern rules in other cultures. Returning to Bourdieu's distinctions, there are those rules which insiders themselves (or some of them) identify; and those which outsiders see but insiders do not.

Unless we believe that the rules that a people claims for itself are always slavishly followed, then their significance is less in prescribing behaviour than in classifying it. However, classifying is a dynamic activity and does not deal with constants. Needham noted this in his attack on the determination of social classifications by common or fixed rather than overlapping or polythetic criteria (1975), and peoples themselves use spoken rules to classify a range of different but apparently inter-related forms of behaviour.

The two main rules by which Darwin Countrymen define indebtedness between patient and helper apply only to serious illness. But the classification of what is serious rather than mild sickness is in the end a matter of collectively agreed interpretation. The application of the behavioural rules (i.e. whether a person is deemed too sick to be able to talk intelligibly and, after recovery, has ceded the right to talk about his illness to whoever helped him), thus legitimizes the classification. There is no prior-existing aetiology to determine whether the rules will apply; rather it is created *in situ*, so speak, by the community deciding whether or not a patient needs special help and whether the helper can thereafter claim this part of the patient's life history to recount as his own (Sansom *infra*: 187-189).

Like most of us, then, Darwin Countrymen can specify behavioural rules in the abstract but cannot state in advance when they will apply, except hypothetically. Similarly, Irvine shows in her study of spirit possession that it is not the properties of the communication code, nor the switch in behaviour, e.g. between ordinary and obscure speech or between speech and silence, nor the switch in context in which speech occurs, that determine what meaning an audience gives to the possessed person's identity. Rather, the audience draws meaning from contrasts in the behaviour of the person: how does his speech or conduct compare with those of his other contexts, and in which contexts can he be said to have a "normal" rather than "abnormal" identity? Identity shifts are created not by a fixed aetiology of spirit possession, even though each culture can specify its own repertoire of speech codes for these situations, but, as among the Darwin hinterland mob, by the interpretive collusion of the audience (*infra*: 257).

The Kasigau of Kenya also recognize a general rule of behaviour which they can specify in the abstract but which takes many forms when practised. The rule is that those Christians who are regarded as "Saved" greet each other as Bwana Okasa (Milton *infra*: 265). But there is considerable contextual variation as to when and between whom this rule should apply: has the person lapsed from religious practice, is the new or aspiring convert really worthy yet of the greeting, does the particular sect to which the person belongs deserve Saved status, and so on? Again, the decision as to whether or not to apply the rule depends on an interpretation of the person's (or his sect's) worthiness, but not on a prior classification of social types. Practicing the rule is a creative process by which identities continually become shaped and re-shaped, yet the over-arching rule remains a constant feature in the abstract.

Here, we may note Milton's assertion that culture can have no meanings of which the actors are unaware. She might reject also the claims of many anthropologists to have discerned cultural rules of which the members of the culture are ignorant. Such rules are, by definition, meaningful to the ethnographer as either a mechanism or, simply, regularity of behaviour. Whether they are meaningful to the actors really depends upon whether they themselves see the behaviour as regular or as contrastable by its irregularity (to refer back to Irvine). If, however, what is regular or irregular to the outsider is not so marked to the insider, then Milton would be right. We cannot impute meaning to the isolated, unconnected, and decontextualized, and it is questionable whether we can even think of phenomena in this way: even "new" events innovate through juxtaposition with the familiar.

The related question of how much people regard what they do as deriving from rules is raised in Williams's discussion of human body movement (*infra*). She suggests that, while the expressive possibilities of body movement are finite, the permutational possibilities are in practice inexhaustible. Hers is the only chapter in the volume which is firmly grounded in an analogy with linguistics: the semasiological body is a "system"; human movements are rule-based, like sound; there is a "grammar" of "positional elements" in body language; and it is our task to try to crack the different codes in order to understand and use a common language of body movements, for there is ultimately a universal structure. She insists, however, that this does not imply that all human movement is alike nor that humans cannot be free to alter their modes of bodily expression. The universal structure makes possible cross-cultural comparison, she says, while the vast number of possible permutations make each cultural system distinctive.

Intentionality and interpretation are critical, however: "The ultimate goal of semasiology is to explain how sequences of a body language are matched with their *correct* interpretations by the users of that body language . . . " (*infra*: 167 my italics). Thus, whereas Williams explicitly proposes a dualistic analytical framework of the *langue* and *parole* type (*infra*: 163-64), her remarks suggest that the process by which she sees bodily movements as becoming meaningful is in fact triangular: the finite limits of bodily expression dictate extrinsic rules; a culture has its own distinctive repertoire at a particular point in time; but the appropriateness of an actor's intention is, in the end, a matter of personal interpretation, which may not in fact accord with those of others watching him. This last element of the interpretative triangle is the slippage which is both necessary for innovation and yet precludes the possibility of a cultural repertoire of acceptable movements, the second element, as ever becoming more than provisional. Since the first element, that of finite rules, is in practice inexhaustible, it is then this third element, the area of interpretive negotiation, which decides what is meaningful, not a dualistic or triangular interaction of independent elements or rules.

From duality and triangle we move closely here to a problem akin to that of the hermeneutic circle (Ricoeur 1981: 211-13, Rabinow and Sullivan 1979: 5; and see Hobart *infra* 47-48, and Salmond *infra*: 74). The meaning of a word can only be understood by knowing the meaning of the sentence of which it is part, yet the sentence's meaning depends both on that of the word and of the text in which it is situated, which both illuminates and is illuminated by the cultural and historical context of the author and readers, and vice versa. We must enter in at some point on the circle, that is, "believe" in it, in order to understand the rest and eventually the whole (Ricoeur 1974: 298).

As ethnographers observing the inter-textuality of events, the question of our entry into the circle can be arbitrary or intuitive, but, in either case, is not reducible to rules, for who is to argue that a particular point of entry should rate above another? Why should a seemingly highly ritualized, heavily attended, exchange of goods take priority as the analytical starting-point over an overhead chance remark of a few words? Either may lead to a similar overall view of the society, or each may yield quite separate pictures. One arbiter is the priority given by the people themselves. Is the collective exchange in fact more of an "event" than the casual remark? They may decide, for it is they, after all, who write the text we call culture. While seeming to favour cultural relativism, this in fact offers the challenge of inter-cultural (or inter-textual) translation.

Consider, for instance, Williams's comparison of the three "kneeling" movements: genuflection, the Muslim "raka", and a woman in a garden (e.g. pulling out weeds). Williams points out that though kneeling is part of all three actions, it does not by itself tell us what each means. We are not interested in the ethological explanation that, say, kneeling denotes submission. We need to know how actions are bounded, yet inter-connect, presuppose, and entail each other, and how much of this is recognized by the actors (*infra*: 169-70). Beyond saying that the first two are religious with different histories, and the last a practical action, Williams lacks the space to pursue these insights. Indeed, for her to do so, would require a much more intensive analysis of each of the specific cultures from which the actions are taken.

There is also the problem of whether the aim of discovering either a universal or cultural language of body movements privileges the linguistic analogy and separates the social and linguistic more than the informants themselves might regard as their own experience. This danger may arise from the very fact that a distinctive feature of many studies of human body movement, especially dance, is the attempt to commit the sequence to notation, an exercise that is necessarily selective. As in the relationship of writing to speech (Derrida 1976), the rule-based notation may come to authorize or determine the relevance of other untranscribed but ever-changing contextual aspects of movement. It will be interesting to see how Williams's pioneering work tackles these problems.

Ardener (*infra*) does focus on one bodily gesture, that of "shaking hands" called *ji aka* among the Ibo of West Africa. But, unlike Williams, he does not analyse the meaning of *ji aka* as part of a meta-language, though such an approach characterized much of his earlier work. (Consider his distinction between paradigmatic and syntagmatic structures (1971a: lxxiv-lxxviii, and 1971b: 465-7) which can be seen as a preliminary to his non-linguistic and more embracing concept of "world-structure" (1975b: 16-20 and 1978: 316-20).) Ardener's intention here is to underline not only how "reality" dissolves the distinction we make between the linguistic and the social, but that, unlike Whorf, we should preserve their simultaneity in our descriptions. The mutuality of the word describing hard-arm (*aka*) and the act of shaking it is in fact as material a phenomenon as one could wish for: a handshake for an Englishman stops short of the wrist; *ji aka* for an Ibo can extend up to just below the shoulder. Yet we translate *ji aka* as handshake in spite of these gestural differences which can, but need not, carry great meaning and even create cross-cultural misunderstanding (see also Chapman *infra*: 134-38). This kind of exercise in comprehending the cultural translations of ourselves and of others, is what constitutes semantic anthropology and is not, therefore, simply to be dismissed as "idealist", as have some critics.

Some might claim that at the level not of handshakes but of supposedly "non-trivial" issues such as war and large-scale exploitation, language classification plays a negligible part in the misunderstandings that arise between peoples. But, apart from this being more assumed than demonstrated (and wrong in my view), there is still the problem of at what point the "trivial" becomes the "serious" and whether the line between them is regarded as the same by everyone. We would hardly expect it to be so, and so the "trivial" has infinite relevance. The "serious" violence in the Liverpool bar, portrayed by Chapman (*infra*: 136-38), could have been avoided if the Englishmen present had known that the Irishmen's murderous threats were "ritual" appeals for the recognition of personal honour as customarily made in rural Ireland, and were not intended to provoke a brawl.

As Ardener points out, neither we nor our informants normally divide our everyday experience into the linguistic and the material: the two inevitably "contaminate" each other (*infra*: 13). To isolate materiality, sometimes as ethological drives and sometimes in the form of cross-cultural statistical regularities, is to drive towards universals which transcend linguistic and cultural differences. Separating out the linguistic eventually leads to a defence of cultural relativism. Separation of the two and their compromised reassembly as generative core and derived variations runs dangerously close to imposing our Western dualistic model on human experience, which for the most part ignores such hierarchisation of practical knowledge. The material *is* the linguistic in use, and so requires translation rather than explanation in terms of "forces".

Why is it, then, that we so often reject the inconclusiveness and indeterminacy of "mere" cultural translation and are instead attracted to the generative premiss of the Western dualistic model in its various guises: that people may not be conscious of the rules of grammar or *langue*, but that it exists in their minds because they can speak the *paroles* which are derived from it?

One possible answer is that we still see human social behaviour as reducible to original causes, searching, so to speak, for valid autochthony. There is an analogy. Some modern literary critics disagree as to whether the meaning of a text should be interpreted ultimately as the author's original intention, or as writing which has become epistemically autonomous of him. The latter reminds us of the depersonalization of structuralism. The former, the notion of original intention, is ambivalent. It can waver between an idea of first cause and that of allowing the text/people to speak for itself/themselves, to which we reflexively respond. It is surely towards the latter that anthropologists are inclined: we concede that a people's history of its origins is part of its continuing translation of what it sees as relevant to the present, but we do not regard it as sufficiently fixed to constitute causal theory.

The so-called repetitions of history are the aesthetically pleasing symmetries that we (ethnographer and informant alike) impose not just to explain but to provide the reassurance of continuity. Ethnographers normally focus on day-to-day repetitions of behaviour. There is of course nothing wrong in identifying apparent regularities of social conduct. But we can make two mistakes. As Bourdieu observes (1977: 29, 36), we may convert our *post facto* observation of the regularity into evidence of it as a rule which prescribed or generated the behaviour. Yet, as the examples which I have cited from this volume show, neither we nor our informants can actually specify when a rule is about to operate, nor what form it will take. The actual conditions and consequences of its operation are indeterminate. The second mistake is that, having converted the regularity into a rule, we may then see it as a compulsory, necessary, and constitutive condition of the social activity. An apparent regularity becomes a general rule and then becomes a cause.

Tropic Creativity

When we perceive social regularities we need not think of them as permanent and fixed features. Social regularities are best thought of as immediate family resemblances: an event is like a preceding event, both called, say, a funeral, by virtue of a few but not all features in common. Successive events add, shed, or rediscover elements as people adjust and counter-adjust to new interpretations of their intentions and purposes. Noting Tonkin's reference to Bourdieu (*infra*: 108, 116), we can see that the regularities that our informants perceive and then call rules in fact come from their *habitus*, or dispositions and practical knowledge of how to carry out tasks. This happens when, in order to seek greater clarity or effect, or simply as play, we refer metaphorically to ourselves, to others, or to events around us. A metaphor may then gain regular currency and become autonomous of and dissociated from its original inspiration.

This displacement through metaphor (Tonkin *infra*: 114) does more than adorn a concept or situation. It may create a new one. Thus established, it is difficult to go back and deconstruct the new concept. We need further displacement to become dislodged from the now regular form we have created. Successive metaphorical displacements are thus chain-like with few ordinary speakers aware of the root form. This is especially so, since, as Tonkin points out, such creativity is never or rarely linguistic alone, but may draw also upon the pre-linguistic and practical thoughts and observations of Coleridge's Primary Imagination. Successive metaphorical extensions can thus be thought of as partial family resemblances, but, like the inter-linking of events, may suggest momentary continuity or regularity.

Habitus can therefore be re-defined as an on-going process of play and experimentation, punctuated by apparent moments of orderliness. This reverses Turner's characterization of structure as the on-going regularities and communitas as the moments which punctuate it (1969). The re-definition also goes beyond Bourdieu's warning not to confuse momentary orderliness with causal rule, for it suggests that orderliness and experimentation are the necessarily complementary dimensions of any creative process.

We see this very clearly in Kendall's analysis of the serious playfulness that characterizes the relationship between Maninka nobles and griots (praise-singers) in Mali in West Africa. Kendall concedes that language use is orderly but argues that this does not imply that it need be based on prescriptive rules. She shows that the orderliness of natural languages comes from the way we bring our speech, bodily gestures, and emotions into some kind of equilibrium, and at the same time adjust this harmonious whole to a particular situation. The griots can hardly plan their language games in advance. They have to balance innovation with social acceptability.

No rule-book on grammar or on speaking can instruct on this, for the creative performance is drawn from an apparently infinite range of possible combinations of bodily gesture, speech, and emotive response. Little can be predicted: what one noble can accept as permissible praise-mongering by the griot, another will reject. One griot may perceive and exploit a sensitive area of a noble's reputation, another may miss it. We may see rules governing the relationship of griot and noble, such that the griot is supposed to be ostentatious and the noble retiring. But the rules are not to be viewed simply as socially compelling. Rather they are counter-balances to experimentation and mark its phases.

In this vein, I have argued elsewhere that it is wrong analytically to isolate fixed from free forms of speech, for the two are only possible through each other and inhere in the presuppositions of all speech and behaviour (Parkin 1980: 62-3), a point comparable to that made by Tonkin, who argues that propositional can never be separated from non-propositional language, and that it is therefore false to analyse its effects as if it can (*infra*: 118).

The most intriguing of Tonkin's suggestions is that the ratiocination by which we understand the world, actually occurs more through non-propositional than propositional means. In other words, performative language, the use of primary imagination, and displacement through metaphors, are actually better confirmatory measures of what the world or "reality" consists of than the true/not-true questions of standard, formal logic. This distinction is reminiscent of that commonly made between the logic of concepts and the logic of imagination. It is the latter, of which poetry is made, which discovers the gaps in our deductive methods of reasoning, often quite accidently, or at least through intuition. While Coleridge's primary imagination sees beyond formal or established concepts simply by dissolving them in order to create new ones, Bergson's intuition both negates the apparently impeccable logic that we feel is somehow not right (1975: 110) and makes graphically acceptable connections between disparate ideas (*Ibid.*: 118-21; and see Milner 1969: 6-9), much in the way that metaphor achieves its effect by both revealing the inadequacy of the parent concept and bringing together otherwise distinct conceptual domains.

This capacity of metaphor and of tropes generally to reason through intuition and the primary imagination may or may not be harnessed by formal logic. But even unharnessed tropes may be assertive as well as evocative, being, as language, more than Sperber's symbols of smells and beliefs (which he also brackets together with the symbolism of irony) (1975: 119-49).

In a penetrating analysis of the extraordinary variety of scholarly approaches to the study of figurative language, Hobart argues optimistically that, even if we find it hard to define tropes, they do seem to make up how we see the world. "They may be treated as ways of perceiving relationships and situations from different perspectives. As such they may cover far broader areas than formal categories and may represent general processes of thinking" (*infra*: 55). He also raises the thorny problem of how much our Western notions of tropes can be applied cross-culturally. If, following Burke (1969), the four major tropes of metaphor, metonymy, synechdoche, and irony, are cognitive examples, respectively, of perspective, reduction, representation, and dialectic, or, in Hobart's own view, of resemblance, relationship, classification, and contrast, then we must indeed satisfy ourselves of the precise nature and status of such processes of thinking in other cultures. Are they in fact universal logical operations which, because they are perceived by us outsiders as "only metaphorical", are then characterized by us as culture-bound metaphysics?

While it may be premature in the absence of adequate data to assess such universality, we have vivid evidence that peoples of other cultures may organize themselves socially through reasoning which appears to us as little more than figurative language. The cosmogony of the Piaroa Indians of Venezuela is a transormational one: human-like mythic beings are produced by and turn into creatures of land and water; they have kinship and affinal relations with each other which are also altered; re-classification constantly occurs. Far from being divorced from what we call the social world, these cosmological transformations provide a language and ontology for describing human social relationships.

Thus, a person's "metaphorical" habitat is either water or land, and denotes his/her descent from one or other of the two main mythic beings. Persons of the same habitat do not exchange with each other and are treated as kin. Persons of different habitats do engage in exchange and refer to each other by a range of affinal terms. But affines also "become" kin. Kinship consists of resemblance which is safe, while affinity consists of difference which is dangerous. To turn affinity into kinship is thus to convert danger into safety. Unfortunately, society is created through difference (e.g. inter-marriage and exchange between different groups), and so danger has to be lived with. Shamans tap this creativity and embody its danger, and so have power for and against society (Overing Kaplan 1982).

Overing Kaplan argues that it is wrong for us to strip off the so-called metaphorical language and then claim to have revealed the underlying logic of a theory of the problems of existence and co-existence. To do so is to deny that the Piaroa themselves understand their own ontology and to deny them their capacity to speak of it intelligibly in their own way. All we have done is to translate the language of their ontology into that of our own. What is "metaphor" for us is "logic" for them. She traces this unprivileged status of other peoples' metaphorical usage to the Platonic idea that metaphors make up rhetoric which is the language of lies and deception. Remove the deceit before you find the truth. But deception inheres not in the words of language but in the uses to which they are put. The Piaroa do not deceive themselves. They even have their own word for metaphor and so are well aware of Platonic fears. On the other hand, figurative language *can* be used to create illusion, if the speaker so intends and the audience is that gullible, just as it can be used to create or re-describe social categories and even peoples (Chapman and Hastrup, both *infra*; and see Halliday on antilanguages (1978: 170-72)).

We have been happy to assess the effects of what we perceive to be figurative language in other cultures. But we have been slow to recognize its use among ourselves. To return to the tribe of anthropologists, Salmond (*infra*) illustrates a striking difference in epistemology between Western anthropologists and Maori elders. Western anthropologists talk of knowledge as a landscape to be explored, conquered, controlled, surveyed, pioneered, and covered by intellectual journies to ever more horizons, etc. Western knowledge is thus seen as inexhaustible. Maori knowledge, by contrast, is regarded as finite, consisting of folk-lore, incantations, genealogies, myths, ritual performances, and language itself. It must be transmitted to succeeding generations with care and guarded with secrecy lest it be lost to outsiders, or to their distortions of it. The metaphor of knowledge as a landscape is not used among them. Instead, knowledge is food for chiefs, treasure, or a cloak (for sheltering the treasure?), and is, moreover, seen by Maori as embodied or fused with places and objects, such as chiefs' houses and property belonging to a descent group. This contrasts with the distance obtaining between Western anthropologists and their subject matter: knowledge is territory out there waiting to be traversed. The two epistemologies do converge in some respects, but in each case much is distinctive.

Salmond notes that a new metaphor can be self-validating by creating as a distinguishable "reality" the object, event, or sentiment to which it refers. The use of "knowledge is a landscape" as a central metaphor in our own epistemology leads to a large number of other metaphorical sets. From landscape we move successively to territory, journey, sighting, facts as natural objects of the environment, the mind as a container, and so on. This inter-locking of metaphors inevitably shapes our intellectual discourse and academic practices (e.g. "in order to make *progress* theoretical *battles* must be *fought* between *protagonists* from different disciplinary *fields*"). The flexibility and ambiguity of such metaphorical usage can also suggest theoretical departures: the contrast made between society as either natural object or as written text is a case in point. The epistemological status of theory itself then becomes open to question. As Salmond notes, thought cannot be separated from observation, since the thinking is itself articulated in the visual idioms of surveying/speculating on fields/areas/domains, etc (*infra*: 73).

She accepts a psychological suggestion that this anthropological proclivity for territorial tropes (shared by many other disciplines) derives from our tendency to root abstract concepts in the language of our "concrete" physical environment (*Ibid*.: 81). By this suggestion we share the concrete logic of the "savage mind". Do the Maori, then, who do not use the landscape metaphor in their epistemology, lack a concrete logic? That they fuse their sources of knowledge and their powers of apprehending it in objects around them suggests that they do have one, but that they employ it differently: as noted above, Westerners distance themselves from the objects that become colonized as knowledge; Maori fill objects with existing, time-hallowed knowledge.

In both cases, a form of objectivity is critical. Objects, however fused they may be with observing subjects, as among the Maori, only have existence in relation to each other in what we can therefore translate as their environment. Their relationships to each other are to that extent spatial. We can therefore re-phrase the contrast in epistemologies: as being explicitly concerned with spatial existence in the case of anthropologists, and as implicit among Maori. This in no way invalidates Salmond's analysis, but draws further on it.

One implication is that among both peoples epistemological thinking rests on spatial disjunctions and continuities but that it is only among anthropologists that this is taken up into the metaphorical language of an inexhaustible landscape.

One possible reason for this difference may be that, for a long time, Western epistemologies have had literature in which to store their knowledge. This has allowed for laterality as well as transmissability. Laterality here comes close to the idea of unending horizons. Laterality can accommodate a wide range of conflicting views, while transmissability without the storage facilities of literature is most efficient when the range of opinions is reduced. The Maori efficiently transmit orally by narrowing their epistemological range; anthropologists revel in widening it to the point, ideally, of idiosyncrasy, and try also to transmit it, though paradoxically much less efficiently (as in the tendency to re-cast old ideas as new). The literary store of knowledge ("laterature"!) becomes in part, then, that of metaphor. Hence our ridicule of the old-fashioned and our propensity to construct new ones: society as organism gives way in turn to the metaphors of machine, language, text, and so on.

An epistemology incorporating metaphors of territory and journeying can certainly also exist among pre-literate peoples. The option is there to be taken up. Quite independently of Salmond, I analysed the language of some East African diviners who use the complementary idioms of journeying from a wilderness to straight paths, and of bodily exploration. The diviner settles on a particular part of a client's body, proclaims it as the source of discomfort, and names the cause and cure. The epistemology is that of moving from wilderness, through paths, to a centre, and from confusion to clarity (1979).

If this is something approaching a semantic archetype found in a wide variety of cultures, then its articulation is certainly variable. Its reference to journey or movement comes up, also, against a contrary proclivity in Western thought. This is what Bergson calls our search for fixity (1975: 15). He takes the example of time and notes that though we experience it only as duration, we can never measure it as such. Rather we treat it as movement which passes us at fixed moments. He blames our language for this. It specifies time as space and, because we assume that language is the conduit of basic thought categories, we assume also that time "really" is movement past fixed points in space. It follows, he says, that our intellect "refuses to consider transition" (*Ibid.*). In fact, the work of Van Gennep and Turner on liminality, and, more recently, by Gell on "lapse" (1979) and "the trance-gap between intention and experience" (1980: 237), have recognized this omission, and such concepts of indeterminacy are regularly associated with the exploration of free will and creativity (see also Denyer 1982). Even so, though we may regard liminality among ourselves and others as a vital topic of study, the language of our own theory has not escaped the presuppositions of fixity.

Why should this be so? Space is "ordinarily" thought of as infinite, while the distances between fixed points within it are thought of as measurable and therefore finite. The spatial metaphors of theoretical language draw very heavily on this finitude (e.g. distinguishing the successive steps of a theory), and may explain more than anything else the sway of positivist assumptions of fixity, set and measurable distance, and of observable objectivity. To talk of "field" or "domain" of enquiry, therefore, is to intimate the possibility of a complete and final solution of a problem. Our inability to find this will mark out a new field but does not eliminate the expectation of a successful quest.

I began this section with a view of metaphor (and, by extension, tropes generally) as benignly creative, of making new concepts and events possible. The examples were taken from other cultures. Yet, in looking at our own theoretical discourse we find that we, too, use figurative language. We accept that others can be metaphorical but expect our own discourse to be literal, and are surprised that it is not. Chapman similarly shows how centuries of 'learned' accounts of other peoples, including more recently the Celts, describe them as rich in verbal imagery but incapable of sustained "analytical" language, yet the accounts themselves are infused with figurative language (*infra*: 128-33). To reveal that we are as non-literal as others is to suggest that, for us, metaphors are masks which parade as objective observation and truth. Are we, then, back to the view of tropes as deceit, after all? Or is it simply that they create or obscure depending on who uses them?

As Ricoeur notes (1978: 251-3), there are certainly those who denounce metaphorical language as illusory, as being guily of "category mistakes". We are reminded also of Sperber's confession that, to him, the word symbol means something false (1975: 3). To argue this for metaphor, however, is to assume that there is a dimension of ordinary language that can in fact portray literal truths. This presupposes that we already know the reality that is so represented. But definitions of reality are always provisional. At least a humanistic science assumes this. Otherwise why continue to search? The absence of a correspondence between language and absolute truth must, then, make language non-literal: we cannot assuredly say what reality is but only what it is like, hence the use of metaphor in theory.

Of course we may speak with varying proportions of "dead" and "live" metaphors: the latter being those which we normally regard as innovative and the former having become part of the polysemy which characterizes all words (Ricoeur1981: 170). Sometimes the dead/live distinction is equated with that of a core/metaphorical meaning (cf. G. Lewis 1980: 119). But this is to assume an ultimate (core) reference created *ex nihilo*, which would be the failure of a purely referential or indexical theory of meaning pushed to its limit.

Ordinary language is, then, metaphorical and, to return to Ricoeur (1978: 251-3), we cannot eliminate metaphorical masks: all we can do is consciously and constantly to replace them. Most chapters in this volume have stressed the non-separability of the linguistic and the social. Given this embeddedness, the creation of new language is the creation of new metaphors which is the re-description of social reality. Ricoeur argues that this referential power of metaphor to re-describe reality comes from its "heuristic fiction" (*Ibid.*) which, put simply, is the capacity to hint at possible worlds not covered by existing epistemological language, and then to convert them into acceptable ones. Sometimes they become unfavourable stereotypes of the other, as Chapman shows has happened in descriptions of the Irish. At other times, unwelcome but convincing discoveries are made, as in the emotional echoes conveyed by poetry. But this is not to deny metaphorical language its potential for "benign" creativity as well: the Icelanders, discussed by Hastrup (*infra*), embraced their newly defined ethnicity, which had first been expressed as their distinctive language and laws; from an evolutionary viewpoint, the metaphorical and analogic application of number may have facilitated more highly abstract (though still ultimately metaphorical) modes of mathematical reasoning (Crump *infra*: 287), after Hallpike 1979: 236; and see also Barnes 1982: 16-20).

There is here another implication of the view that the linguistic and the social are constituted in each other, which concerns the awkward definition of creativity. This is that, being social, new metaphorical language creates not just new references, but new "forms of life" or "events". For Ricoeur, this heuristic fiction of metaphorical creativity turns on the verb "to be" which has two senses: the existential "is" (the rose is red) and the relational, poetic, or metaphorical "is" (the rose is a treasure). Heuristic fiction is used first as a pretence (I am pretending a rose is treasure), then as intention (I intend what I pretend), then as make-belief, and therefore as a statement about a possible world (1978: 252).

As I see it, "being" and "intention" are here linked. The ontology of the former is joined to the intending "I" or subject of the latter, and the result is a re-description and new objectification of reality. From tropic creativity, then, we move to the problem of the relationship of subject to object.

Objectifying Subjects

The last two sections have dealt, respectively, with "their" and "our" rules, and "their" and "our" figurative language. The distinction between the subject as namer and the object as named underlies this separation: "we" ethnographers order "their" activities into analytical categories. "They" are the named or spoken-about objects of "our" investigation. But, as has been clear, the problems and interests are often common rather than separate, and "we", the namers, are often unaware of how identified by our own presuppositions we become.

We might, then, be tempted to dissolve the distinction between subject and object. For particular situations this is indeed appropriate: during and after fieldwork ethnographers and their so-called informants talk about as well as to each other and shape each others' interpretations of themselves, and so are each both subjective namer and objectively named at alternating points in the discourse. Even during the writing-up period, the ethnographer's field experiences in the form of notes and memories talk back to and about him as he coaxes his material into assuming a translation that is acceptable to his colleagues. How often the anthropologist has to revise an agreeable interpretation on discovering some forgotten field notes which contravert it. The notes are irksome but have acquired an independent voice which cannot be ignored. They are no longer the product of his thought but have become dissociated from and challenge it.

When we enter the cosmological world of our informants, also, there may be situations in which the distinction between active subject and passive object seems better laid aside. Among the Giriama of Kenya, among whom I worked, elders speak to the wooden memorial sculptures of certain venerated ancestors. I first saw the sculptures as mere representations of the ancestors: it is "really" the ancestors whom the elders address, and, of course, the ancestors answer back by deed and word, at most only residing in the sculptures. So I thought. But the Giriama insist that these sculptures "become" these particular ancestors for a while, during which they are dangerous or propitious depending on how they are treated and handled. From the Giriama viewpoint the sculptures are at that time not simply wooden containers of spirit, but are fellow conversants. This realization, minor in itself, has implications for understanding their notions of what we distinguish as the material and the animate, and body and soul (1982).

While it is thus legitimate to view an inflexible distinction between subject and object as likely to hinder understanding within and between other worlds, it is in other respects crucial. The key to this claim is the reversible process by which subjects objectify but may themselves be objectified. The question of having to make a choice between either subjectivism or objectivism is then rendered false. Subjectivist attitudes may seem to structure reality, but that same reality becomes metaphorically cast in the role of an environment which "changes" and so "raises questions" and "influences opinion". If opinion *is* influenced by a changing environment, then how can we deny it a subjective role? It is not enough to say that it is only in a metaphorical sense that changing environments (e.g. an ice age or demographic change) influence opinion. This would be tantamount to saying that our own subjectivism is always non-metaphorical which, as we have learned above, is clearly not so. (Consider the way in which the term environment is used by political systems analysts as distinct from geographers.) By admitting that environments act and speak, we are consistent with much of the way we think and reason in everyday life, and also show that we are in that respect little different from our informants: the work of Chinese geomancers is premissed on the reciprocal interaction between buildings and people (Freedman 1969); but Western astrology at both its popular and scholarly levels (Gauquelin 1982) makes similar assumptions about planetary bodies and people. The claim that such assumptions are not central in our lives is questionable: "the economy", "inflation", and "market forces" have so entered the thinking of the Western layman as having an autonomy to which he and his compatriots must respond, that it might be hard to persuade him that they do not exist outside the subjective and highly variable calculations of a small body of experts.

The reversible process to which I referred, by which people, things, and attitudes become objectified, yet may themselves, at another point in time, become active agents, is central both to the language of epistemological argument and to what we normally term belief systems. As regards people, mention has already been made of the way a Darwin "sickfella" becomes defined as losing the power to speak intelligibly and, on recovery, as having permanently lost part of his personal biography. That part of his selfhood becomes someone else's property to tell (Sansom *infra*: 186). But this does not stop him possessing some part of someone else's selfhood. The objectification of patients, children, and social inferiors, is common enough: it is most evident in the use of the third person pronoun to refer to the individual in his presence. But the sick may recover, children grow, and subordinates may rise in the social scale. Similarly, a kind of self-objectification occurs when a person possessed by a spirit talks about and makes demands on behalf of himself. But the spirit eventually leaves the person to speak for himself. Objectification can also be permanent: prejudice against some "aliens" has a long pedigree, as Chapman's chronicle of victims shows. On the other hand particular groups who were once stereo-typed may centuries later do the stereotyping (*infra*: 124-26).

Symbolization has been regarded as the process by which things and attitudes become objectified in our minds as having distinctive qualities, and then, once so constituted, as in turn having effects on our thoughts and emotions (Gluckman 1962; Cohen 1974: 30-31). Once again, the reversible process here shows itself in our theoretical language, an assumption modified but not eliminated by Sperber (1975: 119-149): his assertion that symbols do not "mean" but "evoke" does not remove the implication that they become active agents to which we respond: i.e. we perceive them, they evoke something for us, and we respond to them.

Crump's discussion of numbers and counting suggests a significant way in which this reversibility of subject and object may occur. While noting that the metaphysical use of numbers may have led through their physical application to deductive methematical logic, he notes that the metaphysical is still with us all. For example, we have it weakly in place-names, proverbs, stories, and astrology incorporating the use of seven (e.g. Sevenoaks, The Seven Sisters, etc.), and a little more strongly, in avoidance of the number thirteen as a date with Friday, or for apartments, and possibly in the focus on so-called triangular numbers. Crump presents spectacular examples from other cultures such as the Maya and Chinese calendrical systems (*infra*: 285).

In these and other examples, the particular numbers have intrinsic "mystical" import to which people are assumed to respond. That is to say, these numbers are seen by a people to have autonomous effect. On the other hand, as Crump notes, counting is in fact an objectifying activity, by which serial order is imposed on aggregations. A child eventually learns that the total of any number of objects does not depend on the order in which he counted them, nor how they were laid our prior to counting, nor, indeed, on the identities of things counted, e.g. whether they are a mixture of goats, sheep, and chickens, or all of one species. It is this autonomy of number generally, and the cultural focus on particular numbers, which comes back at the counter, so to speak, and imposes itself on him in ritual and mythic activities, avoidances, and in measuring everyday tasks and goods. The counter becomes the measured.

Modern statistical reports sometimes carry a version of this kind of process. They necessarily eliminate some distinctions between counted objects in specifying common features. They thereby create resemblances or consistency which can never be more than partial but which may be presented as whole instances for persuasive effect. A randomly drawn sample of citizens becomes an illustration of "public demand", and the suggestion of an organized, burgeoning pressure group may be realized. That is to say, people become objectified as numbers, which are converted back into people commonly assumed to be active and united by a single cause, to whom other people respond, and so on. Numbers, as well as illustrating this reversability of subject and object, are clearly also tropes, premissed on the notion of ordering. It is interesting, but probably no coincidence, that Hobart's characterization of the four tropes as resemblance, relationship, classification, and contrast, are easily expressed mathematically.

Crump suggests that the distinction made between traditional and modern numerology is really that between connotation and denotation. The connotation of the number seven in the verse "seven stars in the sky" in the English folk song, "Green grow the rushes, O", is that of a wide range of astrological phenomena, which have no relationship to the numbers of other verses, each of which has its connotation. The denotation in modern numerology is precisely the counting of objects as isolable entities and not allowing their distinctive identities to affect the overall tally. The very rough equations often made between denotation and connotation, extension and intension (Hobart *infra*: 42), and, after Frege, reference and sense, take us more centrally into an area of discussion concerning namers and the named.

Neither Barnes (*infra*) nor Willis (*infra*) consider as adequate Lévi-Strauss's view that names classify either the namer or named, though it remains an important starting-point. Nor is either satisfied with the theory, attributed to J. S. Mill, that proper names are not descriptions and so are meaningless marks. Barnes goes on to elaborate on Frege's doctrine that such names have both reference (*Bedeutung*) and sense (*Sinn*), suggesting after a detailed survey of some native North Americans that it is the various ways in which names are presented in a culture which are the sense of names, and that anthropologists are especially well placed to document ethnographically such sense. His discussion suggests that we should think of a name as transacted according to a variety of cultural rules, each of which contributes to its meaning. Rules of transaction, use, avoidance, and transmission, do not allow us to regard names as having connotation in the strict logical sense, nor does it always follow that a name necessarily denotes a particular object. But the inter-relational quality of names is always present (i.e. who can use which, when and why), and certainly conveys empirical information about the particular world of a culture.

Though the pattern of name bestowal may be complex, Barnes does not explain it simply in terms of an underlying structure of rules. On the contrary, he notes the intentionality of speakers who present and use names, accepting that to do so must indicate both their knowledge of the appropriate social conventions and organization and the necessity for agreement with other persons as to whether existing conventions should be maintained or altered.

Indeed, since proper names derive their meaning both from the fact that they are descriptions (*pace* Mills, Russell *et al.*) and from the ways they are presented and used socially, then they are an aspect of ordinary language use, not set apart from it. Given also the social perpetuity inherent in some naming systems (in some cases substituting, so to speak, for descent (see Riviere 1980: 538-9)), they might even be regarded as an especially marked aspect of language use, subject not only to the ordinary constraints of language use but to the extra constraints emanating from their use in defining the continuities of personhood. As descriptive language, personal names have the "surplus" meaning that comes from polysemy (Ricoeur 1981: 169-70, and Thompson's introduction: 10), yet it is a surplus which offers limited semantic freedom, for the name talks not about persons in general but a specific person and so constantly re-states his distinctiveness. This restricted semantic freedom remains the case even in those systems of personal naming in which, as among the Yoruba, each new-born child is given a newly invented descriptive name, for their allocation and use are still restricted to certain social categories in a way that other descriptions normally are not (Akinnaso 1980). Proper names then become the inverse of new metaphor: both are part of ordinary language use and may have surplus meaning, which, in the case of names, refers intensionally to additional properties of a particular person rather than extensionally to classes of persons in other possible worlds, as can that of metaphor.

Though Willis shares common philosophical assumptions with Barnes, his problem is different. He is puzzled by the extraordinary complexity of Fipa personal naming. He also is dissatisfied with a structuralist explanation which might reduce this complexity to underlying, classificatory rules. He would rather raise the question of "authorial intention": who actually thought up this system in the first place? We can only guess at his or (probably) her identity. But the suggestion that some degree of conscious intention was involved in the development of the system remains reasonable. Persons do, after all, perceive some environmental and social changes affecting them and adjust, however partially, to them.

In the case of the Fipa, the naming system appears to offer a compromise between cosmological and ontological consistencies on the one hand, and changes in the descent and property system on the other. Thus, a continuing feature of Fipa cosmology is the complementary opposition of the "head" and the "loins" associated, respectively, with centrality and authority, and with intrusion and strangerhood. Applied to personal names these two denote patriliny and opposite-sex linkage between alternate generations. By way of a complicated grid of name transmission, a Fipa man or woman can give a formulaic recitation of his/her names which indicate the order of priority of his various identities: paternal, maternal, kindred, and parental, each identity having distinctive cosmological connotations.

This criss-crossing of descent-based identities reflects the way in which names are transmitted but does not disturb the basic cosmological opposition. Fipa cultural continuity is thereby retained yet the change from a unilineal to cognatic system of descent, and the implications this has for defining personhood, are accommodated. Lacking definitive descent group allegiance, persons are admirably suited for the new mobility of the modern market economy. A similar accommodation of individual ambitions is also noted by Barnes as a characteristic of Omaha personal names (*infra*: 223).

If we accept that changes in naming systems are, indeed, ultimately intended by individuals rather than simply generated unconsciously by an underlying structure, then the choices made by a namer reflect on himself as well as on the bearer and those who may or may not use the name. Naming then defines selfhood as well as others' personhood. Putting this another way, the subject objectifies himself through the act of defining or objectifying another.

Here we may share Willis's concern and blame the Western utilitarian emphasis on the atomicity and uniqueness of the individual for the inability of earlier scholars to recognize that it is the transmissability and inter-relatedness of names between namers, bearers, and third parties that should be the focus of analysis, not the names as isolable words or expressions, a point which also underlies Barnes's present and earlier studies. By the same token, definitions of selfhood and person can also suffer from our own cultural presuppositions. A person may be the bodily product of his moral actions and intentions according to Hindu thought, an ontology which denies not only Cartesian duality but also assumptions of discrete fixity in Western notions of the self, individual, or person. Such differences suggest that understanding of selfhood, etc., can only be culturally relative. But we can re-cast the problem in general terms.

Kohák distinguishes (1978: 177-178) between the subject's awareness of himself as the focus of his own action, and his reflection on that action. To be so aware is not necessarily also to reflect. This distinction represents the phenomenological view that we experience before we theorize (*Ibid.*: 3) and that it is in the gap between the two that insight occurs. To this may be added the possibility of losing all awareness of ourselves. Gell describes how, during fieldwork, he accidentally cut his finger and automatically put it to his mouth, completely unaware of the amazed looks of his Umeda informants who, he then was made aware, were shocked that anyone could violate a cultural taboo and actually ingest their own blood. The insight that this produced led Gell to a theory that the prohibitions on the eating of "self" (and by extension animals associated with the self) were a way of preserving it, which reversed the interpretation he might otherwise have had of taboo (1979). In the rapid moment of insight, the subject reflects on himself and his action as object, a fusion that can be longer sustained in certain forms of religious or other meditation and in epistemologies such as that reported by Salmond of the Maori, in which persons identify their knowledge of themselves and their world with such tangible objects as ancestral property and chiefs' houses.

This apparent merging of subject and object, and of unawareness, awareness, and reflection is, in fact, broken by two gaps; that between intention and experience; and that between experience and theorizing (or reflection). These can be part of a sequence: intention – experience – reflection. But as two pairs (intention-experience, and experience-reflection), they each can stand independently: in the first case, I intend to ride that bicycle and, without my awareness of any transition, that intention becomes my experiencing of riding it; in the second, religious experience (for example) is inspired by another but not intended by myself and may be reflected on or theorized either by myself or by someone else (a prophetic interpreter). In the first case the "I" or subject dominates throughout, but in the second he is objectified from the beginning and either recovers his status as theorizing "I" or loses it to a third party who does the theorizing on his behalf. The sequence of intention, experience, and reflection, can be glossed, then, as subject, object, and *either* subject *or* object. Reported experience, then, divides our control of ourselves through our intentions from the struggle to control ourselves or be controlled by others that comes with reflexivity and theorizing. The struggle is nicely instanced in Western society in the often sharply conflicting views of human behaviour held by social scientists (among other professionals) and lay persons. Both are reflexive but it is the reflexivity of the professionals, re-named theory, which is privileged.

Through their epistemological identification with the ancestors, chiefs, and with each other, the Maori limit reflexive disagreement to a minimum and express this in their unity against outside violation. Their so-called "conservatism", then, actually shows greater retention of the original intention to control their own actions and selves. This not only makes perfectly rational a people's claim that its culture originates from the intended acts of some ancestors or mythical heroes, it also shows that the basic phenomenological course of our Western epistemology differs only in that we allow ourselves, through our revelations, to regard some of us as theorizing subjects and others as theorized objects. A "tolerant" society is then one in which the reversability of subject and object, to return to that process, is encouraged and unimpeded, while a fusion of subjects and objects as in Maori epistemology, even if practicable in Western thought, would not necessarily create a 'tolerant' society for it would amount to a ban on disagreement.

Thus, a fusion of subjects and objects can in fact amount to a mutual objectification of the members of society: your opinions must be those that sustain and are sustained by a single view of the collectivity. Alternatively it can be regarded as a prolonged and heightened inter-subjectivity by which all interpretations concur, a condition to which thankfully society rarely even approximates, though clearly there are variations. More common is the objectification by one people of another. This can be read as a statement which the objectifiers are making about themselves, a kind of reflexivity, displacing features which they may find desirable or undesirable in their own society. Or it may be a form of control.

From Chapman's study we can see examples of both types, and of how one may turn into the other. Early documents portrayed the Celts as lacking cultural autonomy and as having either too much or too little emotion, meaning, and imagination of the same kind but never in the same amounts as those who wrote the documents. But the Celts could not read these documents, which therefore affected not them but members of the society in which they were written. Whether cast as noble savage or bestial Caliban, the alien inadvertently came to objectify and so praise or condemn social divisions and ontological possibilities in the "home" society. The reflexivity here has to be unrecognized in order to be effective and so differs from that preceded by awareness. Awareness, when it comes, can be applied with different intent. The harsh stereotypes of the Irish were later, as is all too well-known, used additionally as a means of politically controlling them.

This kind of collective objectification through naming and entitling informs our own theoretical and even ethnographic distinctions as well. Southall shows how the Nuer and Dinka, known locally as the Naath and Jieng, connote "attacker" and "attacked" and are drawn from a range of possible terms in the Nilotic dialects for "person" (1976: 475). Locally the distinction is a subjective one based on an assessment of military dominance, and so it ebbs and flows over time across the same group of people. Yet, in spite of debates about who the Nuer/Dinka "really" are, students are still shown them, inevitably for the most part, as distinct peoples.

Perhaps we are rather like the Icelanders for whom, as Hastrup shows, the use of the ethnic name and the creation of a conscious ethnic distinctiveness were simultaneous. It is true that a propensity for this to happen among the Icelanders arose from the compilation and codification of a distinctive grammar and legal statutes. But, as in cases of Ardener's unspoken "material density" of interaction and practice (*infra*), it is the name that objectifies, often indelibly, and the namer who does the objectifying. In all these situations, subject and object may be reversed, and reversed again. Romans stereotyped Britons who later stereotyped Irish and colonial peoples: the classical object becomes a modern subject seeking a new object.

The reversability of subject and object, replacing the dichotomy of self and other (either individual or collective), plays on the alternation of active and passive as a process and so takes us a significant step away from Western assumptions of individual atomicity and discreteness. "I" and "we" may become not only objectival "me" and "us" but also "you" and even "it" and "them", a transformational process that, in some cultures, goes beyond the pronominal. Even in English the derogatory use of "it" to refer to a person already reduces his humanity, a change that is commonly taken much further in myths and ontologies elsewhere: witches becoming feral beasts, shamans elevated to god-like jaguars, etc.

While such ontological transformation is indeed variously marked in different languages by the power of some to withhold or give names and titles to others, or to assume them for themselves, it is clearly not linguistic alone. The emotional embodiment of language use is noted in a number of the chapters in this volume. They accord with Gilbert Lewis's suggestion that however much we may see a belief system as based on culturally prescribed assertions and affirmations, it is still, in the end, the individual's feelings which predispose him to accept or reject its promises or warnings. The Gnau of New Guinea are not supposed to utter a mother's brother's name. Those who do will be confronted by a particular snake. But it is not enough for us to say that people observe this cultural rule for fear of the consequences of breaking it. That may be partly so. But another restraint is the equivalent of that sentiment by which, in our own society, we often refrain from speaking obscenities in contexts which, we know, will induce no harmful effects on us (Lewis 1980: 195).

Our aesthetic senses, as well as our fears and other emotions, are here inter-twined with the forbidden name, title, or obscenity. On the one hand, as Heelas notes, "language organizes emotional life in conjunction with broader institutions" (1981: 14). On the other hand, the cultural naming that objectifies our 'inner states' for us does not permanently fix our experience of them. As with Coleridge's Primary Imagination, sentiment constantly dissolves and dissipates concepts as we redescribe experiences, often through cross-cultural borrowing of new terms for emotions.

The culturally varying expressions of what we translate as selfhood are aspects of this creative involvement of language with inner states. Rosaldo's detailed study of selfhood in Ilongot society turns on the key emotional concept of *liget* which roughly means "angry" but is favourably associated with striving youth and energetic head hunters. It is positive passion, and it both motivates human head-hunting as a necessary act of burgeoning manhood and creates the wisdom that goes with it (1980: 27). The study thus relates a cultual conception of self to the emotionally framed intentions of individuals who achieve selfhood. But the society has undergone great changes recently, and already the associations of *liget* have shifted, as will the view of desirable selfhood. In describing the Dinka equation of "body" with "self", Lienhardt suggests that they are aware of the common etymology of terms which connote both a part of the body and inner states (e.g. the word for "heart" is also that for "what is inside", "intention", "trust", and "truth"), and so are not predisposed to distinguish thinking and feeling as separable activities as Westerners do (1980: 77-8). Literacy and Christian distinctions of soul, self, and body, may well change this and even convert the idea of involuntary intention as part of the bodily and emotional state (e.g. jealousy as witchcraft) into an explicit separation of subject (self) acting consciously and reflexively upon an object (own body or some other self).

We are, then, back to the contrast between those epistemologies which tend to fuse and those which separate subject and object. As in ethnography, the latter impose on this separation the distinction between "we" and "them".

Ricoeur (1981: 68, 70, 209) draws our attention to the contrast between Dilthey's regard for self-awareness (*Innersein*) as the ultimate epistemological reference, and Gadamer's anti-reflective, historical construction of being (i.e. that it is the individual's prejudices rather than his judgements which constitute him historically). Perhaps there is some reconciliation of the two views in the idea that the fusion, separation, and reversability of subject and object variously make up the different cultural constructions of self and also frame the alternating prejudices that distinguish "us" as a society from "them". That is to say, rather than start with the distinction between personal reflexivity and historical consciousness, we begin with that between who names and who and what is named, and with how the latter demands the former's attention and revises his/their understanding.

Recentring

Since theoretical language is metaphorical we might as well choose our metaphor. Society as text is a useful metaphor in reminding us that ethnographers may try to be cultural translators, that they may focus on the meanings of society as being either intended by cosmological or other "authors", or as infinitely interpretable, and that, as "readers", they may be obliged to take account of their own possible involvement in the text, its degree of coherence, its relationship to other texts (inter-textuality), and even how far it deserves to be judged as an aesthetic work. Other possibilities are suggested. How much is society usefully analysable in terms of a single or of complementary plots? Are the plots of the "normal" linear kind or do they lack clear chronology in their inter-linking of events? To those who would object that the sentences making up a text are fixed, while society is not, Derrida's view of text as ever interpretable wordplay supplies the missing dynamism (1970). As part of this dynamism society-as-text can be aggressively reflexive, attacking the very tenets of its own "language" through narrative (events) that questions more than re-affirms.

The usefulness of the metaphor is in diverting us from any view of society as governed by "laws" of nature or by mechanistic principles. Other insights can certainly be had, especially through the application of the ideas of Derrida himself and of such followers as De Man (1971) and Hartman (1981). In particular, Derrida's strategy of "de-centring" or of abolishing the "transcendental signified" (echoing Nietsche's own abolition of God as original creator/author) turns us away from expecting to find some ultimate system of "causes" in society. Finally, the use of this metaphor fits epistemologically with developments even in the natural sciences where, for example, the challenge from quantum mechanics in the 1920s to Einstein's faith in the ultimate regularity and predictability of elements of the universe has recently been vindicated by an experiment suggesting that the relationship between an atomic nucleus and its surrounding electrons is, after all, random (Aspect *et al.* 1981), just as Gödel's theorem proposing that mathematics can not in fact provide complete proofs has attracted renewed interest (Hofstadter 1980).

Just as uncertainty is now a respectable concept in physics and mathematics, so indeterminacy is respectable in the humanities, whether taking the form of Derrida's "endless signification", of the notion of "finitism" introduced by Barry Barnes, by which we are ultimately free to create concepts and give names to objects (1982), or, as suggested in this volume, of the inseparable yet ever-changing inter-penetrability of language and actions, and ideology and materiality, in the experience and understanding of social events. An allied development is to reject the notion of "permanency" as well as of "ultimate cause" and "predictability" as necessary features of society. "Continuity" remains important for it can accommodate the idea of thematic transformation, i.e. of different realizations of persisting templates of thought and action. But "permanency" is part of what Derrida calls the illusion of a Western metaphysics of presence, which is that things must in some way be "present" in order to exist (see Culler 1979: 161-5): "permanency" has the presuppositional awkwardness of predisposing us to privilege the fixed features of society over those of interpretive free-play.

At this point, we have to curb the metaphor of society as text. If what we really mean is that it is the culture which is the text and which its members interpret (all of which we ourselves interpret), then culture as text has now become object, and its interpreters (we and our informants) have become the subjects. But since culture does not consist of graphically fixed sentences but rather of the interpretations which people place on events, none of which are exactly like the other, then the whole metaphor dissolves in tautology. Culture *is* people interpreting, an activity which necessarily implies at least a degree of conceptual freedom.

The conceptual freedom is, however, limited, for at least a while, by the extent to which an interpretation is acceptable to those to whom we talk. Inter-subjectivity rests on recurrent instances of consensus, a word which entails a notion of conceptual constraint. Society as discourse rather than as text now seems a more suitable metaphor. It retains the attribute of interpretive word-play, but is sceptical of the idea of speech between informants themselves or between informants and ethnographers as totally freed of all con-straints. This is surely closer to Foucault's position that discourse cannot be separated from considerations of power (Foucault 1978; and see Sheridan 1980: 113-134) and to Habermas's that free speech has historically been an ideal which we have sought but not yet truly attained (1972: 9ff.), but which becomes more possible through greater self-awareness of the unacceptable origins and consequences of the beliefs underlying what we say. Such constraints are, it may be noted, of a different order from those variously characterized as "rules" by anthropologists.

Power, then, returns to our centre in social anthropology. But it is not simply the power which rests on the acquisition of land, myth, and material objects, but rather that which comes from unequal access to semantic creativity, including the capacity to nominate others as equal or unequal, animate or inanimate, memorable or abject, discussor or discussed. The struggle to objectify others (i.e. to remain principal or sole agent) is parallelled by the struggle to make acceptable new modes by which this may be done: systems of naming and entitlement; the innovative use of metaphor and other tropes; re-defining an existing epistemology and/or privileging another; providing "definitive" or "authentic" cultural translations; and widening, narrowing, and ranking the available range of communicative codes.

Power struggle of this kind inheres of course in relationships within as well as between cultures and, in so far as it is specifically bound up in the relationship of ethnographer and informant, raises the question of how legitimate it is even to speak of discrete cultures as pre-determining structures of action. It is more immediately a matter between those two persons. Differences of habitus exist between the members of a culture as well as between them and outsiders. That being the case we may say that where mutual intelligibility is possible, it is differences only of degree that separate cultures from one another, and that where mutual intelligibility has become possible then a quantitative has taken the place of a qualitative difference. But that is only from our respective perspectives. Discourse here presupposes as many possible variations in understanding as there are people who can talk to each other, whether they are cultural insiders or outsiders. Indeed, just as the distinction commonly made in ethnography between one neighbouring people and another is no more than an abstraction based on selected features, so it is, at a different level, of two individuals making up a particular so-called social relationship.

It is this selectivity entailed in whatever level of social abstraction that has been the starting-point for our methodologies. Yet, in our ethnographic fieldwork, that is not how we start. The handshake, the sickfella's limp, the griot's playfulness, the sudden talking in tongues, the spurned greeting, the use of a mystical number, the calling of a name, are the events which we happen to witness and which are then talked about and make up our interpretive frameworks. In referring to such events our informants' speech fixes their, to us, chance-like occurrence. We then have the power either to describe in as much context as possible their occurrence, or to convert them into "social facts", "rules", or entrées into a larger web of meaning.

However, whichever we choose, there may be one methodological rule which can be said to distinguish social anthropology: this is that we should identify as far as possible the circumstances by which the apparently chance event becomes an interpretive inspiration. As well as locating the power in our own discourse, this may also tell us in a pre-theoretical way something of that of our informants. It also goes some way to anchoring our and their conceptual freedom in the circumstances of the event.

At root is the question of how discussable power is, both among ourselves and between and among the peoples we observe. This could legitimately be regarded as the discipline's primary interest, for it asks not only how power is talked about and conceptualized but also how much it is a part of those who think and speak it. Such questions are thus ontological even before they are epistemological. I think that it is fair to say that the many studies inspired by Hymes's concept of an "ethnography of speaking" (1962) see as their primary task the description of the rules and procedures which shape speech events (e.g. Bauman and Sherzer 1974: 6-7; Basso 1979: 98 footnote 11). From a quite different perspective, the so-called ethnosemanticists wish to reveal the operational logic in cultural practices through the analysis of lexical co-associations. In their emphasis on "knowing how others do things" these two groups have provided often very sensitive insights into other cultural epistemologies, without necessarily identifying them as such. As a contribution to the understanding of alternative theories of knowledge, this is certainly worth strengthening, with, however, the formalist assumptions of the latter likely to be subsumed in the former's concern with the natural language of everyday use rather than with semantic domains acquired through elicitation.

Epistemological issues are, however, based on the primary ontological question of how the particular usages of natural language simultaneously create or re-create persons, circumstances, moods, and dispositions. Speaking is being before it is procedure. Being entails questions of personal autonomy, self-definition, and power, which only some in any society can ask and answer. In what sense, if any, are those who question and those who answer (and the two may not be equal) privileged to do so? If I answer you under duress that is hardly my privilege, but to do so following your supplication indicates that it is. Similarly, the questions raised by the oppressed mark them out differently from those with the authority or raw power to insist on asking.

Discourse, then, only becomes radical in the interrogative. The structuralist view of speech as one of three main forms of exchange omits this critical feature. Speech without new questions and answers, whether explicit or implicit, can be creative but only within an episteme. This is as true of our anthropological discourse as of the peoples we observe. Evans-Pritchard's implicit theory had its radical impact on social anthropology because it raised questions for others to answer not through a heavy allegiance to a body of hypotheses but through sensitive treatment of the ethnography and with relatively few presuppositions. It is a delicate balance between reporting and interrogation.

Following the pioneering work of Labov (1966) and Bernstein (1971), it might be tempting to phrase the issue in the correlational terms of how much power derives from speech and how much from status in society. That is to say, position in society may confer articulateness, but articulate people may achieve status. But this approach has different objectives. Power clearly is not a correlational phenomenon. It inheres in every act and state. To say that the power or effectiveness of speech depends on acquired or achieved status, is to make it dependent on status. One could as easily argue that some speakers invent new codes and attach statuses to them. If both are more or less "true", then how does correlating them help us understand them? Correlating speech and status fixes each in relation to the other. It makes one more dependent or less powerful than the other, tending to privilege status over speech. But it necessarily omits that other view of speaking *as* being and becoming, as simultaneously creative and re-creative, and as therefore inseparable. Since the correlational view must hold constant selected phonetic or other linguistic items (e.g. Labov's post-vocalic "r"), or selected changes in status, it is to that extent always less complete ontologically, an implication that should at least be considered, however much value there may be in describing past and possible future sociolinguistic trends of an abstract and partial kind. The more complete ontological view is that power inheres in the extent to which speakers can freely ask and answer questions, a view that does not start out by regarding differences of status as necessarily causal. The captured event takes priority over preconceived representations of status. The image of capture is appropriate for this volume, for, in it, we have tried to move towards an "apprehension" of the power in our own as well as others' discourse.

References

Akinnaso, F. Niyi 1980. The sociolinguistic basis of Yoruba personal names *Anthropological Linguistics* 22, 275-304.

Ardener, E. 1971a. The new anthropology and its critics. *Man* (N.S.) 6, 449-67.

—— (ed.) 1971b. *Social Anthropology and Language* (Ass. social Anthrop. Monogr. 10). London: Tavistock.

—— 1975a. 'Language, ethnicity, and population. In *Studies in Social Anthropology: Essays in Memory of E. E. Evans-Pritchard*. (eds) J. Beattie and G. Lienhardt Oxford: Clarendon Press

—— 1975b. The voice of prophecy: further problems in the analysis of events. The Munro Lecture. Edinburgh: Unpublished.

—— 1978. Some outstanding problems in the analysis of events. In *Yearbook of Symbolic Anthropology I* (ed.) E. Schwimmer. London: Hurst; Montreal: McGill-Queens.

Aspect, A., Grangier, P. & Roger, G. 1981. Contribution to *Physical Review Letters 47*, 460. Reported in *The Times* 27th August 1981.

Barnes, B. 1982. *T. S. Kuhn and Social Science*. London: Macmillan.

Barnes, R. 1982. Number and number use in Kédang, Indonesia. *Man* (N. S.) 17, 1-22.

Basso, K. 1979. *Portraits of "The Whiteman"*. Cambridge: Cambridge University Press.

Bauman, R. & Sherzer, J. (eds) 1974. *Explorations in the Ethnography of Speaking*. Cambridge: Cambridge University Press.

Beattie, J. 1980. The self in traditional Africa. *Africa* 50, 313-20.

Bergson, H. 1975. *The Creative Mind*. Totowa, NJ: Littlefield, Adam & Co.

Bernstein, B. 1971. *Class, Codes and Control*. St. Albans: Paladin.

Bourdieu, P. 1977. *Outline of a Theory of Practice*. Cambridge Studies in Social Anthropology No. 16. Cambridge: Cambridge University Press.

Burke, K. 1969. *A Grammer of Motives*. Berkeley: University of California Press.

Burridge, K. 1978. *Someone, No One*. Princeton: Princeton University Press.

Cesara, Manda 1982. *No Hiding Place: Reflections of a Woman Anthropologist*. London: Academic Press.

Cohen, A. 1969. *Custom and Politics in Urban Africa*. London: Routledge & Kegan Paul.

—— 1974. *Two-Dimensional Man*. London: Routledge & Kegan Paul.

Crick, M. 1976. *Explorations in Language and Meaning: Towards a Semantic Anthropology*. London: Malaby Press.

Culler, J. 1979. Jacques Derrida. In *Structuralism and Since* (ed.) J. Sturrock. Oxford: Oxford University Press.

De Man, P. 1971. *Blindness and Insight* New York: Oxford University Press.

Denyer, N. 1982. *Time, Action and Necessity*. London: Duckworth.

Derrida, J. 1972. Structure, sign, and play in the discourse of the human sciences. In *The Structuralist Controversy* (eds). Baltimore: Johns Hopkins University Press.

—— 1976. (1967) *Of Grammatology* (trans.) Gayatri Spivak. Baltimore: John Hopkins University Press.

Epstein, A. L. 1978. *Ethos and Identity*. London: Tavistock; Chicago: Aldine.
Foucault, M. 1978. (1973) Introduction to *I, Pierre Riviere, Having Slaughtered My Mother, My Sister, and My Brother*. London: Peregrine Books.
Freedman, M. 1969. Geomancy. In *Proceedings of the Royal Anthropological Institute 1968*. London.
Gauquelin, M. 1982. *The Truth About Astrology* (trans.) Sarah Matthews. Oxford: Blackwell.
Geertz, C. 1973. *The Interpretation of Cultures*. New York: Basic Books.
Gell, A. 1979. Reflections on a cut finger: taboo in the Umeda conception of the self. In *Fantasy and Symbol* (ed.) R. H. Hook. London: Academic Press.
——— 1980. The gods at play: vertigo and possession in Muria religion. *Man* (N.S.) **15**, 219-48.
Gluckman, M. 1962. Les rites de passages. In his (ed.) *Essays on the Ritual of Social Relations*. Manchester: Manchester University Press.
Habermas, J. 1972. (1968) *Knowledge and Human Interests* (trans.) J. J. Shapiro. London: Heinemann.
Halliday, M. A. K. 1978. *Language as Social Semiotic*. London: Edward Arnold.
Hallpike, C. R. 1979. *The Foundations of Primitive Thought*. Oxford: Clarendon Press.
Hanson, F. A. 1975. *Meaning in Culture*. London: Routledge and Kegan Paul.
Hartman, G. H. 1981. *Saving The Text*. Baltimore: Johns Hopkins University Press.
Heelas, P. & Lock, A. (eds) 1981. *Indigenous Philosophies* London: Academic Press.
Hofstadter, D. R. 1980. *Gödel, Escher, Bach*. New York: Vintage Books.
Holy, L. & Stuchlik, M. (eds) 1981. *The Structure of Folk Models* (Ass. social Anthrop. Monogr. **20**). London: Academic Press.
Hymes, D. 1962. The ethnography of speaking. In *Anthropology and Human Behaviour* (eds) T. Gladwin and W. C. Sturtevant. Washington D.C.: Anthropological Society of Washington.
Kohak, E. 1978. *Idea and Experience*. Chicago: Chicago University Press.
Labov, W. 1966. *The Social Stratification of English in New York City*. Washington DC: Center for Applied Linguistics.
Leach, E. R. 1961. *Rethinking Anthropology*. London: Athlone Press.
Lewis, G. 1980. *Day of Shining Red*. Cambridge: Cambridge University Press.
Lienhardt, G. 1980. Self: public and private. Some African representations. *Journal of the Anthropological Society of Oxford* **11**, 69-82.
Merton, R. K. 1957. *Social Theory and Social Structure*. Glencoe, Ill.: The Free Press.
Milner, G. 1969. Siamese twins, birds and the double helix. *Man* (N.S.) **4**, 5-23.
Needham, R. 1975. Polythetic classification: convergences and consequences. *Man* (N.S.) **10**, 349-369.
Overing Kaplan, J. 1982. Today I shall call him mummy: disorder in Piaroa systems of classification. Paper presented at the London Intercollegiate Seminar (1982), at the School of Oriental and African Studies. Unpublished.

Parkin, D. 1978. *The Cultural Definition of Political Response*. London: Academic Press.

—— 1979. Straightening the paths from wilderness. *Journal of the Anthropological Society of Oxford* **10**, 147-60 (1982 slightly modified version in *Paideuma* **28**, 71-83.)

—— 1980. The creativity of abuse. *Man* (N.S.) **15**, 45-64.

—— 1982. *Speaking of Art: a Giriama Impression* (Alan P. Merriam memorial lecture). Bloomington: African Studies Program, Indiana University.

Pocock, D. 1973. The idea of a personal anthropology. Paper presented to the decennial meetings of the Association of Social Anthropologists, Oxford, 1973. Unpublished.

Rabinow, P. 1977. *Reflections on Fieldwork in Morocco*. Berkeley: University of California Press.

Rabinow, P. & Sullivan, W. M. 1979. *Interpretive Social Science*. Berkeley: University of California Press.

Ricoeur, P. 1974. (1969) *The Conflict of Interpretations* (ed.) Don Ihde. Evanston: Northwestern University Press.

—— 1978. (1975) *The Rule of Metaphor* (trans.) Robert Czerny *et al.* London: Routledge & Kegan Paul.

—— 1981. *Hermeneutics and the Human Sciences* (trans. and ed.) J. B. Thompson. Cambridge: Cambridge University Press; Paris: Editions de la Maison des Science de l'Homme.

Riviere, P. 1980. Dialectical societies (review article). *Man* (N.S.) **15**, 533-40.

Rosaldo, M. 1980. *Knowledge and Passion*. London: Cambridge University Press.

Searle, J. R. 1969. *Speech Acts*. Cambridge: Cambridge University Press.

Sheridan, A. 1980. *Michel Foucault: The Will to Truth*. London: Tavistock.

Southall, A. W. 1965. A critique of the typology of states and political systems. In *Political Systems and the Distribution of Power* (ed.) M. Banton. (Ass. social Anthrop. Monogr. 2). London: Tavistock.

—— 1976. Nuer and Dinka are people: ecology, ethnicity, and logical possibility. *Man* (N.S.) **11**, 463-91.

Sperber, D. 1975. *Rethinking Symbolism*. Cambridge: Cambridge University Press

Sturrock, J. 1982. Differing and deferring (review). In *Times Literary Supplement* of 9 July 1982.

Tonkin, E. 1980. Jealousy names. Civilized names. Anthroponomy of the Jlao Kru of Liberia. *Man* (N.S.) **15**, 653-64.

Turner, V. W. 1969. *The Ritual Process*. Chicago: Aldine.

SOCIAL ANTHROPOLOGY, LANGUAGE AND REALITY

EDWIN ARDENER

The study of classification has a long history in social anthropology.[1]
At many points this interest has closely paralleled and overlapped
with the interests of linguists, both in its general and its particular
applications. A classical instance of common endeavour has, for
example, been in the field of colour classification. Hjelmslev, for
example, long ago noted the discrepancies in colour labels between
different languages (1963: 52-53). Anthropology has multiplied such
instances, so that both the numbers and kinds of colours discrimin-
ated by unit category terms have been shown to be of considerable
variety. Later, some order was brought into the variation by (among
others) Berlin and Kay (1969). There are some general principles
underlying the cultural choices.

These studies raised the issue of relativism versus universals in
social anthropology. Thus, in so far as all classifications partake of
this feature exemplified by colour classification it became legitimate
to ask whether all cultural systems were in principle *sui generis*, even
implying in some sense "separate realities". Whorf, as generally
represented at least, took this question to the point of appearing to
argue that cultural perceptions were not simply mediated by
language, but that language determined the way in which we experience reality. His examples were drawn in part from the kinds of
classification differences referred to already, such as the famous
three kinds of snow of the Eskimo (Carroll 1964: 210). He referred
also to other more general features of language — for example,
presence or absence of grammatical "tense" or of "mood" or
"aspect" — as being some kind of determinant of views of time or
process in particular cultures. Thus, again putting the matter very
simply, a Hopi physics (for reasons of this sort) would differ from a
European physics. I think that Whorf has been misunderstood, but

there is no doubt that the misunderstanding itself has a firm place in specialist thinking about this knotty combination of language, classification, and reality. Consequently much of this work has been judged to have painted itself into a corner, appearing to favour: 1) extreme cultural relativism: 2) separate cultural realities: 3) the cultural determination of both knowledge and "experience": and even, as we have seen, 4) linguistic determination of cultural experience. These extreme positions (if actually held) would obviously make arguments for the existence of cultural universals more difficult, and stand in opposition to ideas of cultural change, as well as to more subtle views of the relation of language to culture and of culture to reality.

Berlin and Kay's work on colour classification was seen by many as restoring universals to the centre of discussion. Thus cultures were "relativistic" in detail but there was some kind of limit to their arbitrary, reality-shaping powers. Some went so far as to argue that at a commonsense level cultural differences were greatly exaggerated, and that the major differences were mystifications deriving from ritual specialists (Bloch 1977). For people with any idea of a universal truth to be taught to all mankind, the exact nature of cultural difference is a serious question. Thus at times both missionaries and historical materialists have led violent attacks on the merest hint of cultural relativism. In Miss Mandy Rice-Davies's phrase, "They would, wouldn't they?" If there are self-evident truths that are to be taught these trusts cannot themselves be subject to any law of cultural relativism. "Cultural realities" must then be rejected on two grounds: 1) if the observer's vision is the truth, then it cannot just be part of the relativity of the observer's culture; 2) if that truth is to be transmitted to others, then cultural "worlds" that differ from it or reject it must be obfuscations of some kind, obscuring the truth. Whether or not one goes on to attribute the obfuscations to simple error, or to self-interest on the part of some portion of the population concerned, is a detail. Fundamentalist missionaries and some development economists have vacillated between both interpretations, while Marxists and historical materialists often tend to favour the latter. That is after all the more universalistic position: cultural classifications thereby become the secondary result, or "artefact", of human universals like power and dominance. As for any kind of role for language — those of "running dog", or at best of "handmaiden" or "lackey", seem to be the most conveniently vacant! So much for any short-lived Whorfian linguistic dreams of empire.

I do not wish to caricature this debate — I think that the

oppositions implied are simply false, although it is easy to see why they should arise. It is, for example, quite obvious that "mystifications" do occur. The literature on the social manipulation of discourse is quite well established: there is really nothing controversial about it. Indeed, it probably seems less problematic to linguists even than it does to social anthropologists. Let us, as it were, assert that when the issues are big enough there is no recourse but to firmly universalistic principles. Yet cross-cultural (or subcultural) misunderstanding on supposedly trivial issues (whatever the possibilities on greater ones) is a very real problem at the level of close interactions between individuals, so much so that it is itself a human universal, and whether we like it or not language looms very large in these situations. This does not only arise in the obvious limiting case, in which the interactors do not share a language. On the contrary, it often seems that the more they *think* they share, the more those "Whorfian" characteristics arise, and in comes the whole baggage of cultural classifications and the rest, all clothed in rich linguistic detail. It is my opinion (see 1971: xix-xxviii), not perhaps widely understood, that this is the point on which Whorf's original insight rests. The self-taught fire-insurance assessor was in the possession of the basic facts of the interpenetration of "language, thought and reality" (Carroll 1964) before he was tempted into the world of the professionals and learned bad habits. The famous programme for linguistic determinism is correctly named the "Sapir-Whorf Hypothesis", for there was no reason why Whorf in his untutored state should have taken that road.

Whorf's problem as a fire-insurance assessor was a *material* one. The insurance company lost if a fire broke out. Any interpretation of the cause of a fire that reduced the incidence of such fires and the amount of such payments was "cost-effective". It might even reduce premiums. We are used to such causes being cast in terms of the physics of combustion. Whorf's insight was to see that the disposition of flammable materials in vulnerable places was often due to a set of underlying linguistic classifications. For him "empty gasoline drums" exploded because they were classed as "empty" (so that people smoked near them) instead of "full" (of gasoline fumes). He found that "spun limestone", and "scrap lead" from condensers (both highly combustible materials), burst into flames when left near rubbish fires, because they were heaped wrongly with non-combustible waste. The mistake was due to the classifications with "lead" and "stone". Whorf's "reality" was inextricably intertwined with human classifications. Physical explosions (he appeared to say) were produced by a careless mixture of categories as well as of chemicals, (Ardener 1971: xxviii). It is the *material* nature of Whorf's basic problem that contains the interesting antidote to his own, and other people's flight into debates on cultural reality. Of course, Whorf's failure to develop an adequate language to discuss his original insight does not absolve him from serious criticism. From any modern point of view it is a great pity that time has frequently to be wasted in denying that this or that study of language and categories of classification embodies merely a culturally relativistic position (Ardener 1971: xxii). Meanwhile, from the point of view of linguistics this often leads to the study of cultural classifications being represented as the collection of cultural curiosities.

Some of these points, including the materiality feature, are here illustrated from the classification of bodily parts. It is well-known that the human body is divided by different criteria in different languages. In the present exposition I shall treat part of such a classification through a simultaneous analysis of thought, language and action, in order to make clearer my arguments.

Let us consider the shaking of hands in England and among the Ibo of south-eastern Nigeria.[2] In both languages there are apparently intertranslatable terms for the gesture (Ibo *ji aka*). Although *aka* is usually translated "hand" the boundaries of the parts concerned are, however, quite different. The English "hand" is bounded at the wrist. The Ibo *aka* is bounded just below the shoulder. The fingers and thumb are called *mkpisi aka*, in which *mkpisi* is "any thin somewhat elongated object" (cf. "a stick" *mkpisi osisi* – *osisi* "tree", "a match" *mkpisi okhu* – *okhu* "fire"). The more open-gestured nature of the Ibo handshake compared with the English handshake is linked in part to this difference of classification. For the English-speaker the extreme, "formal" possibility of presenting an only slightly mobile hand at the end of a relatively stiff arm becomes a choice reinforced by language. For the Ibo-speaker, even if that is a possible gesture it has no backing from language. On the contrary, for him, gripping the forearm and other variants of the gesture are still covered by the concept of shaking the *aka*, and are, as it were, allomorphs of the common gestural morpheme. For the English-speaker such arm-grips are gesturally (that is, not merely linguistically) separate from shaking hands – they are gestures of a different "meaning".

We do not resort to any linguistic determinism if we argue that the gestural classification rests to a certain degree on the labelling of bodily parts. The possibility of a different classification of greetings exists for the English speaker because of the particular placing of a conceptual boundary, which does not exist in Ibo. Thus, on the average of observations, an Ibo in "shaking hands" may involve the movement of an area greater than the "hand" more often than does an English person. Consistently shaking the hand alone, with articulation only at the wrist, might therefore seem to the traditional Ibo a slightly incomprehensible restriction of movement, equivalent perhaps in flavour to being, in the English case, offered only two or three fingers to shake. From the opposite point of view, to the English-speaker "shaking hands" and "arm-grip" are two *kinds* of greeting. To the Ibo they are degrees of intensity, demonstrativeness, of warmth, of "the same" greeting. As a result even a "warm" handshake in the English sense may seem relatively "cool" as a greeting to an Ibo.

Further light is shed by another collocation. The English "help" is translated *nye aka* in Ibo, which appears to mean "give a hand" and thus to be directly parallel metaphorical usage. Yet in close face-to-face cases when a physical "hand" is appropriate, such as when assistance over a large fallen tree-trunk on a path, or up a steep slope, is asked for (*nye m aka* "give me a hand"), a forearm may be offered to be gripped as often as the hand, if in practical terms either may suffice. In an English language context the request "give (or lend) me a hand" in those exact circumstances would only rarely fail to result in the offer of the literal "hand". With regard to the "degree" of helpfulness it is a "warmer" gesture for the English-speaker to be offered a hand then a forearm. The apparent deficiency is thus now on the opposite side of the cultural-linguistic divide.

We may easily ask here, following a respectable anthropological tradition, whether the bodily classifications are not simply determined by the social events the body mediates. One chain of argument might develop from the observation that when the hand is engaged in work, or in preparing palm-oil or food, there is a polite reluctance to offer help or greeting with it. The offering of a portion of the "arm" is, however, still conceptually the "same" gesture, and not a completely "substitute" gesture, as it would have to be in English. Thus, in such circumstances, where an Ibo will offer another part of his *aka*, the English person will have to say "I'm sorry, I can't shake hands". Socially speaking the more extended Ibo *aka* may be determined, let us say, by an overriding requirement that a physical gesture of greeting be made in the maximum number of circumstances. We shall have cause to revert in a different way to this statistical feature. This view implicitly argues that conceptual boundaries are modified like rules: as if a rule with too many exceptions (anomalies) is replaced by a revised rule to accommodate the exceptions. Douglas (1966) was very helpful in relating the idea of category anomaly to the study of social categorization. But, as she herself shows, the existence of anomalies does not lead necessarily to the revision of categories – ambiguity at boundaries, she argues, is, for example, commonly marked by taboo.

It is nevertheless proper to consider our case through the eyes of those who see the body as a map of social interactions. For Douglas and for several other theorists the body is viewed as a main image of society. For them, we would be adding a further reason why the images of the body and of society should be able to coincide. It is possible, on the other hand, to accommodate quite extreme pragmatism, or a kind of behaviourism. For example, to take now the particular use of the *aka* as a "helping hand" it might be that the use of the *aka* as a "rope" to be gripped in an emergency, with the "hand" portion clenched, offers more security, the helped one's "hand" being less likely to slide off – in a hot, sticky and often raining environment in which all helping hands are likely to be slippery. Such pragmatic interpretations are not uninteresting. They lead us, indeed to enquire why two English-speakers' hands should have to make those wild grasping movements towards each other in a similar circumstance. Perhaps a helping *aka* is really more often needed, and the help more often required in more messy and mildly dangerous conditions, than a helping "hand" is. We should encourage all such lines of discussion, in order to show that the material and statistical side of this question is a normal subject for examination. It would be misleading, however, to argue from this pragmatically that the "behaviour determines the language classification". The *aka* classification ignores a possible intermediate conceptual boundary and thereby, we can argue, removes a linguistic criterion that might introduce the possibility of an unwanted choice into the material situation. Once the classification exists, however, it is part of the total experience of unreflecting individuals. There is no "arrow of causation" from behaviour to category, since they cannot be separated. They form a "simultaneity".

It is quite clear then that the *aka* is not a "mere" taxonomic label. Some would echo certain philosophers and say: there are not first of all "objects" and then they are "used" – they are objects *because* they are used. There is a Yoruba proverb which may be translated: "In a forest no-one need fail to fight because of the lack of a cudgel" (Ojo 1966: 34). The forest here is defined as littered with cudgels –- that is a social classification, not a botanical one. We cannot define "use" in a pragmatic sense, therefore (by the way, I am not speaking of the use of *words*, for that would be to prejudge the fundamental question). It seems that *aka* is not a "mere" word in some nineteenth century lexicographical sense. It is attached to the upper limb, but it is a mnemonic for conceptualizations which are not conventionally linguistic or psychological, and which are actualized almost unconsciously as far as the individual is concerned. This is undoubtedly part of the distinction known by the terms "signifier" and "signified" (Saussure 1916). Nevertheless, such a "signified" is too complex for the traditional "linguistic sign" to encompass.

It does seem that persons bilingual or partially bilingual in Ibo and English are prepared to tolerate the rough translation of *aka* as "hand" rather than "arm". The reason lies perhaps in a partly statistical judgment of the relative importance of certain kinds of error. The English "hand" does not easily bear classification as an "arm", but, as we have seen, it is perhaps surprisingly easy to use "hand" for some "arm" interactions. The basic misunderstandings emerge in failed interactions of the rather subtle but materially important kinds that we have been discussing. Different, simpler, more narrowly "linguistic", misunderstandings also occur when (as is usual) animal front limbs are called "hands" by untutored English-speaking Ibo ("hand of dog"). This makes a double misclassification, from an English-language view, since animal front limbs are generally classed as "legs", that is as "rear" not "front" limbs from a human point of view. I would distinguish between cases of misunderstanding of this sort, which are experienced as apparent if puzzling "mis-identifications" (from the point of view of one or other speaker), and the cases of deeper misunderstanding that I have in mind. In the one case the solution is, figuratively, to call for a dictionary (or to make one if it does not exist). In the other the material problem is not experienced as a "misidentification". It is experienced as a social error or a social puzzle, even as some kind of wickedness. Who should be sent for? The difference lies in the fact that only parts of the language-category-object simultaneity are defined as language problems by natural language users. Underestimated as this latter group commonly are, it is worth stressing that such natural users have got the hang of lexical translation. They recognize that there is a common comprehension problem due to using a "wrong" label. They reach frequently for the nearest lexical solution ("That is not a dog's hand but its leg"). The problems we started with, on the contrary, are not seen as linguistic, but as lying in the realm of action. Whorf tried to call them "linguistic", but confused everyone including, very often, himself.

I do not wish to add to the complexities of this case. It is, however, important now to take up the further matter of the "density" of a category. For Ibo-speakers the forearm or lower part of the *aka* is engaged in more socially significant activity than the upper part — as if, as Berlin and Kay argue for colours, the category has a centre of gravity, or a zone most characteristic of its qualities. It may be noted that the Ibo "shoulder" (which we are not discussing here) bounds the top of the upper limb as does a vest or undershirt with a short sleeve, not (as with the English word) as does a garment without a sleeve; in other words, the *aka* is not quite as long shoulderwards as the "arm". It is a fact of common experience that "unit" categories commonly exhibit conceptual sub-gradings (or shadings). We are, for example, clearly aware of this feature with some "unit" kinship terms covering various genealogical specifications. Thus the Ibo *nwa nna* ("father's child") refers to "half-sibling" as well as various "patrilineal relatives". There is always felt to be some degree of semantic density about half-siblings within the category even though half-siblings are also indelibly marked as kinds of patrilineal relative, in virtue of their membership of the unit category. It is worth noting that this is not quite the same as saying that the term *nwa nna* is "extended" from half-siblings to other patrilineal relatives. That is now seen as an ethnocentric error, compounded though it is by the common Ibo-English translation of *nwa nna* as "brother" or "sister".

The "density" gradients of categories must be related to frequency in some ways — perhaps we may put it as frequency of association or interaction with reality. Categories thus contain or coexist with a statistical feature — it is part of their materiality, and we see that the earlier discussion of the possible influence of certain frequencies of social interaction involving the *aka* category has prepared us for such a view. Our perception of the gradients of semantic density, or the possibility of such a perception, is a main reason for denying any simple view that all reality is exhausted by sets of categories. The statistical figure marks irregularities in experience which are not flattened out by unit categories. This is an important point, accounting as it does for the existence of ways of incorporating experience into the category system. We shall wish to recall this later.

To return to our case, the *aka* is more *aka*-like, the lower down the limb we travel. The denser *aka* of the Ibo still includes the forearm, not just the "hand". The next named subdivisions, as we have seen, are the *mkpisi aka*, the "fingers". The biological pragmatist would draw attention to the undoubted saliency of the fingers (and thumb) for all humans. This merely leads us to reflect that the wrist is not anything like so important a subdivision pragmatically, and we may be ready to concede that the real problem may be why the wrist became a boundary in (say) north-west Europe, and not why it fails to be in some other areas (perhaps we shall look forward to a full historical account of these questions from the pens of experts). To subdivide *aka* into "arm" and "hand" is then to reinforce the density gradient at the active end of the limb, but the declaration of terminological independence of the "hand" still does not eliminate a possible perception of the ambiguity of the wrist boundary. For the moment, we may note that the "social" extends so far into the "semantic" here, that the case for a "semantic anthropology" in these terms (Crick) is only a case for a more delicate social anthropology.

For help in making further important distinctions I will allude to the "leg" word *ukwu*, which in a parallel fashion includes the English "foot". Again there are *mkpisi ukwu* ("toes") to match *mkpisi aka* ("fingers"). I have no absolutely equivalent data that bring the *ukwu*/"leg + foot" relationship into prominence, but it is my impression that the classification is susceptible of an equally detailed analysis. The social interventions of the *ukwu* are not subtle, but the "foot" part of the *ukwu* rarely suffers any fate not shared by at least the lower "leg". There is a strong possibility that the uneventful *ukwu* classification reinforces the *aka* classification by the example of a classificatory symmetry. But conversely the forelimb may provide the lively model for the classification of the lower limb. The English system, if we use the new perspective gained from our analysis, is surely *over*-symmetrical? The terminological specification of the "hand" and its "fingers" must be the model for the elaborate separation of "foot" from "leg", and the further provision of "toes" as a separate lexical term to balance the "fingers". We detect here the entry into categorization of a symmetry feature. The failure to provide a unit category term equivalent to "thumb" for the appropriate (big) toe strengthens rather than weakens this impression. The big toe is the only one worth singling out ("I stubbed my toe"), so that the limit to the application of classificatory symmetry is marked by ambiguity.

As we examine the *ukwu* classification beside the *aka* one, new suggestions concerning the different experiential gradients of different terms even inside the same set have arisen. Kroeber long ago (1909) noted the tendency for a classificatory symmetry to tidy up such sets. This is important as indicating that some categories may be "emptier", more decorative, more intellectual, more "cognitive" perhaps, or just more "linguistic", than others. It cannot therefore be the case that the statistical ("frequency") feature we have discussed already, actual determines the categories. On the contrary, through at least the symmetry feature, a certain autonomy appears in category sets. Thus we have been able to catch even bodily terms already taking off into realms of abstraction, their materiality giving way to ideality. In all respects, however, the Ibo system is relatively less advanced than the English one on that road.

I started my account at a point where *aka* was neither behaviour nor text, neither social nor linguistic, but a simultaneity, a unit in total experience. It is now possible to see why Lévi-Strauss's structuralism was able to stumble on the discovery that society *is* text, or that the social is homologous with the textual. As we know, the failure of structuralism in practice was to have no theory to account for the homology. Only a microscopic focus enables us to track the way in which "textuality" peels away from experiential unity. Language is in large measure responsible, no doubt. It is a hybrid medium, its map being partly interior, subjective and rooted in regularities of the "human mind", and partly exterior, objective, and rooted in materiality. Left to itself it intrudes its own arabesques into the perception of materiality: as if a fungus on a lens were to add a galaxy to a record of the universe.

In making an analysis such as the foregoing, I have no opinion on whether other systems which contain a unit "arm + hand" category would have similar detailed features. No other has been made in exactly this way. However, Professor Mihai Pop, on hearing a version of this paper, stated that Romanian usages were remarkably similar. *Mînă*, although from Latin *manus* "hand", is a "forelimb" (the pattern is common in Eastern European languages) and *da mînă* to give a "hand" also (he stated) differs in its realization from the English manner. Dr Andrei Pippidi, the historian, tells me that the use of *braţ* ("arm") has overlaid the *mînă* classification only in the recent history of the standard Romanian language. The *aka*-like features of *mînă* emerge in many standard collocations. The spread of *braţ* is a westernizing feature, exemplified by an indeterminacy about the bounds of the member, as well as by the lack of a symmetrical feature in the lower limb. The "foot + leg" term *picior* is even today undifferentiated. The terms for "finger" and "toe" are also not separated *degetul mîinii* and *degetul piciorului*. Such parallels are, when attested, a bonus, but are also in a sense diversions, as the realities must be explored *de novo* in each case. It is interesting, however, that Roman imperial interactions resulted in the Dacian limb, like the Ibo *aka*, receiving in translation the foreign "hand" term. We cannot pursue these issues here. Even the French terminology bears signs of several reconstructions (cf. von Wartburg

1969: 118, Ullman 1951, Ardener 1971:xxvii). The common Romance "leg" word is a loan in several modern Romance languages (*gamba* > Greek *kambe*). The "finger" and "toe" words remain undifferentiated. The *aka*-type terminology is to be detected in Gaelic and Welsh despite the confusions of English models. Certainly linguistic collections of cultural classifications should be dusted off and restored to the social matrixes from which they were untimely ripped. Many rich results lie in wait for the researcher.

The purpose of this paper, has, however, been to illustrate what is meant by the study of "simultaneities". I wish to indicate that it is possible to derive a multiplicity of social, epistemological, linguistic and psychological theories from a single case. No prizes are offered for their discovery. I am particularly desirous to stress the material features of the reality demonstrated, being tired of the naive assumption that we must here be in an "idealist" discourse. A multiplicity of interpretations is possible because all interpretations start off together in a point source. Certain familiar oppositions take on a healthily problematic air: category/object, structure/event, relativistic/universalistic, collective/individual, and yet there is no collapse by this method of analysis into abstraction.

It will be evident that choosing one part of a body classification instead of a whole body classification (let alone a whole social space) reduces the amount of exotic description, so that it can easily be seen what the anthropology is like. The total space is composed of an infinite series of subtleties of that order. It is also important to demonstrate the very close mesh with reality that I have in mind. The particular case has also some useful corrective features embodied in it. Handshakes and the like belong to an area of human social life which are commonly taken to be the most "observable". Such behaviour can, it is often thought, be relatively objectively described in much the same way as is expected (not always safely) to be done with animals. Indeed, "greeting" in animals is even considered by some to be the same *sort* of phenomenon. Yet even in this simple zone it is clear that the critical humanization has taken place — such that the handshake and the helping hand are "sicklied o'er with the pale cast of thought" mediated by language. We may think the actual instance socially trivial, but in fact the relations of naive English-speakers with naive Ibo-speakers have no more characteristic a framework than this. It is commonplace to draw attention to differences between cultures in complex domains (colour terms and the like). The excellence of such work has perhaps led to the too abstracted view of "cognitive" processes. The classification of the event and the "event" are simultaneous. That is why language penetrates the social. That is also why, by a paradox, linguistics, including socioloinguistics as commonly practised, does not seem to exhaust its significance.

My treatment of Whorf is introduced to show how the absence of a discourse through which to tell of his insights led him ultimately up one of the many blind alleys that start from his initial position. I have often puzzled over why people tend to see only text *or* life, as if each rules out the other. Malinowski too may have started from a similar insight but his blind alley was the theory of context of situation, and the equation of meaning with function (Henson 1974).

Category contains a statistical feature which I have called a "density". This feature accounts for the mathematical possibilities implied in many theories. Start with the extreme view that the cultural categories, linguistically expressed, are the only way we can register experience. Unit categories are then matched to a pattern of frequencies of occurrence which introduces discrepancies both within and between the categories. Thus the *aka* is more involved in interactions the further one travels towards the fingers from the shoulder. The *nwa nna* is realized as "half-sibling" with a particular experiential frequency, within the general pattern of frequency for other patrilineal relatives. The importance of the statistical feature can be illustrated from its bearing on the Berlin and Kay statement concerning colour universals: that colour shades described by subjects as the most typical within unit colour categories are more similar cross-culturally than are the colour *ranges* covered by the categories. The statement is not without methodologically controversial problems, but it matches the notion of frequency and density. The biological features of perception are not abolished by the grid of category: they appear in the density gradients of categories. For the "language is reality" people the existence of the gradients does not change the fact that they are not "present" in the inventory of categories. In addition, as we have seen, the category boundaries intrude their own effects upon the perception of frequency gradients. They are themselves a kind of statistical feature. On the other hand, the "reality is universal" people will pick up frequency gradients corresponding to pan-human experiences which cannot be held therefore to be culturally derived. The important point is, however, that there is in experience no subdivision. For that reason worlds set up by categories bear all the signs of materiality to the untutored human being.[3]

The major contribution of anthropology results from the experience of trying on a multiplicity of cultural spectacles: the illusion of total truth is amended by the revealed discrepancies. Where all the spectacles agree we have a universal. Is it simply a universal of spectacle construction? To find out we try to deconstruct the spectacles. We have added a semantic materialism to the approaches available for such purposes. It is inevitably in part linguistic, for our worlds are inescapably contaminated with language. It is an important advance to learn that the contamination extends into materiality, for that has long been for some the last refuge from language. Conversely, for others language has been a refuge from materiality.

Notes

1. See Ellen and Reason (1979) for recent contributions, and bibliographical references. Durkheim and Mauss (1963) was a founding study.
2. The Ibo live in south-eastern Nigeria, the erstwhile Biafra, and number some 7 millions. The language is conventionally rendered *Igbo*. This spelling is not used here. The *gb* phoneme is not a labiovelar but an imploded bilabial. The spelling *Ibo*, although strictly non-phonetic, thus leads to a less misleading English pronunciation than *Igbo*, which is often mispronounced *Ig-bo*. Ibo is also the normal Nigerian-English spelling. The spelling of examples is simplified here, and is not the official one, in which certain vowels are distinguished by subscript dots, nor an IPA rendering. In the examples, *nye* has an open *e*, the vowels of *mkpisi* are both *i* with subscript dot (a close *e*), *okhu* has undotted *o* (approximately as in *not*) and a dotted *u* (roughly as in *put*), ukwu has dotted *u* in both syllables. Tones are not marked here. *Aka* and *ukwu* both have two high tones. See also Green and Igwe (1963).
3. This presentation is not the occasion to take the matter further, but a hint of the dynamism of the processes concerned may be further exemplified. *Nwa nna* (see above) is contrasted with *nwa nee* ("mother's child" or "full sibling"). This is also used for "patrilineal relative" when closeness of relationship is emphasized. These usages are totally context dependent, but in a regular manner (see Ardener 1954 and 1959). We have then two unit categories each with its own frequency gradient, transferred as a pair to represent relative "nearness" and "distance" of patrilineality. At this new "meta"-level of categorization, the old frequency gradients are now symbolic only. Put oversimply the close associations of *nwa nna* with "half-sibling" and of *nwa nne* with "full sibling", are reduced to degrees of patrilineality defined by other criteria, in different contexts. Here again we catch a category peeling away from materiality with no indication in the linguistic terminology to warn us.

References

Ardener, E. 1954. The kinship terminology of a group of southern Ibo. *Africa* **24**.
———— 1959. Lineage and locality among the Mba-Ise Ibo. *Africa* **29**.
———— (ed.) 1971. *Social Anthropology and Language*. London: Tavistock.

14   *Edwin Ardener*

Berlin & Kay 1969. *Basic Colour Terms, their Universality and Evolution.* Berkeley: University of California Press.

Bloch, M. 1977. The past and present in present. *Man* (N. S.) **12**, 278-92.

Carroll, J.B. (ed.) 1964. *Language, Thought and Reality; Selected Writings of Benjamin Lee Whorf.* Cambridge, Mass: MIT Press.

Crick, M. 1975. *Explorations in Language and Meaning: Towards a Semantic Anthropology.* London: Dent.

Douglas, M. 1966. *Purity and Danger.* London: Routledge & Kegan Paul.

Durkheim, E. & Mauss, M. 1963. *Primitive Classification.* London: Cohen & West.

Ellen, R.F. & Reason, D. 1979. *Classifications in their Social Context.* London: Academic Press.

Green, M.M. & Igwe, G.E. 1963. *A Descriptive Grammar of Igbo.* London: Oxford University Press.

Henson, H. 1974. *British Social Anthropologists and Language*, Oxford: Clarendon Press.

Hjelmslev, B.L. 1963. *Prolegomena to a Theory of Language* (2nd edn of translation). Madison: University of Wisconsin.

Kroeber, A.L. 1909. Classificatory systems of relationship. *Journal of the Royal Anthropological Institute.* **39**, 74-84.

Ojo, G.J.S. 1966. *Yoruba Culture: a Geographical Analysis.* London: University of London Press.

Saussure, F. De 1916. *Cours de linguistic générale.* Published by C. Bally, A. Sechehaye, with Albert Riedlinger. Paris/Geneva: Payot.

Ullman, S. 1951. *The Principles of Semantics.* Glasgow: Jackson.

von Wartburg, W. 1969. *Problems and Methods in Linguistics* (translation of 1943 German edn). Oxford: Blackwell.

ANTHROPOLOGICAL FIELD RESEARCH, MEANING CREATION AND KNOWLEDGE CONSTRUCTION

MALCOLM CRICK

Anthropology is often conceived to be a subject about "the other"; in this paper I am concerned with ourselves. For a professional group skilled in rendering social behaviour intelligible, anthropologists have said little about their own professional practices (Scholte 1980: 78-9; Diamond 1980a: 5), a state of affairs strikingly in contrast with the "sociology of sociology" (Boissevain 1974: 212). The gaps in our discourse about our own habits are striking. In this paper I examine this problem with particular emphasis on fieldwork and the creative activities (both of interpretation and actual writing) which take place in and follow on from fieldwork.[1] I am approaching this topic on a very general level, hence I shall not be making distinctions between different sorts of fieldwork, nor shall I be concerned with the problem of ethics *per se*; for my purpose, epistemological and ethical issues overlap so considerably (Appell 1978: ix) that no separation is required.

The general aim of the paper is to add to that growing loss of epistemological innocence which has been occurring over the last decade or so. "Semantic anthropology" is not the name of a particular branch of the discipline (Crick 1976: 2), it is an attitude to the whole discipline based on the assumption that human meaning-making powers are fundamental and so must be basic in the study of human society. An important part of this attitude is that anthropology must be turned back on itself (*Ibid.*: 163, 167). This paper, therefore, is about our own creativity. The presence of the "us" in anthropological knowledge has always been implicit throughout the history of the discipline, but this presence should be made explicit (*Ibid.*: 153). Anthropological knowledge, after all, is not about "the other", it is generated by the mutual definition of "us" and "other"

(*Ibid.*: 165-9; Dwyer 1979) and is therefore inherently autobiographical. We often speak of the social character of human knowledge, and we ought therefore to be more alive to the social processes at work in the creation of our own professional knowledge. Anthropology too is a conceptual system.

Some of the specific questions I shall be asking in this paper are these: how do meanings get imposed on experiences in the field so as to constitute the data of anthropology? What are the processes by which knowledge is generated by a series of transformations out of this data? Those meaning creation and knowledge construction operations are at the very heart of anthropology, but little is written about the processes involved. Malinowski took great pains in his introduction to *Argonauts* to spell out a number of methodological matters, and these were much discussed by that group he trained. Nonetheless, Berreman was right to speak of a "conspiracy of silence" (1962) on these matters in the sense that such concerns never really became part of the written tradition of our subject. There are now a number of texts available about the experience of fieldwork but a considerable silence still exists about how anthropologising is done – how experiences are registered, how data is organized, how scripts are produced. I am not suggesting that attention to these matters is of equal import for all we undertake, I am also aware that there are limits to the value of the insights to be obtained by self-scrutiny, but our work would benefit from greater reflexivity in this field than has been shown in the past.

Scholte and others have attempted to establish an anthropology of anthropology by studying anthropological "traditions". The reflexive critical attitude involved in this work is fundamental to the semantic outlook. Anthropological knowledge, as Scholte says, is a context-related, culturally mediated artefact; our knowledge is a symbolic form, which among other things, is a symptom of our own society (1980: 66-7). This view obviously has implications for the fieldwork rhetoric of our discipline; we are not dealing with facts simply registered but with highly symbolic, inter-subjective, inter-cultural creations (Scholte 1974: 439-42). We are dealing with marginal communication between strangers, and whatever happens to the data after its initial registration, our resultant anthropological knowledge necessarily bears some of the ambiguity and uncertainty of its intersubjective origins (Schutte 1979).

Dwyer has referred to a fundamental vulnerability in anthropology (1979) which is too seldom frankly talked about. He speaks of a discipline "which shelters, when it does not mystify, itself and its own social system". A sense of this vulnerability combined with a heightened responsibility is part and parcel of accepting seriously a semantic view of our discipline. Bloch (1980) has argued that symbols often function not to reveal but to mystify social realities. Much of our professional discourse is symbolic in this sense and provides much comfort but perhaps not too much insight into what we do. Nader (1976) well states that most of us are not really sure why we do the research that we do.

Ethnographers *do* fieldwork. They also *write* anthropology books (Geertz 1973: 19). These are two very different kinds of activity; in our profession there is a pronounced disjunction between two contexts, two sets of rules, and two types of skills. Between the two contexts, the existential dimension of the discipline is often destroyed as field experience is transformed by the rules involved in the creation of anthropological texts. Dwyer (1977) speaks of the delicate dialogical structure of the meanings created in the field being "resewn" into scripts. The field context is one involving a considerable range of social skills. Understanding is generated from and in a host of relationships (Saberwal 1969: 56); there must be a "playing by ear", patience and intuition are crucial, as is living with the uncertainty of the whole process. Academic life is in many ways a very different mode of being. Indeed, Powdermaker wonders whether preliterate people living all the time in close social groups might not make far better social interpreters than we (1966: 83). Scholte even suggests (1980) that our professional training blunts our normal skills.

The field and writing contexts are not distinct, of course. Clearly what one does, perceives, records etc., in the field are in part determined by what training and interests one takes to the field. We can ask with Tonkin (1971) "What is ethnography?", for it is certainly nothing like observing raw data to which ideas are then added; analytical structurings on different levels of formality are there from the word go. Despite this obvious interconnection of research with theory, however, the difference between the researcher and the writer is still striking. Given two contexts of creativity, the whole nature of knowledge construction in anthropology becomes more intricate. Our vulnerability, too, is highlighted by this duality, for the audiences in the two contexts have in the past normally been different. Those who were informants in the field rarely saw the finished anthropological texts; those for whom the texts were largely written, namely academic colleagues, rarely had knowledge of the precise field situation nor even saw the notebooks from which the anthropologist created his account. Ethnography thus was a "compromise formation" (Crapanzano 1976: 72). The production of meanings and scripts is not much written about; it is the more important that we do this given that the experiential base of our knowledge is constituted in the semantics of the field situation in a context so unlike that in which we write and where the audience is different; it becomes the more important when we realize how many anthropological texts are accepted as knowledge when their authors say virtually nothing about the methods they employed to get their data so that we have no idea what actual events, experiences or facts are the sources of the assertions contained in the monographs (Pelto & Pelto 1978: 5,43; Jongmans & Gutkind 1967: introduction). Without the personal/experiential dimension, we are clearly in a bad position to read the texts adequately and to judge their contents (Paul 1953: 449; Gluckman 1967: xxii).[2]

Things have changed in anthropology as regards consciousness about the fieldwork experience since Laura Bohannan felt it necessary to use an "unprofessional name" (Bowen 1956) when writing "simply as a human being" rather than as an anthropologist, but for a long time Golde's complaint was valid that we presented a *fait accompli* rather than how interpretation, data, and so on, were accomplished (1970a: 1). Talk about life in the field was good for parties, for some seminars, but was rarely written down. This gap has been interpreted in many ways: embarrassment at being candid about failures, elders wishing to preserve secrets from those students undergoing their final *rite de passage* into the status of professional colleague, are two of the most common. Whatever the truth of these views, the consequences for students was a difficulty in finding out how research was actually done. Evans-Pritchard says he was told to take quinine and to keep off women (1973: 1). Beals (1970: 38) related the story of a senior anthropologist who was only advised to take plenty of marmalade. Beattie spoke of the Oxford view as "sink or swim" (1965: 2). Anecdotes abound about fieldwork, which in another breath one is told is the distinctive method and basis of anthropology.[3] 1971 saw yet another reprinting of the Royal Anthropological Institute's strange text *Notes and Queries*. This text, revised many times since its nineteenth century origin, reveals its history very badly, and if read as information about the profession today would put us in a very strange light indeed.

Many gaps in our discourse about fieldwork have now been adequately filled in, women blazing the trail (Okely 1975: 174). Whether this is because of a distinctive female attitude towards experiential realities, or because of a sense of professional oddness is not my concern here. The previous gap need not be explained by any conspiracy or embarrassment, of course, but could be a matter of epistemological naivete. A certain image of scientific practice has led elsewhere to an overlooking of the very important personal and socio-historical components in our work. Despite the number of texts now available to us on the experience of fieldwork, a number of crucial gaps remain. All anthropological knowledge is the result of those processes of transformation and adjustment called "translation" (Phillips 1960: 294,307), but the how, when and why of translation in anthropological knowledge is normally not explicitly talked about — Malinowski, again, was a striking exception in this regard. Another gap on which a great deal more work needs to be done is that of the socio-historical context of anthropological traditions of thought. It is strange that for a discipline which emphasizes "context" in the interpretation of any social phenomenon, that we do not adequately put our own texts into context in the same way. There is also the danger (Dwyer 1979) that if we stress the personal experience of the fieldworker that we shall overlook the fact that the individual is a representative of a discipline which is a symptom of a cultural system. A great deal more scholarly work needs to be done on the history of anthropology so that we have a better contextual grasp of the knowledge we have created. Even with that gap with which this paper is centrally concerned, our writings about the field are often separated from our other publications. This means that the reflexive insights which ought to derive from them are somewhat muted.

I now want to be concrete about vulnerability. Fison once said (in Codrington 1972: vii) that when one has been among an alien people for about two years one may think that one understands, but when one has been there for ten then one is conscious of only beginning to learn. With the constraints of time and money nowadays, of course, even two years is a luxury. What are we doing, then, when we come back from the field after about a year to write a book which purports to be an accurate description of another culture? Barth, for instance, writes about ritual knowledge and secrecy among the Baktaman (1975) after such a field trip. One would have thought the subject of secrecy hard to explore; we know his access to women informants was extremely limited; we also know that his command of the local language for at least half his stay there was extremely basic. Under these circumstances, what status are we to give the monograph? At the end of his research, if only for lack of linguistic skills, an anthropologist is likely on a number of subjects to know far less than a small child from that culture (den Hollander 1967: 18).

The problem we have raised about Barth's work we could pose about any monograph. Radcliffe-Brown's agglutinative work *The Andaman Islanders* consists of ethnological sections and sections put into a theoretical frame which he had not conceived when in the context from which his data were generated. We laud Evans-Pritchard's *Nuer Religion* as a sensitive text, but it appeared over twenty years after its author had left Nuerland. His fieldwork was less than a year and conducted under very difficult circumstances. We do not know what linguistic facility he acquired in this time, but we do know that he had not particularly concerned himself with religious matters while in the field. Maybury-Lewis ends his personal account of fieldwork by first declaring his research a success and then pondering on a central theme in European literature, namely the impenetrability of others (1965: 265).

A very revealing text in this regard is Malinowski's diary (1967), though it is important, as Firth points out in his foreword, to be cautious as to what weight we place on a text of such a character. It is part of the "history" of our discipline that modern anthropology is separated from Victorian by Frazer's "Heaven Forbid!" statement about actually meeting savages as compared with Malinowski's prolonged fieldwork in Melanesia. Reading his diary it is clear that the image of "deep involvement" (Gluckman 1967: xxii) is easily exaggerated (M.L. Wax 1972). That Malinowski was hypochondriacal, arrogant, racist, is not the point. That he spent a lot of time wrestling with sexual urges, read novels to pass the time and had to force himself on occasions to do ethnographic work is all very understandable given the stress under which such research is carried out. The real issue (Geertz 1975a: 47) is epistemological: what understanding can there be when normal empathy and feeling are lacking? If one feels alone when in the presence of others, as Malinowsi confesses, what sort of account can one give of their lives; how can one claim to be seeing things "through native eyes" (Malinowski 1961: 25) or to have knowledge of people at all (Jay 1974).

Malinowski's diary has made us aware of the personal dimension in our research. The researcher is a *part* of the research situation, indeed his self-knowledge is one of his most valuable tools. This is why people advocate studying one's own culture before doing fieldwork (Hsu 1979: 526), getting some psychotherapy or at least undergoing psychological tests to be more aware of one's "personal equation" (Nadel 1951: 48-53; Freilich 1977c: 303). The anthropologist is not the same at the end of his research as at the beginning: there is often a deeply personal learning experience in which one learns a lot about oneself (Gullick 1977: 90; Du Bois 1960: 231).

The individuality of the anthropologist is not a bothersome contaminant in the field situation, it is a fundamental part of it (Nash & Wintrob 1972: 528-9); it is central in the establishment of relationships and in the process of meaning creation and therefore is part of the data. As Gould says (1975: 64-5) every piece of fieldwork is also an exercise in the sociology of knowledge: why has the anthropologist chosen (or sometimes been directed to) this society, to this problem, to this interpretation, and what has "who am I?" got to do with the whole process? Okely argues, therefore, that the individual's self-consciousness must be deliberately put to analytic use in the ethnographic context (1975). It is fairly obvious that when reading an ethnographic work one needs to know something of the author, his training, his interests. But the epistemological point about the semantics of the self is, as Devereux has brilliantly argued, that a vital range of data in any social science context is what is going on in the observer himself (1967). The remainder of this section on fieldwork looks at several aspects of the anthropological self in the ethnographic context.

It is a flattering tale to describe one's fieldwork as 'immersing" oneself in another culture. Mead, who uses such a term (1977: 1) then goes on to tell how in Samoa she resided in the American dispensary along with other whites. Bowen (1956: 207) speaks of the frantic search via letters or books to shield herself from the other culture. Du Bois tells how she lived with her houseboy who in a personal sense remained a complete stranger to her (1960: 212, 221). No doubt the temperaments of different anthropologists (and values of different cultures) lead to different levels of "getting involved" (Paul 1953: 434), but I suspect that most anthropologists retain such a clear sense of their professional goal that the concept of immersion is quite uncalled for. In the colonial situation especially, "participation" would have been play acting since one's membership of the ruling elite was inescapably obvious. Freilich calls anthropologists "marginal natives" which seems presumptuous and impertinent. Anthropologists may make a number of adaptations in order to secure the information they want, but they are in no sense "natives"; in fact one would as like as not be regarded as rude or mad if one did try to act such a role (Wax 1971: 48; Langness 1970: 221). Nadel is right to suggest that our social identity is that of a freak in the group (in Paul 1953: 419). Certainly we do not have either the time nor the social and linguistic competence to participate in all the exchanges that make up social life in another culture. Bleek has also rightly raised the phoney nature of "participation" given the enormous discrepancy of wealth that obtains between the anthropologist and the local people (1979).

One aspect of the ethnographer's position which affects his meaning-making is obviously that of being an outsider. Ethnomethodologists have shown us how much social life takes place against a background of informal unspoken rules. The anthropologist as outsider is not well placed by definition to grasp this tacit fabric. Further, as Bourdieu argues (1977), in adopting the scientific stance the anthropologist distances himself from practical everyday life; this distancing has epistemological consequences. Having separated oneself, practical activities become a spectacle, an object, and as such are liable to be oversystematized and misdescribed because the anthropologist cannot see them as practical because he does not engage in them as practice.

Knowing is rarely solely a cognitive phenomenon. Nash may be correct to suggest that in general anthropologists are good at adapting to other cultures (1963: 158), but it is not without significance that the field experience and so the process of investing events with significance take place in a context of stress for the observer (Wintrob 1969). There is the problem of participant fatigue (Paul 1953: 414). There is the tension between involvement and detachment, the necessity of combining two very different orientations to reality into one attitude (Geertz 1968: 157), the simultaneous operation as "stranger" and as "friend". Of course there are elements of calculation, of closeness and distance in all relationships (Binsbergen 1979: 207), but having to operate in the morally ambiguous context of having several roles simultaneously – of friend, foreigner, scientist, etc. – knowing that one can never at the same time satisfy the audiences for all these roles, is a stressful situation (Kloos 1969). Some fieldworkers no doubt do not find this ambiguity too stressful while others may find any of the fictionalizing which goes with role play upsetting (Appell 1978: 3; Paul 1953: 432). Many anthropologists (Chagnon 1968: 7-8; Briggs 1970: 22) express a great need for privacy in the field. Evans-Pritchard (1940: 13) spoke of the "Nuerosis" induced by all the difficulties the Nuer were causing him. On top of "culture shock" (Oberg 1972) with the stripping away of one's customary props, there can also be "life shocks" (Williams 1967: 15) such as witnessing death and chronic disease for the first time. Along with adapting to a new diet and climate which can upset normal processes such as sleeping, go worries about one's health (Maybury-Lewis 1965: 154), and the need for couples in the field, for instance, to cope with new tensions in their relationship (Mead 1970: 326-7). Also there is the sense of incompetence that attends being in a social and communicational limbo (Wax 1971: 17-19).

From educational achievement as a student one descends to social incompetence, barely able to converse, with a sense of one's skills as a person undermined (Lindstrom 1979: 36; Wagner 1975: 6-7). The professional anthropologist, in short, becomes a cultural amateur. Chagnon wished to give up on his first day (1968: 5). Wax has spoken of the field as an experience where the self is redefined (1960: 174) by the new context and where anxiety sets in while waiting for confirmation by significant others.

Some fieldworkers have likened their research to a second socialization, and in many respects one does have the status of a child in terms of one's minimal cultural competence. Our research experience, like any socialization experience, is bound to be attended by anxiety and this will affect our attitudes and behaviour which, in turn, is bound to affect the data we generate. To add to this is the all-important fact that fieldwork is normally the *rite de passage* into the profession. It can be a "do or die" affair (Golde 1970a: 12): a career may hang on how well one handles adapting to the experience of social incompetence.[4] It is no wonder when so much importance is attached to fieldwork that anthropologists frequently express ambivalence or resentment towards those on whom they are so dependent. Lévi-Strauss is more extreme. For him the field situation induces real philosophical doubt (1974: 43). He went to the ends of the earth (1976: 436-7, 544) to find savages and having finally stood near to them found them mute and unintelligible; his text ends with a painful reflection on the sense of understanding one sometimes has in a chance exchange of glances with a cat.

I now want to turn to the question of rules in fieldwork. Since one of my aims in this paper is to examine the processes involved in our meaning and knowledge creation activities, it is striking that there should be a major controversy within the discipline over rules of procedure in ethnographic inquiry. A number of anthropologists (Levine 1970; Brim & Spain 1974) wax lyrical about field experiments, research design, operationalizing variables, statistical validation, while others adopt the opposite attitude. There are those who talk about rules and methods, and others who talk about relationships and sensitivity. The latter tend to argue that one cannot codify rules for doing fieldwork because it is all a matter of temperament and context (Middleton 1970b: 225; Henry 1969: 46). Cohen and Naroll, more methodologically conscious than most of their colleagues, say that the *lack* of research design has been a major strength in anthropology (1970: 7). Others speak of participant observation as a state of mind rather than a set of procedures (Crane & Angrosino 1974: 63-74), and the Peltos, who have strongly argued for beefing up our practices with a set of techniques, suggest that the sensitivity of the fieldworker as a feedback channel is worth more than any set of rules (1973: 257). Many anthropologists have commented on the role of sheer luck and accident in the field (Crane & Angrosino 1974: 56-7; Wax 1971: 115) and Gould of "sudden unplanned integrative experiences" which are vital in the process of interpretation (1975: 73). While Wax (1971: 285) talks of the farcical nature of writing out detailed research proposals and budgets before doing fieldwork because so much is uncertain, Brim and Spain argue that large research funds should only be given to those who detail hypotheses and variables before going to the field (1974: 93). The Spindlers, in introducing the Brim and Spain volume on research design (1974: vi), suggest that many anthropologists will declare the volume irrelevant to their own work.

The difference of view between the two camps on research activity is striking. If the tough view is correct, then a lot of our work must be shoddy; if the humanists are right about what is important, then one wonders exactly what all the rule talk is about. Of course, in any field situation one may use several different approaches; there is also the obvious difference between what people do and what they say they do: those who speak of relationships do follow certain rules of thumb, presumably those who speak of rules often do not follow their own preaching. Devereux has suggested (1967) that much methodology in the social sciences may be a reaction to the anxiety that social science phenomena create in the observer: the barrage of "methods" may be a way of coping with this. In the extreme situation one ends up with methods which tell one nothing about the object of investigation but a great deal about the scientist's state of mind. Some of the tough rule talk certainly does look like a barricade to prevent rather than facilitate human communication.

The last aspect of fieldwork on which I wish to make a few observations concerns the "context of situation". "Context" does not constitute an adequate semantic theory but it is obviously an important component. If context is useful in working out meanings in general, it stands to reason that a "context of situation" and other literally sociolinguistic approaches may be valuable dimensions to remember when assessing the nature of the utterances made by informants to oneself (Fabian 1979). Freilich has described the ethnographic context as a succession of two episodes: a passive/adaptive phase, followed by an active research phase during which one "gets on with the job" (1977a: 18). This view seems remarkably blind to the inherent fragility and uncertainty of any human relationship,[5] quite apart from the political and other unknowns that surround our work. Salamone acknowledges the personal and subjective aspect of the field context, but so as to control them to produce a more scientific situation (1979). But the lying informant or the paranoid anthropologist are not contaminants in the data which, if removed, would result in objectivity; factors such as the anthropologist's temperament and the informant's motives are what make up the meaning of the encounter.

An important aspect of the "context of situation" is the fact that the anthropologist must create an identity for himself. Although there is an individual element to how one goes about fieldwork, there is also an inevitable historical dimension to the ethnographic presence. The ethnographer has often been construed in terms of how a culture has experienced other types of Europeans: this is why anthropologists may try to shed their "cultural load" (Uchendu 1970: 230-1) so as not to be identified with the missionaries, traders, etc. There is inevitably a power dimension to the ethnographic context, no matter how the individual defines himself (Cassell 1980; Barnes 1979). The important point, apart from realizing this inevitable historical semantics of ethnographic work is that context is defined by two sides. That is, as the ethnographer is theorizing about "the natives", they too are imposing meanings on the situation, for they are speculating about the ethnographer's behaviour. This is what a great deal of the toughest rule talk seems to miss – the fact that the ethnographic enterprise is not a matter of what one person does in a situation but how two sides of an encounter arrive at a delicate workable definition of their meeting. Rosemary Firth has well said (1972: 12) that one's role in the field is very much what "they" allow you to be. Middleton has claimed that his fieldwork was haphazard because what he did was more or less determined by Lugbara interests (1970a: 16). Forge suggests that no matter how much rapport develops, one's role may never be entirely intelligible to one's informants (1972: 296). Wax is certainly right to stress that the role the anthropologist develops will never exactly fit the role structures of the cultures of either of the participants in the ethnographic encounter (1971: 52). Rabinow has gone further and said that in the encounter the anthropologist is not semantically privileged: the anthropologist and "the other" are on the same epistemological level. Whatever the ideal situation, this equality obviously does not obtain. Our informants have never been "full partners" in the study of man as Casagrande writes (1960: introduction). Actually, as Clifford points out (1980) our habits in this respect raise serious questions about authorship for our informants put in such a lot of information yet we call the ethnographic scripts that result our own. Powdermaker (1966: 260) relates her experience on the Copperbelt where she commanded no local language: she describes her main informant as her "alter ego" without whom she could not have written her book; under these conditions it is surely only a power dimension in the anthropological context which makes it possible to avoid acknowledging dual authorship?

There have been several efforts to develop general models of ethnographer-informant relationships. The ethnographer is atypical, marginal and opportunistic; but so, on many occasions, will be the main informants. Rather than utilize romantic mystificatory notions like "rapport", some commentators (Wax 1952; Freilich 1977b) have suggested construing the ethnographic context in terms of a theory of reciprocity (Lundberg 1968). Here it is a matter of both giving, risking and receiving in the exchange of information. Rapport here becomes something of a red herring: people will inform if they are getting something in return (Wax 1952: 34). Hatfield has even argued (1973) that the ethnographic context be seen as one of mutual exploitation. Certainly there are many examples of anthropologists being on the rough end of informants wanting jobs, free rides, medical supplies, money, and even information (Chagnon 1968: 8; McCurdy 1976).

Several factors in the ethnographic context render the relationship even more vulnerable than normal. This is why we must not talk naively about ethnographic facts but rather look at the facticity that represents the accomplishment of the ethnographic encounter (Scholte 1980: 76-7). This context allows a fragile achievement as the result of the dialectic between two ethnologies in marginal communication in which the parties may not share all the rules (*Ibid*:58). The reality of the encounter rather than simply the research is vital (Ennew 1976: 16). Fabian has suggested that objectivity does not reside in a scientific code or in a research attitude, but in a realization that ethnography is produced in a highly contextual, intersubjective situation (1979). This is why the usage of the dramaturgical idiom to describe fieldwork (Berreman 1962) is so revealing: both ethnographer and subject are meaning-making, communicating and concealing information. Geertz has spoken of the situation as an ambiguous collaboration, the maintenance of a working fiction (1968: 150-5), of a context which at any time can evaporate into two separate non-communicating worlds. For informants, after all, any involvement with an ethnographer is bound to be secondary to the rest of their lives, no matter how important "getting on with the job" is to the anthropologist (Rabinow 1977: 47). Rabinow feels the fragility and immediacy of this context so acutely that his reflections on his Moroccan fieldwork are a series of recollections of personal encounters (*Ibid*: 38-9).

Ethnographers not only do fieldwork, they also write anthropology. What is the "product" from the field point of view, namely drafting scripts out of the data constitued by the meanings created in the field, is also the first point in that series of transformations which leads to anthropological knowledge being constructed. There is a major shift here from experience to draft to knowledge, a shift of context, style and audience, but very little is written about it. Many anthropological accounts read as if there had been no field worker present (Beals 1970: 50). A sense of the personal is suppressed, the existential dimension goes under as "I" is superseded by the third person (Crapanzano 1976; Scholte 1980: 58; Kimbal & Watson 1972: 7). Books like *In the Company of Man* (Casagrande 1960) are rare, for factual individuals rarely appear in many types of anthropological account (Jay 1974: 376-7); even one's closest informants sometimes disappear (Casagrande 1960: xii). What is occurring is a reworking in which the individuals observed and the individuality of the observer are eliminated.

The way in which field experience become data and are then written about systematically ought to be a process on which anthropologists have something to say. We see brief references to "presenting data" or to "writing up", but such expressions, which imply a naive empiricism in which no one believes, clearly are not illuminating. Writing up, as Beattie says (1965: 54) is a kind of "conceptual exegesis", it is not a matter of putting interpretations on data, for the data have already been constituted by meaning creating activities. Ennew claims that our ethnographic data are mere "insertions" into our constructions (1976: 44). I have elsewhere (1976: 166) spoken of a text like *Nuer Religion* as forming a "sign" within a semantic field, the articulations of which are made up of the other Nuer monographs, other ethnographic writings on religion, Evans-Pritchard's own religious biography, and so on; given such dimensions and constraints which constitute a text, it is difficult to say exactly how the ethnography does fit in. What actually, then, does happen to our notes? How do they become linked to general notions and marshalled ready for script writing? Little of the struggle for interpretation involved in these processes survives in our writings (Hitchcock 1970: 164) despite the enormous amount of time one spends on what can be enormous quantities of notes (Williams 1967: 39; Boissevain 1970: 83). It is remarkable that explicit discussions of how ethnographic accounts are produced, for instance, the to-ing and fro-ing between embryonic publications and notebooks (Silverman 1972) are so rare. It may be the case that some of these processes may not prove particularly entertaining, but I suspect that few of us share Lévi-Strauss' declared sense of not being actually involved in the writing of his books.

It is not too much of an exaggeration when den Hollander says that because so little ethnography can be checked since others cannot repeat a colleague's work, that most of our anthropology involves *trusting* the accuracy of our colleagues (1967: 29). This trust is remarkable since we are trained to be sceptical about what our informants tell us (Bleek 1980: 292). And as Brown suggests (1981) our "my tribe" territorial imperative serves to make the fact of fieldwork into a kind of local expertise by definition. Let us not forget either that because of the increasing shape and coherence involved with the transformation of notes into articles into monographs, our writings are liable to look persuasive even if they are inaccurate in detail or even fundamentally (Campbell & Levine 1970: 385). Our writing may even involve the deliberate incorporation of inaccuracy in that certain facts about locale, informants, etc., may be changed to preserve anonymity (Barnes 1967: 203).

Scripts, however, are not just the end of the process of meaning creation which occurs in the fieldwork context, for they also purport to be knowledge. It is important that we ask, therefore, how meanings become knowledge. If meanings are seen not as properties but as processes, and data not as given but produced, so too we must look at knowledge in the same light. Knowledge is a social achievement: it consists of meanings that have "made it". Clearly this is not the place to attempt anything like an adequate account of the establishment, maintenance and modification of knowledge structures. It clearly requires looking at epistemological, sociological, psychological and even biological factors (Boissevain 1974: 223). But along with the more customary "sociology of knowledge" frameworks there is another level which contains some elements which will be a part of an adequate framework. This is the level of rules and procedures within an academic profession, and since this paper is about "reflexivity" it is with respect to this level that I shall finish this paper by just briefly hinting at two sorts of ideas which we might find useful.

Recent studies going on under the general label of "social studies of science" may prove useful for directing our attention to some of the issues with which we have been concerned in this paper. Contributions in this field are exposing a great deal of philosophy of science as mystificatory, as disguising the actual operations of scientific research. Latour and Woolgar, in their "anthropology of laboratory life" are concerned to reveal empirically the concrete processes by which science actually gets done, how facts are constructed, negotiated and established, how various social processes play a part in that collective achievement called scientific knowledge. In particular they concentrate on the processes by which the status of "scientific inscriptions" is established and modified (1979: 83). Sometimes, they show, by the most casual of negotiations, meanings can be created for data and the status of interpretations revised. Science, in their view, often looks like a disorderly collection of pieces of practical reasoning involving issues of luck, power and so on.

Any look at academe as a context for knowledge production clearly requires that we go beyond formal rules, publicly stated purposes and the like, to realms of power and covert conventions (Bailey 1977). Bourdieu has, in fact, looked at knowledge production in terms of an economic/prestige/symbol/power model (1975). He sees an academic career as like the acquisition of symbolic capital; as with other symbol systems, transformations are possible. Research might then be looked on as an investment of energy for later reward, for instance publications can be translated into promotion which carries a cash reward as well as prestige. Capital acquired can be used as credit to acquire more; for instance, someone with status tends to get widely cited in bibliographies, thus his reputation is further enhanced. White (1966) claims that Radcliffe-Brown's status really derived not from his ideas at all but from the way he set up pedagogical infrastructures in several places across the globe.

Ideas like those of Bourdieu have been little applied in anthropology, and clearly to amount to more than just an imaginative model and to pass beyond the stage of mere gossip we require a great deal of information about the research, publishing, citation habits, and so on, of members in the profession. Of course there is nothing unique about anthropologists in all this, but we may be up against a hard fact of institutional life that our required level of scrutiny is best performed on the dead rather than on our living colleagues who may not wish for nor see the point of this level of scrutiny of their professional activities. Nonetheless I would see useful insights coming from a closer attention to the symbol/power/ negotiation aspects of academe. To take the issue of revision of work, for instance, Beattie has suggested that it would be wiser to produce a series of articles after one's fieldwork so that one gave ample time for colleagues to make their criticisms before one embarked on the monograph (1965: 52). In fact the number of articles published in our journals which give rise to protracted debate is small. In this sense ethnographic meanings become knowledge through an absence of comment. I do not know how many monographs have benefitted substantially from the process Beattie suggests, nor how many anthropological texts reach a much modified second edition as a result of public scrutiny. Those few cases of outright theoretical challenge to published works (for instance, Needham's reanalysis of Nyoro ethnography (1967), Asad's (1972) reinterpretation of Swat material, Worsley's (1956) reanalysis of Fortes' Tallensi kinship works) have led to heated argument, but stalemate as far as the validity of any of the arguments is concerned.

We can talk abstractly about anthropological knowledge, but anthropological traditions like all paradigms do not float through the air in an intellectual atmosphere unaffected by other sorts of influences. Idea construction, maintenance and change costs money, it involves jobs, it requires the exercise of power. We need to know how departments use their credit to attract students who perpetuate the species; we need to look at how competence is credited by the acceptance of thesis work; we need to be aware of how senior academics can, through their influence on junior members, through the allocation of research leave, funds, promotion, tenure, and so on, create structures in which their own particular interests come to seem increasingly like a definition of the discipline. Some of these factors, the tremendous power of Malinowski in the seminar, the patterns of recruitment to departments, the activities of grant disbursing bodies, should be open to investigation. When it comes to the disbursement of monies or research leave, just as in the case of recruitment and promotion, we may be in a field where there is a considerable discrepancy between formal rules and the actual decision making procedures. The "feudal" structure of academe (Boissevain 1974: 217-8) has been commented on by others, and much that we might analyse in terms simply of the dynamics of knowledge in fact owes much to the exercise of personal power within the institutions concerned. Clearly publications are central status items in our academic symbolic system. Thus to explore the issues indicated here we have to know more about the processes by which referees and readers decide whether to accept an article for a journal or to recommend that a book be published. Such decisions as these are vital, for since publication is a main criterion for promotion, adverse decisions can affect one's career. In the reviewing process, too, to have a book well reviewed enhances one's status; people will then cite one's work and so one's credit will rise further. Citation is a symbolic act, for inclusion is a comment on a colleague's worth; bibliographies are therefore political acts. Of course, given the existence of very different persuasions within the discipline all these remarks about refereeing, reviewing, and so on are the more important, for evaluations may then be more declarations of loyalty to a particular orientation rather than an appraisal of knowledge. In the history of ideas, the emergence of new avenues for writing, for instance the appearance of a new journal, is sometimes vital; given the relationships between power, control and knowledge dissemination, one can see why this is so.

I have not done justice in the space available to the many ideas we might use in looking at knowledge production within our profession. I hope, however, that the discussion will suggest that those like Asad (1979) who find semantic anthropology trivial for its avoidance of issues like power, have misunderstood the scope of semantic anthropology. I believe the critical, reflexive aspect of semantic anthropology to be vital as a means of making us more aware of the nature of our own creative activities. This is not to debunk a discipline in any way, but merely to give us a clearer view of what goes on. Conscious of their meaning-making powers, semantic anthropologists ought to show a more responsible attitude to what, after all, is their own creation. As academe dries up as an employment area for new graduates given the increasing financial pressures to which we are subject, clearly more and more of those we have taught will find themselves outside universities, dispersed through society; this dispersal makes our responsibility of knowing what we are about even greater.

Acknowledgements

I wish to express my thanks to the British Academy and to Deakin University for financial support enabling me to attend the 1982 ASA Conference. I am also grateful to a large number of participants at that conference, in particular Sir Raymond Firth, for making a number of comments which have led to revisions in the original paper.

Notes

1. There is a "personal anthropology" which lies behind the various interests which have converged in this paper. There is a concern with the sociology of academe. Also important is my interest in the "politics of anthropology" which has increased our ethnographic self-consciousness (Nash & Wintrob

1973) given the fieldwork difficulties we now experience in many parts of the Third World and given queries like those by Owusu (1978) about the anthropological knowledge we have produced in the past. Immediately after the ASA Conference I departed for Sri Lanka to do fieldwork, and that research had led me to read widely in the literature on the field experience. One commentator at the conference made the perceptive remark that much of my paper might well be read as a matter of pre-fieldwork anxiety.
2. The Manchester style of "situational analysis" involving concrete cases and actual people is an exception here (van Velsen 1967: 140-1).
3. I do not know how widely University departments in the UK and overseas vary in the extent to which they prepare graduates for the field in linguistics, research methods, and so on.
4. Actually, the importance of one's fieldwork for one's subsequent publishing career is very variable, viz. Evans-Pritchard as compared with Needham. It is also possible to enter the profession and become a member of the ASA without doing fieldwork.
5. Since the "New Ethnography" is a set of methods explicitly designed to elicit knowledge, it is remarkable how blind its practitioners were to how human beings (including themselves) actually make meanings (Manning & Fabrega 1976).

References

Adams, R.N. & Priess, J.J. (eds) 1960. *Human Organization. Field Relations and Techniques.* Homewood: Dorsey Press.

Appell, G.N. 1978. *Ethical Dilemmas in Anthropological Inquiry: A Case Book.* Cross Roads Press, Waltham, Mass.

Asad, T. 1972. Market model, class structure and consent. A reconsideration of Swat Political organization. *Man* **7**, 74-94.

⸺ 1979. Anthropology and the analysis of ideology. *Man* **14**, 607-27.

Bailey, F.G. 1977. *Morality and Expediency: The Folklore of Academic Politics.* Oxford: Blackwell.

Barnes, J.A. 1967. Some ethical problems in modern fieldwork. In Jongmans & Gutkind (eds): 93-213.

⸺ 1979. *Who should know what? Social science, privacy and ethics.* Cambridge: Cambridge University Press.

Barth, F. 1975. *Ritual and Knowledge among the Baktaman of New Guinea.* New Haven: Yale University Press.

Beals, A.R. 1970. Gopalpur 1958-1960. In Spindler (ed.): 32-57.

Beattie, J.H.M. 1965. *Understanding an African Kingdom. Bunyoro.* New York: Holt, Rinehart & Winston.

Berreman, G.D. 1962. Behind many masks: Ethnography and impression management. In Berreman 1972. *Hindus of the Himalayas. Ethnography and Change.* Berkeley: University of California Press.

Béteille, A. & Madan, I.N. (eds) 1975. *Encounter & Experience. Personal Accounts of Fieldwork.* Delhi: Vikas Publishing House.

Binsbergen, W. van 1979. Anthropological fieldwork: There and back again. *Human Organization* **38**, 205-9.

Bleek, W. 1979. Envy and inequality in fieldwork: An example from Ghana. *Human Organization* **38**, 200-5.

———1980. Envy and inequality in fieldwork: A rejoinder. *Human Organization* **39**, 291-3.

Bloch, M. 1980. Ritual symbolism and the non-representation of society. In Foster & Brandes (eds): 93-102.

Boissevain, J. 1970. Fieldwork in Malta. In Spindler (ed.): 58-84.

——— 1974. Towards a sociology of social anthropology. *Theory and Society* **1**, 211-30.

Bourdieu, P. 1975. The Specificity of the Scientific field and the social conditions of the progress of reason. *Social Science Information* **14**, 19-47.

——— 1977. *Outline of a Theory of Practice*. Cambridge: Cambridge University Press.

Bowen, E.S. 1956. *Return to Laughter*. London: Gollancz.

Briggs, J. 1970. Kapluna daughter. In Golde (ed.): 17-44.

Brim, J.A. & Spain, D.A. 1974. *Research Design in Anthropology: Paradigms and Pragmatics in the Testing of Hypotheses*. New York: Holt, Rinehart & Winston.

Brown, P.J. 1981. Field-site duplication, case studies and the "My Tribe" syndrome. *Current Anthropology* **22**, 413-4.

Campbell, D.T. & Levine, R.A. 1970. Field-Manual Anthropology. In Naroll & Cohen (eds): 366-87.

Casagrande, J.B. 1960. Introduction. In Casagrande (ed.): ix-xvi.

——— (ed) 1960. *In the Company of Man. Twenty Portraits by Anthropologists*. New York: Harper & Brothers.

Cassell, J. 1980. Ethical principles for conducting fieldwork. *American Anthropologist* **82**, 28-41.

Chagnon, N. 1968. *Yanomamo. The Fierce People*. New York: Holt, Rinehart & Winston.

Clifford, J. 1980. Fieldwork, reciprocity and the making of ethnographic texts: the example of Maurice Leenhardt. *Man* **15**, 518-32.

Codrington, R.H. 1972. *The Melanesians, Studies in their Anthropology and Folklore*. New York: Dover Publications Limited.

Cohen, R. & Naroll, R. 1970. Method in cultural anthropology. In Naroll & Cohen (eds): 3-24.

Crane, J.G. & Angrosino, M.V. 1974. *Field Projects in Anthropology. A Student Handbook*. Morristown: General Learning Press.

Crapanzano, V. 1976. On the writing of ethnography. *Dialectical Anthropology* **2**, 69-73.

Crick, M. 1976. *Explorations in Language and Meaning*. London: Malaby Press.

Den Hollander, A.N.J. 1967. Social description; the problem of reliability and validity. In Jongmans & Gutkind (eds): 1-34.

Devereux, G. 1967. *From Anxiety to Method on the Behavioural Sciences*. The Hague: Mouton.

Diamond, S. 1980a. Anthropological traditions, the participants observed.

Diamond (ed.): 1-16.

—— 1980b. (Ed.): 1980. *Anthropology. Ancestors & Heirs*. The Hague: Mouton.

Du Bois, C. 1960. The form and substance of status. A Javanese-American relationship. In Casagrande (ed.): 211-32.

Dwyer, K. 1977. The dialectic of fieldwork. *Dialectical Anthropology* 2, 143-51.

—— 1979. The dialectic of ethnology. *Dialectical Anthropology* 4, 105-24.

Ennew, J. 1976. Examining the facts in fieldwork. Considerations of method and data. *Critique of Anthropology* 7, 43-66.

Epstein, A.L. (ed.) 1979. *The Craft of Social Anthropology*. Oxford: Pergamon Press.

Evans-Pritchard, E.E. 1940. *The Nuer*. Oxford: Clarendon Press.

—— 1973. Some reminiscences and reflections on fieldwork. *Journal of the Anthropological Society of Oxford* 4, 1-12.

Fabian, J. 1979. Rule and process: Thoughts on ethnography as communication. *Philosophy of Social Science* 9, 1-26.

Firth, R. 1972. From wife to anthropologist. In Kimball & Watson (eds): 10-32.

Forge, A. 1972. The lonely anthropologist. In Kimball & Watson (eds): 292-7.

Foster, M. Le C. & Brandes, S.H. (eds) 1980. *Symbol as Sense. New Approaches to the Analysis of Meaning*. New York: Academic Press.

Freilich, M. 1977a. Fieldwork: an introduction. In Freilich (ed.): 1-37.

—— 1977b. Fieldwork: Problems and goals. In Freilich (ed.): 255-89.

—— 1977c. A guide to planning fieldwork. In Freilich (ed.): 301-11.

—— (ed.) 1977. *Marginal Natives at Work. Anthropologists in the Field*. New York: Schenkman Publishing Co.

Geertz, C. 1968. Thinking as a moral act. Ethical dimensions of anthropological Fieldwork in the New States. *Antioch Review*, 139-58.

—— 1973. Thick description: towards an interpretative theory of culture. In Geertz 1975b: 3-30.

—— 1975a. On the nature of anthropological understanding. *American Scientist* 63 (Jan/Feb), 47-53.

—— 1975b. *The Interpretation of Cultures*. London: Hutchinson.

Gluckman, M.G. 1967. Introduction. In Epstein (ed.): xv-xxiv.

Golde, P. 1970a. Introduction. In Golde (ed.): 1-15.

—— 1970b. Odyssey of encounter. In Golde (ed.): 65-93.

—— (ed) 1970. *Women in the Field. Anthropological Experiences*. Chicago: Aldine Publishing Co.

Gould, H.A. 1975. Two decades of field work in India. Some reflections. In Béteille & Madan (eds): 64-82.

Gullick, T. 1977. Village and city field work in Lebanon. In Freilich (ed.): 89-118.

Hammond, P.B. (ed.) 1975. *Cultural and Social Anthropology. Introductory Readings in Ethnology*. 2nd edn. New York: Macmillans Publishing Co.

Hatfield, C.R. 1973. Fieldwork: Towards a model of mutual exploitation. In Hammond (ed): 426-33.

Henry, F. 1969. Stress and strategy in three field situations. In Henry & Saberwal (eds): 35-46.

—— & Saberwal, S. (eds) 1969. *Stress and Response in Fieldwork*. New York: Holt, Rinehart & Winston.

Hitchcock, J.T. 1970. Fieldwork in Gurkha country. In Spindler (ed.): 164-93.

Honigmann, J.J. (ed.) 1973. *Handbook of Social and Cultural Anthropology*. Chicago: Rand McNally.

Hsu, F.L.K. 1979. The cultural problem of the cultural anthropologist. *American Anthropologist* **81**, 517-32.

Hymes, D. (ed) 1974. *Reinventing Anthropology*. New York: Vintage Books/ Random House.

Jay, R. 1974. Personal and extrapersonal vision in anthropology. In Hymes (ed.): 367-81.

Jongmans, D.G. & Gutkind, P.C.W. (eds) 1967. *Anthropologists in the Field*. Assen: Van Gorcum & Co.

Kimball, S.T. & Watson, J.B. (eds) 1972. *Crossing Cultural Boundaries. The Anthropological Experience*. Chandler Publishing Co.

Kloos, P. 1969. Role conflicts in social fieldwork. *Current Anthropology* **10**, 509-12.

Kroeber, A.L. (ed.) 1953. *Anthropology Today*. Chicago: Chicago University Press.

Langness, L.L. 1970. Entrée into the Field. Highlands New Guinea. In Naroll & Cohen (eds): 220-5.

Latour, B. & Woolgar, S. 1979. *Laboratory life. The Social construction of scientific facts*. Beverly Hills, Sage Publications.

Lévi-Strauss, C. 1974. *The Scope of Anthropology*. London: Jonathan Cape.

—— 1976. *Tristes Tropiques*. Harmondsworth: Penguin.

—— 1978. *Myth and Meaning*. New York: Schocken.

Levine, R.A. 1970. Research design in anthropological fieldwork. In Naroll & Cohen (eds): 183-95.

Lindstrom, M. 1979. Americans on Tanna. An essay from the field. *Canberra Anthropology* **2**, 36-45.

Lundberg, C. 1968. A transitional conception of fieldwork. *Human Organization* **27**, 45-9.

Malinowski, B. 1961. *Argonauts of the Western Pacific*. New York: E.P. Dutton.

—— 1967. *A Diary in the Strict Sense of the Term*. London: Routledge & Kegan Paul.

Manning, P.K. & Fabrega Jr., H. 1976. Fieldwork and the "New Ethnography". *Man* **11**, 39-52.

Maybury-Lewis, D.H. 1965. *The Savage and the Innocent*. London: Evans Brothers Ltd.

McCurdy, D. 1976. The medicine man. In Rynkiewich & Spradley (eds): 4-16.

Mead, M. 1977. *Letters from the Field 1925-75*. New York: Harper & Row.

Middleton, J. 1970a. *The Study of the Lugbara. Expectation and Paradox in Anthropological Research*. New York: Holt, Rinehart & Winston.

—— 1970b. Entrée into the field. Africa. In Naroll & Cohen (eds): 225-30.

Nadel, S.F. 1951. *The Foundations of Social Anthropology*. London: Cohen & West.

Nader, L. 1976. Professional standards and what we study. In Rynkiewich &

Spradley (eds): 167-82.

Naroll, R. & Cohen, R. (eds) 1973. *A Handbook of Method in Cultural Anthropology*. New York: Columbia University Press.

Nash, D. 1963. The ethnologist as stranger. An essay in the sociology of knowledge. *Southwestern Journal of Anthropology* **19**, 149-67.

———— & Wintrob, R. 1972. The emergence of self-consciousness in ethnography. *Current Anthropology* **13**, 527-42.

Needham, R. 1967. Right and left in Nyoro Symbolic Classification. *Africa* **37**, 425-51.

Oberg, K. 1972. Contrasts in fieldwork in three continents. In Kimball & Watson (eds): 14-86.

Okely, J. 1975. The self & scientism. *Journal of the Anthropological Society of Oxford* **6**, 171-88.

Owusu, M. 1978. The ethnography of Africa: the usefulness of the useless. *American Anthropologist* **80**, 310-34.

Paul, B.D. 1953. Interview techniques and field relations. In Kroeber (ed.): 430-51.

Pelto, P.J. & Pelto, G.H. 1973. Ethnography. the fieldwork enterprise. In Honigmann (ed.): 241-88.

———— 1978. *Anthropological Research, The Structure of Inquiry*. Cambridge: Cambridge University Press.

Phillips, H.P. 1960. Problems of translation and meaning in fieldwork. In Adams & Preiss (eds): 290-307.

Pocock, D.F. 1973. The Idea of a Personal Anthropology. TS.

Powdermaker, H. 1966. *Stranger and Friend. The way of an anthropologist*. London: Secker & Warburg.

Rabinow, P. 1977. *Reflections on Fieldwork in Morocco*. Berkeley: University of California Press.

Royal Anthropological Institute, 1971. *Notes and Queries on Anthropology*. Sixth-edition. London: Routledge & Kegan Paul.

Rynkiewich, M.A. and Spradley, J.P. (eds) 1976. *Ethics and Anthropology. Dilemma in Fieldwork*. New York: Wiley & Sons.

Saberwal, S. 1969. Rapport and resistance among the Embu of Central Kenya (1963-1964). In Henry & Saverwal (eds): 47-62.

Salamone, F.A. 1979. Epistemological implications of fieldwork and their consequences. *American Anthropologist* **81**, 46-60.

Scholte, B. 1974. Towards a reflexive and critical anthropology. In Hymes (ed): 430-52.

———— 1980. Anthropological traditions. Their definition. In Diamond (ed.): 53-87.

Schutte, A.G. 1979. Ethnography. The Elementary Form of Sociological Knowledge? TS.

Silverman, M.G. 1972. Ambiguation and disambiguation in the field. In Kimball & Watson (eds): 204-29.

Spindler, G.D. (ed) 1970. *Being an anthropologist. Fieldwork in eleven cultures*. New York: Holt, Rinehart & Winston.

Tonkin, J.E.A. 1971. The uses of ethnography. *Journal of the Anthropological*

Society of Oxford **2**, 134-6.

Uchendu, V. 1970. Entrée into the field. A Navaho Community. In Naroll & Cohen (eds): 230-7.

Van Velsen, J. 1967. The Extended Case Method and Situational Analysis. In Epstein (ed.): 129-49.

Wagner, R. 1975. *The Invention of Culture*. Englewood Cliffs: Prentice-Hall.

Wax, M.L. 1972. Tenting with Malinowski. *American Sociological Review* **37**, 1-13.

Wax, R.H. 1952. Field Methods & Techniques. Reciprocity as a fieldwork technique. *Human Organization* **11**, 34-7.

—— 1960. Twelve years after. An analysis of a fieldwork experience. In Adams & Preiss (eds): 166-79.

—— 1971. *Doing Fieldwork Warnings & Advice*. Chicago: University of Chicago Press.

White, L. 1966. The social organization of ethnological thought. *Rice University Monographs on Cultural Anthropology* **25** (4). Houston.

Williams, T.R. 1967. *Field Methods in the Study of Culture*. New York: Holt, Rinehart & Winston.

Wintrob, R.M. 1969. An Inward focus. A consideration of psychological stress in fieldwork. In Henry & Saberwal (eds): 63-76.

Worsley, P.M. 1956. The Kinship system of the Tallensi: a revaluation. *Journal of the Royal Anthropological Institute* **86**, 37-75.

MEANING OR MOANING? AN ETHNOGRAPHIC NOTE ON A LITTLE-UNDERSTOOD TRIBE

MARK HOBART

Meaning is what essence becomes when it is divorced from the object of reference and wedded to the word.

Quine — Two dogmas of empiricism.

Was it the Queen of Hearts or Humpty Dumpty who liked changing the rules to suit their position? An unworthy doubt sometimes creeps into mind that "meaning" is so slippery a word that those who use it may find they are unwittingly wearing Lewis Carroll's cap. The history of anthropology is littered with the wreckage of theories, the ambiguity of the core concepts of which was as essential to their initial appeal as it was to their eventual decline. But anthropologists, understandably, prefer their working concepts on the hoof, so to speak, and are suspicious if they are neatly stuffed for inspection. There is a drawback though to the comfortable stance that what is meant by meaning should be evident to an idiot. Not only does this let idiosyncratic interpretations of culture pretend to infallibility, but it may make what is being talked about quite obscure. The term itself has a curious ancestry. As Harold Bloom remarks "the word *meaning* goes back to a root that signifies 'opinion' or 'intention', and is closely related to the word *moaning*. A poem's meaning is a poem's complaint . . ." (1979: 1, italics in the original; see also Onions 1966). In fact still more lies behind the usage.

A short survey of popular theories of meaning may help to highlight some of the problems, and the unstated presuppositions. Like the tiger's tail, it is quite possible — if dangerous — to seize upon a convenient notion without bothering about what it may entail and commit one to what it may. Ethnography poses a double difficulty.

Research requires the study of indigenous categories and cultural assumptions, while anthropology itself is part of a changing, and internally diverse, Western academic tradition. This makes the problem of translation in its broadest sense more serious than is often recognized. It is easy to assume that our academic, and cultural categories are self-evident and to overlook how far a "double hermeneutic" is inescapable.[1] A more critical ethnography would have, as it were, to confront both aspects (e.g. Needham 1976). Sadly space does not permit a full demonstration of the argument.[2] So I shall confine myself to the less evident part of the problem. The issue may be cast into striking relief by treating Western philosophers and their work, not as beyond scrutiny, but more familiarly as the rather pedantic elders of a little known tribe on which the ethnographic record is slim.

My argument in short is that meaning, as it tends to be used, is a weak notion as it is far from clear, and indeed far from culturally neutral. Among the different intellectual traditions in the West, those of most immediate interest may be glossed a little simplistically as the Anglo-Saxon analytic, the German hermeneutic, and the French semiological. As we shall see, despite differences all run into similar kinds of problem. What is remarkable to an outsider is how far certain key concepts are at times regarded as unproblematic. Most theories also tend to have an Achilles' heel. For they rely at some point upon culturally specific, and questionable, metaphysical assumptions (in Collingwood's sense, 1939 and 1946), which may be at odds with those of the culture under study. It is a matter of debate whether it is legitimate to ignore the existence of such possible differences.

This issue is not new, of course. Recent attempts to present the problem in epistemological terms (Foucault 1967, 1970; Kuhn 1962, 1977), or to rephrase it by deconstructing the analyst's categories (Derrida 1972, 1976), run into difficulties of their own however (Culler 1981; Lakatos & Musgrave 1970; Putnam 1981; Newton-Smith 1981). It is arresting to see meaning itself as an aspect of an epistemic shift (Foucault 1970); and there has been a trend towards seeing figurative language in particular as somehow central to issues of meaning, or even constitutive of knowledge (Lakoff and Johnson 1980; Ortony 1979). This may hide a paradox: if all utterances are structured figuratively, why should the analyst's utterance be exempt? A currently voguish approach to meaning may then be hoist on its own petard. If this kind of relativism has shortcomings, it does not follow that the opposite extreme is any better. The argument that events are appreciated in the buff tends to require a view of language as transparent and the observer's categories as simply congruent with reality. On one view the weakness of this position is that in translation, rather than being a conveniently neutral medium, reality lands up becoming a further language, so doubling the steps of translation (see Gellner 1970: 24-5 below). It is increasingly hard these days to live in an uncomplicated world of facts admired impartially by judges of impeccable taste. The drawback of such cheerful philistinism is nicely described in the popular Malay proverb:

> *Seperti katak di bawah tempurong*
> Like a frog under a coconut shell
> (he thinks that he sees the whole world)

Meaning has many senses in English. It is "a very Casanova of a word in its appetite for association" (Black 1968: 163; for some reason, meaning inspires sexual metaphors). So it may help to look at

TABLE I

Common English uses of "to mean"

	Example	Approximate Synonym	Comments
1.	I mean to read this book.	Intend (Ba, P2, L2, L7)	cf. L6
2.	He never says what he means.	? (L3)	2 & 3 are
3.	She rarely means what she says.	Intend ? (L4)	related but far from identical
4.	What did he mean by wrinkling his nose?	Signify ? (Bc)	
5.	Those black clouds mean rain.	Sign (P3) Signify (Bb; L9)	cf. L8. This is also a necessary condition
6.	$m = 2n$. That means that m is even.	Shows (Bg)	
7.	Fame and riches mean nothing to a true scholar.	Have no value/ significance (L8, P1)	Note significance v. signify
8.	. . . he, I mean the Bishop, did require a respite.	Refer to (Bd)	
9.	It was John I meant, not Harry.	Refer to? (L10)	
10.	The Latin word "pluvia" means "rain".	Symbol (P4) Stands for	cf. L1

For convenience of reference all my examples are taken from well-known works. The code is:

B = Black 1968: 163.
L = Lyons 1977: 1-2.
P = Parkinson 1968: 1.

The first reference is that of the source; subsequent ones are similar examples from the sources cited.

vernacular use as a start. Some of the more obvious are given in Table I. From this alone "to mean" is roughly synonymous with: intend, signify, show, have value (or significance), refer to, stand for. Meaning also stretches to cover causation. Clouds are a necessary condition of rain, not an arbitrary signifier. This issue of the "motivation" of signs will crop up in due course. It should be apparent though that English usage (as those of other European languages) may include several senses and distinct kinds of relationship.

Meaning may also be applied to quite separate aspects of discourse. We may need to distinguish between the meanings of words, sentences and whole texts. To Ricoeur the whole difference between semiotics and semantics is that between simple signification (what he dismisses as the "unidimensional approach") and the almost infinitely variable relationship between subject and predicate by which all propositions are formed (1976: 6ff.) Beyond that there is a clear sense in which the meaning of sentences cannot be taken out of context. Context, however, presents some unpleasant problems of its own. For the present it is useful to note that the different levels at which it is possible to speak of "meaning" are often muddled.

If uses of meaning appear confused, perhaps an analytical approach of the kind favoured in British or American philosophy may help? There are at least seven main theories. A short summary may be useful as it separates some of the central issues; and if we distance ourselves a little by treating philosophers ethnographically, we find that they unwittingly offer all sorts of clues as to their presuppositions which might otherwise escape notice.

Perhaps the most plausible view is that words are a way of talking about things. In "Denotation Theory" words have meaning by denoting things in the world, the object being the meaning (Russell 1905; cf. Lyons 1977: 177-215 on confusions between denoting and referring). Matters are not so simple however. For how does one speak, for instance, of past events and imaginary objects? It is hard, by this approach, to cope with words like "and" or "if", which have no physical counterparts, but being logical connectives ought be included in a comprehensive theory of meaning. The stress on physical objects turns out not to be accidental. The same object may be appreciable in different ways; and it is common to distinguish between the reference and the sense of a term (Frege 1892, translated 1960) which may be variously interpreted but is widely treated as close to the difference between extension (what a word denotes) and intension (what it connotes in J.S. Mill's parlance).[3] The dichotomy between semiotics (semiology) and hermeneutics can be related to these two ways of defining things (cf. Guirard 1975: 40-44). Intensional meaning is often expressed in terms of properties which may be described further as subjective, objective or conventional in their link to an object (Copi 1978: 144). It is possible to trace intension, with its emphasis upon essential properties, back to Greek theories of essence (Quine in my opening quotation). So the link between words and things is not as straightforward as might seem; but the history of the connexion is ancient. If words do not simply refer to things, what then is meaning? On one reading:

> Once the theory of meaning is sharply separated from the theory of reference, it is a short step to recognizing as the primary business of the theory of meaning simply the synonymy of linguistic forms and the analyticity of statements; meanings themselves, as obscure intermediary entities, may well be abandoned. (Quine 1953: 22).

If words do not simply name things, do they name ideas instead? This view, which goes back to Locke (e.g. Staniland 1972: 28-52), was more recently espoused by Sapir (1921) where he tied meaning to the mental images of objects. Images of a thing vary, however, between people; and many words cannot be imagined at all. One version of "Image Theory" substitutes "concept" for "image" and on this de Saussure based his theory of language (for good critiques see Black 1968: 152-6; Kempson 1977: 16-17). For his distinction of *significant:signifié* is that of sound:concept (Baldinger 1980: 1-7; Lyons 1977: 96-98). The reliance of de Saussure and some of his successors upon a rather steam-age theory of meaning is rarely made explicit.

The two approaches so far discussed try to fix the meaning of words. The next set are concerned with sentences, or propositions (what may be wrong with reducing the former to the latter is discussed in Quine 1970: 1-14). These theories seem to ground themselves in some form of "reality" or, as Putnam put it "a world which admits of description by One True Theory" (1981: xi). The crudest version, "Causal Theory", tries to derive meaning from causation. The meaning of a statement is the response(s) it induces (Stevenson 1944). One way of whiling away a dull afternoon is in inventing expressions to which no sane man could possibly respond.

A more serious contender is "Verification Theory". This sets out to define the meaning of a proposition by its correspondence with reality. In its classic form "the meaning of a proposition is the method of its verification" (Schlick 1936). This view has an obvious appeal in the natural sciences; but it is harder to see how it would comfortably fit cultural discourse. There are many things which are

[handwritten marginalia: only have one theory – can we not use a synthesis of these approaches to accommodate meaning.]

[handwritten marginalia (left margin): Why does under-lying meaning]

beyond verification even in principle, such as past, or unobservable, events. The original version has been refined in various ways (a "weak" version of the criterion of verifiability has been proposed by Ayer 1936) perhaps the best known being Popper's preference for "falsifiable" over "verifiable". So, for a sentence to have meaning, what it says must in principle be falsifiable by facts. This is potentially a useful way of scrutinizing certain kinds of theory (see the debate between Kuhn and Popperians in Lakatos & Musgrave 1970) but, on at least one interpretation, it would leave every novel, poem or religious belief as meaningless. It would seem then that theories of meaning may at best only work for a given problem. If so it might be inappropriate to try to apply them generally.

The work of the Logical Positivists points to a fascinating problem. Members of the school such as Carnap set out explicitly to produce a system free of metaphysical assumptions (the title of one work was "The elimination of metaphysics through logical analysis of language" 1932, translated 1959), and further held that all metaphysical statements were meaningless. It is questionable whether they succeeded in this. If one is empiricist enough it is perfectly possible to regard physical objects as metaphysical assumptions in their own right. For instance:

> Physical objects are conceptually imported into the situation as convenient intermediaries — not by definition in terms of experience, but simply as irreducible posits comparable, epistemologically, to the gods of Homer . . . in point of epistemological footing the physical objects and the gods differ only in degree and not in kind. Both sorts of entities enter our conception only as cultural posits. (Quine 1953: 44).

If the philosophical elders are not unanimous, it seems at least that most have strong, and partly assumed, beliefs of a distinctive kind.

All this might seem far from anthropological *terra firma* (if that it be). Not only is knowledge of our own ideas beginning to seem increasingly relevant to a study of meaning, let alone in other cultures; but it seems that our ideas are collective representations which impose stark limits on what we think. This comes out clearly in the most elegant of the reality-based of the "Correspondence Theories". Rather simply put, a true proposition is in correspondence with reality, a false one not. The argument developed by Tarski (1944) and Davidson (1967) is too complex to discuss here (for good accounts see Lyons 1977: 10-13, 154-173; Kempson 1977: 23-46). Several points are relevant though. First translation is held to be possible by virtue of it being possible to specify conditions of truth valid for all possible worlds (presumably this ought to include the ethnographer's culture of study; one trusts this is not an impossible world). Second the theory applies to sentences, not propositions, so it is necessary to remove the ambiguity of the former. To cope with this demand, it is necessary to focus on the truth or falsity of sentences under a given interpretation. Other sentences may have indeterminate reference. So, to fix the meaning of a sentence, we have to posit, however temporarily, a separate interpretation, or specify a reference. If ambiguity still remains, this is held to be the fault of the component expressions, or of grammatical structure (Lyons 1977: 169-70). Language it seems must be made transparent whatever the cost. Procrustes and his bed-technique seem kind by comparison.

The difficulties of correspondence theory have been neatly put by Gellner:

> Language functions in a variety of ways other than "referring to objects". Many objects are simply not there, in any obvious physical sense, to be located: how could one, by this method, establish the equivalences, if they exist, between abstract or negative or hypothetical or religious expressions? Again, many "objects" are in a sense created by the language, by the manner in which its terms carve up the world of experience. Thus the mediating third party is simply not to be found: either it turns out to be an elusive ghost ("reality"), or it is just one further language, with idiosyncracies of its own which are as liable to distort in translation as did the original language of the investigator. (1970: 25).

The difficulties include then how truth is to be understood and the problems in moving from sentences in actual (natural) languages to notionally context-free true propositions. The loss is that all religious, moral and aesthetic statements become beyond the pale, which leaves us poor anthropologists driven back to ecology, with even such trusty standbys as power looking distinctly green at the gills.

The last approach we need to consider puts meaning firmly within culture and habits of language use; for which reason perhaps it has a degree of popularity among anthropologists. After proposing, in his complex "Picture Theory", that meaning was achieved by a homology between reality and the structure of language, Wittgenstein emerged with his second, or "Use Theory" (1958, 2nd edn 1969; 1953, 2nd edn 1958; in each case the latter differs slightly). It has kinship links with verification theory in the stress upon method, but improves on it by locating meaning in the use of words in a language. So meaning is not a kind of object in the natural world, but a part of cultural convention. Language is used in a rather special sense though. For, in any society, there are many different systems of verbal signs, each with rules of proper use. Meaning depends then not on a pan-cultural convention, but upon employment in a particular context (Wittgenstein 1969: 17). Wittgenstein refers to each set, and "also the whole, consisting of a language and the actions into which it is woven (as) the 'language game' " (1958: I, 7 my parentheses). These games include: giving orders, describing objects, reporting events, forming hypotheses, making up stories, translating, praying etc. (1958: I, 23). "The speaking of language is part of an activity, or of a form of life" (1958: I, 23) and "what has to be accepted, the given, is − so one could say − forms of life" (1958: II, 226e). Different sets of terms cannot be directly compared; for language use depends on a context.

Once again Gellner is conveniently on hand to note the drawbacks.

> If "meaning = use", then "use = meaning" . . . if the meaning of expressions is their employment, then, in turn, it is of the essence of the employment of expressions (and by an independent but legitimate extension, of other social behaviour), that it is meaningful. (1973a: 55).

The danger has a parallel with Durkheim's link of morality with society. If what is moral is simply social, then the social is *ipso facto* moral, or at least no institutional practice can ever be questioned on moral grounds. Here, it becomes impossible to question meaning. Other theories had too little, this has too much. Gellner also remarks on difficulties in grounding the theory. For

> . . . forms of life" (i.e. societies, cultures) are numerous, diverse, overlapping, and undergo change. (1973a: 56)

> . . . the point about forms of life is that they do not always, or even frequently, accept themselves as given . . . On the contrary, they often reject their own past practices as absurd, irrational, etc. (1973a: 57)

Wittgenstein may well have intended "form of life" to refer to narrower contexts than a whole culture (1958: II, 174e; Winch 1958: 41 applies the term to institutions such as "art" or "science"), but this may not escape Gellner's trap entirely, For, while the diversity of uses of words in different activities is important, it raises awkward questions about how activities are linked. The theory appeals to an unanalysed notion of "context". As it is used here context takes at least three forms: the place of any term within a semantic field, or contrast set; the place of this set within a system of activity; and the place of the activities within an encompassing culture.[4] To invoke context as "given" may be a starting point, it is hardly a conclusion.

The purportedly "hard" Anglo-Saxon analytical philosophy has difficulty in defining meaning because of a bad tendency to do so by reference to ostensibly self-evident constructs (reality, truth, life) which invariably turn out to be dubious. Is it possible that approaches which were designed specifically to study meaning fare any better? Hermeneutics started out as biblical exegesis but has been developed into a general science of understanding (Schleiermacher 1838), into the methodological basis of *Geisteswissenschaften* (Dilthey 1958), into a way of understanding human existence (Heidegger 1927), and even into a method of studying social action as text (Ricoeur 1979). In its most simple formulation it looks promising (Geertz 1973; cf. Hobart 1983) provided one does not look too close.

The difficulty is that the different schools, apart from internal shades of emphasis, are in bitter disagreement on what, in fact, meaning is and how (far) it can be known at all. One view is that the observer cannot escape the historical, or social, circumstances in which he lives and which limit his understanding (Bultmann 1957; Gadamer 1965). So there is no privileged position from which meaning can be known "objectively". Against this, and closer to Dilthey (and his disciple Betti 1962), Hirsch has recently sought to counter this argument by distinguishing the significance of a work in any possible context, from its meaning, here understood philologically as the original intention of the author, which is in theory at least open to validation (1967: 8ff.). To confuse matters, Ricoeur, while preferring the traditions of Schleiermacher and Dilthey, has the task of rescuing hermeneutics as a general theory of understanding (*Verstehen*) of culture, from the narrow philological grip of his apparent ally (who rightly saw the dangers in prostituting the concept; on Ricoeur, see his 1979: 88ff.). The fury of the debate between rival, and sometimes allied, schools (see Kermode 1981 on Juhl 1980) makes it clear that if hermeneutics can provide a clear statement about meaning it will be over the dead bodies of its own proponents. As a schoolboy I heard a popular rumour that Charles Atlas, the original body-builder, had strangled to death due to the overdevelopment of his neck muscles. The growth of hermeneutics threatens at times to bring about its suffocation in much the same way.[5]

There is an interesting connexion between hermeneutics and the use theory of meaning. In the notorious notion of the "hermeneutic circle" the interpreter is faced with the apparent paradox that the meaning of the words depends upon the meaning of the sentence of which it is part; while the sentence meaning depends in turn on its constituent words. So understanding is circular and, to compound the metaphors, requires an intuitive leap to grasp whole and part together (cf. Ricoeur 1981: 57, on the subject "entering into" the knowledge of the object). Similar problems apply between sentence and text; and presumably between text and culture. To approach meaning requires "pre-understanding" by the interpreter (Bultmann 1957: 113; cf. Betti 1962: 20-1 who objects to this whole idea) of the context of any utterance. So, once again, context descends as the *deus ex machina* to resolve the seemingly intractable problems of meaning. Text being philoprogenitive, it has spawned con-text and, for general edification, pre-text and inter-text (Culler 1981: 100-118; if pre-text = pre-understanding, does text = understanding?). Gellner, among others, has made the point that the distinguishing feature of most social anthropology — typified by functionalism — is its stress on context in analysis (1970; 1973a; 1973b). It is not unamusing, therefore, to see hermeneuts and philosophers find the answer to their problems in a concept which anthropologists have been enthusiastically dissecting in numberless specialized ways for decades. There are, it would seem, Frankensteins afoot hoping to breathe life back into the dismembered corpse of context.

In view of the difficulties in getting the semantic band wagon onto the road, it will hardly come as a surprise that much of the successful work has been phrased in terms, not of meaning, but of signification. (Wilden has argued that signification is simply the digital counterpart of meaning in analogic coding, 1972.) There will be, I fear, a sense of *déja vu* when it turns out that those who agree that language, and indeed culture, should be approached semiotically disagree as to how signification is to be understood (see Lyons 1977: 95-119; also Baldinger 1980). The problems may be exemplified by a short look at the work of de Saussure, because of his great impact in anthropology. Just how closely apparently unrelated schools are actually providing alternative formulations of similar problems comes out in the following citation.

> . . . semiotic systems are "closed", i.e., without relations to external, non-semiotic reality. The definition of the sign given by Saussure already implied this postulate: instead of being defined by the external relation between a sign and a thing, a relation that would make linguistics dependent upon a theory of extra-linguistic entities, the sign is defined by an opposition between two aspects, which both fall within the circumspection of a unique science, that of signs. These two aspects are the signifier — for example, a sound, a written pattern, a gesture, or any physical medium — and the signified — the differential value of the lexical system . . . In a word, language is no longer treated as a "form of life", as

Wittgenstein would call it, but as a self-sufficient system of inner relationships. (Ricoeur 1976: 6)

Here we find a third possibility. Meaning is no longer to be defined by either an external "reality", or an external context. Instead it is to be defined within language itself by splitting the latter according to a questionable connexion (see Image Theory). The effect, in fact, is just to shift the problem of context from an external one to an internal. Chronos only swallowed his children; Logos seems to have swallowed his mother.

In view of its importance, it is useful to examine some of the details of de Saussure's scheme more carefully. For a start, what exactly is the signified? On examination it turns out to be nothing other than our old friend "concept" *en haute couture*. If I may introduce Ogden and Richards' "triangle of signification" (Lyons 1977: 96-99; Baldinger 1980) it becomes clear that the third angle (the reference) is largely ignored which distracts attention from the nasty problem of what it is in things that are indicated by concepts. Once we ask about the properties of objects, we are plunged into ancient, but still thorny, controversies about universals and particulars (e.g. nominalism versus realism) and definitions (whether essential,, linguistic or prescriptive) which have raged singe the great Greek philosophers. In sticking their heads in the semiotic sand, anthropologists leave the large, and juicy, part delectably exposed to predators.

On another score, it has become a cliché of structuralist argument that the link between signifier and concept is arbitrary. This assertion is worth looking into. The arbitrariness of the linguistic sign is often treated as synonymous with the conventionality of the relation of form and meaning. As Lyons notes, however, the two terms are far from identical. For instance, in England the association of wisdom and owls is conventional but certainly not arbitrary (1977: 104-5). The possibility that the relation of sign and object was not arbitrary was recognized by Pierce in his notion of "icon" (that he should describe the resemblance as "natural" is illuminating, but inaccurate as it depends on cultural definitions of natural). Much attention has been given to these non-arbitrary, or 'motivated', connexions (e.g. Ullmann 1962: 80-115) between form and meaning, maybe because they held out the promise of being able to reduce meaning to hard, unambiguously definable, relations. (There is another set of relations, closely related, but more resistant to pigeon-holing – namely those between meanings, which are customarily sentenced to the woolly world of figures of speech.) Once again the opposition between de Saussure and Pierce is not without deeper, if often unremarked (cf. Boon 1979), philosophical roots. As Benoist has made plain, the problem was aired as long ago as Plato's dialogue, the *Cratylus*, as to whether the relation of names and things is natural or conventional; whether they are based in *physis* or *nomos (techné)*.

> Hermogenes versus Cratylus, Saussure versus Pierce: western knowledge since the Greeks has always put, and tried to solve, the question of the relationship between culture and nature. Is culture rooted in nature, imitating it or emanating direct from it? Or, on the contrary, is culture at variance with nature, absolutely cut off from it since the origin and involved in the process of always transforming, changing nature? The matrix of this opposition between culture and nature is at the very matrix of Western metaphysics. Metaphysics constitutes it, or, in virtue of a circular argument, whose name is history, is constitued by it. (1978: 59-60).

At every turn the close link between meaning, or signification, and notions of essence, truth and so forth have lurked near the surface of discussion, Benoist brings out clearly just how much current debates depend on conveniently forgotten, or worse unrealized, philosophical conundrums. Our intellectual ostrich seems to bury his head ever deeper.

No account of signification would be complete without reference to the work of Lévi-Strauss, the more so as he has often been held to dismiss meaning as unimportant to his style of analysis. Sperber has, rightly, questioned how seriously the parallel between linguistics and structuralism should be taken. For

> . . . despite a terminology borrowed from linguistics, symbols are not treated as signs. The symbolic signifier, freed from the signified, is no longer a real signifier except by a dubious metaphor whose only merit is to avoid the problem of the nature of symbolism, not to resolve it. (1975: 52)[6]

Further

> . . . the fundamental question is no longer "What do symbols mean?" but 'How do they mean?' . . . (but) the question 'how' presupposes the knowledge of 'what'. Saussurian semiology therefore does not *in principle* constitute a radical break, but rather a shift in interest . . . I say 'in principle' because in fact, Saussurian semiologists have completely left aside the what-question, and have studied not at all 'How do symbols mean?', but rather 'How do symbols work?' In this study they have established, all unknowing, that symbols work without meaning. Modern semiology, and this is at once its weakness and its merit, has refuted the principles on which it is founded. (1975: 51-2, emphases in the original)

The logical glue which holds together symbols, signs and meaning seems in danger of dissolving. It also seems that metaphor, for which Lévi-Strauss has a penchant in his analyses, may also be an un-acknowledged part of his own method.

It is increasingly common to speak of a "paradox" in structuralist, and semiotic, perspectives. After all "what is it that enables one to say that language speaks, myth thinks, signs signify?" (Culler 1981: 31). At this point meaning once again creeps in.

> Treating as signs objects or actions which have meaning within a culture, semiotics attempts to identify the rules and conventions which . . . make possible the meanings which the phenomena have. Information about meaning . . . is therefore crucial . . . (1981: 31)

Certain forms of communication may be reflective (cf. Jakobson 1960; Hawkes 1977: 81-7; Guirard 1975: 7) and threaten to violate the codes on which they are founded, as may happen in poetry or literature. In so doing it

> . . . reveals a paradox inherent in the semiotic project and in the philo-sophic orientation of which it is the culmination. To account for the signification of, shall we say, a metaphor is to show how the relationship between its forms and its meaning is already virtually present in the systems of language and rhetoric . . . Yet the value of metaphor . . . lies in its innovatory, inaugural force. Indeed, our whole notion of literature makes it not a transcription of preexisting thoughts but a series of radical and inaugural acts . . . The semiotics of literature thus gives rise to a 'de-constructive movement' in which each pole of an opposition can be used to show that the other is in error but in which the undecidable dialectic gives rise to no synthesis because the antinomy is inherent in the very structure of our language. (Culler 1981: 39)

My apologies for this long citation. It serves the purpose, though, of making clear that the elegancies of post-structuralism look at times very much like the more palaeolithic versions of the hermeneutic circle.

Why should approaches to meaning, however egregious they set out to be, land up looking so similar? The reason may be that they depend upon similar implicit metaphysical assumptions. Lyons touches the point neatly when he asks simply whether the signifier should "be defined as a physical or a mental entity?", or indeed "what is the psychological or ontological status of the signified?" (1977: 99). While semiotics may have started out as a critique of the view that "concepts exist prior to and independently of their ex-pression" (Culler 1981: 40), they end up falling into the opposite trap, for "expression now depends on the prior existence of a system of signs" (1981: 40).[7] So, what status does what have? It is on this question that that impenetrable writer, Derrida, to my mind makes one of his most useful suggestions. It is a pervasive "metaphysics of presence" which creates these seeming paradoxes, or contradictions.

The problem may be seen to lie in the western tendency to construe being (what exists) in terms of what must be experienced as present. The notion of meaning, Derrida argues, stems from this metaphysics. For we tend to think of meaning as something present to the awareness of a speaker (one might add the idea of awareness itself is compounded of presence) as what he "has in mind" (Culler 1979: 162) without recognizing how metaphorical our observation is. The difficulty is that the image of container (mind) and contents (meanings, thoughts, ideas etc.) is dangerously misleading as there are no grounds seriously to hold this position except as metaphor. Yet the two notions conveniently imply one another (Derrida 1979: 88ff.). If the relation of signifier and signified is not simple substitution, but rather involves mutual supplementation as well, then it no longer becomes self-evident that the proper sense of words, rather than the figurative, is original (Benoist 1978: 29). Put another way, how much is the priority we give to literal meaning over, say, metaphorical due to our sense that the former is somehow more "real" or present? The supposed paradoxes of semiotics become expressed in terms of figurative speech.[8] It seems that we must pack our bags yet again.

So far two themes seem to run through approaches to meaning. Each theory tends to be grounded in another domain, so displacing the focus of inquiry. Saussurean schools of thought escape this in part and make clear the dichotomy between internally and externally defined models. More generally, whatever the approach, at each turn we are faced with problematic distinctions which have their roots in the history of Western philosophy: the reality of the physical or the mental; the relation of focus and context; natural law against cultural preferences; the essential or the nominal.

Figures of speech would seem to by-pass the hybrid problems of form versus content by being centred about content, or meaning. They offer a classification of possible forms of resemblance, and association, and so a potentially unambiguous language of critical evaluation. This promise obviously depends on exactly what figures of speech, or tropes, are or do; and the assumptions on which they rest. With the tropological phase at its peak, figures of speech are being hailed as the new philosopher's stone — gall-stone to some — and the problems tend to be shoved aside. Tropes may be brought to bear on almost anything not only within the study of discourse, but they are used to threaten the foundations of our knowledge. They are seen as the key to epistemological shifts (Foucault 1970); they may be constitutive of all our thought (Ortony 1979; Lakoff & Johnson 1980); to the delight of many they offer to turn Lévi-Strauss's gay new structural dog into a mangy mongrel with a promiscuous pedigree reaching back to Quintilian and Aristotle (Culler 1981; Derrida 1976, 1979; Sapir 1977, cf. Crocker 1977).

The problems start when we try to find out quite what tropes are. Rhetoricians commonly hold the vast range to be reducible to four main forms: metaphor, metonymy, synecdoche and irony (the order is important as a sequence to Foucault). In Sapir's scheme, metaphor has two varieties: internal based on shared properties; and external (or analogy) where properties are secondary to the formal congruence of relationships. This latter, he argues, is central to Lévi-Strauss's analyses (1977). Metonymy is often treated as contrasted to metaphor: contiguity not shared property (Culler 1981: 189ff.). Synecdoche is the possible permutations of wholes (genus) and parts (species), and underpins classifications (Sapir 1977: 12-19). Irony is often held to stand apart. There are two obvious questions. What kinds of relationship fall to each trope? And how are the tropes related? For Sapir cause and effect, for instance, are metonymic (1977: 19-20); for Burke they are clear examples of synecdoche (1969: 508). The difficulty stems from how the major tropes themselves are to be defined. Jakobson reduces synecdoche to metonymy (1956). The Belgian rhetoricians in Liège, Group μ, after detailed review of the field, concluded that all metaphor can be reduced to synecdoche (1970 French edn; 1981 English). In the same year however, Genette traced synecdoche, metonymy and all other tropes back to metaphor (1970). Since then Eco has completed the confusion by deriving all metaphor from spurned metonymy (1979). One might be forgiven for thinking that whom God wishes to destroy, He first makes mad.

Why should such distinguished scholars disagree so strikingly? One reason is that the classical sources themselves started from different positions (Aristotle 1941; Quintilian 1921). What kind of entity (sic) are tropes in fact? Often they are treated as a simple classification of types of association: "butterfly-collecting" in Leach's sarcasm. Many of the difficulties noted above seem to stem from taking a taxonomic view of tropes. Behind this lurks the now-familiar catch. Metaphor seems to be defined in terms of "essential properties"; metonymy as the workings of chance. Once again we seem pulled towards the abyss of western metaphysics. Since Aristotle, in Derrida's view, categories themselves have been seen as the means by

> . . . which being properly speaking is expressed in so far as it is expressed through several twists, several tropes. The system of categories is the system of the ways in which being is construed. (1979: 91)

Figures of speech seem to bring us back to the old problems of what are properties? what is essential? what indeed is accident? Derrida would push it further and see tropes as underlying those "basic" kinds of category — substance, action, relation, space, time, accident — through which western philosophers try to capture being.

Tropes seem to have more immediate uses in creating words and images, where none were before. "Metaphor plugs the gaps in the literal vocabulary" and so is a form of catachresis — the putting of new senses into old words (Black 1962: 32). Such extensions may be almost totally constitutive when conceiving the relation between events in terms of ideas like time. This raises the possibility that language itself may be construed metaphorically. In English, Reddy has argued that our impressions of language are largely structured by the image of language as a container, the contents being ideas, thoughts, feelings, or indeed meanings (1979: 289). By pointing out that alternatives are available to what he calls the "conduit metaphor", Reddy makes a strong case for the catachretic nature of many of our core concepts (those noted above). Foucault has sought to generalize this kind of argument by applying it to how we structure relations between classes — such as the sane and mad (1967) — or even how our basic ideas of what constitutes an explanation are made up (1970). In this view it is the image of irony which is now dominant. This produces a contrast between a surface and an interior, such that the superficial is to be explained by a deeper structure, as in the Freudian model of mind or in structuralism. The doubling will allow alternative styles of analysis: the search for formalism (perhaps Needham 1978; 1980) as against some (hidden) meaning (Geertz 1973). Metaphor seems then to make up how we see the world and how we set about studying it — even if we are not sure what metaphor is.

This is not quite the end of the tale. With their Nietschean heritage, the French post-structuralists — in a mood of *fin d'épistème* — see no escape from the web of words, or tropes, what Jameson called "the prison-house of language" (1972). This gallic gloom may be a little premature. To reverse Davidson (1980), let us wonder whether, to use a principle of lack of charity, the turgid and convolute style of these writers does not serve to obscure their own Achilles' heels.

If relationships and abstract issues are conceived catachretically, why should this not hold good as well for the relationship between image and referent in Foucault's and Derrida's own models? We seem near to the self-referential paradox. What exactly is the relationship between an episteme and what it structures; or language and to what it relates? There is no reason that this must be confined to the image of a prison by which thought is kept in place. It seems that their discourse carries within it its own unexplored metaphor. Lovelace's prisoner wondered whether iron bars made a cage. Why should they not make a jemmy for a burglar, or a jail-breaker?

There is another way in which tropes may be understood. They may be treated as ways of perceiving relationships and situations from different perspectives. As such they may cover far broader areas than formal categories and may represent general processes of thinking. Burke, for instance, sees the four major tropes as examples of the more encompassing operations of: perspective, reduction, representation and dialectic (1969). This would go some way to explaining how, if they are treated as classes to be defined extensively, they run into problems.

This is not, however, how tropes are understood by most writers. Around the terms for the main tropes seem to cluster all those metaphysical problems in Western thought which have dogged meaning throughout. Even the classification is fluid. For the same distinctions may be linked to different figurative terms according to one's point of view. For instance, the accidence often associated with metonymy may link the latter to metaphor (through essential as against contingent properties), or to synecdoche (contingent opposed to necessary connexion). At one level tropes come close, it would seem, to simple modes of discrimination and association. As they are defined in so many ways it is hard to find neat fit, but the four master tropes involve recognition respectively of resemblance, relationship, classification and contrast.[9] If the familiar problems are posed (what is being talked about: essences, properties, names etc.?), we seem to be back to the rondo of confused classes of the rhetoricians.

Studying Western thought with the aid of tropes may be highly informative. For both are home-grown within the same culture. On what grounds, one might ask, is it legitimate to export them to the tropics? A horrible possibility occurs as to why structuralism should have the appearance of being so widely applicable. Is it that the main tropes are truly cross-cultural? This has yet to be shown; and there are endless disputes as to how they are to be defined anyway. Or is it just that most (perhaps all?) cultures have certain cognitive operations in some form? It would be hard to imagine a society with no notion of resemblance (and so presumably the rudiments for making connexions which look like metaphor). Might it not be the ostensible congruence of these kinds of operation which allows apparent translatability? Is the structuralist claim to be able to decode myth accurately from Indonesia to South America then false, because the constructs it uses register only gross parallels? I suspect so. One would be foolhardy indeed to assume, for instance of resemblance, that exactly what it is about a thing, or event, that enables it to be compared is necessarily the same in all cultures. In short, can we presume that other cultures have precisely the same formulations of resemblance, relationship, class, contrast and so on? Or are their views of what is essential, accidental, necessary and more sufficiently identical to our own that translation is unproblematic? There is sufficient *prima facie* evidence that ideas vary quite enough — in classical Indian metaphysics as one example (Inden 1976; Potter 1977) — for it to be folly to assume one's own cultural constructs apply across cultures instead of arguing the case. There is, after all, no reason why translation should be an all-or-nothing business. Why can there not be degrees of understanding and misunderstanding? Part of the trouble comes, it seems to me, from treating the notion of "communication" as simple fact, not sometimes as ideal only partly achieved. Because we dimly perceive something through the crude homology of formal operations in different cultures, we should not dupe ourselves that we understand very much. I think this is why tropes seem to offer a panacea, and make the formidable problems of translation look spuriously easy. If this is so, the sooner we move into a post-tropological age the better. Western philosophers may be excused ethnocentrism. Can anthropologists?

What, if anything, comes out of this look at the philosophy of meaning? The most surprising feature is how much is assumed, and how much of this disclaimed. The elimination of metaphysics — perhaps, like marital fidelity, devoutly to be desired — seems less an actuality than wishful thinking. Does what we know fare any better then than what we hold to exist? There is, I think, a case to answer that the lenses in our academic spectacles are forged more figuratively than we often chose to admit. On these grounds the slightly facile image of an ethnography of philosophers will have served its purpose if it has helped to change a tired perspective.

There are other bugbears afoot. Wittgenstein's idea of the language game may have its drawbacks, but it does describe rather well what academics sometimes do. Can we really talk of theories in general, for instance of meaning, when some of the more successful work at best in limited situations? (This may be a simple aspect of Quine's point (1951) that the entities which any theory assumes to exist are those which constitute the range of the theory's variables.) Theory may have to be very narrowly defined where successors on a single subject interpret it such that it has different ranges of application. For example Burke's processual view of figurative language saw it as framing most thought; whereas Sapir read Burke, or figures of speech, as a formal classification of symbolic associations. A more disturbing problem is what exactly is implied in the apparent universality of application of our theoretical constructs. Is it, in fact, evidence of the superior power of our analytical frameworks? The scale of Western academic resources are so great (Gellner 1973a), compared to the societies most anthropologists study, that it is possible to obliterate the nuances of a culture while seeming to explain it. What criteria are we to use to decide between rival theories, or translations (Hesse 1978)? It is easy to import our own principles of elegance, metaphysics or whatever to resolve the matter. In the end, how sensitive will Lévi-Strauss's analysis of South American myth turn out to be, and how much *lèse-majesté*?

The tension between alternative positions may be reflected in differences between philosophy and anthropology. Hollis has stated one aspect of the problem clearly. He has argued that we are obliged to assume identical criteria of rationality in other cultures, as we would, in fact, be unable to know it, should alternative logics exist (1970). An analogous argument could presumably be made for meaning, but its implications are frightening. What would be the point of anthropology if, *a priori*, we could never know if other cultures had different ideas of reason or meaning, *even if they did*? Part of the impasse stems from different concerns. As I understand Hollis the philosopher's brief is to argue for parsimony, to prevent the world becoming unnecessarily, even hopelessly, complicated. The more empirical anthropological brief is to keep as much as possible of the subtlety, and lack of clarity even, of cultural discourse as she is spoke. Might it be that we try falsely to generalize issues beyond the enterprises in which they were postulated? At any rate the cost to anthropology if we accept Hollis's argument is so high that it might well be preferable to sacrifice universal notions of rationality, meaning or whatever instead.

One aspect of the metaphysics of presence is that argument is sometimes read as claim to truth. This is strange. Usually only works of such monumental dullness that no one can be bothered to question (or read?) them remain unchallenged. The better the argument, often the more it provokes debate and eventually its own refinement or rejection. In this spirit let me phrase a conclusion in an extreme form, not because it is correct but in the hope that it will stimulate others to produce better.

In taking meaning as the theme, I chose one of many loose threads which threaten to unravel the sweater of contemporary anthropological equivocation, cynically called theory. My arguments are hardly new (Evans-Pritchard, among others, has put the case far more subtly). If they have any value though, then failure to consider the possibility that other cultures have other philosophies is, at the least, a ghastly epistemological blunder. Western philosophy seems hopelessly caught in its own toils and anthropology is — as I am sure its wiser proponents realized — our one chance of escaping the sheer tedium of our own thought. Anthropology stands little chance though so long as it is bent upon castrating itself on every rusting knife of intellectual fashion. As every anthropologist knows, the life of the subject hangs on ethnography, as this is our outlet from onanistic ethnocentrism. Ethnography is not much use if it is not critical; and this critisicm has two aspects. Its obvious face is the reflective consideration of what to select from the richness of human action and discourse. Its hidden, almost shunned, face is the possibility of reflecting on our own categories, our self-evident assumptions — call them philosophy or metaphysics if one will — by which we can question the dreary shuffle which passes for the "rational" growth of knowledge. This is not a forlorn search for Shangri-La. For as most ethnographers know, we glimpse through the dark glassily real, and seemingly different, worlds. Otherwise there is the grim prospect of peddling filched fashions which become, like the Cheshire Cat, long on face, short on body. Then talk of meaning turns to moaning.

Notes

1. My special thanks must go to Professor Martin Hollis who suggested this expression and offered many useful comments; and to Dr Ruth Kempson who gave helpful criticism. The idiocies which remain are, of course, my own.
2. This version is roughly the first half of the original paper, which was too long for the present format. In the second part some simple ethnography on Balinese ideas of meaning and intentionality was introduced to argue that the kinds of difference with western views were such as to have led to wildly ethnocentric interpretations of Balinese culture.
3. cf. Lyons 1977: 177ff. where the relationship between naming, reference,

denotation and sense is looked into, for purposes of theories of linguistics.
4. The more recent work on speech acts and conversational implicature are not included in these remarks and will receive fuller treatment in a forthcoming paper on context.
5. There are so many different formulations of the hermeneutic circle that it would seem to need a critical analysis all of its own. My aim is simply to disabuse the more trusting reader of the fear that hermeneutics is some esoteric orthodoxy on which he somehow missed out. The debate within the broad tradition of hermeneutics is too rich to serve as a fossilized doorstop for "Interpretive Social Science" (Rabinow & Sullivan 1979).

   Restating the terms of the debate does not help much. To read context as a set of propositions raises Collingwoodian problems of freedom from presuppositions and Quinean ones of theory dependence. One may define the hermeneutic circle in similar language as: to understand X, one must know what state of affairs would be described by X, and to know that one must first understand X. This puts great weight on "know" and "understand". (One might argue backwards that the hermeneutic circle stems from the attempt to reconcile the two notions.) "Understand" has always seemed a problematic idea to me and to be tinged with the metaphysics of presence discussed below.
6. The relationship of code, or context, to signs and symbols receives interesting treatment. ". . . in contrast to what happens in a semiological decoding, it is not a question of interpreting symbolic phenomena by means of a context, but — quite the contrary — of interpreting a context by means of symbolic phenomena." (Sperber 1975: 70).
7. As Benoist points out, the structuralists seem for the most part to have borrowed naively from linguistic models without considering how far these are rooted in western metaphysics. Derrida goes on to consider how de Saussure's stress on the spoken word as against the written is a product of his assumption that the primacy of the former is somehow linked to its greater "presence" to the experiencing mind (Benoist 1978: 28; Culler 1981: 40-1; Derrida 1976). The idea that experience is a kind of pre-cultural given might need defence in the light of the above. Culler (1979: 162-3) gives a delightful introduction to how Derrida copes with some of Zeno's paradoxes by trying to show how far they depend on presence as really real.
8. One many reach a similar position by way of "motivation". Lyons, discussing the work of Porzig, shows that the direction in which the meaning of a lexeme will be generalized cannot be determined by reference to motivation alone, but depends upon metaphoric extension (1977: 264), itself a problematic notion.
9. By contrast I refer to the range of intelligible, indeed informative, comparisons such as bitter-sweet, but hardly bitter-blue.

References

Aristotle 1941. Poetics (trans.) I. Bywater. In *The Basic Works of Aristotle* (ed.) R. McKeon. New York: Random House.

60 *Mark Hobart*

Ayer, A.J. 1936. *Language, Truth and Logic*. London: Gollancz; 2nd edn 1946 Harmondsworth: Pelican.

Baldinger, K. 1980. *Semantic Theory*. Oxford: Blackwells.

Benoist, J.-M. 1978. *The Structural Revolution*. London: Weidenfeld.

Betti, E. 1962. *Die Hermeneutik als allgemeine Methodik der Geisteswissenschaften*. Tübingen: Mohr.

Black, M. 1962. *Models and Metaphors: Studies in Language and Philosophy*. Ithaca and London: Cornell University Press.

—— 1968. *The Labyrinth of Language*. London: Pall Mall

Bloom, H. 1979 The breaking of form. In *Deconstruction and Criticism* (Bloom *et al.*). London: Routledge & Kegan Paul.

Boon, J.A. 1979 Saussure/Pierce à propos language, society and culture. In *Semiotics of Culture* (eds) I.P. Winner & J. Umiker-Sebeok. The Hague: Mouton.

Bultmann, R. 1957. *History and Escatology*. Edinburgh: Edinburgh University Press.

Burke, K. 1969. *A Grammar of Motives*. Berkeley and London: University of California Press.

Carnap, R. 1959. The elimination of metaphysics through logical analysis of language (trans.) A. Pap. In *Logical Positivism* (ed.) A.J. Ayer. London: Allen & Unwin.

Collingwood, R.G. 1939. *An Autobiography*. Oxford: Oxford University Press.

—— 1946. *The Idea of History*. Oxford: Oxford University Press.

Copi, I. 1978. *Introduction to Logic* (5th edn). London: Collier-MacMillan.

Crocker, J.C. 1977. The social functions of rhetorical forms. In *The Social Use of Metaphor: Essays on the Anthropology of Rhetoric* (eds) J.D. Sapir & J.C. Crocker. University of Pennsylvania Press.

Culler, J. 1979. Jacques Derrida. In *Structuralism and Since* (ed.) J. Sturrock. Oxford: Oxford University Press.

—— 1981. *The Pursuit of Signs*. London: Routledge & Kegan Paul.

Davidson, D. 1967. Truth and meaning. *Synthese* **17**, 304-23.

—— 1980. *Essays on Actions and Events*. New York: Oxford University Press.

Derrida, J. 1972. Structure, sign and play in the discourse of the human sciences. In *The Structuralist Controversy* (eds) R. Macksey & E. Donato. London: The John Hopkins University Press.

—— 1976. *Of Grammatology*. London: The Johns Hopkins University Press.

—— 1979. The supplement of copula: philosophy *before* linguistics. In *Textual Strategies* (ed.) J. Harari. London: Methuen.

Dilthey, W. 1958. *Gesammelte Schriften*. Stuttgart: Teubner.

Eco, U. 1979. *The Role of the Reader*. Bloomington: Indiana University Press.

Foucalt, M. 1967. *Madness and Civilization: a History of Insanity in the Age of Reason*. London: Tavistock.

—— 1970. *The Order of Things: an Archaeology of the Human Sciences*. London: Tavistock.

Frege, G. 1892. Uber Sinn und Bedeutung (trans.) P. Geach & M. Black as "On sense and reference" in *Frege: Philosophical Writings*. Oxford: Blackwells.

Gadamer, H.-G. 1965. *Wahrheit und Methode* (2nd edn). Tübingen: Mohr.

Geertz, C. 1973. *The Interpretation of Cultures.* New York: Basic Books.

Gellner, E. 1970. Concepts and society. In *Rationality* (ed.) B. Wilson. Oxford: Blackwells.

——— 1973a. The new idealism: cause and meaning in the social sciences. In *Cause and Meaning in the Social Sciences* (eds) I.C. Jarvie & J. Agassi. London: Routledge & Kegan Paul.

——— 1973b. Time and theory in social anthropology. In *Cause and Meaning in the Social Sciences* (eds) I.C. Jarvie & J. Agassi. London: Routledge & Kegan Paul.

Genette, G. 1970. La rhétoric restreinte. *Communications* **16**, 158-171.

Group μ. 1981. *A General Rhetoric.* London: The Johns Hopkins University Press.

Guirard, P. 1975. *Semiology.* London: Routledge & Kegan Paul

Hawkes, T. 1977. *Structuralism and Semiotics.* London: Methuen.

Heidegger, M. 1927. *Sein und Zeit.* Halle: Niemeyer.

Hesse, M. 1978. Theory and value in the social sciences. In *Action and Interpretation* (eds) C. Hookway & P. Pettit. London: Cambridge University Press.

Hirsch, E. 1967. *Validity in Interpretation.* London: Yale University Press.

Hobart, M. 1983. Review of C. Geertz *Negara: The Theatre State in Nineteenth-Century Bali.* In *Journal of the Royal Asiatic Society* 1983, No. 1.

Hollis, M. 1970. The limits of irrationality. In *Rationality* (ed.) B. Wilson. Oxford: Blackwells.

Inden, R. 1976. *Marriage and Rank in Bengali Culture.* Berkeley: California University Press.

Jakobson, R. 1960. Closing statement; linguistics and poetics. In *Style in Language* (ed.) T.A. Sebeok: Cambridge, Mass: M.I.T. Press.

Jakobson, R. & Halle, M. 1956. *Fundamental of Language.* The Hague: Mouton.

Jameson, F. 1972. *The Prison-House of Language.* Princeton: Princeton University Press.

Juhl, P.D. 1980. *Interpretation.* Princeton: Princeton University Press.

Kempson, R.M. 1977. *Semantic Theory.* Cambridge: Cambridge University Press.

Kermode, F. 1981. Review of P.D. Juhl *Interpretation.* In *London Review of Books* **3**, No. 8.

Kuhn, T.S. 1962. *The Structure of Scientific Revolutions* (2nd edn enlarged 1970). London: University of Chicago Press.

——— 1977. *The Essential Tension.* London: University of Chicago Press.

Lakatos, I. & Musgrave, A. (eds) 1970. *Criticism and the Growth of Knowledge.* London: Cambridge University Press.

Lakoff, G. & Johnson, M. 1980. *Metaphors We Live By.* London: University of Chicago Press.

Lyons, J. 1977. *Semantics* (2 vols). Cambridge: Cambridge University Press.

Needham, R. 1976. Skulls and causality. *Man* (N.S.) **11**, 71-88.

——— 1978. *Primordial Characters.* Charlottesville: University Press of Virginia.

——— 1980. *Reconnaissances.* Toronto: Toronto University Press.

Newton-Smith, W.H. 1981. *The Rationality of Science.* London: Routledge &

Kegan Paul.

Onions, C.T. (ed.) *1966. The Oxford Dictionary of English Etymology*. Oxford: Clarendon Press.

Ortony, A. (Ed.) 1979. *Metaphor and Thought* Cambridge: Cambridge University Press.

Parkinson, G.H.R. 1968. Introduction. In *The Theory of Meaning* (ed.) G.H.R. Parkinson. Oxford: Oxford University Press.

Potter, K. 1977. *Indian Metaphysics and Epistemology*. Princeton: Princeton University Press.

Putnam, H. 1981. *Reason, Truth and History*. Cambridge: Cambridge University Press.

Quine, W.V.O. 1951 On what there is (*Aristotelian Society Supplementary Volume*). Reprinted in *From a Logical Point of View* 1953.

―――― 1953. Two dogmas of empiricism. In *From a Logical Point of View*. London: Harvard University Press.

―――― 1970. *Philosophy of Logic*. Englewood Cliffs, N.J.: Prentice-Hall.

Quintilian, 1921. *Institutio Oratoria* (trans.) H. Butler. Cambridge, Mass: Harvard University Press.

Rabinow, P. & Sullivan, W.M. (eds.) 1979. *Interpretive Social Science: a Reader*. London: University of California Press.

Reddy, M.J. 1979. The conduit metaphor: a case of frame conflict in our language about language. In *Metaphor and Thought* (ed.) A. Ortony. Cambridge: Cambridge University Press.

Ricoeur, P. 1976. *Interpretation Theory: Discourse and the Surplus of Meaning*. Fort Worth, Texas: Texas Christian University Press.

―――― 1979. The model of the text: meaningful action considered as a text. In *Interpretive Social Science: a Reader* (eds) P. Rabinow & W.M. Sullivan. London: California University Press.

―――― 1981. *Hermeneutics and the Human Sciences* (trans. and ed.) J.B. Thompson. Cambridge: Cambridge University Press.

Russell, B. 1905. On denoting. *Mind* 14, 479-493.

Sapir, E. 1921. *Language*. New York: Harcourt, Brace & World.

Sapir, J.D. 1977. The anatomy of metaphor. In *The Social Use of Metaphor: Essays on the Anthropology of Rhetoric* (eds) J.D. Sapir & J.C. Crocker. University of Pennsylvania Press.

Schleiermacher, D.F.E. *1838. Hermeneutik und Kritik: mit besonderer Beziehung auf das Neue Testament* (ed.) F. Lucke. Berlin: Reimer.

Schlick, M. 1936. Meaning and verification. *Philosophical Review* 45, 339-369.

Sperber, D. 1975. *Rethinking Symbolism*. Cambridge: Cambridge University Press.

Staniland, H. 1972. *Universals*. London: MacMillan.

Stevenson, C.L. 1944. *Ethics and Language*. New Haven, Conn.: Yale University Press.

Tarski, A. 1944. The semantic conception of truth. In *Philosophy and Phenomenological Research* 4, 341-75; reprinted in his *Logic, Semantics and Metamathematics*. Oxford: Oxford University Press 1956

Ullmann, S. 1962. *Semantics*. Oxford: Blackwells.

Wilden, A. 1972. Analog and digital communication. In *Systems and Structure: Essays in Communication and Exchange*. London: Tavistock.

Winch, 1958. *The idea of a social science and its relation to philosophy*. London: Routledge & Kegan Paul.

Wittgenstein, L. 1953. *Philosophical Investigations* (trans.) G.E.M. Anscombe. Oxford: Blackwells; revised 2nd edn 1958.

—— 1958. *The Blue and Brown Books: Preliminary Studies for the "Philosophical Investigations"*. Oxford: Blackwells; 2nd edn 1969.

THEORETICAL LANDSCAPES
On Cross-Cultural Conceptions of Knowledge

ANNE SALMOND

It is often supposed, in anthropology and other disciplines, that language is primarily an instrument of literal assertion, and that under conditions of proper control, precise and unambiguous descriptions of reality are feasible. In such a view, the main linguistic difficulties that any science might meet are likely to be those of definition — the features of its terminology must be specified, and correlated as accurately as possible with features discerned in the real world. Repeated trial and error testing of specified terms will decide, finally, whether they are capable of leading to definitive descriptions of reality: this is the empiricist criterion of meaning.

This paper arises from a different set of premises about language. Here it is supposed that language is an instrument for the negotiation of meaning, and that contexts of utterance and pre-existing knowledge are important both in saying, and in interpreting anything that is said. Since structures of contexts, language and knowledge may vary (within uncertain limits) cross-culturally and even across disciplines, it is held that the absolute verification of descriptions is not feasible, and their acceptance or rejection may be influenced by epistemological, situational and rhetorical factors as well as by physical experience. This is an interpretive account of meaning, which applies as much to scientific language as it does to everyday talk; and it has the effect of directing our attention as anthropologists to our own interpretive activities as well as to those of others, and to the complex interactions between our interpretations, theirs and "the real world".

Recent writings in philosophy and linguistics have carried the debate between the empiricist and interpretive accounts of language into discussions of metaphor, and a number of scholars (Lakoff &

Johnson 1980; Ortony (ed.) 1979, and Sacks (ed.) 1979) have suggested that metaphor plays a central role in language, thought and
action, and that much and perhaps most of our talk is tropological.
W.V. Quine has said in a recent brief statement:

> It is a mistake, then, to think of linguistic usage as literalistic in its main
> body and metaphorical in its trimming. Metaphor, or something like it,
> governs both the growth of language and our acquisition of it. What comes
> as a subsequent refinement is rather cognitive discourse itself, at its most
> drily literal. The neatly worked inner stretches of science are an open
> space in the tropical jungle, created by clearing tropes away (in Sacks
> 1979: 160).

His own statement shows clearly enough that cognitive discourse
is not always literal, and that tropes may trespass freely in philosophical talk. Mary Hesse and others (Hesse 1963, 1964; Boyd in
Ortony (ed.) 1979) have shown that they are also important in
natural scientific discourse, and the role of organic, mechanical and
other analogies are well attested for the social sciences (e.g. Pepper
1942). All of this creates considerable trouble for an empiricist
account of language, for tropes are semantically shifty and resist
definition, and cannot be made to stand beside features of reality
in any reliable manner. Worse still, there might be no independent
reality for them to stand beside, for as Max Black has suggested it is
possible that "a metaphor might be self-certifying, by generating the
very reality to which it seems to draw attention" (in Ortony 1979:
37).
    In this paper I want to suggest that not only do we frequently use
metaphors in scientific talk; we also speak of the scientific enterprise
itself and its products, knowledge and understanding, in metaphorical terms. The examples I will discuss are taken from recent texts in
anthropology and from more casual talk about knowledge, so they
cannot claim historical or cross-disciplinary application; all the same
it appears that some of these metaphors have ancient antecedents in
the West, and it is probable that a study of discourse about knowledge in other periods, other disciplines and other Western languages
would enrich and elaborate the argument of this paper.[1] It also
seems likely, from a comparison with Maori talk about knowledge
and truth, that our epistemological metaphors are (at least partially)
culturally specific, and that our knowledge of knowledge is therefore
(at least partially) culturally constrained.

> Ethnology — like any science — comes about within the element of
> discourse. And it is primarily a European science employing traditional
> concepts, however much it may struggle against them. Consequently,

whether he want to or not — and this does not depend on a decision on his part — the ethnologist accepts into his discourse the premises of ethnocentrism at the very moment when he denounces them. This necessity is irreducible; it is not a historical contingency. (Jacques Derrida 1978: 282)

A close inspection of anthropological texts shows that our discourse about knowledge characteristically elaborates a series of metaphors about location in a physical landscape, where the space-time properties are those of commonsense Western perception (and not say, those of Western science). These metaphors mirror either the landscape itself or physical activities upon it, and the properties which lend them value, far from maximizing definitional precision, appear to include flexibility, a capacity for ambiguity and rich resource for variation. Discussions (e.g. Needham 1972) of terms with such characteristics in scientific talk often end by suggesting their deletion; in this paper, on the contrary, I would argue that these metaphors and words like "belief", "mind", "meaning", "knowledge" and "culture" are indispensable to our questioning of the universe, just because their ambiguity generates puzzlement and so talk, and that schemes for their censorship are bound to be frustrated. On the other hand, such terms do belong to a "web of meaning" that is characteristically English, (since only texts in English[2] have been consulted here), and it is important to consider how they may limit our approaches to the anthropological project of "knowing" and "understanding" life in other societies.

A somewhat arbitrary entry to these metaphors might begin with the presupposed claim, *knowledge is a landscape*. This claim does not stand on its own but enters into a series of entailments [*knowledge is a landscape* entails that *knowledge is territory* entails that *knowledge has spatial existence*], and it is linked with a series of related metaphors including *intellectual activity is a journey* (and so *knowledge is a destination*); *understanding is seeing* (and so *knowledge is clear sight*); *facts are natural objects* (and knowledge is their possession); *the mind is a container* (and knowledge is stored in it); *language is a conduit* (and knowledge is transmitted by it); *intellectual activity is work* (and knowledge is its product), and metaphors about relative height, width, depth and closure. Each of these metaphors works out a different theme in our (non-physical) reflections about (non-physical) knowledge, but always in a metaphorical context of physical activity in a physical environment.

I shall discuss these metaphors in turn, drawing upon examples from commonplace expressions in theoretical talk and quotations from a more-or-less random selection of theoretical texts in anthropology — Claude Lévi-Strauss *Structural Anthropology*

Volumes 1 and 2, Maurice Godelier *Perspectives in Marxist Anthropology*, Stephen Tyler (ed.) *Cognitive Anthropology*, Edmund Leach *Rethinking Anthropology* and Malcolm Crick *Explorations in Language and Meaning* among others; and shall suggest what some of their possible pragmatic implications might be. I begin with one of the higher-order entailments of *knowledge is a landscape*, i.e. *knowledge has spatial existence*. Consider the following expressions:

> the theoretical *universe* of Marxism
> the semantic *sphere*
> a *global* structure

and this quotation:

> In granting the science of language its correct *place within* the overall study of speech, I have at the same time *located* linguistics as a whole. (Saussure 1974: 17)

Here the spatial existence of knowledge is simply presupposed, and a metaphorical elaboration based on the commonplace characteristics of (Western) space can begin.

In the next-order entailment, *knowledge is territory*, theoretical writers speak of "territory", "regions" and "areas", for example

> The semantic style *covers* all the *territory* which was included in the older functional social anthropology . . . we shall have to wait to see how semantic anthropology recasts these areas which have so far been virtually *untouched* . . . (Crick 1976: 125)

Now the metaphor focuses more precisely upon land, and a whole complex of implications based on our physical and cultural experience of land begins to emerge. Land is taken to have a surface (which can be "covered") and "ground"; and some of its physical features are evoked in the entailment *knowledge is a landscape*, as in the following expressions:

> conceptual *landscapes*
> an intellectual *climate*
> a *landmark* in the development of anthropology
> in view of the *gulf/chasm* between them
> an epistemological *horizon*

Land is three-dimensional and more or less static in the Western conception, and so movement and change (and the passage of time) are represented by the flow of air and water across the earth's surface:

> in the *mainstream* of the French sociological school

into his works *flow* at least two distinct traditions
he *launched* a number of major changes
the *currents/winds* of change,

while interrupted change is expressed in metaphors of sinking and stagnation:

> Societies of the "Asiatic" type *sinking* into a thousand-year *stagnation* (Godelier 1977: 120).

Before a theoretical landscape is subject to human occupation it is taken to be wild, untamed, uncultivated and chaotic (as for instance, in Levi-Strauss' phrase about the "uncleared sectors of social life" (quoted in Godelier 1977: 216)), and so a first stage in theoretical development is often phrased in metaphors of "exploration", "pioneering", "staking claims" and "clearing away the undergrowth":

> a publication that *explores* and *searches* and questions (Leach 1961: vii)

> I am, as far as I know, a *pioneer*, or rather a *backwoodsman*, in the work of *clearing* and *opening up* what I called semiotic (C.S. Peirce, quoted in Robey 1973: 59).

I shall return to this theme later in the paper, for it has strong and obvious links with the metaphor *intellectual activity is a journey*. Suffice it to say now that in this process of exploration, new *discoveries* are made, and the terrain is *charted, mapped* and so brought under cognitive control:

> It is better to assemble reminders on this subject piecemeal by *exploring* a diversity of *terrains* . . . In the *explorations* below, we can see how in different *maps*, language can *chart*, constitute or *disguise* a *landscape* (Crick 1976: 129)[3]

From cognitive control, metaphors of political control may follow, and so theorists speak of

a world-renowned *authority*
law governed domains
a *realm* of communication *rules*
a scientific *revolution*.

The question of demarcation now holds political implications, and so *boundaries* between *domains* are drawn, *borders* and *frontiers* are established, and *barriers* may be built to guard them:

> *breaking down barriers* between science and art
> "messages which *stand on* the *frontiers* of language" (Barthes 1967: 23)

those branches which wish to *go beyond* the *boundaries* of existing disciplines (Crick 1976: 106).

Lévi-Strauss elaborates this metaphor in speaking of the relations between anthropology and linguistics:

> For many years they have been working very *closely* with *the* linguists, and all of a sudden it seems to them that the linguists are *vanishing*, that they are *going* on the other *side* of the *borderline* which *divides* the exact and natural sciences *on the other*. (Lévi-Strauss 1963: 69)

In their recent work *Metaphors We Live By*, Lakoff and Johnson discuss in some detail the metaphor *argument is war* (4-7, 61-65, 77-82), which emerges in such expressions as *indefensible claims, attacking weak points* in a *position, demolishing* an argument, using *strategies, winning* or *losing ground*. They suggest that this metaphor does in fact affect our perceptions of arguments and the way in which they are practised. An argument, in our society, has a scenario of speakers adopting different opinions which come into conflict. They each plan how to win their "protagonist" over to their "side" by asking questions which "attack the other's position", and making statements that "defend" their own, deliver a "counter-attack" and perhaps eventually "withdraw" in a "retreat". An argument can end in a "stalemate", "truce" or a "surrender", it is said to be "won" or "lost". Here we begin to address the question of whether metaphors such as *knowledge is territory* and *argument is war* affect practice. Lakoff and Johnson are prepared to argue forcefully that they do.

It is the combination of these two metaphors, *knowledge is territory* and *argument is war* that leads to talk of intellectual "imperialism" in theoretical texts:

> Science progressively *invades* the *domain* of the arts (Guiraud 1975: 11)

> the flexibility, even the *surrender*, of formalist theses by their own *defenders*, provide us with an inkling that the *quarrel* over a definition of economies that has *raged* for over 20 years . . . (Godelier 1977: 21)

> explosions of academic *wrath* (Leach 1961: 21)

So theorists speak of *raids* on other fields, the fruits of *plunder, combat zones, arenas, taking up cudgels*, loosing *lethal shafts/broadsides*, and other such bloodthirsty expressions. They defend their own discipline against "trespass" and "invasion", and anyone who has seen a practitioner of one field face an audience of experts in another will not suppose that this language is merely fanciful. Nor is it likely that our single-minded search for *laws, rules* and *control* in Western science is accidental. I suggest that the organization of *areas* of study into *disciplines* and *domains*, the consequent production of university departments, subject texts and specialist practitioners, and our whole style of academic discussion and debate owes much to the way in which the geo-political organization of knowledge is conceived in theoretical talk.

Now I wish to turn to the metaphor, *intellectual activity is a journey*. This follows logically from a spatial conception of knowledge, and it generates a great number of expressions that we would not normally notice as metaphorical:[4]

> the first *step* in this analysis
> we will *proceed*
> this *leads* me to postulate
> an important consequence thus *follows*
> we will *return* to this *point*
> we *arrive* at the concept of . . .

In such language it is presupposed that intellectual activity (and more specifically, a theoretical discussion) proceeds along a "path" with a specific "direction" and final "goal", and this may be generalized to the description of how theories are developed:

> But linguists and anthropologists *follow* their own *paths* independently. They *halt*, no doubt, from time to time to communicate to one another certain of their *findings* . . . (Lévi-Strauss 1963:32).

In this conception a scholar must "keep up" with "progress" in his field or "fall behind" and be "overtaken" by others. His way may be difficult, beset by *false trails, detours, blind alleys, wrong tracks* and *pitfalls*, and an unwary traveller may *fall into a trap, go in circles, take a backward step* or be *lost* altogether.

The leaders on such a trail are spoken of as *explorers* and *trailblazers*, who *open the path* and *pave the way* for those who *follow* and act as *guides* and *leaders* for the less intrepid; and their journey may be conceived of as a *guest*, a *search*, a *pursuit* or a *hunt*.

These metaphors are a favourite source for rhetorical elaboration in theoretical writing:

> the disciplines have their *place* well-*marked*, and . . . in a multi-*dimensional space* to each one there corresponds an original *path* which sometimes *crosses*, sometimes *goes along* other *paths*, and sometimes *parts* from them . . . One may *discover* logically possible *paths* . . . which would set *the course* of those sciences yet unborn (Lévi-Strauss 1976: 298).

In English, there appears to be a whole series of metaphors which place high value on a movement "forward" and "up"[5] : *conscious is up, unconscious is down* (get *up*, *wake up*, he *sank* into a coma); *having control is up, being under control is down* (I have control *over* her, on *top* of the situation, he is *under* my command); *future is up* (what's coming *up*?) and forward (*forth*coming events); *rational is up, irrational is down* (we *raised* the *level* of the discussion, he couldn't *rise above* his feelings); and *forward is superior* (he's *ahead* of the others, *forward*-thinking). If one combines these metaphors with the claim *intellectual activity is a journey*, it is not too difficult to understand the persistent appeal of notions of intellectual *advancement* and the inexorable *progress* of science in Western thought.

Intellectual activity is a journey also seems to underlie many of those linguistic expressions used to organize theoretical discourse. I suggest a term "marker posts" for phrases which locate different stages in the progress of an argument:

this *starting point*
from this it *follows*
we will *go further* with our analysis
how far have we come?
so far . . .
we shall *return* to this point
we shall not *linger* long
now — and *here* we *arrive* at the very crux of our research . . .
we now *come to the end* of our discussion.

They may also serve to point out features of the intellectual landscape as the discussion proceeds:

As Malinowski has *pointed out*
there we can *clearly see*
Notice that . . .
Let us *look* at their contradictions
here we recognize/find
on one *hand . . . on* the other.

Such expressions function as a form of "ostension" in academic discussion, and they may be followed by brief "naming ceremonies" for the phenomena so located:

I propose to *term* this . . .
this we may *call/label* . . .

For complex structures simple ostension may not be enough, and they may have to be "sketched", "outlined", "mapped" and "modelled", sometimes quite literally in diagrammatic or three-dimensional presentation. The metaphor *intellectual activity is a journey*, then, is worked out in the most elaborate detail in theoretical talk, and it appears to be a major device for presenting abstract ideas in an orderly manner. At this rhetorical level at least, it does have practical effects.

The next metaphor to be considered, *understanding is seeing*, has already entered the discussion when we talked about ostension. If knowledge is a landscape that is traversed in theoretical accounts, it follows logically that we will look about us as we travel, and notice features of the terrain. From any given *vantage-point* or *position*, the viewer has a particular *outlook, orientation* or *view*. If he is high up on the landscape, his *perspective* will be *wide* and relatively *distant*, whereas if he is closer to the *ground* the *scope* will be *narrower* and he can take a *close look* at specific features:

> Structuralism is neither a theory nor a method, but *a way of looking at things*" (Leach in Robey 1973: 37)

> It would require a profound *shift* in *perspective* to see the limitations of this *view* (Crick 1976: 6)

> let us *focus* on this point
> from a *wider point of view*

It is this notion that understanding is essentially a way of *looking at things* that underlies all accounts of "objectivity", for it encourages us to think of the viewer and the viewed as separate, distanced entries, and the physical existence of the "object" as not in doubt.

This metaphor of "seeing" also underlies our conception of fieldwork as an activity located in the particular, and theory as a "high level", relatively *remote view* of a *wide range* of phenomena:

> The ethnographic study of society must have a *concrete*, almost *microscopic* character . . . A systematic, comparative and *generalizing perspective* must complement the *close-range view* (Lévi-Strauss 1963: xi)

And yet, an interpretive approach to anthropology would suggest that this sort of distinction between theory and ethnography is fundamentally misleading, and that thought and observation cannot be separated in this way — least of all in our reflections upon life in other societies.

Closely related to *understanding is seeing* is another metaphor, *explanations are light sources* (Lakoff and Johnson 1980: 48)

> What a *brilliant* idea!

> each type of explanation *throws illumination* on appropriately selected case material. (Leach 1961: 23)

> *in* the *light* of the structural principle
> a *flash of insight*

and failures of explanation are spoken of as failures of sight:

> this notion *obscures* rather than *illuminates*

> his consequent *eclipse* has *hidden* much of value *from our view* (Crick
> 1976: 35).

Thought is described as a form of light projection, by reflection, refraction, or the casting of images:

> thought constructs a giant *mirror*-effect, where the reciprocal *image* of
> man and the world is *reflected* ad infinitum, perpetually decomposing and
> recomposing in the *prism* of Nature — Culture relations (Godelier 1977:
> 213)

and description is visual reproduction — sketching, surveying, outlining and charting:

> I shall *draw* my *illustrations* in *sharp contrast*, all *black* and all *white*
> (Leach 1961: 2)

I think it is possible that much theoretical innovation in anthropology (and other fields) depends upon such metaphors in quite a direct way. Different theoretical orientations are expressed just so — as different vantage-points in epistemological space. Structuralism, according to Lévi-Strauss' account, views other societies from a height, at such a distance that the people seem like ants. This account is not surprising, given the metaphorical associations of rationality and control with height. The ethnoscientists, on the other hand, seek to "see the world through the eyes of the native" by "getting inside his head". They try to replicate his *world view* by adopting his precise vantage-point. In hermeneutic theory it is taken for granted that the theorist and those he seeks to understand will have different perspectives, but the process of reflexive interpretation (through the "hermeneutic circle" — based on *intellectual activity is a journey*) is an attempt to bring about a "merging of horizons", so that the viewpoints of self and other progressively overlap and understanding is achieved as shown diagrammatically in Fig. 1.

There are marked differences in supposed relative status between anthropologist and other in each of these accounts — in structuralism the analyst is hierarchically superior, in ethnoscience he seeks to efface himself, and hermeneutic theory presents itself as an exchange between equals. I do not want to make too much of this, but it does seem an interesting outcome of the metaphors of orientation, and it is at least possible that such conceptions will affect practitioners' styles of fieldwork and the presentation of accounts.

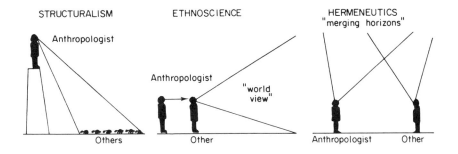

STRUCTURALISM   ETHNOSCIENCE   HERMENEUTICS "merging horizons"

Anthropologist

Anthropologist   "world view"

Others   Other   Anthropologist   Other

Fig. 1

A further metaphor, *facts are natural objects*, follows from *knowledge is a landscape* and *understanding is seeing*. If we walk around in a theoretical landscape and look about us, we are likely to see things, and in this account the "things" that we see are pre-eminently "facts". Facts are depicted as hard, solid, concrete and tangible — they are to be found on or under the "ground" and can be *picked up, collected, gathered, dug up, sorted, sifted, weighed, balanced, arranged* and *looked* at:

> the *hard* facts of the matter are . . .
> a *mass/cluster/bundle* of facts
> a *grounded* theory is one *based* on facts

> he tried to secure the co-operation of colonial administrations in *collecting* cultural and linguistic information, even proposing a new ethnological journal for *storing* it (Crick 1976: 16).

Facts are objects, described in group nouns, with a physical existence and of natural origin. They come from the wild, and must be sorted and ordered by man. They belong to the earth, for someone in close touch with facts is said to have his *feet on the ground*, to be *down to earth* and *close to the grass roots*. A fact may be mineral, to be mined or excavated, or vegetable, to be "gathered" and "preserved", cultivated and even cooked (from *raw* facts to be half-*baked* theories). This is the true metaphorical basis of "objectivity", presupposed in our everyday talk about what is. It is also the linguistic rationale for the persistent idea that *fieldwork* is data-*gathering*, as though the important features of another society will be lying about on the ground for our collection. If this is so, the ethnographer need only know enough to recognize the odd facts, the rare and the representative, and have the techniques at his command to preserve these "facts" and carry them back home for leisurely analysis. It is at least one possible explanation for the otherwise incomprehensible ignorance of local languages (for when one can *see*, why talk) that has been the feature of so much anthropological fieldwork.

In parenthesis, I suggest here that there is a root sequence of metaphors in English which describe the logistics of empiricism. The first of these, *facts are natural objects*, accounts for the finding and collection of facts, and their existence independent of context or cognition. The second, *the mind is a container*:

At the *back* of my mind
he's *full of* information
empty-headed
I'm *cramming* for my exams
it's *gone* right *out* of my head

suggests that facts are collected from external reality and packed inside one's head, and the third, *language is a conduit,*[6] accounts for the passage of information from one person to another:

that was a *loaded* remark
don't *force* your meanings *into* the wrong words
you need to *put* that concept *into* words very precisely

Some linguistic parcels may be too difficult to open, and so communication fails:

that remark is completely *impenetrable*
metaphorical *unwrapping*

This metaphorical description of perception, thought and communication influences us to talk as though these processes involve a simple gathering, packing, sending and unpacking of facts and "information", it assumes that their objective existence is beyond all reasonable doubt, and suggests that our interpretive power as rational beings is no more complex that the logistics of a parcel post. It contradicts much of what has been learned about human communication and interpretation of reality, and yet it is unavoidable in our descriptions of these complex, reflexive and dialectical exchanges. It is no wonder that logical positivism and "objectivity" seem so sensible to most speakers of English.

By contrast with facts, *theories are cultural products*, and much less substantial and solid in nature. They are located above ground, and thinkers are said to have their *heads in the clouds*, to be *up in the air* or living in an ivory *tower*. The great challenge of thought is to *grasp* the intangible — ideas, structures, consequences and relations, and to give it substance. Thus theories must be *grounded* in facts, and theoreticians gather facts from the wild and domesticate them, bringing order out of chaos and making epistemological space fit for human habitation. Intellectual *work* is above all a process of production — it is not play or amusement for dilettanti in our conception — and so the structural characteristics of Western production should apply to the production of knowledge as well. And if Sahlins' dictum, "production is the realization of a symbolic scheme" (1976: 181) is anything like accurate, it should apply, and perhaps preeminently, to the processes of epistemological manufacture.

There is an irony here, however, for in our talk about knowledge we have scarcely arrived at the industrial state. A "hunter-gatherer" mode of intellectual subsistence has already been briefly described in the account of fact *finding* and *gathering* and in metaphors of "hunger" and "thirst" for knowledge, but most of our metaphors about theoretical activity depict it as a form of sedentry agriculture:

the recent popularity of ethology has resulted in a great amount of poor *work* in (this) *field* . . . (Crick 1976: 101)

to *cultivate* an understanding
a *neglected field*, which has not reverted to *wilderness*.

Ideas and theories may be *propogated*, and *transplanted* from one field to another, and there is a constant concern with fertility and growth:

a *productive* are of speculation

Malinowski's linguistic work was not *fruitful* (Crick 1976: 8)

fields which are *ripe* for the most advanced mathematical investigation (Lévi-Strauss 1963: 55)

a *fertile* relationship with language.

This even flows over into metaphors of personal fertility for important thinkers:

Lévi-Strauss' most *seminal* suggestion (Crick 1976: 41)

It was not Engels who *gave birth* to this dogmatism (Godelier 1977: 102)

and images of an *infant* science which will eventually grow to maturity.

Explanatory failure is conversely described as impotence, sterility, emasculation and death:

sterile philosophical debates

neo-evolutionism adds its own *impotence* to the limits of empiricism (Godelier 1977: 90)

we shall not be able to get rid of the difficulties involved in the content of the concept of science;

we cannot silently *bury* it with a mere *death* sentence (Godelier 1977: 95-6)

Because successful thought is seen to be productive, knowledge may be spoken of as wealth and ideas as resources to be borrowed, exchanged, traded and acknowledged in accounts of intellectual debt and credit; and some of this wealth may be invested in the construction of theoretical monuments.

to the memory of the founder of "Année Sociologique": That famed *workshop* where modern anthropology *fashioned* part of its *tools* (Lévi-Strauss 1963: v)

the *master-builders* of anthropology as we know it today (Lévi-Strauss 1976: 4)

building models/theories/systems
laying the groundwork/foundations for a theory
the *cornerstone/building-blocks* of a theory

we admire the *elegance* of this *construction* (Lévi-Strauss 1963: 15)

a *collapse* of the classic themes in cultural anthropology (Godelier 1977: 39)

the *demolition* of totemism

Lévi-Strauss performs some remarkable rhetorical flourishes on this theme in his tribute to Durkheim in *Structural Anthropology 2*:

This doctrine has not ceased to astonish us by its imposing *proportions*, its powerful logical *framework*, and the *vistas* it *opens* onto *horizons* where so much is yet to be *explored*. The mission of Mauss was to *complete* and *fit up* the prodigious *edifice* conjured from the *earth* at the passage of the demiurge. He had to exorcise a few metaphysical ghosts who were still trailing their chains *there*, and the *edifice* had to be shielded once and for all against the *icy winds* of dialectic, the *thunder* of syllogisms, the *lightning flashes* of antimonies (Lévi-Strauss 1976: 5-6).

The Marxist notions of *infra-structure* and *superstructure*, and Lévi-Strauss' account of *concrete* logic and the savage as "bricoleur" are elaborated from this metaphorical base, *theoretical systems are buildings*.

Now we come to the question of a network of implications about space in English semantics. Space in commonsense English is three-dimensional and static, forming a backdrop for movement and the passage of time. It is divisible and quantifiable in standard measures, and most of our ordinary talk about space assumes a human location on a physical surface (the earth). Relative to this surface there are a series of orientational continua – vertically placed on it and marking relatively "high"/"low", vertically below it and marking "deep"/"shallow" or "surface", horizontally on it and marking "wide"/"narrow", and relative to some physical entity and marking "in"/"out", "on"/"off", "front"/"behind", "central/ "peripheral" and "near"/"far".

I have not studied this aspect of English semantics in any detail, but it does appear that speakers of English place valuations upon these continua, so that "high", "wide", "deep", "forward", "far" and "central" for instance, appear to be associated with "good", especially in our talk about cognition:

high minded	*low* minded
broad minded	*narrow* minded
a *deep* thinker	a *superficial* thinker
forward thinker	a *backward child*
far-sighted	*short*-sighted
a *central* argument	a *peripheral* argument

I think one can suggest some ways at least, in which these continua and the valuations placed upon them, have affected the construction of theory in anthropology and related fields.

Consider, for instance, the prevalence of talk about "levels" in theoretical discussion. Notions of social stratification, evolution and abstraction are all based on a hierarchy of levels:

high and *low* status groups
high (complex, advanced) cultures and *low* (simple, primitive, archaic) cultures
high and *low* levels of abstraction.

Given that height is associated with rationality, control, superiority and power in English (Lakoff and Johnson 1980: 14-21), it is not really possible to use hierarchical accounts in any neutral sense, and attempts to grade societies from "high" to "low", or types of reflective thought (say, fieldwork and theory) on a stratified model will inevitably suffer from a semantic "warp" in which movement from low to high is interpreted as progress or advance. This "warp" has proved treacherous in much of anthropological thought:

a *regressive* people, that is, one that *descended* from a *higher level* of material life and social organization (Lévi-Strauss 1963: 105) a *low level* of development in productive forces (Godelier 1977: 183)

though nowhere *elevated* to the *status* of an absolute rule (Leach 1961: 74)

The notion of height in cognition is closely associated with that of breadth, presumably reflecting the physical experience of one who climbs to a high point on a landscape and looks down. So a "wide scope" is valued in theory construction:

the *widening* of sociolinguistics *along these lines* would clearly be a welcome *advance* (Crick 1976: 65)

the sheer *range* of his interests, *breadth* of vision

Douglas has long criticized the *narrow* conception of the *scope* of witchcraft studies, and has suggested that *advance* to a *broader* frame of reference . . . (Crick 1976: 111)

The other continuum which is a continual source of inspiration to theorists is that of relative depth. *Deep* structures, patterns and logic are held to be difficult of access, fundamental or "elementary", unconscious, perhaps universal to all human cognition and hidden from sight. *Surface* structures, by contrast, are easy to see but chaotic and confusing, conscious but delusory and deceptive. The great challenge of theoretical activity is to think *deeply* and *penetrate* to those patterns which lie behind the surface of human life, and by explanation bring them to the light. In this we can recognize the metaphorical source of Lévi-Strauss' "elementary structures", Chomsky's "deep" and "surface" structures, and major elements in the thought of Marx and Freud. If the metaphor is applied specifically to the earth, it is elaborated in notions of digging and uncovering the concealed (Foucalt's *Archaeology of Knowledge*), and if to water, in expressions about "sinking" and being "submerged":

we must *sink* to the *level* of the unconscious where science *locates* truth (Crick 1976: 39)

(Marx) undertook the study in *depth* of one form of society . . . he dismissed empiricism and *going beyond* a system's *superficial appearance*, sought those *deeper* structures which can *reveal* a logic both *hidden* and *obscure* (Godelier 1977: 76)

I have not attempted in this paper to offer any exhaustive lists of the use of these metaphors of knowledge in anthropology, because that is not possible. Such metaphors are open-ended and creative, and the theoretical innovations that arise from their use are at once familiar and so intelligible, and yet novel and provocative. They are not used according to any strict criterion of logical consistency – it seems that writers (and even more, speakers) may move rapidly and quite freely from one of these related metaphors to another:

> *At first glance* the theme of this essay might seem excessively *narrow* . . .
> Firstly, it . . . *lies* at the very *heart* of anthropological kinship and theory.
> Secondly, it is a *branch* of kinship theory . . . Thirdly, it is a *field* to which
> . . . (Leach 1961: 55)

> we have *stirred* up from the *depths* of anthropology's discourses and texts,
> a contradictory and theoretical *dead-end* (Godelier 1977: 93)

> Lévi-Strauss . . . unquestionably opened up . . . a *field* which had long
> been *stagnant* (Crick 1976: 50)

Much of the richness and piquancy of theoretical talk, and many of its new departures seem to arise from the flexibility and ambiguity of such non-literal use of language.

There are some comments of a more general nature that can be offered now. The development of the metaphor *knowledge is a landscape* appears to dominate our talk about knowledge to a remarkable extent. I found only a few minor and peripheral metaphors that seemed unrelated to it. Some writers spoke of an intellectual "genealogy" where ideas were *inherited* from *ancestral* figures – this might derive from the personal fertility metaphor discussed earlier. There is also a religious metaphor of *followers, disciples, dogmas,* and *revelations*, and an educational one of *schools* of thought, but these are not much elaborated in theoretical discussion.

Why landscape, then? David Rumelhard, a psychologist, suggests that "nearly always, when we talk about abstract concepts, we choose language drawn from one or another concrete domain" (in Ortony 1979: 89), and orientation in a physical environment is at once our most complex and our most direct experience of "the real world". It would seem, then, as Sahlins has suggested in another context (Sahlins 1976: 166-204), that concrete logic is by no means the prerogative of savages, and that even in our "highest level" talk about theory and explanation, we remain quite firmly "grounded".

At the same time, there is no literal sense (at least as far as I'm aware) in which knowledge does resemble the physical environment, spatially or in any other way, and so these landscape metaphors present major difficulties of explanation for "similarity" or "analogy" theories of metaphor. I have already quoted Max Black as suggesting that "a metaphor might be self-certifying by generating the very reality to which it seems to draw attention" (Ortony 1979:

37), and if we find scholars ordering their material into fields, adopting theoretical positions, fighting pitched battles, and building theories on strong or shaky foundations and at high and low levels of abstraction, it can only be because this is the case, for there is nothing in knowledge itself which suggests that such activities should follow.

In the final section of this paper I want briefly to discuss some of the ways in which Maori speech accounts for knowledge, to open the question of how far our own epistemological metaphors may be universal or particular. This is a discussion that I hope other anthropologists will join, bringing to bear their thoughts and experiences of other socieities.

The English metaphor *knowledge is a landscape* suggests that knowledge is something inexhaustible, based on a "ground" that can be worked and reworked, viewed from many different vantage-points and traversed on an infinite series of pathways. Knowledge is endlessly producible, for there are always new facts to be discovered, new fields to be created and brought into production, and new theories to be built. The Maori metaphors of knowledge (*maatauranga* or *waananga*) on the other hand, draw upon notions of *oranga* (necessity for life) and *taonga* (cultural wealth), and here knowledge is depicted as above all exhaustible and destructible, a scarce resource, conserved within the group, guarded by chosen individuals and never to be squandered. Those who held knowledge were often reluctant to "give it out", a caution which is made very clear in a text by a Ngati Maru scribe who had been commissioned (probably by John White) to collect information from his elders in the second half of the nineteenth century:

> I will say this: the old people will not divulge their incantations, or allow them to be written on paper, nor will they divulge the incantations respecting the dead or funerals, nor will they divulge the ceremonies and incantations for the birth and baptism of a child, nor the ceremonies and incantations of war, nor any other ceremonies and incantations. Perhaps they feel that such things are too sacred to be given. Even the incantations chanted at the planting and harvesting of the kumara they will not divulge. Nor do they even like to give the ancient history of the wars, unless they have tobacco or a few shillings given them . . . You can see by the long time I have had your book that the old men do not like to speak of these matters . . .
>
> When I ask some old chiefs they distinctly refuse to tell about the deeds of old, but answer by saying "How tiresome it is!" So then I lay the book on one side; and thus I have had this book five years in my possession. (White 1888: 183-4).

Once knowledge (including valued technologies) comes into man's possession however, from elders, ancestors and gods, the task is to pass it down to succeeding generations, and to keep its sacred power intact by ensuring that the conditions of transmission are *tika* or correct. So the elders speak of knowledge as a *cloak*, as *food for chiefs* and a *treasure* — something rare, prized, and touched with the powers of *tapu* and *mana*, and always to be cherished. If a man teaches all he knows to a younger man, his sacred powers may soon dwindle away, and yet certain forms of knowledge (particularly those termed *kura* and *waananga*) were not a personal possession, but something that must be passed on to chosen members of the group. In traditional terms this meant that such knowledge was taught in seclusion, often in the dark and well away from food, women and other polluting influences. Those who disregarded such precautions would at the very least not learn, and more likely fall prey to some serious misfortune or die.

As I understand it, the most valued forms of knowledge were intimately associated with ancestral power and efficacy; for instance *waananga* might refer to a medium (through whom ancestors spoke) or an altar on which gods come into the presence of their descendants, as well as to knowledge of creation and tribal accounts, genealogies and *karakia* or incantations; and *kura* as well as referring to knowledge also meant the sacred colour red, a treasure of something cherished, and a chief or man of powers. Other terms for knowledge and belief had connotations of abundant resources and hospitality, the attributes of a man of *mana*; and *kuuware* or "ignorant" also meant "unimportant" and "low in the social scale".

It is perhaps not surprising then, that truth (*pono*) was closely tied to situational factors. To make truth claims was also to make claims of power, and so it was important who made an assertion, to whom, on what occasion and in what ritual conditions. *Tika* appears to be pre-eminently a notion of contextual truth, where appeal to ancestral precedents and powers might lead to affirmation, or equally politically, contradiction and assertions of disbelief. Each descent group held a rather different set of ancestral accounts from every other, and knowledgeable men were not only well aware of alternative versions to their own but had evolved strategies to deal with them:

Te Matorohanga, priest of the school of learning at Wairarapa to his pupils, 1865:

> Attention! O Sirs! Listen! There was no one universal system of teaching in the Whare Waananga (school of learning). Each tribe had its own

priests, its own college, and its own methods. From tribe to tribe this was so; the teaching was led astray by the self-conceit of the priests which allowed of departure from their own doctrines to those of other schools of learning. My word to you is: Hold steadfastly to our teaching; leave out of consideration that of other (tribes). Let their descendants adhere to their teaching, and you to ours, so that if you are wrong (hee), it was we (your relatives) who declared it to you (and you are not responsible); and if you are right (*tika*), it is we who gave you this treasured possession (*taonga*). (Smith 1913: Vol. I, 84)

The Maori management of knowledge (as a rare good, a descent-group possession, infused with sacred power) is at once quite unlike, and in some ways very like, our own. We do have a secondary metaphor *knowledge is wealth* in our own theoretical talk, and knowledge is often jealously guarded, difficult of access and treated with caution in the Western tradition of science. I suppose that our attitudes to certain very potent scientific technologies would offer the closest parallel to the tribal guarding of esoteric information in Maori society. At the same time there is no extended elaboration of spatial metaphors about knowledge in Maori speech. People do talk of thinking *deeply (kia hohonu nga whakaaro)* and seeing *clearly (kia marama te titiro)* in speaking about understanding, and there are associations of knowledge with heights (e.g. *toi*: art, knowledge, summit, citadel of a fortified hilltop village) but these themes are not taken far.

And yet it would not be true to say that landscape and buildings have no epistemological significance in tribal thought – quite the contrary. Landmarks and certain buildings are critical to group structures of knowledge in Maori society. It is not so much that knowledge is projected onto an imaginary landscape or into a metaphorical building process; rather, specific knowledge is "bound into" specific landmarks and chiefly houses, carvings and heirlooms belonging to the descent group, in a direct and immediate relationship.

In recent discussions of naming (Kripke 1972; Putnam 1975) metaphors of "dubbing" and "naming ceremony" have been suggested for the ways in which natural features or "kinds" can be given linguistic labels by ostension. These metaphors apply literally to the Maori case, where knowledge and power could be "talked into" physical objects (say, in the blessing of a building, a carving, a weapon or ceremonial ornament) and fixed there by a name. In the accounts of any descent group (its histories, songs, players, proverbs and oratory), stories are told of how ancestors claimed territory, naming landmarks after parts of their bodies; how they travelled across that territory, leaving names behind them; the fishing grounds and rocks and eeling pools, trees, bushes, streams, waterfalls, rivers, patches of bush, hills, caves and ridges are all named, and most of the names evoke ancestral histories. A child would often be taught a particular account *in that place*, so that the place and its knowledge were one, and the place and its name became a guarantee for the truth-value of the account — "I know it is true, because I have seen that very rock." At the same time the place serves to bring the account into present time (much as documents serve us in Western histories) so that the past has existence in the present. Places, carvings and chiefly houses are not symbols or representations of past history in tribal understanding — that puts them too far apart; rather, knowledge is bound into them with a power of naming that locks them together, and collapses distance in space-time.[7]

Chiefly houses may be greeted as ancestors and spoken to on ritual occasions, and heirlooms may be wept over and addressed. Man's relationship with what Europeans would gloss as "objects" and the "physical environment" is not detached, but premised on a shared descent that is spelled out in the origin accounts. Men addressed the world in ritual talk and invoked ancestral powers to get a suitable reply — good crops, fine weather, success in fishing and finding game. It is difficult to imagine a philosophy based on a distinction between an "internal" subjectivity and an "external" objectivity being elaborated in such a system of thought.

One could argue that Maori talk about knowledge is more in keeping with an interpretive, dialogical approach to anthropology than our own spatial metaphors. The "landscape" account presents the anthropologist as a detached intelligence, working to domesticate and master an objectified world, whereas in Maori thinking, truth is always contingent upon situational factors, knowledge claims are tied to power, the environment has a right of reply and one is vulnerable to its rebuttals. This is, I must say, a close account of my experience of working as an anthropologist in New Zealand.

It is not possible to draw any serious philosophical conclusions from this first tentative approach to a cross-cultural account of knowledge, except to suggest that it may offer some support for a position of limited relativism. Our own conception of knowledge, based as it is upon a metaphorical set that Maori speech does not share, cannot be claimed a universal, and yet it works in a way that has some parallels in Maori practice. Although the Western and Maori descent group epistemological worlds are clearly not the same, they can (with intense interpretive effort) preserve some measure of intelligibility.

Scholars in the two traditions do not understand knowledge alike, but I think it at least possible that they might come to understand one another.

Notes

1. I thank Ralph Grillo for suggesting some possible avenues for exploration.
2. Texts in English translation are regarded as part of English anthropological literature for this analysis.
3. It is relevant here to note how spatial metaphors have been elaborated within semantics itself. Epistemological *space*, semantic *fields* and *domains* with *sharp* or *fuzzy* boundaries, cognitive *maps* and taxonomic *partitions* are commonplace expressions. They present a one-dimensional "container" account of meaning which does scant justice to the complexity of semantic pattern.
4. The distinction between "live" and "dead" metaphors may be troublesome in this context. The point is simply that our language about journeys and our language about intellectual activity employ many of the same expressions; and this commonality of linguistic resources forms the base for elaborations which most speakers of English would recognize as metaphorical.
5. For an extended discussion of these metaphors, see Lakoff and Johnson 1980: 14-19.
6. See Reddy, The Conduit Metaphor, In Ortony 1979: 284-324.
7. The Maori concept of "space-time" is of a medium (*waa*) in which intervals are marked out (*taki*) by ritual, genealogy, and acts of revenge. [*taki*: "distributive prefix, take to one side, recite (genealogies), challenge/make a speech (in rituals of group encounter"; *takitaki* "provoke, avenge, trace out, fence"; *waa*: "space, interval, area, region, time, season"; *waawaa*: "picket, stake of fence, be distributed, separated"; *takiwaa:* "defined district, space, time, period, be separated by an interval".] Also note *tawhiti*: "distant, widely separated in space or time".

References

Barth, F. 1975. *Ritual and Knowledge among the Baktaman of New Guinea.* Oslo: Universitetsforlaget
Barthes, R. 1967. *Elements of Semiology*. London: Jonathan Cape.
Crick, M. 1976. *Explorations in Language and Meaning*. London: Malaby Press.
Derrida, J. 1978. *Writing and Difference*. London: Routledge & Kegan Paul.
Gadamer, H.-G. 1976. *Philosophical Hermeneutics*. Berkeley: Univ. of California Press.
Geertz, C. 1971. *Myth, Symbol and Culture*. New York: W.W. Norton.
—— 1973. *The Interpretation of Cultures*. New York: Basic Books.
Godelier, M. 1977. *Perspectives in Marxist Anthropology*. Cambridge: Univ. Press.
Guiraud, P. 1975. *Semiology*. London: Routledge & Kegan Paul.

Heidegger, M. 1978. *Basic Writings*. London: Routledge & Kegan Paul.

Hesse, M. 1963. *Models and Analogies in Science*. London: Steen & Ward.

—— 1965. The explanatory function of metaphor. *International Congress for Logic, Methodology and Philosophy of Science 1964*. Amsterdam: North Holland.

Kripke, S. 1972. *Naming and Necessity*. Oxford: Basil Blackwell.

Lakoff, G. & Johnson, M. 1980. *Metaphors We Live By*. Chicago: Univ. Press

Leach, E. 1961. *Rethinking Anthropology*. London: Athlone Press.

Lévi-Strauss, Claude 1963. *Structural Anthropology* New York: Penguin.

—— 1976. *Structural Anthropology 2*. New York: Penguin.

Macdonald, G. & Pettit, P. 1981. *Semantics and Social Science*. London: Routledge & Kegan Paul.

Marcus, G. & Cushman, D. 1982. *Ethnographies as Texts*. Houston: Xerox, Rice University.

Needham, R. 1972. *Belief, Language and Experience*. Oxford: Basil Blackwell.

Ortony, A. (ed.) 1979. *Metaphor and Thought*. Cambridge: Univ. Press.

Pepper, S. 1942. *World Hypotheses*. Berkeley: Univ. of California Press.

Putnam, H. 1975. The meaning of "meaning". In *Language, Mind and Knowledge* (ed.) K. Gunderson. Minneapolis: Univ. of Minnesota Press.

Quine, W. V. O. 1960. *Word and Object*. Cambridge, Mass: M.I.T. Press.

Ricoeur, P. 1976. *Interpretation Theory: Discourse and The Surplus of Meaning*. Fort Worth: Texas Christian University Press.

—— 1977. *The Rule of Metaphor*. Toronto: Univ. Press.

Ridley, B. K. 1976. *Time, Space and Things*. New York: Penguin Books.

Robey, David (ed.) 1973. *Structuralism: An Introduction*. Oxford: Clarendon Press.

Rosaldo, M. 1980. *Knowledge and Passion*. Cambridge: Univ. Press.

Sacks, S. (ed.) 1979. *On Metaphor*. Chicago: Univ. Press.

Sahlins, M. 1976. *Culture and Practical Reason*. Chicago: Univ. Press.

Sapir, J. D. & Crocker, J. C. (eds) 1977. *The Social Use of Metaphor*. Philadelphia: Univ. of Pennsylvania Press.

Saussure, Ferdinand 1974. *Course in General Linguistics*. London: Peter Owen.

Smith, S. P. 1913. *The Lore of the Whare Wananga* Vols. I and II. New Plymouth: Polynesian Society.

Turner, V. 1974. *Dramas, Fields and Metaphors*. New York: Cornell University Press.

Tyler, S. 1969. *Cognitive Anthropology*. New York: Holt, Rinehart & Winston.

Ullman, Stephen 1977. *Semantics*. Oxford: Basil Blackwell.

White, J. 1888. *The Ancient History of the Maori* Vol. V. Wellington: Government Printer.

Wilson, B. R. (ed.) 1979. *Rationality*. Oxford: Basil Blackwell.

MODELS, MEANINGS AND REFLEXIVITY

STEPHEN GUDEMAN and MISCHA PENN

Models have enjoyed widespread use in anthropology, and in the social sciences generally. In many fields, for example, the human body has been used as a model to portray the parts and functioning of society. Anthropologists have been especially imaginative contributors to the reservoir of model concepts. Radcliffe-Brown (1977), in a well-known passage, once suggested that sea shells could serve as the model for whole societies; but Leach (1961) modelled Radcliffe-Brown himself as a collector of butterflies, and suggested that we think of societies as stretchy plastic sheets. From Lévi-Strauss we have learned of kaleidoscopes, pumps and camshafts, while in addition to "models of" and "models for", Geertz offers us the model of the text which is to be distinguished from Turner's model of life as drama. Since Morgan, anthropologists have modelled lineage organizations in the pattern of Linnean classifications, but as Evans-Pritchard (1940: 202) reported, the Nuer actually model their lineages as a set of lines all meeting at a common point.

By contrast to the many examples of model use in anthropology, theories about the model are fewer in number and not highly developed. (Nutini 1970; Caws 1973). Most fall into one of three currents, although common to all is a distinction made between model and social facts. In "realist" theories, advocated by Lévi-Strauss and others, the model is said to have an independent reality which is not determined by the particular "facts" being modelled. Because the model contains an internal and independent pattern of its own, it provides an explanation for facts which cannot otherwise be understood. "Nominalist" theories, in contrast, would deny that models have an inherent, formal reality. The emphasis here is shifted to the factual level. Radcliffe-Brown (1957), Nadel (1957) and others have maintained that models are constructed on the basis of inductively linked observations of social phenomena; the empirical relations among observable data determine the structure of the model. Such models are said to describe but not explain the facts under observation. A third position is represented perhaps by Leach's attempts to account for the model in anthropology. He has adopted primarily a critical perspective. For Leach (1964a, 1964b) models do not possess the detached formal existence sometimes claimed for them by realists, but neither are they concrete entities drawn directly from empirical facts. Models, he has argued, are a kind of fiction. Despite Leach's critical position, his perspective is akin to the others in that he also offers a two level view; the formal model must be an approximation to the ethnographic facts.

Our views about models run contrary to most of the accepted arguments. For us, a model is a symbol or set of symbols. Anything can serve as a model, just as the same "object" can itself model different phenomena. A leaf, for example, could model bilateral symmetry of the body or of a social organization; alternatively, its growth, coloration and dessication might model the human cycle of life to death; yet again, its internal patterning might be seen to model a genealogy. There exists no necessary of *a priori* connection between a model and that which it models. Above all, a model is not the structure or the essence of the phenomena for which it serves as model.

A model is a human construction, the product of a constitutive activity. The thesis we advance is that anthropologists habitually engage in two fundamentally different types of modelling activities and employ two types of models. One we shall term the "universal model" (U-model). This form of model has received greatest theoretical attention, for it is a product of the dominant discourse in Western society. The universal modeller reconstructs data by use of a given model type. Originally developed in the natural sciences, this modelling activity has gained widespread use in other fields including anthropology. A second tradition, however, offers a different form, the "local model" (L-model). The recognition that a people construct their own or local models calls for a different activity on the part of the anthropologist. The practical utility of and Western concern with universal models has sometimes diverted anthropologists from seeing the contribution they have made to twentieth century thought through their use and development of the local model concept. In fact, we shall be led to argue that U-models are themselves simply a species of L-models.

Two Traditions

In spite of the modernity of the concept of the local model, the distinction we draw has a foundation that reaches back through several centuries of Western thought. Historically, universal models have been crucial in the development of the natural sciences. Models of this type are the principal legacy of the Galilean-Cartesian tradition which has shaped our conception of Western science. In this tradition, it was believed that physical phenomena have a "structure" expressible in terms of mathematical relations. These relations, the so-called "primary qualities," which stand in contrast to sensory or "secondary qualities," underlie the appearance of all things. Such structural explanations are free of contamination by chaotic and ephemeral secondary qualities; they are independent of social and historical change. These facets of the Galilean-Cartesian vision help account for the important role that universal models have played in scientific explanation. Their deductive character makes it possible to view physical laws as necessary truths rather than expressions of the fortuitous occurrence of specific causal factors. The use of a language whose terms and categories are systematically defined in geometrical fashion, together with inference rules for the derivation of global laws, provides a vision of the essential nature of all things.

Descartes also argued that his account of the nature of formal, mathematical thought could be extended to human nature. To be certain, he did not hold that it could be used to explain history and social existence; rather, he argued that judgemental thinking, independent of time and place, could be explained by invariant rules. The essential character of human beings can be discovered by examining the judgements and reasoning of mathematicians and logicians.

We are not claiming that universal models, as we find them in contemporary anthropology, are the direct descendants of this tradition. But we do maintain that anthropological models have inherited certain crucial features, specifically the requirement that they consist of at least two levels; a "core" and a "derived" language. To this feature we shall return.

The Galilean-Cartesian view has not rested without criticism. Vico is usually credited with having launched the first systematic attack. He argued that while structural explanation affords a precise and elegant understanding of physical reality, the study of human beings involves the interweaving of historical, cultural and social factors. Vico did not impugn the Cartesian account of the validity and exemplary character of mathematical knowledge. He urged, however, that the rules which safeguard inferences do not exist independently of the creative activities of mathematicians. Only because the rules and definitions are themselves a part of the various activities which we associate with doing mathematics do proofs appear incontestably certain. Vico also rejected the view that all genuine knowledge must possess the linear order found in mathematical demonstration. Not all human activity, for example, possesses the pattern or purposes of mathematical injury. Myth, poetry and the development of social institutions represent alternative sources for understanding the idea of "structure". These human products lack the deductive symmetry and the core properties associated with Galilean models. They consist of elements which are neither deductively related, as "rationalists" have maintained, or contingently linked by causal variables, as "empiricists" have urged. For Vico, knowledge, whether of saddle-making or of geometry, meant participation in activities; and it was this doing or making which provided the grounds for conventional human truths. Human truths are not matters of "fact" or "logic" but belong to a different order of things.

Universal Models

Universal models in anthropology have their roots in the Galilean-Cartesian tradition. A fundamental characteristic of all U-models is the presence of two analytical levels, although the precise relation between these "levels" takes different forms. A U-model contains a "core" language consisting of a set of defined elements. All relevant features of the model-object are prefigured in the model's core language. It is a "purified" language in that it designates a set of common, uniform features which underlie social behaviour. In general, the terms of this language are said to capture the essential characteristics of the processes, events or things in the world which are to be modelled. Universal models do not single out specific on the ground practices, such as rituals or economic behaviour. The goal of devising the model is to isolate the essential features within or underlying the behaviour, no matter how variegated it appears "on the surface." Universal models presuppose the existence of a single, monolithic and comprehensive "logic" of social activity. A puzzling counter-instance to the U-model's assumption of an overarching social logic would be Malinowski's account of the differences in Trobriand behaviour while fishing in the lagoon as opposed to the open seas in that it illustrates the parallel existence of two divergent orders of meaning (Malinowski 1948).

In addition to a core language, there exists a second level made up of the problematic, undefined elements. Universal models present strategies for the discovery of relations among these designated features of the system to be modelled. When it can be shown that the undefined terms of the model may be derived from its core language, the model may be said to represent all and only those properties which account for the role and operation of the system to be modelled. All U-models, thus, contain at least two levels, a core language and derived elements, the former providing specific meanings and rules for inferring relationships among the latter. In this sense, U-models are believed to capture invariant and essential properties.

Before attending to other features of the U-model, let us examine some illustrations from the anthropological literature. For lack of space we must be brief, and we shall confine our examples to kinship and economics. But at the outset, we would emphasize that the frequently cited opposition between those anthropologists viewed as "empiricists" and those seen to be "rationalists," between the two sides of the Channel, between − to put it more crudely − the "followers" of Radcliffe-Brown and Lévi-Strauss is a misleading issue (Leach 1976). From our standpoint, both sides have their footing in the same Western intellectual tradition. Furthermore, our interest is to uncover various uses of the universal model, regardless of whether it is applied intra- or interculturally.

In kinship, two forms of the U-model may be found by examining the work of Lounsbury and Fortes. Both use a two-layered model, but the character of the relation between the levels varies.

Let us begin with the elegant and influential work of Lounsbury. As one might expect, his assumptions are clearly set forth in one of his earlier and well-known essays. "A Formal Account of the Crow- and Omaha-type Kinship Terminologies" (1964). Directly we ask the reader's indulgence on two counts. First we shall quote at length from Lounsbury, for he has presented an excellent account of the model he constructs; but we also ask the reader to believe that we set forth the main features of the U-model before recalling the Lounsbury work. For Lounsbury:

> A "formal account" of a collection of empirical data has been given when there have been specified (1) a set of primitive elements, and (2) a set of rules for operating on these, such that by the application of the latter to the former, the elements of a "model" are generated; which model in turn comes satisfactorily close to being a facsimile or exact replica of the empirical data whose interrelatedness and systematic nature we are trying

to understand. A formal account is thus an apparatus for predicting back the data at hand, thereby making them "understandable", i.e. showing them to be the lawful and expectable consequences of an underlying principle that may be presumed to be at work at their source (1964: 351).

Lounsbury's explication of his model corresponds to our description of the universal model. The method yields "lawful" results because it is deductive; and one formal model can be matched against another on the basis of "sufficiency" and "parsimony," two criteria which also have historical roots in the Galilean-Cartesian tradition. In addition, to justify the levels of the model, Lounsbury invokes both Murdock and Malinowski. From Murdock, Lounsbury draws the "core language": the "assumption of the . . . near universality of the nuclear family." Malinowski's idea of the extension of primary relationships helps to justify his "derived language" (1964: 381). In the Lounsbury model, the core meanings of kin terms are first specified, and to these terms expansion rules are then applied. As we now know, the method has sparked lengthy debate among anthropologists over the "nature" of kinship (Scheffler and Lounsbury 1971; Schneider 1972, 1976). In fact, much of the kinship debate centers precisely upon whether or not there exist core meanings of kinship, whether these meanings are cross-culturally or universally valid, and whether or not extension (or reduction) rules have sociological validity. We rest with the observation that Lounsbury's model is clearly essentialist in that it exhibits the general characteristics of all U-models — a body of isolated core meanings, derivation rules which permit prescribed logical operations upon the former, and a guarantee that, assuming the model's adequacy, it will ultimately reveal "underlying principles" or "sources."

It is not accidental that Meyer Fortes has at times (1969) alluded to the work of Lounsbury in support of his own position; yet, the Fortesian universal model is, in some respects, fundamentally different from that proposed by Lounsbury. Fortes distinguishes two levels in kinship systems. At the base are "Mendelian-like" genes which are "segregated in their operation but . . . (combined) in different ways in specific kinship systems." These "limited number of general principles rooted in the universal facts of parentage" underlie all kinship systems (*Ibid*: 35). Counterposed to this primary level is that of the actual or encountered phenotype. "Phenotypically, kinship systems are generated which are suited to maintain the social organization required by particular communities" (*Ibid*: 35). This latter form of organization, which is the product of specific historical societies, depends on the "recognition" given by a social group to the "natural genealogical connections" which underlie any kinship system (*Ibid*: 49). To designate this relation between "elementary features" and "structural logic" (*Ibid*: 52), Fortes proposed the term "innucleation." "Genealogical connections are *innucleated* . . . in kinship relations but are nevertheless precisely distinguishable from them" (*Ibid*: 54). To be certain, Fortes argues that genealogical connections are recognized in diverse ways, in culturally divergent forms, but the elementary connections always serve as the "building blocks" of a kinship system (*Ibid*: 68).

The relation between the two levels of Fortes' model is, therefore, not one of derivability as in Lounsbury's, but of "replicability" or innucleation. A kinship system has a structure which is not "reducible" to the economy or polity; nevertheless the system is constructed out of certain units. For Fortes, uncovering the relation between genotype and phenotype, or exposing the building blocks, is a matter of laborious, inductive, empirical analysis.

The classificatory method, the project of building more and more refined typologies (Middleton and Tait 1958), is one index of the use of this type of model. "Observed" facts are arranged and rearranged, refined and combined in order to generate typologies. But these are not simply devices of convenience. The classifications are constructed in the hope that true building blocks will be discovered; the discrete classifications are constructed on the premise that essential factors exist. But, as the last half century has shown, the empiricist journey seems never to reach a finality, a resting place, for new "facts" and new solutions constantly appear to upset the entrenched principles of ordering. If we may use the term, the "mystification" of the empiricist is that essential units exist to be discovered.

Thus, like Lounsbury's model, the Fortesian one consists of the two analytic levels we have found characteristic of U-models generally. Differences subsist in the relation between the "levels" of their models and in the selection of elementary units. In place of the core and derived components of Lounsbury's model, and their relation of deductive necessity, Fortes emphasizes an inductive relation between factors which are in principle "observable." But the pattern inherent in both models remains similar: the complex world of kinship must be supplemented and clarified by "genotypes," "underlying principles" or "sources," whether given or inferred.

Let us now turn, again briefly, to certain arguments within economic anthropology, specifically the formalist-substantivist opposition. There are several ways to grasp the differences between the two views. Certainly, substantivism falls in the framework of institutional approaches to the economy; formalism offers an atomistic, individualistic view. If one starts at the macro-level, the other tends to emphasize the micro-level (Cancian 1966; Kaplan 1968). But we would again point to the fact that both positions, with an exception (Polanyi 1968: 175-180), rely on universal models. The formalists might be compared to the Lounsbury mode, the substantivists to the Fortes style.

Polanyi (1968: 140) once characterized the two approaches as beginning from either "fact" or "logic." Substantivism commences with the observed fact that life is based upon material use. Humans derive their maintenance, they must have an exchange with, the environment. This empirical observation was itself about humans in their capacity as organizers of sense impressions to satisfy material needs.

By contrast, the term "logic" refers to a means-ends, decision-making framework. The building blocks in this approach are the assumption of scarce means, choice among the means, alternative but comparable ends, and a linking of means to ends according to logical rules. Whereas the inductive substantivist method deals with "laws of nature," the deductive formalist method is based on "laws of the mind" (Schneider 1974: 24).

But this seeming division between substantivist as empiricists and formalists as rationalists requires further exploration. Consider first the formalist position. Formalists begin with a set of realistic or heuristic assumptions about human behaviour. These constitute the core language. (The elemental language itself is derived from nineteenth century utilitarianism; its grounding is in a Western code.) This core language is then applied cross-culturally. All human economic actions become understood on the basis of a derivational logic; the method is deductive. One of the most sustained and recent attempts to use this model has been offered by Harold Schneider, and we may use his approach in illustration. Again, a lengthy quotation may best illustrate the modelling activity, which ideally would match that of Lounsbury in precision and reliance on form. Schneider cites with approval, and as charter, the general position of Frank Knight:

> Defending economics, Knight's argument emphasized the *deductive* nature of economic analysis in contrast to the *inductive* orientation of Herskovits. In the nature of deductive reasoning the approach to the study of economic behaviour is not through the ethnographic facts but by means of "universal principles," logico-mathematical in form, springing from

the imagination. Generating the logical system necessary to deductive economics requires no cross-cultural data or facts from *any* system, except perhaps common sense knowledge of the empirical realm to which the theory is to be applied (Schneider 1974: 23).

Here again is expressed the Cartesian deductive model. From a core language is to be derived a specific model. Schneider even adds the Lounsbury provision that the data at hand should be succintly predicted: "It is well to be sure that the theory has some relation to the world it intends to explain and is not just a theoretical toy if one expects to use it to explain the real world" (Schneider 1974: 23).

This same viewpoint was expressed earlier by Cook. He argued for the use of models that simplify analysis, and a method of successive approximations to "reality" (Cook 1966: 335-6). The nub of the argument hinges on a distinction drawn between subject and object. We test models on "concrete situations," on given data. Neither Schneider nor Cook takes account of the fact that data are not raw; they are constructed by models.

Our portrayal of Karl Polanyi's position as a form of universalism will, perhaps, be controversial; but a close reading reveals that he rather consistently utilized an "innucleation" form of the universal model. Unravelling Polanyi's argument, however, requires several steps. To begin, Polanyi consistently attempted to rid his argument of an economistic perspective, both by urging that the economy is embedded in society and by holding that individual motives are themselves derived from institutions. The latter is, in fact, the linchpin of his theory. For Polanyi there exists in the individual no fundamental, inherent economic experience. "No human motive is per se economic. There is no such thing as a *sui generis* economic experience in the sense in which man may have a religious, aesthetic, or sexual experience" (1968: 63). Motives become economic, they are so labeled, only by or within a specific social organization. In his praise of Aristotle, Polanyi pointed out that "with him once and for all, human needs presupposed institutions and customs" (*Ibid.*: 99). Polanyi, thus, deconstitutes the individual, he rids the argument of individual intentions as an invariable source or essence in the economy.

But this obliteration of the economistic individual is achieved only by positing a different core or essence. Human motives are derived from, we might say they signify, institutional arrangments. For Polanyi the invariable core of all human provisioning was land and labour. Over and over he returned to the theme that land and labour provide a kind of constancy or bedrock in all societies. It was this view which allowed Polanyi to claim that in market society land and labour are fictitious commodities. Real commodities are produced, but the true feature of land and labour is that they are not produced; they have a precultural existence (*Ibid.*: 31-36). Therefore, to pretend that they are produced is to warp, to fictionalize, something that is given to society.

Upon these assumptions rest the other parts of Polanyi's model. Anthropologists often have referred to Polanyi's well-known modes of exchange and nonexchange: reciprocity, redistribution, the market and householding. Each of these patterns of integration was itself based upon an institutional form: symmetry, centricity, price-making and autarchy. These abstract or formal institutional arrangements were modes of group organization, irreducible patterns in themselves. But which institutional form prevailed, which form was dominant, depended entirely upon the degree to which it encompassed land and labour. In other words, for Polanyi land and labour were like genes; the phenotypic level was the observed level of institutional form and patterns of exchange. The relation between the two levels, as in Fortes, is not one of derivation. The "fit" between core and surface is asserted but not shown. Significantly, the fundamental comparative activity for substantivists also turns out to be classification, the construction of typologies built on one or another empirical feature (Dalton 1972; Halperin 1977).

Thus, although Polanyi posed a strong argument against formalism he did not, for the most part, transcend the universal model; he only shifted the core language as well as the relation between its two levels. Still, it must be noted that Polanyi also espoused a slightly different, more semantic, view; to this we will return.

Reflexivity in the Universal Model

Why has the universal model proven so attractive to anthropologists? In general, it holds out the possibility that a precise and objective "reconstruction" of the data may be accomplished. Lévi-Strauss in particular has appeared to operate with this presupposition, another legacy of the Galilean-Cartesian tradition which itself culminated in the analyses of the Vienna Positivists. But more is involved than the pursuit of objectivity. The notion that, when properly devised, models of this type embody invariant properties seemed a way to undercut the reflexivity inherent in various modes of inquiry. Lévi-Strauss, it seems clear, distinguished between two kinds of knowledge: the knowledge which a people may have of their social order (the home-made model) and the knowledge which satisfies various canons of scientific legitimacy (1963: 120-163). The former, equated with secondary qualities, he believed to be reflexive, while the latter which was founded on the idea of primary qualities was seen to represent genuine, non-reflexive knowledge.

Lévi-Strauss seems inclined to treat folk thought as a species of perceptual knowledge. In the Cartesian tradition, perception was considered an imperfect reproduction of what is given in experience, a fragile "image" of the secondary qualities of things. Distortive and illusory, the latter is a vague and fleeting copy of the sensations in which it is grounded; and though illusory, judgements based on such experience also are accompanied by an impression of certitude that they are, in fact, based upon reality. Similarly, the structuralist sees folk thought as a mode of perception in which the history of a people and their social organization is subtly elaborated. The "secondary qualities" in this case correspond to conscious participation in rule-accordant behaviour. Like sense qualities, norms and values project themselves as irreducible facts, grounded in reality. The home-made model to which Lévi-Strauss (1953) refers is a mechanism for the interminable recycling or reproduction of social experience.

For Lévi-Strauss then, home-made models are mystifications, being conscious representations based upon sensory experience of the social world. Only a model delineating the unconscious structure, he argued, would be free of the distortions yielded by the reflexive dimension of the intellect. Mechanical and statistical models (1953, 1969) are based upon primary and therefore nonreflexive qualities; home-made models are a reflexive, "secondary elaboration" upon these.

We argue, by contrast, that any core language is itself a reflexive projection by the anthropologist, like an eye which looking through a periscope encounters itself. With universal models there is always a "secondary elaboration" deriving from the assumption that our own knowledge constitutes the primary core language for others. However secondary and distorting conscious representations sometimes may be, the presupposition that they are underlain by another, deeper level accessible only to the anthropologist, and corresponding to his discourse, surely must be seen as a rationalization of the anthropological activity of modelling.

We maintain, furthermore, that the structuralist "escape" from folk reflexivity through the universal model has been achieved at the cost of introducing another form of reflexivity; let us call it "systemic" reflexivity. A universal model contains two levels, a core set of *a priori* meanings and rules, and a derived language. But this second language, if in fact it is derived, must reflect the core. The derived language can never contain anything more than that which is prescribed and allowed by the core and its operations (Gödel 1930). Thus, kinship terminologies will always encode alliance for Lévi-Strauss and extensions for Lounsbury. The two levels in a universal model stand in a reflexive relationship, one to the other.

Anthropologists as modellers assume that their universal models "refer to" or "stand for" a "chunk of reality" (Bunge 1973). But the fact that a universal model may be said to represent the underlying features of different kinship or economic systems is not given by the model itself. There is nothing in the relations obtaining among the symbols in the model which "point" it in the direction of this or that parcel of reality. To phrase it differently, the relation between model and model-object is not inherent. We are sometimes bewitched into thinking that the "standing for" relation between model and modelled is an intrinsic feature of the model. But it is just one among a number of activities involved in the practice of modelling.

Modelling is a craft, and involves the purposes and assumptions as well as the skills of the modeller (Aris & Penn 1980). The universal modeller brings to the core language his own codes, his own outlooks, just as formalist models in economic anthropology draw on nineteenth century utilitarianism. In this respect, the anthropologist has no assurance that his universal model is anything more than a mirror of himself. Universal models are nothing other than one culture's local models projected elsewhere; they have a form which serves this purpose admirably.

Local Models

Let us turn from anthropologists to ethnography. We would direct attention to local models. Folk thought and action themselves constitute models, for they construct the past as they yield schemas for the future. Perhaps, following Vico, we should think of local models on the order of works of art, paintings or the collage. Each has a particularity, built as it is out of disparate codes and things, without a given form. Despite the particularity, can we isolate some features of the local model, and find examples of its use in kinship and economics?

Universal models are said to "represent," "be about," or "stand for" something which is independent of them. But we suggest that local models — indeed, all models — are constructions of reality. There is no "objective" world outside them, except as constituted by another model.

This nonreferential character of models was experienced by one of the authors during fieldwork. When eliciting directions from villagers in Panama, he received what seemed to him to be landmark or referential information. People would speak of working near "Green Tree" or living near "Pretty View." The anthropologist, at first, understood these terms to be names which pointed to specific features in the real world. Only after several futile attempts at landscape navigation and sighting did the anthropologist realize that the terms lacked arrows pointing them toward an independent, external reality. They were only bits of a systematic, local map that could hardly be said to point to anything other than itself. The map had to be understood as a local model, not as a mapping or reflection of a given, external world (Gudeman 1979). In this sense, local models, like universal ones, are reflexive, but (paradoxically) the models do no more than "represent" themselves.

The internal form of a local model also may differ radically from Western expectations. It would be *a priorism* at its worst to assume, as have the "rationalists" and "empiricists," that the "parts" are causally or deductively linked. In this respect, adopting a "reconstructive" methodology, which as we have observed is a survival of positivism, can be misleading. A local model must be "deconstructed." For example, according to either neoclassical or Marxian theory, the "production" of material goods comprises a fundamental category referring to real world processes; and productive activity itself is conceived as "instrumental behaviour" in which the linking of means and ends is to be understood in causal or deductive terms. But when we look about us, we find that there are many local models in which what we call "production" is modelled quite differently. In rural Panama, for example, agricultural activities are presented in the image of barbering the hair; among the Gogo of Tanzania, cattle raising is modelled in the image of female reproduction, and vice-versa (Gudeman n.d.). No causal or deductive model could possibly reconstruct the complexity inherent in these forms of life. They must be "deconstructed" if their significance is to be understood.

Local models, therefore, need not possess a clean, deductive form. Consider, for example, the economic model proposed by the Physiocrats. Their model seems to contain an "irrational" fissure; for the Physiocrats, agriculture was conceived as a causal, productive activity, but artisanry was imaged as a combinatorial, nonproductive activity. From the standpoint of the model of neoclassical economics, Physiocracy represents failed science; from the viewpoint of a Marxist model it is a mystification. But when viewed as a local model built upon natural law doctrines, the patterning of the Physio-crats' model can be explicated for the modern observer, even if that involves a shock to his own ingrained "linear" orientation (Gudeman 1980).

These examples suggest the further feature that many models lack levels. Perhaps this is part of the message in Malinowski's (1961) "total" portrayal of the Kula, or in Bateson's (1958) rather different way of elucidating the Wau-Lau relationship among the Iatmul. A local model view of kinship is perhaps advocated by David Schneider, but his analytic schema itself is composed of various levels (1972, 1976, 1980).

Instead of hierarchically ordered languages, in local models we might expect to find intertwined codes or "semantic envelopment." Human models are reflexive in the fundamental sense that they make those who make them; they are not made *from* something but made. The profound insight in the Vichian tradition is precisely that folk thought is a work of art. Like a poem or painting, the particularity of the local model consists in that fact that it encom-passes disparate pieces from disparate codes: the private and the public, the inner world of experience and the outer world of things, cultural artifice and natural process. Its intertwined nature means that the local model must cut across our normal categories, just as Malinowski contended that the Kula is neither pure ceremony nor pure economics but something between the two.

But Malinowski was not the only one to hint at such views. We may, for example, return to Karly Polanyi who, at times, also entertained a constructivist, semiotic view of the economy.

> What occurs on the process level between man and soil in hoeing a plot or what on the conveyor belt in the constructing of an automobile is, *prima facie* a mere jig-sawing of human and nonhuman movements. From the institutional point of view it is a mere referent of terms like labor and capital, craft and union, slacking and speeding, the spreading of risks and the other semantic units of the social context (1968: 127).

This local model vision of the economy is revealed most clearly in Polanyi's writings on money, which he explicitly saw as a semantic system, similar to writing and language. Here Polanyi came close to proposing "family resemblances" as a method of cross-cultural comparison (Needham (1975). Money, he argued, has no defining essence, no attribute which is consistent from one culture to another. It is only a symbol with many and divergent uses. After surveying various money uses, Polanyi concluded: "Numerous combinations of these variants occur. No one rule is universally applicable, unless it be the general one that money uses are dispersed between a multiplicity of objects" (1977: 99).

The anthropological perspective, however, may be linked to other trends in Western twentieth century thought. One source for our antiessentialist view of models is Wittgenstein's *Philosophical Investigations* (1958) but in the Preface to this work Wittgenstein (1958: vi) offers unique and singular praise to the stimulus and impact which Piero Sraffa had upon his thoughts. We are led, therefore, to ask: Why did Wittgenstein thank Sraffa? Why did a twentieth century philosopher find himself in intellectual debt to the editor of the Ricardo papers and the author of a brief economic critique? To put it differently, what is the relation of Sraffa's work to our discussion of models (Fann 1969: Roncaglia 1978)?

Sraffa's own work or model (1960) is a critique. Initially, it was seen to be a critique only of the foundations of neoclassical economics. By means of his model Sraffa was able to show that capital as a quantity has no existence "prior to" profit. As a value unit, capital is not a separate factor of production, measurable independently of distribution. The size of capital, as a quantity, is related to the price level. The link between capital and profit is not causal; rather, size of capital, profit, rate of profit, wage level and prices must all be seen in an interdependent noncausal relation.

It was also first thought that Sraffa had provided a new solution to the Marxian problem of transforming values into prices (Robinson 1965). In Volume I of *Capital*, as is well-known, Marx begins with labour value; by Volume III he tries to show how this value level "underneath" may be transformed logically into the apparent real world of prices. Marx tried to derive prices from a "core language." But this attempt was not successful; more strikingly, recent studies based on the work of Sraffa suggest that no deductive relation exists between labor value and market price (Lippi 1979; Steedman 1977). Prices cannot be derived consistently from labour values. There is no reason to assume an underlying reality beneath prices, a reality grounded in natural laws.

What is the impact — or should we say the "sting" — of Sraffa's model? On the one hand, it constitutes an attack on the neoclassical, causal model, by demolishing the idea of capital as a characterizable essence; on the other, it is an attack upon the Marxian deductive model in that the value "level" becomes otiose. The critique of both models is the same in that for both the existence of core and derived languages (either causal or deductive) is denied. The Sraffian model repudiates the existence of specifiable essences in the economy. Summarizing briefly, the Sraffian model is nonreferential and contains no levels or atomistic units. We suggest it is this perspective that links Sraffa to Wittgenstein. But this returns us to the problem of defining the characteristics of local models. Here perhaps the philosopher must be "silent" in that local models can be defined only by what they are not. The anthropologist, on the other hand, has worlds to explore.

We draw to a close with the observation that our discussion of universal and local models does not imply that these are simply alternative types. We would, in fact, invert the standard view. According to the accepted wisdom, universal models are superordinate to local models, the latter being degraded, imperfect or false copies of the former. They lack the vaunted "clarity" of the derivational model. We hold, by contrast, that models of the "Euclidian" kind are themselves local models and that their universal use is a secondary elaboration. Other local models become mystifications only when we operate under the fiction that the Galilean-Cartesian one has universal status. Social orders are models in the sense that they contain a people's intentions and actions that provide a plan for future behaviour. Recreating these orders by way of our own is only to assert that our model has an unimpeachable grasp on the essential characteristics of human behaviour. But perhaps our task is limited to a deconstructive clarification of "other" models.

In some respect, we are returning to Vico's distinction. At best we can only model the natural world, but humans live models they have made. The Galilian-Cartesian model is an example of this making, however it has no privileged claim to reality. A certain "savagery" in our thought has led us to use it cross-culturally (Wittgenstein 1979), but an explicit recognition of the importance of the local model may help us escape this bewitchment.

References

Aris, Rutherford & Penn, Mischa 1980. The mere notion of a model. *Mathematical Modelling an International Journal* 1, *1-12.*

Barnes, John 1971. *Three Styles in the Study of Kinship*. London: Tavistock.

Bateson, Gregory 1958. *Naven* (2nd edn). Stanford: Stanford University Press.

Bunge, Mario 1973. *Method, Model and Matter*. Dordrecht: Reidel.

Cancian, Frank 1966. Maximization as norm, strategy and theory: a comment on programmatic statements in economic anthropology. *American Anthropologist* 68, 465-470.

Caws, Peter 1973. Operational, representational, and explanatory models. *American Anthropologist* 76, 1-10.

Cook, Scott 1966. The obsolete "anti-market" mentality: a critique of the substantive approach to economic anthropology. *American Anthropologist* **68**, 323-345.

Crick, Malcolm 1976. *Explorations in Language and Meaning*. New York: John Wiley.

Dalton, George 1972. Peasantries in anthropology and history. *Current Anthropology* **13**, 385-407.

Evans-Pritchard, E. E. 1940. *The Nuer*. Oxford: Clarendon Press.

Fann, I. T. 1969. *Wittgenstein's Conception of Philosophy*. Oxford: Blackwell.

Fortes, Meyer. 1969. *Kinship and the Social Order*. Chicago: Aldine.

Gödel, Kurt (1930). 1967. Some metamathematical results on completeness and consistency. On formally undecidable propositions of Principia Mathematica and related concepts I, and on completeness and consistency. *From Frege to Gödel: A Sourcebook in Mathematical Logic* (ed.) Jean van Heijeuvoot Cambridge: Harvard University Press.

Gudeman, Stephen. 1979. Mapping Means. In *Social Anthropology of Work* (ed.) S. Wallman (Assoc. social Anthrop. Monogr. **19**). London: Academic Press.

—— 1980. Physiocracy: a natural economics. *American Ethnologist* **7**, 240-258.

—— n.d. "A Dual Model of Production".

Halperin, Rhoda 1977. Conculsion: a substantive approach to livelihood. In *Peasant Livelihood* (eds) R. Halperin & J. Dow, pp. 267-297. New York: St. Martins.

Kaplan, David 1968. The formal-substantive controversy in economic anthropology: reflections on its wider implications. *Southwestern Journal of Anthropology* **24**, 228-251.

Leach, Edmund 1961. *Rethinking Anthropology*. London: Athlone Press.

—— 1964a. Models. *New Society* (14 May).

—— 1964b. *Political Systems of Highland Burma*. Boston: Beacon Press.

—— 1976. *Culture and Communication*. Cambridge: Cambridge University Press.

Lévi-Strauss, Claude 1953. Social Structure. In *Anthropology Today*. Chicago: University of Chicago Press.

—— 1962. *The Savage Mind*. Chicago: University of Chicago Press.

—— 1963. *Structural Anthropology*. New York: Basic.

—— 1967. *The Elementary Structures of Kinship*. Boston: Beacon Press.

Lippi, Marco 1979. *Value and Naturalism in Marx* (trans.) H. Steedman. London: NLB.

Lounsbury, Floyd 1964. A formal account of the crow- and Omaha-type kinship terminologies. *Explorations in Cultural Anthropology* (ed.) W. H. Goodenough. New York: McGraw Hill

Malinowski, B. 1948. *Magic Science and Religion*. New York: Free Press.

—— 1961. *Argonauts of the Western Pacific*. New York: Dutton.

Middleton, J. & Tait, D. (eds) 1958. *Tribes Without Rulers*. London: Routledge & Kegan Paul.

Nadel, S. F. 1957. *The Theory of Social Structure*. London: Cohen & West.

Needham, Rodney 1975. Polythetic Classification: convergence and consequences. *Man* (N.S.) **10**, 349-69.

Nutini, Hugo 1970. Some considerations on the nature of social structure and model building: a critique of Claude Lévi-Strauss and Edmund Leach. *American Anthropologist* **67**, 707-731.

Polanyi, Karl 1968. *Primitive, Archaic, and Modern Economics*, G. Dalton (ed). Garden City: Anchor.

Radcliffe-Brown, A. R. 1957. *A Natural Science of Society*. Glencoe: Free Press.

—— 1977 (1953). Letter to Lévi-Strauss. In *The Social Anthropology of Radcliffe-Brown* (ed.) A. Kuper, p. 42. London: Routledge & Kegan Paul.

Robinson, J. 1965. Piero Sraffa and the Rate of Exploitation. *New Left Review* **31**, 28-34.

Roncaglia, Alessandro 1978. *Sraffa and the Theory of Prices*. Chichester: John Wiley.

Scheffler, H. & Lounsbury, F. 1971. *A Study in Structural Semantics*. Englewood Cliffs: Prentice Hall.

Schneider, David 1972. What is kinship all about? In *Kinship Studies in the Morgan Centennial Year* (ed.) P. Reining. Washington, D.C.: The Anthropological society of Washington. pp. 32-63.

—— 1976. Notes toward a theory of culture. In *Meaning in Anthropology*, (eds) Basso and Selby. Albuquerque: University of New Mexico Press.

—— 1980. *American Kinship* (2nd edn). Chicago: University of Chicago Press.

Schneider, Harold K. 1974. *Economic Man*. New York: Free Press.

Sraffa, Piero 1960. *Production of Commodities By Means of Commodities*. Cambridge: Cambridge University Press.

Steedman, Ian 1977. *Marx after Sraffa*. London: NLB.

Wittgenstein, Ludwig 1958. *Philosophical Investigations* (trans.) G.E.M. Anscombe. New York: Macmillan.

—— 1979. *Remarks on Frazer's Golden Bough* (trans.) A. C. Miles (ed.) R. Rhees. Atlantic Highlands: Humanities Press.

LANGUAGE VERSUS THE WORLD: NOTES ON MEANING FOR ANTHROPOLOGISTS

ELIZABETH TONKIN

Semantics for anthropologists

The meanings of meaning are many, as the innocent anthropologist who looks at the literature soon discovers.[1] Meaning is of course a philosophers' domain; it has, also, after a long absence, become an important subject for linguists. No one who is seriously interested in meaning can remain ignorant of all this work, and that means struggling to grasp complex and formally presented arguments in what are, for social anthropologists, unfamiliar frameworks silently underpinned by equally unfamiliar presuppositions.

In this volume, Hobart discusses many of the problems of meaning's meaning (*infra*: 39-63). I shall not pay explicit attention here to theories in semantics, but they are important. I believe anthropologists could avoid many definitional errors by studying, for instance, Lyons' (1977) scrupulous distinctions, not only of kinds and theories of meaning, but especially in what can be meant by terms like "utterance", "word" and "concept" and the relationships which are posited with them.

Nevertheless the richness and complexity of current semantics easily makes one miss a crucial point. Most of it is focused on what is, quantitatively, a small part of language, and it frankly ignores most forms of understanding and response (see e.g. Lyons 1977: 56, 94). The category most writers attend to is so-called propositional language, but it can be argued that this does not exist in the pure state posited by analytical philosophers and accepted by many linguists (see e.g. Schon 1967; Lakoff & Johnson 1981 for simply-put critiques of "the dominant views of meaning"). Again, this paper is not argued as an explicit contribution to that debate. What I am trying to do is simply to suggest *a framework in which anthro-pologists could study meaning.* Such a preliminary exercise has I think to ignore existing definitions not least because the residual categories of others are not necessarily substantive categories for us. So, Lyons sets "the social" and "the expressive" apart from each other *and* from "the meaningful". Anthropologists will feel unhappy with these divisions as they are exemplified, logically they should also feel unhappy with the premises on which the divisions are based.

Connected to this objection is a second one. Existent semantic definitions refer to language; indeed for many, meaning is a purely linguistic phenomenon. I agree that only people mean, but do they mean only with language? Like linguists and philosophers, anthro-pologists also study language, but they concern themselves too with acts, symbols, rituals — with events and objects that are not confined to language or do not contain it. Is it possible to study meaning across such diverse media of human thought? Maybe not, but it might also be worth trying to in the first place, at least so as to be able to draw demarcation lines from experience and not to assume they exist on terms which may not fit anthropology's proper questions. So, meaning is here broadly and variously interpretable, and may include "feel", "evoke" (cf. Sperber 1975) and "under-stand". Of course, other languages will not allocate terms as English does: anthropologists are in the business of interpretation from the start.

As much as studying *meaning*, then, we are trying to understand *thought*, since most anthropologists have accepted Lévi-Strauss's claims that non-linguistic things are *bonnes à penser.* I also want to connect perception and praxis, and I would like to think that my framework, which demands such a connection, is on the whole consonant with Bourdieu's "outline of a theory of practice" (1977).

In What Ways are Anthropologists Typically Involved in Meaning?

Even if "meaning" is not their specific topic, anthropologists neces-sarily make meanings, since they try to a) *understand* (e.g. something, otherness); b) *interpret* (otherness to myself or other readers); c) *explain* (how/why something/otherness is).

Broad as these aims are, they include very considerable further translations, they are academic-species-specific as well as universal, and different as they can be in principle they often fuse in practice. *Understanding* as opposed to "knowing" implies *interpretation.* Observation and description are always informed and directed by presuppositions, which an anthropologist tries to make as explicit as possible and structure into analogies, models or theories of a conscious and well-formed kind.

Yet there are huge differences between a) types of experience (including verbal and non-verbal), b) an experience and an interpretation of it, c) specialist and stereotypic, insider and outsider interpretation. The distance between, say, others' nonverbal experiences and special outsider's explanation is no less great because the anthropologist's familiar job is to try and cross it. *Meaning* (verb and noun) is a part of an outcome of such journeys, part of continual, often simultaneous transpositions from experience to interpretation, or interpretation to explanation. Writing (in any language) is itself a process of translation and a change of medium. Once we set out in full the steps between observation and scholarly article or report — only tangentially noted here — it is clear that they occur through an experiencing reporter. This is a major objection to positivist theories of social analysis which assume that the reporter is a motiveless agent who simply meters some supposedly real (direct?) input from the world[2] .

Any anthropological focus on *meaning* is likely to encounter — and may explicitly try to resolve — fundamental questions, such as: Do the processes of analysis practised by anthropologists replicate the processes of meaning? Do anthropologists simply raise to consciousness their own thought processes when they are trying to get at what I've called "an otherness"? Is there any way they can find out whether they do so or whether their subjects' meaning processes are truly different? If one argues that symbolic thinking, say, exists only through *construal*, then all meanings are contingent, none final. Cf. Lévi-Strauss: "The unity of the myth is . . . a phenomenon of the imagination, resulting from the attempt at interpretation" (1969: 5). Any special validity claimed for one or another type of analysis of meaning has to be judged in the light of these possibilities, which are likewise presuppositions of some analyses.

The anthropological activity of ethnography is similarly problematic, perhaps especially so if it is an attempt to report other theories of meaning or other philosophies. Since the analyst has only been able to understand through analogy, the report includes comparative references to "Western" learned models, and therefore a convergence of analysis usually occurs. How else, for instance, to investigate philosophies, where these can be deduced from practice but are not stated as such? Must philosophical theories only be held to exist in the Western forms which have been institutionalized through a particular social history? In so far as philosophies are *lived*, they frame and direct meaning much more fundamentally than scholarly explanations do. But how to explain what seems possibly a universal dialectic between action and assumption if its condition seems precisely unreflective and unanalytic?

The last question is of course a general one. It does not seem to be problematic to theorists of several persuasions. To them, the argument that any analysis of meaning simply replicates their own thought processes is more defeatist than its possible corollary, that every analysis simply disintegrates actual "Gestalts" of meaning and does not describe, let alone explain them. Given the great number of sequential translations which any anthropological account represents, the anthropologist who rejects hermeneutic or ethno-methodological approaches, or simply refuses to accept that anthro-pology is an infinite regress into solipsism or relativity, has neverthe-less to accept that his or her accounts of meaning may quite transform what is described.

In the context of this paper, I suggest a) that since we in practice deduce meaning from the unarticulated, we need a justification for doing so, and a language or model with which to analyse what we are doing. Such a model would have to show how linguistic and non-linguistic experience are connected. b) Although I've described an apparently sequential "movement" of meaning, it is not a simply linear one from simple to complex, cause to consequence. It involves processes of analogy, displacement, and apparently simultaneous understanding and glossing.

Clearly anthropologists have no models with which adequately to represent the *interaction* of all these processes, the ways in which they fuse and as it were jump from one level (of analysis) to another. Consequently, we cannot fully describe them. But I think the human ability to extrapolate from one type of understanding and apply it to another, and the non-linear processes of everyday meaning, must somehow feature in anthropological analysis. At present perhaps we are only at the stage of specifying the inadequacies in the models we have.

As a brief illustration of the sort of abilities I'm trying to con-sider, imagine the ways you can look at a painting. It can be enjoyed in its totality, or in selected parts — the representation of clouds at the top, the detail of grass in the bottom right-hand corner — the pattern of selected parts may be noted as repeating in the whole — and so on, and so on. Anyone can shift attention, can foreground or background aspects of the painting in this way, without neces-sarily being able to articulate or comment on the process. Anthro-pologically, this is interesting because such abilities are always in operation, working to ignore as well as to pay attention (under what social circumstances is the choice made?) through practice (when does the discursive glossing develop?) and constituting socially recognized ways of interpreting events. Language itself shows these features — as in the actual variability in production of phonemic contrasts, so that people can ignore these and other kinds of "deviation" — but most types of linguistic analysis do not concentrate on them.[3]

Is Meaning only Linguistic?

The hoary question "can there be thought without language?" is not so popular as it used to be, but that is not because there is now a convincing answer. Confining "meaning" to language is one way of by-passing it. Taking meaning in its broadest sense, I make the fiduciary assumption that meaning is a human apprehension (this is also an atheistic assumption, else there would be transcendent, God-given meanings) and that it is not inherent in things. For me, therefore, God is not in the quad whether other people are or not, and though music on the radio continues to play unheard, it affects the owner only by the extra cost of batteries. But, when it is listened to, does music mean? Certainly responses to music vary individually, as well as culturally — its expressiveness is not an inherent attribute, just as its forms are historically and culturally varied (cf. Eades 1982).

One can consider the question broadly — without necessarily answering it — by refusing again to privilege language. Is music, like language, a form of social exchange? Both are materially produced and audited and consist of sounds systematically contrasted, produced in time and therefore irreversibly. They are also both pulsed, paused and varied in pitch, but in contrast to the polyphonic riches of music, language uniquely fuses different patterns simultaneously which we call phonological, syntactical, lexical — though they are all realized in *sound*. In order to further understanding this fusion has been left aside by linguists because it seemed more fruitful to separate out language 'levels', but it is I think more complex than the harmonies of music which Lévi-Strauss used as an analogy/description of larger forms constructed with language ("myths").

It is language's specific ability to carry *content*, meaning in the sense of argument, description, directives and so forth, and even to reflect on itself ("meta-language") which is usually held to define it. I have argued elsewhere (Tonkin 1979) that language, complex as it is, is nevertheless only one aspect of the operations of the Primary

Imagination, which as Coleridge described it "dissolves, diffuses, dissipates in order to create". I suggest that one can add many verbs to this list: compares, contrasts, applies, transposes, shifts, frames, condenses . . . The processes are many, the elementary principles of discrimination are few and the resultant combinations almost infinite. (I accept that some of my verbs may prove to represent higher-order combinations of elementary principles.) They can be discerned in patterns of action (kinship rules are a favourite example) and in phonology; they are used to mark out the world, but they are not simply structural oppositions. Oppositions are as it were "nouns" compared with the "verbs" which I am trying to stress. Sperber argues that symbolization is not a semiotic process: I would agree but would put it rather that *evoking* and sign-making ("matching"?) are two of the ways in which different relationships are constituted in the primary imaginative process.

It is noticeable that Coleridge's verbs are much richer in suggesting relations than the structural matrices to which anthropologists have become accustomed. These appear to be outcomes of processes, whereas Coleridge's verbs or Sperber's "evocation" are only a few of the processes which will result in structure. Given that human beings exist in time and evidently act on one another and on the world by various means including talk, models of process seem prior and more appropriate. They require however a notion of *processing subjects* as the agents of these variable powers. I call them variable powers to indicate the difference between the human abilities to monitor, to pay attention, to ignore, to relegate, to focus on, to sediment into what Polanyi called "tacit knowledge". (They are also a few of the verbs one could add to those already given.) Such words label perceptual or cognitive abilities, abilities which prove universal and which may enable language as a special development, without the need of hypothesizing any innate language mechanism. How far they are innate or learned abilities is being investigated by psychologists and is a matter of great importance for anthropology. Their existence suggests that thought is not confined to language — a hypothesis with evident consequences for the study of meaning.

Constituents and Characteristics of Meaning

Even if language is a special development of abilities which are also universally put to use in other dimensions (literally!) it is a development which transformed human beings, a tool which altered consciousness, conserved knowledge, became a means of thought and its medium. Its structuring also enables the exercise of several functions simultaneously and these clusters of functions can include the condensed and multiple relations of poetry or the social markings and uses which have been investigated in socio-linguistic studies.

"Things" may have intrinsic attributes as well be associated with values and meanings arising from their uses in other domains. Cows may say more than money because they are not "just" symbols. Evans-Pritchard commented that one would come to different conclusions about the Nuer if one believed their cows didn't exist! (1973). Cows are different from "cows", that is the word or sign, whose actions are confined to the airwaves (sticks and stones may break my bones . . .). It is true that in their proper, social context some utterances are performative and their use may even authorize a death; they may also be treated as powerful in themselves when authoritatively said. Here I stress simply that a proper activity of anthropologists would be to try and distinguish the modes of meaning in particular cases, without prior assumptions of what "meaning" should be, and given that verbal glosses are not necessarily the meaning itself.

Because of the arbitrary character of its semiotic, language is a relatively standardized medium of exchange; but this has costs as well as benefits. Leach rightly points out (1982: 174) that a sacrificial allocation or array of bridewealth gifts can "say" more than money, a single, undifferentiated means of exchange. The same can be true of language, compared with *choses bonnes à penser*". A major achievement of social anthropology is its demonstration of how richly – and implacably – worlds are created by the perceptual and cognitive abilities of humans, using their environment in many ways so that society itself can be defined through and enacted by reference to "concrete thought". So-called body language indeed is in some ways more powerful, since, though it is just as much learned culturally, it is generally even less conscious and treated as more authentic; it partly constitutes the self from moment to moment.

We act on the world through thinking with it, as well as about it. Such thought is also synaesthetic, with human relationships and other objects of our sense impressions understood in terms of one another. It is worth noting that language does likewise. Metaphor, as many writers have shown, is not just an adornment of language but a means of the very ratiocination which is often distinguished from it. Anthropological arguments are like others in their constitution, as Salmond shows (*Infra*: 64-87). As metaphors are built (*sic*) on metaphors, argument is produced.

In a lucid and fascinating explication, Schon used the term *displacement* for the process of concept development, in the sense that such "concepts have been displaced to situations outside of their ordinary patterns of use and they have been transformed in the process. Through their displacement they have been extended. They have been made to include a new kind of instance" (1969: 30-31).

Displacement itself is a metaphor.[4] At the risk of obscuring a diversity of distinct though related operations under one term (I think Wagner's 1978 use of the similar "obviation" does this) one can see displacement in the constitution of speech (one element successively displaces another) in psychological shifts and transpositions – that is in the substitution of one form of action for another, or from one mode to another, e.g. from "rebellion" to "ritual".

Replacements/displacements modify, but they do not necessarily extinguish what has gone before: the crucial point to investigate is what forms of modification occur. In the syntagmatic chains of speech, in narrative, in drama and presumably in all rites – certainly in political action – the significance of each step depends on what has gone before. Successive narrative displacements effect resolutions and reformulations of moral contradictions (cf. Sapir's analysis, 1977, of a West African tale). In a rite of passage a person may be put through successive displacements (often themselves metaphorical or analogical) which effectively alter his or her social state.

So far I have not tried to distinguish language from non-language but rather have tried to show that there are omnivorous human processes of analogy, transposition and displacement which are not confined to language, but in which language, itself operating the same way, can be used. Language is a form of action, and we should note that very often one can choose between linguistic and non-linguistic forms. If I remark that it is cold, you may agree with me in a form of words – or disagree – or close the door. Or you may ignore me.

I choose this example as a reminder that meaning *in language* can not be tied to "grammatical" form. Social context may determine meaning – "we" means "you" but only if I'm your superior, as Ervin-Tripp remarks in an interesting survey of some of these possibilities in American English speech (1976). Ardener's and Kendall's articles point out how there is "interpenetration of language, thought and reality" (Ardener *infra*: 3). One can distinguish languages through the differences of level in which kinds of meaning are carried, thus in English there is distinction of subject and object by word order, in Latin by morphological form. They are different

in the ways they encode the social (e.g. the uniquely English connotations of "accent" which may located in remarkably few markers).
I think one can also show that parallel acts in two cultures can be
verbal and non-verbal. An example I have mentioned elsewhere in
reference to naming (Tonkin 1980) is that whereas in some West
African languages babies who are thought to die repeatedly may be
called "Rubbish Dump"; some Kru people may actually put such a
baby on the rubbish dump when it dies.

Just as J. R. Firth argued that linguistic meaning is immanent in
all the levels of language, and there is syntactical, lexical etc.
meaning, so one could argue that components of meaning occur
through human structuring of events, as well as in the structures of
response which they evoke. It is hard to describe this dual process,
first because it is *not* verbal, and secondly because anthropologists
have paid little attention to the structures of responses – as I found
when I tried to explicate masking (1979). The linguistic models – or
rather the types of structural linguistic models used by many anthropologists – are not appropriate, as Kendall explains (*infra*).

There seem always to be ways of framing action, switching its
significance or shifting it into another plane.[5] This can occur through
the most trifling of means. A brief phrase may be the password (cf.
Bellman 1980: 74). Where Afikpo masqueraders set their sticks
they make a stage. They therefore do more than some structuralists
would say they are doing. They don't just separate special from
non-special space. They make a section of space special, they *mark*
it in the linguists' sense and they redefine themselves socially too:
they reconstitute the people present into masqueraders and ordinary
human audience.

There must therefore always be switching or framers to constitute
drama and ritual, as "a temporary sphere of activity with a disposition all its own . . . in a marked off space". The words are
Tambiah's, and derived from Huizinga's *Homo Ludens*. It is part of
cultural knowledge to recognise switches, and it is powerful to use
them, either because one has the right to do so, or the ability.
Skilled members can thus be wise, witty or astute, unskilled ones
incompetent, foolish or even dangerous. A really powerful person
is powerful sometimes through overriding or negating the
conventions/displacements which constitute ritual space, as
Alexander did when he cut the gordian knot in the temple at
Gordion.

Subjects and Socialization

Anthropologists have generally, and sometimes specifically, rejected the *subject* and preferred theories of system and structure. I think the subject has to be considered, and can be without reversion to those sociological depravities "voluntarism" and "subjectivity". I have argued that meaning cannot be understood as an outcome alone, and that the different processes which generate these outcomes are the operations of perceptual and cognitive abilities, which help to constitute consciousness. (Many, however, are not confined to human beings.) A focus on "subject and verb" is more powerful than one on "object" alone, and it permits kinds of understanding hardly possible with systemic paradigms. These include the construction of self (see e.g. Gell 1979), and understanding of history and change (cf. Thompson 1978) and of socialization, a vital topic which simply cannot be understood within existing paradigms either of systemic theories or of individual-centred interactionism or social psychology (Tonkin f/c). How many of the "verbs" I have listed are *learned* operations, and in what ways are they tied to already determined occasions, or transformed from bodily postures learned in very early social interaction into "meanings" like the meanings of authority figures, demonstrations of force?

Bourdieu's theory of practice is one theory that does permit the investigation of these questions. He argues that the social organization of space, labour, inequality, gender identity and so forth are internalized by children so that they simultaneously come to recognize them and learn to use them to understand other aspects of their world. Since the means and the meanings are acquired as aspects of each other, the new members reproduce and sustain their "habitus" and it is from and with the habitus that rules can be generated. But these are secondary, derived rules, which do not really constitute the habitus itself; though "it is because each agent has the means of acting as a judge of others and of himself that custom has a hold on him" (1977: 17).

Does Bourdieu's approach to socialization repeat the errors of earlier ones by giving no possibility of *change*? Just as anti-Marxist functionalism has to make socialization invariantly ineluctable, so does Marxist functionalism make "hegemony". However, Raymond Williams, trying to escape from this trap, argues that "the hegemonic process . . . is in practice full of contradictions and unresolved conflicts" (1977: 118). Bourdieu points out that these exist in hierarchised and unequal societies, whereas when there is a quasi-perfect correspondence between the objective order and the subjective principles of organization (as in ancient societies) the natural and social world appears as self-evident . . . The political function of classifications is never more likely to pass unnoticed than in the case of relatively undifferentiated social formations, in which the prevailing classificatory system encounters no rival or antagonistic principle (1977: 164).

It is in these "egalitarian" conditions, then, that there is a sort of totalising control, a one-class hegemony.

It is, I think, nevertheless possible to argue that the social, which is a species characteristic, depends on choice, and thus implies inclusion and exclusion, while the developmental cycle gives rise to discontinuities and conflicts of interest within every unit of production and consumption. It is at this level of practice that the operations of perception and abstraction may be developed, and in the particularities of the habitus as defined by Bourdieu. Since they involve — I have argued — the ability to displace concepts and to acquire language, humans acquire tools of thought which can, intrinsically, permit escape from social givens. It is at this very fundamental, as it were prelinguistic level, that the so-called infinite creativity of language actually exists. Actual forms of speech and their sequencing are far more constrained. Yet parents are again and again staggered to find how soon their children turn parental language against their parents. Shakespeare makes Caliban cry to Prospero

You taught me language; and my profit on't
Is, I know how to curse . . .

Although Caliban curses his gift, it has taken him from prelingual innocence to experience with its griefs; we could even say that in this example the language of the conqueror has given the conquered a chance to articulate his exploitation.

Is Arthritis a Disease of Language or is it Confined to People?

I have not focussed on theories which argue that meaning can be deformed, reality misrecognized, ideologies misrepresent, "muting" sustain subordination. This is not because I reject such theories, far from it, but I think they cannot be applied fruitfully without very careful attention to *what* is being shaped or blocked by social or economic actions. Unless meaning is first sorted out in some of the ways suggested here, one cannot for instance think about *consciousness*. How elemental is the consciousness that is said (in more than one theory) to be formed by social relations?

Just as available linear and structural models are incompetent to analyse the displacing character of meaning, so the available models which treat language and society either as simply parallel or caused by one another are quite incompetent to specify relations of linguistic production and those limitations on the construction of social reality which we recognise intuitively or simply take for granted. Does an elaborate hierarchy of address terms, for instance, infallibly indicate a concomitant social hierarchy, is it a dependent outcome of such hierarchy, or part of the ideology it generates, or an actual constituent of such hierarchy? One may find any of these views asserted (and wonder if the reporter on it really deduced the social hierarchy partly from the terms). There are probably several relations simultaneously in dialectic. To take an example where hierarchical forms of address are *not* used (Tonkin 1980), other evidence suggests that an egalitarian practice disguises real inequalities, yet — like Caliban — the inferiors may understand very well where power lies. And yet again, if inferiors are able to address superiors in the same ways as each other, and without any show of deference, should we not decide that the inequality is *in these respects* diminished?

Maurice Bloch has given some very convincing examples of how certain kinds of discourse can be used to restrain change and block opposition (1974, 1975). However, the linguistic reasons he gives for this happening can easily be rejected. Briefly, propositional language is not the only meaningful language. Bloch's is the old "enlightened" position that verbal rationality is the only *true* way to understand the world. As I have pointed out, ratiocination occurs through "non-propositional" means. Language is not only propositional and illocutionary, and performatives are only so when they are contextually appropriate and socially legitimate. (Otherwise, I can say "I name this ship *Queen Elizabeth*" forever; no champagne bottle will break nor any ship glide into the sea.)

Bloch wrongly opposes formalized to free speech acts. Terms like *register* and *style* remind us that languages may have elaborately diversified resources: this plenitude entails limitations on use, and, as J. R. Firth remarked some years ago, much apparently free conversation is highly predictable. We could say that it is the options of follow-on, rather than the linguistic features (lexical, syntactical, phonological) which are more or less open, but this draws attention to the fact that it is social rules of turn-taking and skills in manipulating style, register and subject matter which are at issue. There is nothing inherent in discourse *as such* which enforces inequality, but the social presuppositions which underpin it may be authoritarian. It is because humans "embody" language in Kendall's sense (*infra*: esp. 13-15), that authority is often potential until actuated in discourse; if there is a right to speak which is "properly" taken, authority is exercised, but if not, it is lost. Certain aspects of language may be especially appropriate, culturally, to gain certain kinds of control of a situation (and most situations include speech), but as I point out in the example of address terms, a set of linguistic forms is not *simple* evidence of authoritarianism. Like other historical outcomes, too, it constrains the generation born into them, but it need not do so absolutely.

Bloch's argument falters where the wrong underlying cause is selected to explain properly identified effects. But his is a slippery subject, since almost any aspect of language can become a social marker or used in the same way as non-linguistic means to alter events. Then, as Kendall says, "when two definitions of a situation are in conflict, the winning definition resides in the hands of those who have 'power' " (from original paper). But one interlocutor's short term loss may be a long term gain for, as she also implies, "power" is a label which like "language" needs careful specification according to context, and may cover components that should be distinguished (cf. Tonkin, 1979).

In this "framework in which anthropologists could study meaning", meaning itself is not definable *a priori* in a single, finite way. In this I differ from Milton, for instance. She agrees that meanings are meanings for people (*infra*: 261); from my framework it follows that single true meanings do not exist, be they analysts' or analysands'. There are many conditions in which only one type and content of meaning (*vb*) is held to be true by all the participants: it is our job to investigate these conditions.

Several contributors to this volume note that our need is to bring together aspects of the world made separate (or irrelevant) in current social analyses. This should mean relating, not suppressing, real differences. Thus, the power of subjects has to be related to the varying linguistic habitus which partially form them; individual speakers are socialized into repertoires of language varieties which differ in scale and functionality quite apart from being differentially accessible. (One may be born "into" a national language or a minority one or be socially confined to the "low" variety in diglossia.) Mass literacy and the mass media may mean mass changes in consciousness. At points in history particular social groups establish (switch into) what they then believe are special forms of life; the markers of this could be metaphorical displacements from old occasions and they may thereafter become definitions of new ones. Each choice implies closure and exclusion and the individual may not be able to change the social conditions which in turn would alter the "meaning outcomes" so created. To sum up, "meaning" turns out to be like any other anthropological topic. It does not label a universal characteristic but a focus for questioning, and our answers can only be plausible if they reconcile structure, history, and the conditions of human creativity.

Notes

1. Of course anthropological attention was early paid to this subject. See e.g. Malinowski's contribution to Ogden and Richard's *The Meaning of Meaning* in 1923 (cf. Tonkin, 1971). Sir Raymond Firth pointed out at the conference that *Mencius on the Mind* (Richards 1932) was a text for him and his contemporaries: it should still be so.
2. Anthropologists are only beginning to theorize their practice (see e.g. papers for the SSRC Workshop on Participant Observation. September 1979; Lowry 1981). "Observation" alone labels many relationships – see, e.g. Stanley's study of Mass Observation (1981).
3. Linguistics changes its dominant models in the same way as other social sciences and they are akin in emphasis and succession. The unit of analysis has changed from the word (peaking with Saussure?) to the sentence (Chomsky?) but now increasingly is discourse – stretches of language whose structures are not the same as that of the sub-units. It can be argued that analysis of language only became possible through literacy, which permits the detachment of language from its speakers, and that this autonomy of language remains a dominant, "required" assumption for linguistics. Despite the generative revolution only some linguists focus on production and interpretation, (e.g. Halliday, who treats language acquisition as the acquisition of operators with which to carry out functions). The second technological revolution for linguistics has been sound recording, but this too was at first seen as enabling structural analysis (e.g. of phonemic contrasts); the opportunities it gives to study production are, it seems to me, only just being exploited, apart from acoustic phonetics.
4. "Each of these two spaces [of the Kabyle], inside and outside, can be derived from one another by means of a semi-rotation, only on condition that the mathematical language expressing such operations is reunited with its basis in practice, so that terms like displacement and rotation are given their practical senses as *movements of the body* . . ." (Bourdieu, 1977: 118).
5. My use of "framing" is somewhat different from Goffman's. It is the action I stress (cf. Goffman's Ch. 8, "the anchoring of activity"). As Barley says, we create "art" by *framing* it (sometimes literally), simultaneously backgrounding and depreciating functional aspects as "design". This process *may* match indigenous interpretation insofar as some artefacts are themselves *framed* by their use in "clearly demarcated festivals and ceremonies" (1981: 6). The term "shifter" has also been given rather different senses, as

in Silverstein's (1976) account, hence I suggest "switch."

References

Ardener, S. (ed.) 1975. *Perceiving Women*. London: Malaby Press.
Barley, Nigel 1981. The linguistic image in the interpretation of African objects. Summary for Conference: Visual Art as Social Commentary. SOAS Nov. 30/ Dec 1. University of London.
Basso, Keith H. & Selby, Henry A. 1976. *Meaning in Anthropology*. Albuquerque: School of American Research and University of New Mexico Press.
Bellman, Beryl 1980. Masks, societies and secrecy among the Fala Kpelle, *Ethnologische Zeitschrift Zürich* **1**, 61-79.
Bloch, Maurice 1974. Symbols, song, dance and features of articulation: is religion an extreme form of traditional authority? *Archiv. Europ. Sociol.* **15**.
—— 1975. Introduction. In *Political Language and Oratory in Traditional Society* (ed.) M. Bloch. London: Academic Press.
Bourdieu, Pierre 1977. *Outline of a Theory of Practice* (trans.) R. Nice. Cambridge: University Press.
Coleridge, S. T. 1956. *Biographia Literaria* (1817). London: J. M. Dent.
Eades, J. S. 1982. Dimensions of meaning: Western music and the anthropological study of symbolism. In *Religious Organization and Religious Experience* (ed.) J. Davis (Ass. social Anthrop. Monogr. **21**). London: Academic Press.
Ervin-Tripp, Susan 1976. Acts and social learning. In *Meaning in Anthropology* (eds) Keith H. Basso & Henry A Selby. Albuquerque: University of New Mexico Press.
Evans-Pritchard, E. E. 1973. Some reminiscences and reflections on fieldwork. *J. Anthrop. Soc. Oxford* **4.1** (H.T.) 1-12.
Firth, J. R. 1957. *Papers in Linguistics 1934-1951*. London: Oxford University Press.
Gell, Alfred 1979. Reflection on a cut finger: Taboo in the Umeda conception of the self. In *Fantasy and Symbol* (ed.) R. H. Hook. London, New York etc: Academic Press.
Goffman, Erving 1975. *Frame Analysis*. Harmondsworth: Penguin.
Halliday, Michael A. K. 1976. Early language learning: A sociolinguistic approach. In *Language and Man* (eds) W. C. McCormack & S. A. Wurm. The Hague/Paris: Mouton.
Huizinga, J. 1949. *Homo Ludens* (trans.) R.F.C. Hull. London: Routledge & Kegan Paul.
Lakoff, George & Johnson, Mark 1980. *Metaphors We Live By*. Chicago & London: University of Chicago Press.
Leach, Edmund 1982. *Social Anthropology*. Fontana Masterguides Series: Fontana Paperbacks.
Lévi-Strauss, Claude 1970. *The Raw and the Cooked* (trans.) J. & D. Weightman (Mythologiques I 1964). New York: Harper & Row.
Lowry, Joanna 1981. Theorising "observation". *Communication and Cognition*

14.1, 7-23.

Lyons, John 1977. *Semantics* Vols I & II. Cambridge: University Press.

Ogden, C. K. & Richards, I. A. 1923. *The Meaning of Meaning.* London: Routledge & Kegan Paul.

Ottenberg, Simon 1975. *Masked Rituals of Afikpo.* Washington: University of Washington Press.

Polanyi, Michael 1967. *The Tacit Dimension.* London: Routledge & Kegan Paul.

Richards, I. A. 1932. *Mencius on the Mind.* London: Kegan Paul, Trench Trubner & Co. Ltd.

Sapir, David 1977. The fabricated child. In *The Social Use of Metaphor* (eds) J. D. Sapir & J. C. Crocker. Philadelphia: University of Pennsylvania Press.

Sapir, David & Crocker J. C. 1977. *The Social Use of Metaphor.* Philadelphia: University of Pennsylvania Press.

Schon, Donald A. 1969. *Invention and the Evolution of Ideas* (first published as *Displacement of Concepts*, 1963). London: Tavistock.

Silverstein, Michael 1976. Shifters, linguistic categories, and cultural description. In *Meaning and Anthropology* (eds) K. H. Basso & H. A. Selby. Albuquerque: University of New Mexico Press.

Sperber, Dan 1975. *Rethinking Symbolism* (trans.) Alice Morton. Cambridge: University Press.

Stanley, N. S. 1981. "The Extra Dimension": A study and assessment of the methods employed by Mass Observation in its first period, 1937-1940. PhD Thesis (CNAA, Birmingham Polytechnic) June 1981.

Tambiah, S. J. 1981. A performative approach to ritual (from *Proc. Br. Academy* **LXV**, 1979). London: British Academy.

Thompson, E. P. 1978. *The Poverty of Theory and Other Essays.* London: Merlin Press.

Tonkin, Elizabeth 1971. "Some aspects of language from the viewpoint of social anthropology, with special reference to multilingual situations in Nigeria". DPhil Thesis, Oxford.

—— 1978. Masks and powers. *Man* (N.S.) **14.2**, 237-248.

—— 1980. Jealousy names, civilized names: anthroponomy of the Jlao Kru of Liberia. *Man* (N.S.) **15.4**, 653-664.

—— Rethinking socialization f/c *J. Anthrop. Soc. Oxford.* **13**(3), 1982.

Wagner, Roy 1978. *Lethal Speech: Daribi Myths as Symbolic Obviation.* Ithaca & London: Cornell University Press.

Williams, Raymond 1977. *Marxism and Literature.* Oxford: University Press.

"SEMANTICS" AND THE "CELT"

MALCOLM CHAPMAN

This paper concerns Celts, the meeting of incommensurate category systems, and the way in which the former have been created, to some degree, by the latter. This may sound rather arcane, but it will, I hope, be found acceptable as "semantic anthropology".

I suggest two interpretations of what semantic anthropology might be. On the one hand, we have a new label for anthropology as a whole; the label, itself perhaps only tactical and temporary, implies an attempt to achieve an intelligent and self-aware empiricism: this will be neither idealist nor materialist, but prepared to study human reality in words, ideas and things, without ascribing arbitrary theoretical priority to any of these (see Ardener 1971 and Crick 1976 for some background). It is with this semantic anthropology that I ally myself. On the other hand, we have "semantic anthropology" as a subdivision of anthropology as a whole; as such, it will be concerned with words and symbols and classifications, and with an obviously idealist bent (see Chapman 1978a). I approve of the former, and hope that my work might contribute to it. My paper will bear, tangentially, upon the latter.

What I wish to do here, is to discuss a problem raised by the anthropological material with which I am most concerned. In doing so, I will be refining upon arguments already made elsewhere (see Chapman 1978b), and there will unfortunately not be time here for a recapitulation of these. I hope, nevertheless, that what I have to say here will be at least nearly capable of standing on its own. My work concerns "Celts". Celts are, like semantic anthropology, a privileged location of meaning; meaning, in the Celtic fringes, comes in barrowloads. This, I should emphasize, is not an observation that is the fruit of my own ethnographic experience; rather, my ethnographic work, in Scotland and in Brittany, has been in part an attempt to explain why, from the great bulk of commentary on Celtic matters, it is the impression one receives.

The Celts, and their various etymological and functional cognates (Keltoi, Celtae, Galatoi, Galatae, Galli and so on), served, for classical antiquity, to fill the ethnological space to the north and north-west of the civilized world. The Celts were a people beyond the boundaries of rule and order and knowledge, and as such were a semi-mythological creation of the classical imagination. In some commentaries, they share the pages with creatures that we now regard as unequivocally mythical, and they share some of their characteristics. Diodorus Siculus, writing in Greek in the middle of the first century B.C., comes to a consideration of the Gauls in Book V of his *Bibliotheca historica*, having passed through, in Books III and IV, Ethiopia, the Amazons of Africa, the inhabitants of Atlantis and the origins of the first gods, the principal Greek gods, the Argonauts, Theseus and the seven against Thebes. Diodorus is considered to have drawn uncritically on many sources, and we can take what he says as a summary of what the classical imagination had come to find conventionally acceptable as a description of the northern barbarian. He refers to their tendency to excess when given wine (V, 26: 167), to their failure to appreciate the proper value of the gold that they find lying about their country, and that they use abundantly in personal adornment (V, 27: 167-9), to their fairness of skin and hair (V, 28: 169), and to their erratic, perverse and lustful sexual habits (V, 32: 183). Most interestingly, however, for semantic anthropology, he says the following:

> The Gauls are terrifying in aspect and their voices are deep and altogether harsh; when they meet together they converse with few words and in riddles, hinting darkly at things for the most part and using one word when they mean another; and they like to talk in superlatives, to the end that they may extol themselves and depreciate all other men. They are also boasters and threateners and are fond of pompous language, and yet they have sharp wits and are not without cleverness at learning (V, 31: 177).

There is a tendency to treat classical authors as having access to a pure and unmixed observation of the world, not simply because they were writing before sociology and politics could have entered into and biased their view, but also because the world that they had before them was itself pure and unmixed. The races and cultures that we now treat as *fons et origo* of the modern world were mostly given their names by classical authors, and seem, in the period, to be still fresh from the showroom. There is little justification for this notion, however, except in that it provides us with an excuse for treating as fact writings that, if subjected to critical historiographical and anthropological treatment, might largely dissolve. Diodorus, while an admirer of the Greek and Roman civilizations, put into his appreciation of the Gaul a nostalgia for the Homeric Greek past that was, when he was writing, already over six centuries behind him. He says of the Britons, using themes that were to be later greatly exaggerated by Tacitus in his *Germania*:

> As for their habits, they are simple and far removed from the shrewdness and vice which characterise the men of our day. Their way of living is modest, since they are well clear of the luxury which is begotten of wealth (V, 21: 155)

and further:

> They use chariots, for instance, in their wars, even as tradition tells us the old Greek heroes did in the Trojan War (V, 21: 155).

In Gaul:

> Brave warriors they reward with the choicest portions of the meat, in the same manner as the poet introduces Ajax as honoured by the chiefs after he returned victorious from his single combat with Hector (V, 28: 171).

I introduce the Homeric note simply to show that there never was a time when *theory* about society did not enter into the *observation* of society. Empirical material has always, even as far back as we can go, been taken up into theory, and made secondary to it.

Other classical texts confirm the picture offered by Diodorus. Strabo says:

> The whole race which is now called both "Gallic" and "Galatic" is war-mad, and both high-spirited and quick for battle, although otherwise simple and not ill-mannered (Strabo, 4, 4, 2: 237).

> In addition to their trait of simplicity and high-spiritedness, that of witlessness and boastfulness is much in evidence, and also that of fondness for ornaments; for they not only wear golden ornaments — both chains round their necks and bracelets round their arms and wrists — but their dignitaries wear garments that are dyed in colours and sprinkled with gold. And by reason of this levity of character they not only look insufferable when victorious, but also scared out of their wits when worsted (Strabo, 4, 4, 5: 247).

Caesar says that "as a nation the Gauls are extremely superstitious" (or "given to religion") (*De Bello Gallico*, vi, 16), and "the god they reverence most is Mercury" (*Ibid.*, vi, 17). Tacitus says of the

the Britons, comparing them to the Gauls:

> they show the same daring in seeking danger, and when the crisis comes, the same timidity in drawing back (*Agricola*, 11: 59).

of the Germans, he says:

> They have fierce blue eyes, red hair, and large frames, only capable of sudden effort. They endure labour and service less patiently than we, and cannot support thirst and heat (*Germania*, 5: 91);

> They worship Mercury more than any other of the gods (*Germania*, 9: 94);

> (. . .) from a strange contradiction of character, they love idleness yet hate peace (*Germania*, 15: 98).

Cato says of the Celts of Cisalpine Gaul: "they have two great passions, to be brave in warfare and to speak well" (cited M. Dillon 1973: 32). Myles Dillon sums up the Classical response to the Celt:

> The Celts impressed the ancient historians as being impetuous and fearless in battle, easily roused and with a high sense of honour, arrogant in victory and desperate to the point of suicide in defeat, delighting in ornament, in feasting, in the recitation of poetry, *admodum dedita religionibus* "much given to religion" (*Ibid.*).

It may already be obvious to anybody that knows anything about typical views of the Celt or the Irishman in our time (and that must surely include everybody brought up in English in Britain), that there is a significant continuity between the classical texts, and modern commentary on the Celts, both popular and academic. We can move directly to the nineteenth century, and find there British politicians, ethnologists, and historians, all united in ascribing to the Irish:

> (. . .) unreliability, emotional instability, mental disequilibrium, or dualistic temperament. The stereotypical Irishman was a kind of Celtic Jekyll and Hyde; he oscillated between two extremes of behaviour and mood; he was liable to rush from mirth to despair, tenderness to violence, and loyalty to treachery (Curtis 1968: 51).

Disraeli called the Irish "wild, reckless, indolent, uncertain and superstitious" (cited, *Ibid.*). Yeats, in praise rather than blame, said of the Celts that:

> Men who lived in a world where anything might flow and change, and become any other thing; and among great gods whose passions were in the flaming sunset, and in the thunder and the thunder show, had not our thoughts of weight and measure (Yeats 1924: 219);

They had imaginative passions because they did not live within our own strait limits, and were nearer to ancient chaos (*Ibid.*: 220).

(. . .) a thirst for unbounded emotion and a wild melancholy

(*Ibid.*: 227).

Before we go any further in exploring the continuity of imagery over this two thousand year period, let me put aside an issue that often seems to intrude into discussion of such commentaries, but which is for immediate purposes of little importance. I refer to the question of whether the opinion voiced of the Celt is favourable or unfavourable, complimentary or rude. Piggott distinguishes between these two attitudes to the Celt, calling them "hard primitivism" (unfavourable, rude), and "soft primitivism" (favourable, complimentary) (see Piggott 1968: 92). Curtis' study of anti-Irish prejudice in England in the nineteenth century is in large part a liberal denunciation of English "prejudice", that led to the construction of an unfairly unfavourable opinion of the Irish character (Curtis 1968). I do not personally find it profitable to distinguish in principle between those commentators who praise the Celt, and those who offer him dispraise, for I do not think that this opposition between praise and dispraise is fundamental to the ideas that we are discussing. For as long as there have been commentaries on the Celts, there have been ambivalent, biased, prejudiced, rose-coloured or self-seeking positions from which these commentaries have been made. Of the people that I have quoted, Diodorus was writing with a great admiration for the classical civilization of which he was a part, while maintaining a taste for Homeric simplicity; Caesar was writing to extol the Celts, in order that his conquest of them should seem all the more praiseworthy; Tacitus was writing in praise of the barbarians in order, through the contrast, to mount a fierce attack on the manners of Rome's ruling classes; Disraeli was unambiguously hostile to the Celt, in the context of agitation for Irish home rule; Yeats was in love with the Celt; Dillon picked out only the complimentary aspects of the metaphors used by classical authors because he too, was writing in compliment; Curtis dwells at length on the unfavourable aspects of metaphors used by "Anglo-Saxons" in the nineteenth century to describe the "Celts", in order to rebut the racialist slur, and to throw criticism back at the English society that generated such evil ideas. While all these positions have their justification and interest, I am not concerned here with whether the opinion formed of the Celt is good or bad. In an extended study of the metaphors that have been used to describe the Celt, I said:

Since the eighteenth century, the Celtic fringes have posed for the urban intellectual as a location of the wild, the natural, the creative and the insecure. We can often find it said, with warm approval, that the Celts are impetuous, natural, spiritual and naive. I try in what follows to make it clear that such an approval is drawing on the same system of structural oppositions as is the accusation that the Celt is violent (impetuous, emotional), animal (natural), devoid of any sense of property (spiritual), or without manners (naive). I include the bracketed terms as effective synonyms of the words that precede them, that we would use to praise rather than deride (. . .). We are dealing here with a rich verbal and metaphorical complex, and I have not thought it very important to distinguish between those who find a favourable opinion of the Gael within this complex, and those who dip into it to find the materials for derision. In both cases the coherence of the statements can only be found at their point of origin, the urban intellectual educated discourse of the English language, and not at their point of application, the Celt, the Gael, the primitive who is ever-departing, whether his exit be made to jeers or to tears (Chapman 1978b: 18).

Picking out the qualities of the Celt that are of significance for this paper, we can create the same verbal and moral balance. If we take the "emotional instability" of the Celt, then we can either paraphrase it as "excitable and high-spirited", or as "unreliable and moody"; if we take the Celt's manifest inability to call a spade a spade, then we can speak either of his "eloquence and subtlety", or of his "evasiveness and uncertainty"; if we speak of the Celtic inability to organize, then we can call it "independence and individualism", or we can call it "incompetence and selfishness". The pictures may seem to differ, but for my present purposes I am indifferent to the contrast. It does not matter whether we call the Celt "unreliable, moody, evasive, uncertain, incompetent and selfish", or "excitable, high-spirited, eloquent, subtle, independent and individualist". The polarity of moral judgement that separates these two views I am treating, for the moment, as trivial, when set beside the metaphorical consistency that unites them.

I do not intend to try to fill the two thousand year gap that separates, say, Diodorus from Yeats, or Caesar from Disraeli, or thoroughly to discuss how consistencies and continuities might organize themselves over such a period. There are several possibilities, all of which have probably been partly true. We might suppose that the idea of the Celt that we are considering was invented arbitrarily in antiquity, and has been simply handed down in continuous cultural tradition. We might argue rather that these ideas were reappropriated from newly available classical texts in the seventeenth and eighteenth centuries, to become once again common intellectual currency; the supposed arbitrariness of the vision might remain, with eighteenth century commentators merely reproducing, for no other reason than respect of antiquity, the ideas that were given them; given the exaggerated classical bias of eighteenth and nineteenth century scholarship, this must certainly be a part of any explanation of continuity and consistency of ideas from antiquity through to the present. We might argue that Celts have always and everywhere been the same, and that the consistency over two thousand years stems simply from right observation of their habits. We might, and here I begin to feel some personal sympathy for the arguments that I am putting forward, argue that the writers of classical antiquity and of eighteenth and nineteenth century Europe were speaking for a social and intellectual polity that defined itself as ordered, rational, civilised and right, and that the Celt served them both as a figure of opposition, a mythical alter-ego which they used in pursuit of their own self-definition. That is more or less the view of the modern history of Celtic commentary that I have taken (see Chapman 1978b), and the arguments found there can be applied, without much difficulty, to the classical Celt.

Within the logic of this last argument, we can treat the Celt as, in origin, an entirely fictional creature, owing his existence not to a physical presence or to its observation, but to metaphorical activity at the centre of majority society. The Celt, from this point of view, is a product of theory, and observational confirmation of the theory, and physical location and discovery of the Celt so created, are secondary to the theory, and not essential to it. This argument works very well, and there is not much in the Celt that we can not explain by this means (see, again, Chapman 1978b).

What I wish to do here, however, is to explore the possible observational bases that might provide empirical foundation for, and empirical confirmation of, the theory of the Celt. It is not easy here to disentangle observation and theory, for as I pointed out above there has never been a time when observation has been pristine and innocent; empirical evidence in this field has always been theory laden. I want to try to imagine, however, a theoretically innocent observational basis for the image of the Celt that we have had handed down to us. To do so, I am going to begin with a linguistic analogy.

Early attempts at the notation of non-European non-written languages by European linguists and ethnographers were hampered by what seemed, to the ear of the investigator, to be the uncertain and wavering pronunciation of the native speakers. Henson summarizes this problem, speaking of:

> (. . .) the frequent tales of indeterminate and wavering pronunciations, where the language under description did not correspond in its phonemic

system to that of the investigator. To give an example, a Scottish missionary, the Reverend Hugh Goldie, wrote of the Efik language: "B is
frequently interchanged with p; or rather, a sound between the two, is
very frequently employed. D has often r as a substitute, or rather, through
imperfect enunciation, has the sound of r given to it. It is occasionally
substituted for f" (Henson 1974: 11; the citation is from Goldie 1868:
5-6).

Many examples of this kind can be found, and the exact details
of the languages concerned, and of the observed phonetic imper-
fections, are not important here. The essential point to note is that
the ears of one phonemic system observed, in the speech of another,
wavering and uncertainty. We can imagine a category system (such
as a phonemic system), at its simplest, as a unidimensional and
continuous physical reality, upon which divisions have been
arbitrarily imposed, thus rendering the physical reality down to
significant units. Let us take a fragment of "physical reality", and
divide it up differently, according to two incommensurate and
culturally different category systems:

The horizontal line is a physical reality, which the category systems
A and B have divided up differently. The vertical lines are
"boundaries" between the "categories", and the categories are
represented, for system A, by arabic numerals, and for system B,
by roman numerals. Since this is a "model", and one simplified to
the point of absurdity, then exactly what fragment of physical
reality the horizontal line represents is not immediately important.
It could be, however, to choose relatively simple examples, a range
of possible human vowel sounds (divided into phonemes), the light
spectrum (divided into colours), a range of sound frequency (divided
into the notes of non-homologous musical scales), or the human
arm (see Ardener, *infra*). None of these would exemplify exactly
the simple and symmetrical lack of fit that I have imposed in my
diagram, but I am interested in a generality here, and the detail can
wait. What system "A" observes, when confronted with system "B",
is not a different kind of order, but a disorder: category (i) is
observed as a wavering and uncertainty around the boundary
between categories (1) and (2); category (ii) is observed as a wavering
and uncertainty around the boundary between categories (2) and
(3). What I wish to argue is that the wavering and uncertainty that
one phonemic system finds in another, has its analogues at every

level of human reality, in the confrontation of one culture with another.

I have spoken of the division into significant units of "physical reality", as if this were primarily what "categories" were all about. This is, even for the simplest "physical" examples, a misrepresentation (see Arderer, *infra*), and I do not in any case wish the argument to be considered to be particularly about "physical reality" at all. Rather, I take it that a "culture", or a "society", is a many faceted complex of systems of meaning, all of which are "category" based; from the phoneme to the symphony orchestra, from sign-language to general elections, "culture" is meaningful categories in action. And wherever there are categories and these are incongruent from one culture to another, then there is the possibility that one system will find, in another, the same kind of indeterminate wavering that one phonemic system can find in another. The nature of the particular categories will determine exactly how indeterminate wavering will be perceived, and what conclusions will be drawn from it. The adjectives "indeterminate" and "wavering" that Henson uses to describe the phonemic example provide, however, an analogy that will help us to account for the most regular and consistent, and at the same time most elusive, feature of the Celtic character, as it has been observed over the centuries. I refer to the sense of a critical absence at the centre of things, a lack of solidity where reality ought to be, and at the same time, an abundance of change, of excess at the edges of the world, of paradoxical duality and mood-shifting and things being other than they seem. If we return to the category system "A" and "B" above, when "system A category (2)" looks directly at "system B", what it finds where there ought to be stable reality, is a boundary between categories (i) and (ii), from which "reality" falls away on either side; where there is a boundary in system A between categories (2) and (3), where there is a discontinuity in the world, there is, instead, in system B, an untroubled unity, that is equally unsettling to system A. These ideas are not, even within such an impoverished system as I have presented, easy to express. We can sympathize with the attempts of those, from antiquity on, who have tried to put into words an apprehension that is so evasive and fleeting, and yet at the same time so omnipresent; an apprehension that, though solidly rooted in observation, yet exists not in reality, but in the moment when realities meet:

> when they meet together they converse with few words and in riddles, hinting darkly at things for the most part, and using one word when they mean another; and they like to talk in superlatives (. . .). They are also

boasters and threateners (Diodorus, V, 31: 177); The whole race (. . .) is war-mad, and both high-spirited and quick for battle, although otherwise simple and not ill-mannered. And therefore, if roused, they come together all at once for struggle, both openly and without circumspection (. . .) because they always share in the vexations of those of their neighbours whom they think wronged (. . .) (Strabo, 4, 4, 2: 237); In addition to their trait of simplicity and high-spiritedness, that of witlessness and boastfulness is much in evidence (. . .). And by reason of this levity of character they not only look insufferable when victorious, but also scared out of their wits when worsted (Strabo, 4, 4, 5: 247); As a nation they are extremely superstitious (Caesar vi, 17; cf. Tacitus, *Germania*, 5); they show (. . .) daring in seeking danger, and when the crisis comes, (. . .) timidity in drawing back (Tacitus, *Agricola*, 11); They have fierce blue eyes, red hair, and large frames, only capable of sudden effort. They endure labour and service less patiently than we (Tacitus, *Germania*, 5); (. . .) from a strange contradiction of character, they love idleness yet hate peace (*Ibid.*, 15); Prone to exaggerate, they describe everything in the strongest colours; which of course renders their speech picturesque and figurative. Figurative language owes its rise chiefly to two causes; to the want of proper names for objects, and to the influence of imagination and passion over the forms of expression (Blair 1765: 4); à la fois naifs et sagaces, ennemis de tout détour et pénétrant aisement les détours d'autrui, rudes et fins, enthousiastes et moquers, imitateurs et spontanés; ils pussent, dans leur discours, d'une brièveté énigmatique et sentencieuse à une éloquence impétueuse et intarissable en figures hardies; leur mobilité singulière en ce qui concerne les personnes et des choses extérieures ne tient pas seulement à la vivacité de leur imagination, mais aussi à leur indomptable personnalité, toujours prête à réagir contre le despotisme du fait (Martin, 1855: 258); L'élément essentiel de la vie poétique du Celte. c'est l'aventure, c'est-à dire la poursuite de l'inconnu (Renan (1854) 1947-64, Vol. IX; p. 258); comparée à l'imagination classique, l'imagination celtique est vraiment l'infini comparé au fini (*Ibid.*); An organization quick to feel impressions, and feeling them very strongly; a lively personality therefore, keenly sensitive to joy and to sorrow (. . .); it may be seen in wistful regret, it may be seen in passionate penetrating melancholy; but its essence is to aspire ardently after life, light, and emotion, to be expansive, adventurous, and gay (Arnold, (1866) 1891: 84); (. . .) the expansive, eager, Celtic nature; the head in the air, snuffing and snorting (. . .); for good or for bad, the Celtic genius is more airy and unsubstantial, goes less near the ground, than the German(*Ibid.*: 85); wild, reckless, indolent, uncertain and superstitious (Disraeli, cited Curtis 1968: 51); unreliability, emotional instability, mental disequilibrium, or dualistic temperament. (. . .) he oscillated between two extremes of behaviour and mood; he was liable to rush from mirth to despair, tenderness to violence, and loyalty to treachery (*Ibid.*); The beauty of the Irish landscape lies in the never-ending change of colour. A momentary break of sun transforms the sky from dull yellow to bright, rain-washed blue. It lights a hillside to brilliant green, or mottles its brown and green and mauve. A moment later it disappears, dashing the sky back again to mournful purples and misty greys. So it is with the Irish character Arensberg 1937: 16); where there is an ever present sense of the reality and existence of the other world of spiritual and psychic experience (Campbell 1960: 24); Norman men are sensible and have more trust than the Breton. On the other hand, the Breton is livelier and expresses his feelings. The Norman is pacific but the Breton, after several glasses of eau-de vie, becomes argumentative and often violent (a Norman waiter, *Sunday Times* magazine, March 21st, 1982: 69);

I have argued that the lack of fit between two category systems provides a real, observational and experiential basis for the kinds of judgement that are cited above. I have given the phonemic example as a model. Most of the events, however, within which such judgements might be formed, are the product of events occuring in a multi-dimensional social space, with many different orders and systems of category intervening. It will be observed that many of the judgements cited above refer to emotional states, and to moods and character, and this deserves comment. None of the people whose views of the Celt I have cited above are, or were, properly speaking native-born Celts and native Celtic speakers. With the possible exception of Diodorus, however, they have all had extensive first hand experience of the people of whom they speak, variously as soldiers, politicians, administrators, travellers, scholars and so on. Of them all, only Campbell, to my knowledge, learnt a Celtic language to complete fluency, although a few others of them probably had a limited competence in one or another of the Celtic languages. Where linguistic communication is bound to be absent or limited, contact between "Celts" and "non-Celts" is going to be mediated not through language, but through the many possibilities, intentional and unintentional, of non-verbal signification. It must have been largely through such channels that, over the centuries, the most casual and the most frequent impressions of the "Celts" have been formed.

It will be clear that the possibility for misjudgement and mis-interpretation, of the kind that I have described, is very great in "non.verbal" matters. Character, emotional states, and changes of mood, are judged and expressed according to a great diversity of non-verbal "semantic" phenomena, including bodily posture, gesture, stress or rapidity or pitch in speech, frequency or rapidity of move-ment of the body, avoidance or seeking of bodily contact, and so on. All these things are semantically loaded, rule governed and category based, and vary greatly from culture to culture. There is not, however, any serious popular conception that such things require "translation" from one culture to another. Most people, when faced with an unintelligible foreign language, will recognize the need for "translation"; non-verbal "language" gestures, and generally semantic use of the body, of the person, or of groups of people, are not usually granted the same status as language in this respect. Translation will not be thought necessary. In general, an "English-speaker" will interpret the gestures of, say, a "Breton-speaker", a "French-speaker", or a "Gaelic-speaker", according to an entirely "English" set of rules of interpretation, without feeling any need to go to the bother of "translating". We can look at a few examples of the kind of misinterpretation that can occur when non-verbal category systems meet:

In general, an Englishman shakes hands with other Englishmen only rarely, usually on occasion of high formality, such as the introduction of strangers. Friends, at least in the circles that I move in, do not shake hands, except, say, on occasions of mutual congratulation, at the sealing of a bet, or before or after long separation. In the normal run of things, a shaking of hands would introduce a formality that would distance the actors, rather than bringing them together. One of the ways in which friends show that they are friends is by not shaking hands when they meet. Kissing is similarly restricted. In the urban Yorkshire society and class in which I was brought up, the circle of acquaintances that a man normally kisses is very small indeed, all female, and includes perhaps only girlfriend, wife, mother, sister, daughter, grandmother and granddaughter. A man from such a milieu usually only folds a woman into his arms for the purposes of amorous embrace, or perhaps (although not by any means necessarily) at leavetaking and meeting between the kissable relatives already listed. If we put this Englishman, on holiday in Brittany perhaps, into party A of, say, half a dozen young Breton people with whom he has made friends, then he might experience the following: he will be walking in the street with the six young people (3 men and 3 women, say), when they will meet another group of six young people (similarly composed); two or three of the first party will claim acquaintance with two or three of the second party, and all will stop to greet one another. The men of party A will all shake hands with the men of party B; the women of party A will embrace the women of party B, exchanging four kisses, two on each cheek; the men of party A will then embrace the women of party B, and the men of party B the women of party A, all exchanging four kisses, two on each cheek. Verbal introductions of the strangers in each party may or may not form part of all this activity. After all this is over, two or three sentences may be exchanged, about the weather or the price of petrol, and it will then be time to start the whole round of kissing, embracing and handshaking again, this time in leavetaking rather than in greeting. If we include the bemused and embarrassed Englishman in this maelstrom of intimate bodily contact, then we can count, over the space of perhaps three or four minutes, and with our thirteen actors, twenty four handshakes, sixty mutual embraces, and four hundred and eighty kisses. Sometimes the men will embrace one another for good measure. Even though there are often minor defections and derelictions in the performance of these rituals of greeting and parting, the programme is as I have outlined. It is clear that the Englishman could be forgiven for concluding, from the event of which he has been a part, that the French are a very emotional people, and a curious mixture, at once punctilious and sexy. Furthermore, when, half an hour later and alone, he meets one of the women that so short a time before he was evidently fondling with intimate caress, and she cuts him dead, even though she clearly "recognizes" him, then he can be forgiven for going on to think that the French are not only emotional, but that they are also extremely capricious of mood.

It is worth pursuing the handshaking theme further, particularly since the Breton example will in some sort complement the detailed discussion, in Ardener's paper (*infra*) of the hand and hand-shaking. Breton men shake hands very frequently, when meeting casually during the day. Usually one hand-shake for the first meeting of the day will do for the whole day, but later, if one becomes involved in a round of handshaking, in a bar perhaps, then one may shake the same hand again. I learnt to shake hands with something like the right regularity and frequency, although I often made mistakes, accidentally ignoring proffered hands, or eagerly offering to shake hands where I had already done so only a few minutes before. Clearly, in my behaviour, there would have been grounds to cause a Breton to think that I was a) reserved; b) over-friendly; c) capricious and unsure of my mood. When I was at sea for a month in a tuna-fishing supply boat with a crew of about thirty, I learnt eventually that one was expected to shake the hand of everybody on board once on the first meeting of the day. The days then became a kind of Kim's game for me, as I tried to remember whose hand I had shaken and whom I still had not met. The engineers, keeping peculiar watches and emerging rarely from the bowels of the ship, posed me particular problems. The sailors, however, most of whom had decades of experience of this social nicety, seemed to have no problem in remembering. A sailor coming into the midday or even the evening meal would, without any appearance of forethought or perplexity shake the hands of those people around the table that he had not already met that day, ignoring those with whom he had already exchanged this greeting. I simply could not perform this feat of memory, and must, again, have appeared oddly tempered to those subjected to my failures of judgement.

A sailor, particularly a fisherman, often has hands and forearms covered in oil or fish-blood and scales. Handshaking is still carried on, however. A fisherman with dirty hands will offer his forearm; one with dirty hands and forearms will offer the tip of his elbow; I have even seen a fisherman, who had been delving around in the bilges and was filthy to half way up his upper arm, offer what can only be described as his shoulder. Handshaking is always done with the right hand, and a clean left hand can not be substituted for a dirty right. While in the fishing village in Brittany, I once made the mistake of trying to open an oyster with the pointed tip of a very sharp clean knife (a stupidity that, incidentally, people from a non-oyster eating culture like my own tend to go in for). The knife slipped and, since I am left-handed, I drove the knife point an inch into the ball of my right-hand thumb. Shaking hands with my right hand was out of the question for a week or so, and I was anxious to avoid anybody's gripping me by the right hand, and so tended to hold it back. What I *should* have done was offer my right forearm. Because, however, I come from a culture where handshaking is not particularly important, and certainly not important enough to drive the classificatory hand right up to the shoulder in circumstances where the "hand" itself was injured or otherwise unavailable, I shook hands far less than I should have. The Englishman was "reserved". Once or twice, purely on impulse, when I was faced with an unavoidable handshake, I offered a curiously twisted left hand; this was, to judge from the expression that clouded the face of the recipient, a very strange thing to do. Not only "reserved", then, but rather odd with it.

Let us now leave Brittany, and go to Ireland in pursuit of the fighting Paddy. My example here is anecdotal, in that I cannot remember where I read it, and so cannot supply the reference. It has an engaging symmetry, however, that makes me want to risk presenting it even without reference. Consider the case of the Irishman, in the bar in his home village somewhere in the rural depths of western Ireland. A few drinks have been drunk, and a simmering resentment between two adult men erupts into crisis, perhaps over some real or imagined insult. Protagonist 1 leaps to his feet, and says something like "I'll kill him! Hold me back, someone, for I'll not be responsible for what I do to him if I get my hands on him". Protagonist 2 voices similar sentiments, expressing his eager desire to fight, and his hope that somebody will hold him back, and thus prevent him from killing protagonist 1. The two will threaten to square up to one another, at the same time maintaining their pleas to the world in general that somebody hold them back. In normal circumstances, and according to the local patterns of kinship, friendship and obligation, people will appear from the background to hold the two men apart. Once the two men are safely held back, they can then make eager attempts to get away from those that are holding them back, in demonstration of their burning desire to get at one another's throats, and fight it out. Eventually, the holders-back will manage to persuade the two that they should not fight, and the protagonists will reluctantly agree, out of respect for the judgement and feelings of their holders-back, that they will put off their quarrel to another day. Honour is satisfied on all sides, and no blood spilt. Such is the regular course of fights in this small bar in Ireland. The "fight" is an elaborate means for the expression, resolution and determination of local conflicts, personal prestige, alliance of kin and friends, and so on; there is little of what an English court would call "physical violence".

We can now take one of the men from the village, and put him in a bar in Liverpool. He is visiting relatives, perhaps, or is over to look for a job. He goes to a pub, and a few drinks are drunk. Somebody gives him cause for offence. Others have heard the insult, and it can not be ignored without loss of face. He leaps to his feet, saying something like "hold me back somebody, or I'll kill him!". The other drinkers in the pub look contemplatively at the ceiling, or take thoughtful pulls from their pint pots. Henceforth, everything is upside down. The Irishman, in order to persuade somebody to hold him back, emphasizes at length the truly appalling consequences that will follow if he is not contained, such a fighter and hot-tempered man he is. The audience remains unmoved. The more he boasts in order to persuade somebody to stop the fight, the more inevitable does it become that he will be honour-bound to force a fight in order to make good his boast. Nobody holds him back. There is a fight.

The English people in the bar could not fail to find in this confirmation of all they had ever been told about the hot-tempered, impetuous, over-emotional, belligerent, red-haired Paddy. The Irishman, in his turn, might be appalled by the cynical lovelessness of a people prepared to sit by and let a perfectly peaceable, self-respecting Irishman get his head broken.

I have chosen the two examples given above, not because they present any ethnographic novelty or subtlety, but rather because of their accessibility and banality. I have also done them much less than justice, for such events often take longer to describe than they do to happen. I have only sketched in the barest outline of the greeting in Brittany, saying nothing of the nuances of formality, warmth, affection, toleration, dislike, and celebration that can be expressed by variations of the handshake, embrace or kiss. The Irish fight, similarly, would demand half an ethnography for its proper description. Nevertheless, such events, and others like them, can, in situations of culture-contact, happen dozens of times a day for the same person; unnoticed, or only half-noticed, their cumulative effect can be nevertheless impressive. It must surely be the case that culture-specific misinterpretations of the kind that I have described lie behind Tacitus' "from a strange contradiction of character, they love idleness yet hate peace" (*Germania*, 15), or Strabo's "by reason of this levity of character they not only look insufferable when victorious, but also scared out of their wits when worsted" (4, 4, 5: 247). We cannot know enough to reconstruct the social realities that gave rise to these conclusions, but they have sufficient in common with modern commentary to justify a general inference. From Strabo's "the whole race (. . .) is war-mad" (4, 4, 2: 237) to the Ireland of Donnybrook Fair and the Kilkenny Cats, from Diodorus' "using one word when they mean another" (V, 31: 177) to Thomson's "the fun, the cleverness with words" (Thomson 1976: 166), from Caesar's "as a nation they are extremely superstitious" (vi, 16) to Campbell's "ever-present sense of the reality and existence of the other world of spiritual and psychic experience" (Campbell 1960: 24), there is a significant similarity; we might almost call it a continuity − one category system looks at another, and finds there uncertainty, wavering, paradox, lawlessness, drama, rhetoric, semantic over-excitement, too much and too little.

I hope that it will be clear that the kinds of "category" that I have been talking about, while they are unavoidably "semantic", are often of a conceptual complexity of which "words" and "physical reality" are themselves only subsidiary parts (see the discussion in Ardener, *infra*). The example of the greeting in Brittany is, for example, not just about the "handshake", but also about a whole system of conceptual categories concerning emotion, friendliness, sexuality, formality and so on. If we look again at Diodorus' description of the Gauls, we find an inventory of themes that crop up again and again, and none of these is simply about "verbal categories". Diodorus refers to the Gauls' tendency to excess when given wine (V, 26: 167), to their flamboyant use of gold in personal adornment (V, 27: 167-9), to their strange hair and skin colour (V, 28: 169), to their erratic and lustful sexual habits (V, 32: 183), and to their riddling, hinting, boasting and threatening (V, 31: 177). If we add to this Ceasar's reference to their excessive super-stition and religiosity (vi, 16), then we have a fairly good summary of the main themes that dominated not only classical appreciation of the barbarian, but that also form the history of modern ethno-graphic description throughout the entire world. If we look at wine, gold, pigmentation, sex, riddling, fighting, and religion, then we find that every one is, from the first, conceptually complicated, and every one offers the possibility of conceptual mismatch of the kind that I have described; for each of them, this could be demonstrated throughout the history of the non-Celtic/Celtic con-frontation. And while this confrontation is one, on both sides, of conceptual complexity, the observations that the confrontation provokes, the realities that present themselves, seem to be empiri-cally innocent. The "stereotype" of the other, while it probably always has a purely theoretical component, is nevertheless "observed".

A concentration on "non-verbal" categories stems partly from a desire to emphasize, should there have remained any doubt, that such categories are as "semantic" as language; it also stems from the belief that confrontation of culturally different "non-verbal" cate-gory systems has probably been more productive over the centuries of ideas such as those concerning the Celts, than has that between verbal categories (cf. Ardener, *infra*: 11-12): everybody can misread "non-verbal" categories; only the linguistically privileged are very likely to get involved with verbal category problems. It is worth, nevertheless, giving consideration to language, since it is the most obviously "semantic" of semantic systems. Verbal category systems, the lack of fit between the verbal categories of one culture and another, and the various anomalies and ambiguities to which verbal classifications can give rise, are now relatively familiar ground for the social anthropologist. It is clear to us now, I think, that one set of verbal categories, when looked at from another culturally different and incongruent set, will appear, according to the specific lack of fit between the two systems, to have words that mean "too much", words that mean "too little", words that are evidently capricious and aberrant in their use, and so on. An alien language will appear, as did "primitive languages" to the early ethnographers, to be subject, paradoxically, both to strange fits of generalization, and to inexplicable tendencies towards detail. Such observational phenomena are clearly a part of the more general problem of the meeting of category systems that I have been discussing.

In general, the layman, even the bilingual or polyglot layman, is not capable of dealing in any anthropologically or linguistically sophisticated way with the problem of the lack of fit between the semantic categories of different languages. He may never, indeed, notice the lack of fit, until "reality" itself starts to misbehave before his eyes, and even then he may well suppose that he has only "made a mistake", in one language or another. He may, if he is thoughtful, conclude that his second language is oddly defective, that words mean "more" or "less" than they ought, or that words have "extended meanings" and oddly metaphorical usages (see Muller 1856: 369; Henson 1974: 21). We need not sneer at the layman here, for such have been, to a very great extent, the conclusions of anthropology. If we take what has been the foremost issue through which the problem has been discussed in British social anthropology, that of alien category systems for the classification of kin, we find that it was a long time before anthropology was able to cope with them. Until relatively recently, when a kin term did not correspond, in the range of its usage, to the English term, it was argued to be, through various logical and developmental routes, an "extension", a kind of metaphorical elaboration, of the English term (for considerations of this, see Henson 1974: 25; Needham 1972). Even when the attempt was made to grant to alien kinship nomenclatures their own systematic integrity, the idea developed that we were dealing with "classificatory" systems, as though our own were in some sense not classificatory.

It was, and remains, imaginatively difficult to accord to alien category systems their own autonomy, their own right to be considered, from their own point of view, fundamental and normal, and not extended or metaphorical or demented or semantic. In general, when we come across a word in a foreign language that means all of the word as we translate it in English, but also some more besides, then there is a great temptation to regard this "more" as somehow extended or metaphorical or symbolic with regard to the rest of the meaning. Much of our excitement when faced with alien classificatory systems, and much of our argument about how to deal with them, arise from a failure to deal with this problem properly. Our language and conceptual system have their own way of dealing with meaning in English, and of dividing "real" meanings from meanings that are secondary, fictional, expressive, metaphorical, symbolic and so on. While we can assume that all languages and cultures have ways of distributing relevance and trenchancy to, say, the various different usages of the same word, we discover nothing about these simply by applying our own criteria, and assuming "symbolic" significance, with all the excitement that that implies, wherever the categories of English literality are disturbed. I make this point partly to express a suspicion that it is precisely this kind of "extra" meaning that lies behind the appeal of semantic anthropology, in its status as a subdivision of anthropology as a whole; in this sense, semantic anthropology might be said to owe its origin to the same kind of classificatory over-excitement that has led commentators over the centuries to find the Celts eloquent, excitable, temperamental, dualistic and so on. Meaning is not necessarily meaningful at all, if what we are after is a proper understanding of native reality. Meaning is not a gloss on reality; it is, rather, reality itself. As such, it is as banal, or as exciting, as it is for the natives. Our own reactions to alien category systems provoke us to find interest where, in a sense, there is none. I make this point also because it bears again on the idea of the Celt. We have seen that the Celt has been viewed as a peculiarly metaphorical and capricious creature, and I have tried to show why this might have been so. One of the ways in which this idea is propagated today is through the notion that Celtic languages, because the words in them do not always have the same semantic range as those in English or French are somehow "rich in imagery". This idea is popular in language-learning circles, and McDonald (1982) gives an account of how, in Breton-learning courses and classes, lexical and grammatical mismatches are used to support this and other equally gratifying conclusions about the Breton language, the Bretons, and the Celts. The existence, for example, of the anthropologically familiar mismatch of colour categories as between "Celtic" and "non-Celtic" languages, is used to argue a metaphorical perception, a natural unity of imagery; the existence, conversely, of extensive technical vocabulary concerning, say, wind directions, or ways of cutting peat, is argued to represent a richness of language and perception that English and French have somehow "lost". Semantically, the Celts have got something that we haven't. As I said above, in the Celtic fringes, meaning comes in barrowloads.

It is not only semantic anthropology that has responded to the meaning and metaphor that sparkle on the edges of the world, but anthropology itself. When Strabo and Diodorus were writing, there was no doubt that the centre of civilized order in the world lay on the northern shores of the Mediterranean. It was to the south, in

Africa, and to the north-east and north-west, in Europe and Asia, that moral, political and semantic insecurity were located. When the moral centre of gravity of Europe moved northwards in the modern period, so the ethnology of Europe, and its glamour and insecurities, re-organized themselves, at least for the British commentator. Macaulay wrote:

> The Irish (. . .) were distinguished by qualities which tend to make men interesting rather than prosperous. They were an ardent and impetuous race, easily moved to tears or laughter, to fury or to love. Alone among the nations of Northern Europe they had the susceptibility, the vivacity, the natural turn for acting and rhetoric which are indigenous on the shores of the Mediterranean sea (Macaulay (1849) 1883: 33).

In noting that the Celts and Mediterraneans were "interesting", and at the same time ardent, impetuous, susceptible, vivacious, dramatic and rhetorical, Macaulay might have been preparing the field for the European anthropologist. In one of my "A-level" biology text books there was a picture of a man with the relative size of different parts of his body determined according to the amount of brain that was given over to their control. He had huge lips, eyes, tongue and ears, grotesquely large hands and fingers, feet and toes, and an otherwise shrivelled trunk and limbs. We could draw a similar picture of Europe, with the size of its parts determined by the proportion of the collective anthropological brain that has been devoted to their study. If we included, in the determination of the relative size of the different parts of Europe, a demographic adjustment to express the reciprocal of the attention that the various parts *ought* to have received on account of their population size, then the map that we produced would be grotesque indeed. It would be largely composed of mediterranean coastline and islands, and of a few colossal islands in the north Atlantic — Iceland, Ireland, the Faroes, the Hebrides, the Orkneys and Shetlands; Lewis would be, perhaps, fifty thousand times bigger than greater London; England would be a shrivelled appendage to Scotland and Wales; north-eastern France would be barely noticeable next to the looming bulk of Brittany, the Basque country and the Languedoc. There can be no doubt that European anthropologists have followed the "interest" and the "rhetoric" that Macaulay found, and have gone to areas where, as Macaulay would surely have agreed with Muller, words had a tendency to say "more than they ought to say" (Muller 1856: 369).

References

Ardener, E. W. 1971. Introduction: social anthropology and language. In *Social Anthropology and Language* (ed.) E. Ardener (Ass. social Anthrop. Monogr. 10). London: Tavistock.

—— 1982. Social anthropology, language and reality. This volume.

Arensberg, C. 1937. *The Irish Countryman. An Anthropological Study*. London: Macmillan.

Arnold, M. (1866) 1891. *The Study of Celtic Literature*. London: Smith, Elder.

Blair, H. 1765. *A Critical Dissertation in the Poems of Ossian*. Dublin.

Campbell, J. L. 1960. *Tales of Barra told by the Coddy*. Edinburgh, for the editor: Johnston & Bacon.

Chapman, M. 1978a. Reality and representation. *Journal of the Anthropological Society of Oxford* IX (1), 35-51.

—— 1978b. *The Gaelic Vision in Scottish Culture*. London: Croom Helm.

Crick, M. 1976. *Explorations in Language and Meaning*. London: Malaby.

Curtis, L. 1968. *Anglo-Saxons and Celts: A Study of Anti-Irish Prejudice in Victorian England*. Connecticut: University of Bridgeport.

Dillon, M. (& Chadwick, N.) (1967) 1973. *The Celtic Realms*. London: Sphere.

Diodorus Siculus. Loeb edition, Vol. III (1970); Books IV, 59 to VIII.

Goldie, H. 1968. *Principles of Efik Grammar*. Muir and Paterson.

Henson, H. 1974. *British Social Anthropologists and Language*. Oxford: Clarendon Press.

Julius Caesar. *The Conquest of Gaul* (trans.) S. A. Handford. Harmondsworth: Penguin (1951).

Macaulay, T. (Lord) (1849) 1883. *The History of England*. Vol. I. London: Longmans.

McDonald, M. 1982. Social Aspects of Language and Education in Brittany". D. Phil thesis, Oxford (in preparation).

Martin H. 1855. *Histoire de France* (Vol. I). Paris.

Müller, M. 1856. Comparative Mythology. *Selected Essays,* Vol. I (1881). Longmans, Green and Co.

Needham, R. 1972. *Rethinking Kinship and Marriage*. London: Tavistock.

Piggot, S. 1968. *The Druids*. Harmondsworth: Penguin (1977).

Renan, E. 1854. La Poésie des Races Celtiques. *Oeuvres Complètes*, 1947-64, Vol. IX. Paris: Calmann-Lévy.

Strabo. Loeb edition, Vol. II (1969); Books III to V.

Tacitus. *Agricola and Germania* (1926). London: Macmillan.

Thomson, D. 1976. *Nua-Bhàrdachd Ghàidhlig* (ed.) D. Macaulay. Edinburgh: Southside.

Yeats, W. B. 1924. *Ideas of Good and Evil*. London: Macmillan.

ESTABLISHING AN ETHNICITY

The Emergence of the "Icelanders" in the Early Middle Ages

KIRSTEN HASTRUP

Introduction

To establish an ethnicity as an analytical unit of social anthropology presents one with a whole range of theoretical and empirical questions. The answers to these questions are linked through the semantics of ethnic classification, which integrates the analyst's view with the people's self-identification. That is, the meaning of ethnicity cannot be sought out in a purely deductive manner, it requires the cooperation of the people involved, so to speak, because they themselves "play the part of theoreticians in this field" (Ardener 1975: 346).

This, at least, is the point of view taken here, and the aim of the present paper is to demonstrate how it is that a semantic analysis of ethnicity may integrate empirical realities of social discontinuity with theoretical reflections on the bounding of analytical wholes. I contend that as far as the concept of ethnicity is concerned, we find ourselves in an associative field where real and nominal definitions will ultimately merge (cf. Southwold 1978: 157). I would contend further that perhaps this perspective is what characterizes a "semantic" anthropology at a general level. In this sense the semantic endeavour of present day social anthropology may be understood as a search for a new language in which to carry out the dialoque between empirical and theoretical realities without violating either. A language in which the meaning of the concepts used is found in a reciprocal and reversible relationship between the nominal and the real definitions, to paraphrase Ullmann (1962: 57).

In this language, one of the entities to be spoken of is "ethnicity".

In my discussion of this concept, I take my point of departure in two works of Ardener concerned with the relationship between language, ethnicity, and population (1975, 1974). In this connection, I shall only mention that one of the more important issues raised is the matter of self-definition as a constitutive element in the classification of people. I intend to show how self-definition occurred at a particular point in time in a historical process, in the hope of clarifying the relationship between ethnic classification and history with reference to a particular case. In that sense my work is tallying with recent attempts to define ethnicity in a European context (cf. for instance Beck and Cole (eds) 1981). Further, I intend to show how naming propensities are actually involved in the creation of particular "peoples", and in that way we get close to one of the main topics of this volume, namely the formative role of language. In choosing the case of ethnic classification, my aim may be seen as to illustrate what Ardener calls "the close match of the classifying process with the workings of language itself" (Ardener 1975: 346), and perhaps through this illustration contribute to a more detailed understanding of this "match".

Empirically my case is located in medieval Iceland, and in dealing with a remote historical society we are faced with slightly atypical problems of validation. However, this is not the place to discuss these problems, which I have dealt with elsewhere.[1] Yet a brief account of the historical framework of this particular society is appropriate.

Iceland was uninhabited until the last part of the ninth century, when the Viking expansion towards the north-west hit this remote island.[2] Most of the settlers came from Norway or from the Norse colonies in the British Isles. According to the native Icelandic tradition of the time, the reason for leaving Norway was to flee the tyranny of king Harald Fairhair, who, in the attempt to make up a united kingdom of what had until then been a lot of lesser chiefdoms, seized the allodial land of the free farmers. One of the first men to reach the shores of the North Atlantic island, known by a variety of names, was a certain Flóki Vilgertharson, a "great viking", and it is to him that the island owes its present name, according to the author of the twelfth century "Book of settlements".[3] Flóki arrived about A.D. 870, and although he himself did not stay, the name of Iceland persisted, and soon the settlers began to arrive in great quantities. It is assumed that in the period from 870 to 930 some 40,000 individuals came to Iceland equipped for a new life, yet carrying with them their old Norse language and traditions as well as their livestock and other provisions.[4] They established themselves with private ownership of land, a little barley cropping, and with animal husbandry as their main living. They lived in extended families, had an essentially cognatic system of kinship yet with some traces of a patrilineal ideology in certain contexts,[5] sacrificed more or less steadily to the ancient Norse gods, Othin, Thórr, and Freyr[6], kept their thralls as they had always done, and were probably quite busy in making this virgin land liveable.

Although the settlers in Iceland virtually "isolated" themselves, they were very much tied into the general social, political, and mercantile development of the early Middle Ages, as travelling and commerce remained for a long time an integrated part of their life. As far as religious matters were concerned, Iceland met with the Christian mission shortly after mainland Scandinavia, resulting in a formal acceptance of Christianity as the "national" faith in the year A.D. 1000. Although we have to use inverted commas in speaking of an Icelandic "nation" of the time, the term being rather anachronistic, we should note that in 930 a constitution had been agreed upon, which made of the country an autonomous political construct, which was to last until 1262, when Iceland came under Norwegian supremacy. It is this political construct which is here referred to as the Icelandic Freestate, and it is the society and the period of the Freestate which is the historical frame of the present analysis.

Rules and Social Action

The constitution of 930 marked the beginning of a social "experiment", which even today seems fascinating. In this section of the paper we shall devote ourselves to an account of this experiment, as narrated in terms of legal rules established and meaning created through social action.

The constitutive event of the Freestate was the establishment of the Althing, or people's assembly, being from 930 onwards the centre of legislation and jurisdiction in Iceland. With the Althing (*althingi*) an elaborate constitution based on the institutions of people's assemblies and chieftaincies was created, and all of it was summed up in the making of a law, which effectively transformed the community of settlers into a society. In Viking Age Scandinavia the "law" was synonymous with "society", and probably this ancient idea of social unification was part of the inducement for the settlers to make up their own law.[7] Apart from this it is hard to determine what caused the farmers of the first part of the tenth century to think out a constitution of that scale, yet it is certain that through a collective act they defined a social structure which was unique.

Based as it was on a hierarchy of *things*, with the Althing at the top and the Spring *things (Várthing)* at the bottom, it was unparallelled in Scandinavia, even if the *things*, or people's assemblies, were found in other places, too. It is this hierarchy, (in which the Althing is thought to comprise the 12 Spring *things*), which make of the Althing a sort of "national" *thing*, which was unprecedented. When in 965 a third level of *things* emerged between the former two with the establishment of Quarter *things*[8], the idea of unity through hierarchy was even more clearly expressed.[9] In 1004 the Althing was enriched by what was then conceived of as a "fifth court" (*fimmtardómr*), which was to function as a supreme court, or the ultimate court of appeal. With the establishment of the "fifth court" the Icelandic constitution was complete, and although many new laws were made after that, the constitution of the *things* remained the same until 1262, when Iceland became part of the kingdom of Norway. The highest office in the country was the office of the Lawspeaker (*lögsögumathr*). He was checked for three year periods, during which he had to recite all laws obtaining in the society, at three successive Althing assemblies. Part of the law, namely that part which related to the constitution and the *thing*-organization, had to be recited every year. Among the recurrent duties of the Lawspeaker were also to state the calendar for the year to come, and to act as the supreme interpreter of the law in cases of doubt.[10]

If the Lawspeaker thus acted as the chairman of the Althing, the actual administration of the law was left with the different courts at various levels of the hierarchy, and responsible for the functioning of these courts were the chieftains (*gothar*). At the bottom level of the hierarchy of *things*, the *gothar* ruled over the Spring assemblies, while at the top level, the 36 of them constituted the *lögretta*, the legislatory body of the Althing. With the Lawspeaker acting as chairman, the *lögretta* adjusted old laws and made up new ones as need arose. As far as the chieftaincies (*gothor*) were concerned, they were a curious mixture of private property and public office, and as such they could be bought, sold, aquired through force, or inherited according to the circumstances. But whatever they were in our terms, they were certainly a cornerstone in the constitution of the Icelandic society. There were 36 of them, 12 for each quarter (*fjorthungr*), and three for each Spring *thing*, of which there were four in each quarter.[11] Every free farmer had to affiliate himself with a particular *gothi*, and through him the members of his household and the tenants and cotters on his land were linked to the wider society.

Let us now subject the law to closer inspection. It will be recalled that the "law" was more or less synonymous with "society", but as far as the law as a system of rules goes we should note that it did not exist in a codified form outside the memories of the administrators of the law. Until 1117, the law was orally transmitted, and if we are to localize it anywhere it is in the Lawspeaker, who personified the society, therefore, when he once a year "spoke" the law in front of the Althing assembly.

Essentially the law is a rule system, but the rules of a legal system are of two kinds (Hart 1961: 91-2). There is

> a primary set of rules which relate positively or negatively to different types of actions, and a secondary set which belongs to a different logical type. They relate to primary rules, but over such question as precedents, interpretation and changes in the law . . . The primary rules . . concern actual events, while the secondary rules play a basically semantic function (Crick 1976: 99)

This dual dimensionality of law is of extreme importance when one considers the creation of Icelandic law. There was no precedence at any level. Through an imaginative social action, or a creative social event, the island dwellers decided that a rule system governing social behaviour was wanted, yet they had no pre-existing code, or no secondary rules, of which they could say that they warranted particular procedures or primary rules, or implied certain social sanctions. They had an "idea of law" as in some way defining society, but the historical situation in which they found themselves differed radically from the Norwegian background, and they certainly had to translate this idea of the law into a distinct social reality. Of course, the distinctiveness of this reality was thereby further underlined.

Characteristically, the law was first formulated in terms of particular cases, stating procedures and sanctions to follow particular deeds, or rights and duties to obtain in specific circumstances. As observed by Foote, in discussing the style of old Icelandic law, matters are "spun out in pragmatic fashion, more by accumulation than by systematization" (Foote 1977: 48). The point is that it could not be otherwise, given the fact that the law had to be made from scratch and with no general rules preexisting. Evidently, in formulating the primary rules, even in the casuistic style so typical of Icelandic law, a deeper semantic level was concurrently established. Yet there was no way in which the semantic relationships obtaining at this level could be formulated as general principles or the like, since there was no precedence. The meaning of the law had to be gradually established through action, through the dealing with particular social events, and through passing sentence in particular court cases. Thus we may say, with a slight turn of Professor Foote's wording, that through accumulation at the level of primary rules, systematization gradually occurred at the level of secondary rules. It was only through precedence in action that the imaginative constitution of a particular social structure could be followed by the creative definition of a particular system of meaning.

Once a particular system of meaning had been established as a basis for interpretation, particular rules could be "measured" against this system. This means that once some such system of implicit meanings had become part of the collective representations of society, the road was open for changes as well. If this seems paradoxical, it is, nevertheless, obvious that changes cannot occur if there is nothing to be changed *from*; the notion of change simply makes no sense in that case. However, once a particular rule had been established it could also be changed if it no longer seemed justified. This applies equally to primary and secondary rules. As far as the first ones are concerned changes can often be read directly out of the text, as "old" paragraphs are sometimes followed by an additional section explicitly acknowledged as *nymaeli*, that is a "new law" or, literally, a "new speech". Some new "speeches" had greater repercussions at the level of secondary rules than others, and conversely, some changes at the level of semantic relationships led to more adjustments at the level of events. I shall not belabour this point here, but make the general statement that changes at these two levels were discontinuous in relation to each other.[12] What is more, they still had to be specified in action. From today's perspective we register changes, not in action, but in the consequences that new actions had for the further development of the law.

Language and Ethnic Identification

At a certain point in time in the process of social development writing was introduced. In Iceland, as elsewhere, this happened in the wake of Christianity. The first pieces of writing were religious texts, and in Latin. However, written Icelandic appeared in the middle of the eleventh century, when it was probably still used mainly for translating religious texts (Turville-Petre 1953: 75-6). However, in about 1100 writing became of broader usage, as it was now used to write down genealogies, and laws. In 1117 it was decided at the Althing that the corpus of laws was to be put into writing as a whole. Formulated as a new law, the decision to write up the entire body of laws registered as just one more step in the process of social development. But it was to have immense consequences for the concept of law, as held by the inhabitants of Iceland. It is beyond the scope of the present paper to demonstrate this, however (see Hastrup 1979a). What I want to show here is that almost at that very point in time, when the laws were written down, an ethnic category was established on the pillars of social structure. The "Icelanders" emerged as a self-declared people.

In the laws there is no reference to an ethnic category. The population of the law consists of "men", "tenants", "heirs", "adulterers", and the like, or, if contrasted to foreigners, they are "men of this country". Thus the individuals encompassed by the law were simply, and tautologically, members of the Icelandic society. In those few contexts where reference to a particular cultural heritage was made, the diacritical feature was the language, that is the language known as *dönsk tunga*, "Danish tongue". To be a member of any court, the person had to be a native speaker of "Danish" (Grágás Ia: 38). As a contemporary name for the common Scandinavian language, the concept of *dönsk tunga* points to Denmark as the point of reference for the more or less shared Norse culture (Haugen 1976: 135), while at another level it also points to a conception of unity between the Nordic countries. The point at issue here is that as far as the inhabitants of Iceland were concerned, they had not yet appeared as a people when the laws were written down (in 1117-18), if by a "people" we understand a group made up through naming.[13]

Very shortly after, however, this people was created in a historical work written by Ari *inn fróthi* about 1120. And the name was given to the "Icelanders" with retrospective application as from the beginning of social life in Iceland, that is from the first constitution some 200 years before. The place where the naming occurred was Ari's *Íslendingabók*, the "Book of the Icelanders", which is a piece of history covering the years 870 to 1118.[14] In this work, which is generally considered a reliable source of the hitherto unwritten history of the inhabitants of Iceland, we are told of the making of the constitution, the succession of Lawspeakers, changes in calendar, the advent of Christianity, the discovery of Greenland, and much more. As a narrative of events taking place within a chronological frame *Íslendingabók* is also a statement of historical continuity amidst the changes and achievements of the Icelandic society during the recorded period. The continuity is established with reference to the name of the Icelanders, who thereby emerged as an ethnic category defined as a people with a separate history.

One could not wish for better evidence of a shared history defining an ethnicity, but the force of the Icelandic case does not stop here. Another piece of writing was composed shortly after *Islendingabók*. This was a work of linguistic scholarship, which for want of a proper name is normally referred to as the "First Grammatical Treatise", written about 1140.[15] It is a remarkable piece, being the only known grammatical work in a vernacular (non-Latin) language of the period. The author states that he was prompted to write the treatise because reading and writing had become common by then; and he wanted to facilitate this reading and writing of, as he says, "laws, genealogies, religious works, and the learned historical works, which Ari has written with great acumen"[16] (FGT: 20). This statement is packed with information, belonging to several levels of reality, and we may for the moment let it speak for itself.

Of the *First Grammatical Treatise* as such we may say that as far as the linguistic content goes, it is no less interesting or informative. In a thoroughly scientific manner the First Grammarian, as the anonymous author is conveniently called, identified what would today be called the phonemes of the Icelandic language (Haugen 1976: 197). Demonstrating the inadequacy of Latin letters for expressing the sounds of Icelandic, he subsequently suggested an alphabet for, as he formulates it, "us, the Icelanders" (FGT: 21). It will be recalled that at the time the common term for all the Nordic languages was *dönsk tunga,* "Danish tongue". This label was used to distinguish the Norsemen from the rest of the world, also in Iceland. The First Grammarian still used this term for the spoken language, but he indirectly claimed that Icelandic was a specific branch of Danish for which a particular written language was needed. Speech was still mutually intelligible between the Nordic countries, but from about the time when the *First Grammatical Treatise* was composed, the development of the Scandinavian languages split into several histories (cf. Haugen 1976). The establishment of separate written languages was part of the reason for this.

The obvious philological value of the work aside, the *First Grammatical Treatise* deserves anthropological consideration precisely because of its stress on linguistic and cultural particularity. But we have to be careful now. Although language is generally thought of as one of the main distinctive features in the definition of ethnic groups, there is no mechanistic one-to-one relationship between language and the establishment of separate identities. As noted in a recent paper, language is not really an index of ethnic identity, but it may be used as a means for establishing or changing that identity (Gal 1981: 104). We shall return to this below.

Generally speaking language relates to culture in at least two ways, belonging to discrete levels of reality. At one level language is part of culture, at another level, it "expresses" culture (Ardener 1973, 1975). In other words, language is related to culture in both a metonymical and a metaphorical way. In the first sense, the writing of such a work as the First Grammatical Treatise is but one sign among others of the social development and scholarly achievements of the old Icelanders. In the second sense, the creation of a particular Icelandic alphabet on the basis of an identification of the phonemes of spoken Icelandic can be read as a metaphor of a consciously recognized cultural identity. This is where the *First Grammatical Treatise* becomes a most important statement of ethnicity.

At a certain level, the name of the "Icelanders" is just a word, which quite unobtrusively was, or became, part of the natural language. However, once the category had been established as the name of a particular people, it generated a new reality, also as far as the definition of the "natural" language was concerned. The linguistic reality of continuity between the spoken languages of the Nordic countries was punctuated by a conscious effort on the part of the First Grammarian. As a consequence "Icelandic" appeared as a separate language spoken by the "Icelanders", as retrospectively defined by their historian, Ari, to whose works the First Grammarian referred so reverently.

In this sense the cleaving off of Icelandic from the common Scandinavian language became a further means of establishing their ethnic identity. This is where the naming of the Icelanders quite clearly was much more than a linguistic event. At a more general level this is also where we can now venture the opinion that the primary significance of language in ethnic identification is not in its being, mechanically and metonymically, an index of a particular identity, it is rather in its being in particular historical circumstances a powerful metaphor of a separate reality.

Creativity and Intentionality

As I read the Icelandic case, of which you have been given a brief and selective account, it is evidence of the establishing of an ethnicity through a kind of creativity which is in part linguistic. At first there was only a community of settlers, but after a few generations this community was turned into a society by way of a collective social action. The establishment of the Althing and the conscious creation of a specific Icelandic law were the constitutive events. While an autonomous political and legal structure thus came into being at one stroke, it was only through action and social process that this structure was gradually transformed into a system of meaning. Apparently this system of meaning was a prerequisite for the establishment of a separate identity, which was declared by way of naming. At this stage, the creativity registers mainly as a linguistic faculty, yet once the name was produced as a label for a particular social space, new meaning was created within it and even retrospectively so. Thus, once the Icelandic society had been declared a separate reality, it also emerged as a distinct semantic space which generated its own "events". In that sense, the ethnic identification of the Icelanders changed their historical fate.[17]

The point to be made here is that creativity, as a distinctive feature of human society, "unfolds" at many levels of social reality, conscious or unconscious, and with both overt and covert consequences. This raises the question of intentionality, and I think that it may be answered in relatively simple terms. At the level of events, and of individuals acting, the making of the first constitution and the (later) writing of the history of the Icelanders probably were "intentional". That is, these acts had clearly defined purposes, namely to create a set of (primary) rules for social behaviour and to record the development of a particular society. Yet, at another level, where the formulation of rules implicitly led to the creation of a unified semantic space, and where the historical narrative implied the invention of a people, there was no, and could not be any, deliberate purpose, or "intentional meaning". Meaning at this level was wholly "implicational".

The distinction between intentional and implicational meaning, which is owed to Hanson (1975: 8-11), is useful, I think, because it allows us to place "intentionality" at the level of the events themselves, that is at the level of explicit purpose. At the level of implicit meanings neither the "causes" nor the "consequences" of particular creative events are to be found in a particular intentionality. At least not unless we speak of societies as goal-seeking systems.[18]

Though even then the "intentionality" of the system is better understood as a particular kind of rationality — "better", because it allows for redefinition of the course of history, read as a discontinuous string of more or less overlapping semantic spaces in contrast to a continuous series of evolutionary stages.

Ethnicity and History

With these last few remarks on history we have come back to the general problem of establishing ethnicities. We have seen how in the Icelandic case, identity was first stored in action. Later, when the "experiment" had turned into shared experience, the identity became stored in a common history and in a name. It was at this point that the identity became an ethnicity in the sense of being based on an explicit identification vis-á-vis others. At a more general level we may sum up the case in the statement that the self-declaring propensity of humanity (Crick 1976: 169) seems to find one of its expressions in the identification of ethnicities.

In the announcement of a separate Icelandic reality, history and language were both formative aspects of the identification, yet belonging to different dimensions. The linguistic declaration of separateness was a statement of identification belonging to a spatial dimension, in that it punctuated a linguistic continuity appertaining to the Nordic countries as a whole. New conceptual boundaries were thereby introduced in this larger sociogeographical space. As for the historical definition of the Icelanders it worked both in a spatial and in a temporal dimension. It was, therefore, a more inclusive statement of a separate reality than the one made in terms of language. I concede that this must always be the case, even if the identification of a *shared* history is as much a matter of definition as the naming of a particular language may be.

Perhaps we are now in a position to isolate the "idea of history" (cf. Collingwood 1946) as the ultimate prerequisite of ethnicity. Whether the history actually referred to as "shared" in a particular ethnic identification covers a shorter or longer period in time is of less moment; what matters is that an idea of a shared history exists. Without it, an ethnicity cannot be declared, even if at another level ethnicity may still be just a way of speaking of political relations.

If by this statement we give back ethnicity to history, we certainly also give back history to the people, because we take our point of departure in the people's own conception of their history. We do so for good anthropological reasons. As pointed out by Wendy James in a discussion of great relevance for my proposition: "indigenous tradition represents in some degree a *whole* point of view of the past, based on historical experience and a particular cultural representation of it" (James 1977: 129). Thus, it is by way of taking native concepts of history into consideration that we may remain faithful to our holistic claims, also as far as the dimension of time is concerned. This also applies to the establishing of ethnicities as bounded wholes extending in both time and space.

With this view of history we end up by seeing it as a string of more or less disconnected, discontinuous and yet overlapping semantic spaces located both in time and in geographical space. I propose that we use the term "state" to speak of such spaces.[19] With this notion we are in a field of associations, where we can easily conceive of both the synchronic and the diachronic dimensions.[20] What is more, we are sure that our object (that is the "state") is defined with due reference to semantic properties. As I see it, the Icelandic "Freestate" is such a state, in relation to which the particular events taking place in the period gain meaning.[21]

Among the events taking place during the Freestate was the making of the inhabitants of Iceland a "people". Through this the society became an ethnicity, by definition – their own as well as ours. It is at this point that the ethnic classification makes the empirical and the theoretical bounding of the relevant whole merge, "relevance" measured in relation to social experience and to semantic analysis, respectively. Thus it is with the aid of the Icelanders themselves, or any other people for that matter, that we are able to establish a particular "state", meaningful to both the people and the anthropologist.

Acknowledgements

In writing this paper I have once again come to realize my great intellectual debts to Edwin Ardener of the Oxford Institute of Social Anthropology, who supervised my graduate research.

Thanks are also owed to Jan Ovesen who made useful comments on a preliminary draft of this paper.

Notes

1. The main body of work is found in Hastrup (1979a); for more special issues I refer to Hastrup (1979b, 1980, 1981a, b, c). As far as my general position is concerned I may refer to Hastrup (1978), and to Hastrup and Ovesen (1980).
2. For a general account of the Viking expansion, see for instance Foote and Wilson (1970), Sawyer (1962), or Jones (1964, 1968).
3. The "Book of settlements" or *Landnámabók* has appeared in several editions. I here refer to the edition of Jakob Benediktsson, in *Íslenzk fornrit*, Vol. I, 1968. For a survey of the relationship between the various rescensions transmitted see for instance Rafnsson (1974).
4. The actual number of settlers is hard to determine as it has to be established by inference from secondary figures. Thus estimates vary from 20,000 to 70,000, with most of them clustering around 40,000.

   As for the Norse origin of the settlers this is probably statistically quite true for the most part, but there is certainly also an element of "over-communication" of a particular cultural heritage built into this. The influence from the Celtic fringe of the British Isles should not be underestimated, especially not as it appears in even some of the more important themes of old Icelandic culture.

5. The slightly anomalous kinship system in Medieval Iceland has been discussed by Barlau (1981), Rich (1976, 1980), Merrill (1964), and by myself in Hastrup (1979a, 1981b). Compare also Meinhard (1975).
6. For an outline of Norse mythology, see for instance Dumézil (1959; trans. 1973), Holtsmark 1970. For an analysis of cosmology and mythology I refer to Meletinskij (1973) and Hastrup (1981b).
7. This will be well known from the notion of "Danelaw", for instance, and from the ancient proverb *meth lög skal land byggja,* "with law shall the country be built", or even ". . . made inhabitable", which opens most Scandinavian laws transmitted from the early Middle Ages. The notion of law-as-society has received fuller treatment in Hastrup (1979a), and has also been dealt with in (1981b). This is in its "anthropological" consequences. The references to this concept in history and philology are numerous.
8. It is a matter of some dispute whether the quarter *things* were ever actually established as separate *things.* But they certainly existed through their distinct court functions, even if at the Althing site. The quarter courts had to settle cases that involved people from two or more Spring *things* within the quarter. The courts operated on the basis of a "segmentary" principle.
9. This concept of hierarchy derives from Dumont (1966).
10. Our knowledge of all this stems from the transmitted body of laws, collected in *Grágás.* Grágás was first edited and published by Finsen in 1852 (IA, IB), 1879 (II), and 1883 (III). They were reprinted in 1974 by Odense University Press.
11. By the refinement of the constitution in 965, the number of *gothar* was actually enlarged from 36 to 39, because of the establishment of an extra Spring *thing* in the northern quarter. However, in the present context, we may leave it at the neat duodecimal system, on which the first constitution was based.
12. For a relevant discussion of this with direct bearing to the anthropological study of changes at various levels, see Ardener (1973).
13. This idea of a people made up by naming, in contrast to a population which is made up by numbering, is owed to Ardener (1974, 1975).
14. *Islendingabók* (ed.) Jakob Benediktsson, 1968.
15. *Den Fφrste Grammatiske Afhandling,* Dahlerup and Jónsson. eds. 1886. In the text it is referred to as FGT.
16. See also Haugen (1976: 197, 242-3).
17. Perhaps it ought to be said here, that once a particular people had been defined through naming, it could also be "defined out". That is, in a way, the semantic "drawback" of the definitional propensity.
   In the case of Icelanders this actually came to happen, when in 1262 they were "redefined" as (again) the inhabitants of a particular Norwegian province.
18. See for instance Wilden (1972: passim) for a discussion of "goal-seeking".
19. In order to situate the concept of state in a larger context it may be useful

to compare it to another recent suggestion. In an attempt to reformulate the theory of social evolution, Friedman and Rowlands define what they call "stages" in this evolution, as sections of a continuous transformational process in which a particular social form dominates material reproduction (Friedman and Rowlands 1977: 267). In contrast to the neat series of analytically identifiable stages in a continuous process, the string of states which in my view constitutes history, builds up a discontinuous picture of more or less inclusive (in terms of both time and space) wholes, which are defined as much by reference to semantic properties (that is with a view to an internal, or indigenous, conception of the whole). It is this dual definition (analytical and empirical) which makes me believe that the analytical results of the semantic approach display a higher degree of "historicity" than in the case of the evolutionary theory, even if both approaches are attempts to come to grips with the dimension of history.

20. These terms are here used in a direct Saussurean sense (Saussure 1916). See also Ardener (1971).

21. Actually, we have now reached the point where the notion of Freestate gains additional meaning. In itself it is a rather anachronistic term, being a nineteenth century Danish construct (*fristat*) invented by national liberalists. Yet, no contemporary term exists for this society, save for the indirect reference to it in the notion of *vár lög,* "our law". (cf. Note 7). Today the Icelandic term used is *thjothveldith,* which perhaps is best translated as the "commonwealth". For the reason just indicated, I prefer the notion of Freestate, however.

Also it was with reference to the Freestate, as the original 'free' state, that the Icelanders of the nineteenth century created a nationalist movement, leading to the attainment of sovereignty in 1918; until then Iceland had been under Danish supremacy since 1380, when Denmark seized Norway, and, with it, Iceland. (see Hastrup 1981d). This not only makes the notion of "Freestate" even more pertinent, it also adds to our discussion of the position of history in ethnic identification.

References

Ardener, Edwin 1971. Social anthropology and the historicity of historical linguistics. In *Social Anthropology and Language.* (ed.) E. Ardener. (Ass. social Anthrop. Monogr. **10**). London: Tavistock.

—— 1973. Some outstanding problems in the analysis of events. In *Yearbook of Symbolic Anthropology I.* (ed.) E. Schwimmer. London: Hurst.

—— 1974. Social anthropology and population. In *Population and its Problems: A plain man's guide* (ed.) H. B. Parry. Oxford: Clarendon Press.

—— 1975. Language, ethnicity, and population. In *Studies in Social Anthropology. Essays in Memory of E. E. Evans-Pritchard* (eds) J. Beattie & G. Wenhordt. Oxford: Clarendon Press.

Barlau, Stephen 1981. Old Icelandic kinship terminology: An anomaly. *Ethnology* **20**, 3.

Beck, Sam & John Cole (eds) 1981. *Ethnicity and Nationalism in South-eastern Europe*. Papers on European and Mediterranean Societies 14. Amsterdam: Anthropologisch-Sociologisch Centrum.

Collingwood, R. G. 1946. *The Idea of History*. Oxford: University Press.

Crick, Malcolm 1976. *Explorations in Language and Meaning: Towards a Semantic Anthropology*. London: Malaby Press.

Dumézil, Georges 1959. *Gods of the Ancient Norsemen* (trans.) E. Haugen. Berkeley (1973): University of California Press.

Dumont, Louis 1966. *Homo Hierarchicus. The Caste System and its Implications*. (trans.) M. Sainsbury. London (1970): Weidenfeld & Nicolson.

FGT Den første og anden grammatiske afhandling. Udg. V. Dahlerup & F. Jónsson. København 1866: Samfund til Udgivelse af gammel nordisk Litteratur.

Foote, Peter 1977. Oral and literary tradition in early Scandinavian law: Aspects of a problem. In *Oral Tradition, Literary Tradition. A Symposium* (eds) H. Bekker-Nielsen *et al*. Odense: University Press.

Foote, Peter & David Wilson 1970. *The Viking Achievement. The Society and Culture of Early Medieval Scandinavia*. London: Sidgwick & Jackson.

Friedman, Jonathan & Michael Rowlands 1977. Notes towards an epigenetic model of the evolution of "civilization". In *The Evolution of Social Systems*. (eds) J. Friedman & M. Rowlands. London: Duckworth.

Gal, Susan 1981. Language and ethnicity in Austria: Correlational vs. Interactional Approaches. *Ethnicity and Nationalism in Southeastern Europe* (eds) S. Beck & J. Cole. Papers on European and Mediterranean Societies 14. Amsterdam: Anthropologisch-Sociologisch Centrum.

Grágás. Islaendernes Lovbog i Fristatens Tid. Udg. V. Finsen, 1852, 1879, 1883. Reprinted 1974: Odense University Press.

Hanson, Allan 1975. *Meaning in Culture*. London: Routledge & Kegan Paul.

Hart, H. 1961. *The Concept of Law*. Oxford: Clarendon Press.

Hastrup, Kirsten 1978. The post-structuralist position of social anthropology. In *Yearbook of Symbolic Anthropology I* (ed.) E. Schwimmer. London: Hurst.

—— 1979a. *Cultural Classification and History: With Special Reference to Mediaeval Iceland*. Unpublished D Phil Thesis, Oxford University 1979. (Forthcoming).

—— 1979b. Classification and demography in medieval Iceland. *Ethnos* **44**, 3-4.

—— 1980. The social anthropology of a medieval society. The Icelandic Freestate A.D. 930-1262. Paper presented at Nordisk Forskerkursus on Historical Anthropology, Copenhagen 1980.

—— 1981a. Between history and anthropology. Paper presented to The Swedish Association of Historians, April 1981.

—— 1981b. Cosmology and society in medieval Iceland. A social anthropological perspective on world-view. *Ethnologia Scandinavica*.

—— 1981c. Kinship in medieval Iceland. *Folk* **23**.

—— 1981d. Creating a nation. Nationalist trends in 18th and 19th century Iceland. Paper presented at IUEAS Intercongress, Amsterdam, April 1981.

Hastrup, Kirsten & Jan Ovesen 1980. *Etnografisk grundbog*. Copenhagen: Gyldendal.

Haugen, Einar 1976. *The Scandinavian Languages. An Introduction to their History*. London: Faber & Faber.

Holtsmark, Anne 1970. *Norrøn Mytologi. Tro og Myter i Vikingetiden*. Oslo: Det Norske Samlaget.

Islendingabók. Jakob Benediktsson (ed.) 1968. *Islenzk Fornrit* 1. Reykjavik.

James, Wendy 1977. The Funj Mystique: Approaches to a Problem of Sudan History. In *Text and Context. The Social Anthropology of Tradition* (ed.) R. K. Jain. Assoc. Social Anthrop. Essays in Social Anthropology 2. Philadelphia: Institute for the Study of Human Issues.

Jones, Gwyn 1964. *The North Atlantic Saga*. London: Oxford University Press.

―――― 1968. *A History of the Vikings*. London: Oxford University Press.

Landnámabók. Jakob Benediktsson (ed.) 1968. *Islenzk Fornrit* 1. Reykjavik.

Meinhard, H. H. 1975. The patrilineal principle in early teutonic kinship. In *Studies in Social Anthropology. Essays in Memory of E. E. Evans-Pritchard* (eds) J. Beattie & G. Lienhardt. Oxford: Clarendon Press.

Meletinskij, E. 1973. Scandinavian mythology as a system. *J. Symbolic Anthrop.* 1 & 2.

Merrill, R. T. 1964. Notes on Icelandic kinship terminology. *Amer. Anthropologist* 66, 867-872.

Rafnsson, Sveinbjorn 1974. *Studier i Landnámabók*. Lund: Bibliotheca Historica Lundensis.

Rich, George 1976. Changing Icelandic kinship. *Ethnology* 15.

―――― 1980. Kinship and friendship in Iceland. *Ethnology* 19.

Saussure, Ferdinand de 1916. *Course in General Linguistics*. (trans.) W. Baskin. London (1974): Fontana/Collins.

Sawyer, P. H. 1962. *The Age of the Vikings*. London: Edward Arnold.

Southwold, Martin 1978. Definition and its problems in social anthropology In *Yearbook of Symbolic Anthropology* (ed.) E. Schwimmer. London: Hurst.

Turville-Petre, Gabriel 1953. *Origins of Icelandic Literature*. Oxford (1975): Clarendon Press.

Ullmann, Stephen 1962. *Semantics. An Introduction to the Science of Meaning*. Oxford (1972): Basil Blackwell.

Wilden, Anthony 1972. *System and Structure. Essays in Communication and Exchange*. London: Tavistock.

SEMASIOLOGY

A Semantic Anthropological View of Human Movements and Actions

DRID WILLIAMS

Introduction

The term "semasiology" (see Williams 1976) is used as a label for certain new procedures and methods in the study of human movement[1], some of which are outlined (others only alluded to) in this paper.[2] The term also implies certain assumptions about the nature of human beings: that they are rule-following, role-creating, meaning-makers. Older definitions of humanity, i.e. "tool-maker", "imperial animal", "fallen angel", "weapon-maker", "political animal" and the like lead to different styles of analysis and ultimately, to different conclusions. The assumptions made about humanity by semasiologists are encoded in the definition of the word "action" as it is used in our theoretical context.[3]

Culture and Human Movement

Chapman rightly observes that where we recognise a need for the translation of unintelligible foreign spoken languages, body languages are not granted the same status: "Translation will not be thought necessary" (*infra*: 134). Semasiology begins from the premiss that translation *is* necessary; that human body languages, i.e. the semantic uses of the body and the spaces in which it moves, have largely eluded us, for a start, because movement has been a nonliterate medium of human expression. Our theory of human actions is tied into a transcription system (see Williams 1977), some examples of which appear in this writing.

The introduction of written texts into the study of human

movement is a subject that merits examination on its own, but it will suffice to say here that transcriptions of actions pushes Geertz' notion of "thick description" to its limits – and perhaps beyond. This is due to the fact that in transcribing actions, one specifies what is being transcribed in different ways than are apparent on examination of transcriptions of vocal acts. In this paper, as in all of our researches, the same status is accorded to transcriptions of bodily acts as to vocal acts: we begin by recognizing that both speak*ing* and mov*ing* are non-material phenomena.

In fact, like the concept of human "culture", human movement is not itself a material phenomenon. Human movement is a cognitive and semantic organization of a material phenomenon: the human body (or bodies) in a four-dimensional space/time. Just as there is a sense in which "culture" can be seen as a cognitive, and ultimately meaningful, organization of material phenomena and the external environment, so human actions in any of their manifestations are cognitive, and ultimately meaningful, organizations of bodies and the structured spaces in which they move.

Act*ing*, like danc*ing*, or mov*ing*, is essentially the termination, through actions, of a certain kind of symbolic transformation of human experience (see Williams 1972). Where the more familiar terminal symbols of speech are expressed in words, sentences and paragraphs, the less familiar terminal symbols of movement are expressed in action signs, action utterances and an impressive variety of structured systems of meaning that include deaf-signing, dances, martial arts, liturgies, ceremonies of all kinds, manual counting systems, systems of greeting and many others. We merely reiterate an anthropological truism when we say that from the outset, we are considering a global array of human body languages; an astonishing variety of systems.

There is *intra*-cultural variation as well as *inter*-cultural variation such that some comprehension of the sociolinguistic facts of these constitutes an important first step towards a semasiological understanding of human movement.[4] If the "code" of the body language is not understood, then the empirically perceived "messages" will be misunderstood (see Pouwer 1973: 1-13). To facilitate understanding of what human movement *is*, we must recognize the non-material conceptual boundaries that are placed on it, and this is why we require rather elaborate theoretical and methodological means whereby we can assure ourselves, and others, that our analytical re-descriptions are both accurate and truthful.

One of the consequences of our interest in *variation* among human body languages is the idea that systems of body languages are *not* unitary phenomena. That is, they cannot adequately be described by only one set of organizing principles, although at a structural meta-level, we can postulate certain invariant features of (a) the body, (b) the space in which it moves, and (c) certain transitive and intransitive features of an hierarchy of human choice, such that we can say that there are elements of these body languages that are in complementary distribution in the world, and so do not, *at this level*, conflict with one another.[5]

Our method(s) of approaching the vast field of human movement studies consists, not of a unitary descriptive "grid" into which we force highly variant cultural data. Rather, we aim to encourage the point of view that "unity" will perhaps emerge from seeing the ordered relations between variants and contexts. This is possible only if one sees "variety", including sometimes incompatible ideologies and beliefs perceived in the systems "on the ground", not as deviations from an assumed "norm", but as manifestations of intricate sets of *rules* that, at base, can be seen to reiterate a linguistic truism: the medium (in this case, movement) is the message.

"Unitary descriptions", then, will usually be produced by semasiologists — by anthropologists of human movement. It is social anthropology, like theoretical physics and other sciences, that can produce semasiological accounts of body languages as "unitary phenomena" governed, say, by the law of hierarchical motility or the structure of interacting dualisms (see Williams 1976: 214). Ecology, theology and ethology also produce unitary descriptions, but ours are not like these. We do not, as anthropologists, offer a meta-theoretical level of explanation that consists of motivational, behavioural or religious explanation of what human movement consists.

In fact, each individual user of a body language may have a unique, personalized, model of what his or her movement experiences and manifestations consist. Each user may or may not be cognizant, even of other models of actions held by other members of other cultures far less his or her own. But, it is just here that neo-Durkheimian preoccupations with the relation between individual and society become important. They are important to us as trained investigators insofar as they are couched in the Saussurian notion that in separating (body) language from moving, acting, dancing, we are at the same time separating (1) what is social from what is individual and (2) what is essential from what is more or less accessory or accidental, "Body language", as we conceive of it, is not a function of the individual mover, actor or dancer: it is a primary social fact.

Whilst it is true that many "movers", like most speakers, behave *as if* only a limited number of ways of acting exist, this does not alter the fact that it is the semasiologist who, as a result of discipline and training, plus a far greater than average visual and spatial awareness, is able to transcend these particular models; who is able, in a clear and elegant manner, to describe and explain to others of what these systems consist.

The "theory" here is not so much, then, a "theory of movement" comparable, say, to kinesiological theories about measurements of latent kinetic energy and muscular movements, as it is a "theory of culturally and semantically laden actions" couched in theories of various idioms of dancing, singing, liturgy, greeting systems, martial arts and such. It is in some sense more rightly understood as a "theory of descriptions" of these phenomena (see Williams 1982). Part (and only part) of what we mean by "description" is the writing of the actions in Laban script, of which a few minor examples appear in this paper.

At the simplest level of our enquiries, we start by asking, "how would the people of some other culture or the users of some other body language expect me to behave if I were a member of that culture or wanted to use their body language?" We ask this because we believe that to explicate the rules of the body language of "x" is to provide a few beginning answers to that question and at the same time lay the groundwork for a low-level "theory" of that body language. Because we advocate a self-critical style of anthropological study, we constantly compare the rules of "x" with the known rules of our own idioms, thus the knowledge that emerges is of a basically reflexive nature.

It is thus that the description of the rules of "x" body language (dance, signing system or what-you-will) itself constitutes a "theory" of that culture or of some part of a culture, because it represents *the conceptual model of organization* used for the body language of that culture. We "validate" our theories by our increased abilities to anticipate successfully how "x" people would expect us to behave if we were members of that culture, and we can, if challenged, provide "validation" on other, more recondite levels as well.

It is an axiom of semasiology that the medium of movement in the human realm is as profoundly rule-based as is the medium of sound as it is used in human speech.

Meaningful Rules

I draw attention, for example, to the significance of permutational analysis (Williams 1981: 214-217) by pointing to the finite character of the expressive possibilities of movements of the human body: the semasiological body itself is thus conceived of as a system. Constraints on this system's capacity to move are considered important because it is just here that the semasiological definition of "rule" begins: at the level of "meta-rules" where we comprehend the laws and principles of movement that are paradigmatic to the whole expressive bodily system. Given the numerical potential that actually exists (Williams 1981: 215), we know that no human system of body language exhausts, through usage or in practice, all of the potential of which that system is capable.

At an observational level, we know that a body language, or any subset thereof, will have a grammar of positional elements and movement elements that are used over and over in a variety of ways that identify it as that particular body language (or "code") and no other. It will have rules for deletion, inclusion and spatial manipulation that are distinctive features of it as an identifiable idiom of structured, meaningful movements.

The body language will also have rules for combining elements from the smallest "emic" units (see Kaeppler 1972 & 1978) or "motifs" into larger and larger combinatory units.[7] Movement sequences also have rules for conjoining and embedding phrases into larger sequences. It may be that ". . . it is the rules themselves that define just what [a body language] is . . ." (Myers 1981: 263). We know that the locally Euclidean space wherein all human movement takes place is rule-bound (see Durr & Farnell to 1981). The structures and semantics of human actions are irrevocably connected (see Puri 1981a). Without the rule-bound, language-like characteristics of human actions, communications on a non-vocalized level[8] would be a tedious business indeed. Without rules (even if the rules are the absence of rules), we would be reduced to a kindergarten "show and tell" level of comprehension in our daily affairs that would impede our activities and understanding greatly — or else "action" and "ritual" semiotics would be confined to the confused state of affairs described over a decade ago by Ardener (1971: xliii-xlv).

All social anthropologists understand the interdependence of linguistic, social and movement elements in the human domain: we offer nothing "new" with reference to our preoccupations, surely, but we do offer new methods of conceiving of, reconstituting and interpreting movement data. Our understanding of the facts, grounds and consequences of this interdependence is not simply "intuitive". Perhaps this was anticipated by Sapir who said:

Gestures are hard to classify and it is difficult to make a conscious separation between that in gesture which is merely of individual origin and that which is referable to the habits of a group as a whole . . . we respond to gestures with an extreme alterness and, one might almost say, in accordance with an elaborate and secret code that is written nowhere, known by none, and understood by all (1949: 556).

One would prefer to change the word "understood" in the Sapirian formulation to "used by all" because one doubts that the "unwritten codes" and rules of body languages are even vaguely understood by many. There is a sense in which it is the so far successful attempts to "crack the codes" that justifies semasiology's existence.

Social-Theoretical Issues

In the theoretical and methodological world of semasiology, we do not hold the assumption that better knowledge of the semantically void fields of physics and kinesiology of human movement, rather than of the sematically-loaded, intentional, reflexive, rule-bound nature of movement is going to permit a more humanistic — or "scientific" — analysis of human actions. Whilst we recognize various levels of rules, starting from our meta-level of structures of interacting dualisms, of the degrees of freedom of the semasiological body and all the rest (see Williams 1976: parts I and II), we see human actions as they exist on an empirical level as structured, semantic spaces (closely akin to the "moral spaces" of Crick (1976: 113-115)). These spaces exhibit all of the features of unpredictability, teleology, transaction and obligation that characterize human domains.

Semasiology postulates certain *structural* invariants with reference to the human body and the physical spaces in which it moves (and our analytic re-descriptions are informed by a model of mathematical degrees of freedom of the body, enabling us to do legitimate cross-cultural comparisons), but we do not, because of this, fall into what we think of as the "determinists' trap". That is to say that our "meta-rules", "transformational rules" and the like do not project us — or the rest of humanity — into a positivistic, behaviouralist universe where human actions are seen simply as necessary responses to external stimuli. Nor do we see semantically dense spaces solely as the results of "social forces" that are external to individual decisions.

To treat human actions as instances of manifestations of known structural laws of the expressive human body-instrument is *not* to treat *all human conduct* as instances of ill-defined "laws" of human society or conventions, and this point can hardly be over-stressed. Semasiology does not teach that all human *conduct* is determined by a "structure of interacting dualisms" or by the degrees of freedom of the semasiological body: it does affirm the idea that all human conduct and actions are generated out of a finite field of movement possibilities. To postulate universality of structure does not, in our view, simultaneously provide evidence that all human actions — far less human "nature" — is alike, or that human freedom is non-existent.

Our preoccupation with questions like these stems from our deep concern over what "the dance" and "ritual" consists of. If human beings are creatures driven totally or even partially by external stimuli, then "ritual" consists of actions that are no more likely to attain *human* ends than any other action we might think of. On the other hand, if human beings are creatures who, given their unique natures, powers and capacities, have the freedom to choose activities, obligations, responsibilities and such in a basically unpredictable universe, then ritual consists of freely assumed obligations to attain specific ends and they are not therefore strictly equatable with "habitual", routinized actions. To put matters in brutally simple terms, we ask, "can brushing one's teeth and attending a religious or political ceremony be classified equally as 'ritual' actions?"

Synonymy and the Semantics of Movement

The ultimate goal of semasiology is to explain how sequences of a body language are matched with their correct interpretations by the users of that body language, be it the Dominican post-Tridentine Mass, the Indian *hasta-mudra* system, North American Indian sign languages, social dancing, deaf signing systems or any other movement system. Like many other social scientific goals, this one has yet to be achieved. The significance of our program at New York University in the Social Anthropology of Human Movement certainly finds one of its foci here, and we have made some inroads with research that is presently in hand.[9]

Seen from an international perspective, questions that seem to have been answered by semasiology's predecessor's[10] turned out, in the end, to have more questions (and yet more profound questions) lurking behind them. One of the basic concepts that badly wants investigation, for example, is that of synonymy in body languages. To say that two different sequences of body language or even two gestures from different codes "have the same meaning" is to claim that they are synonymous, or that they in some sense "paraphrase" one another. Great carelessness has been exhibited in the usage of these concepts regarding body languages.

For example, a true case of synonymy would be as shown in Fig. 1. Clear examples of this kind are relatively hard to come by. If

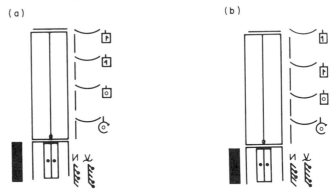

Fig. 1   (a) Catholic sign of the cross. (b) Orthodox sign of the cross.

other examples are considered, say, the act of kneeling (see Fig. 2) the answer has to be preceded by the phrase "it depends", which is

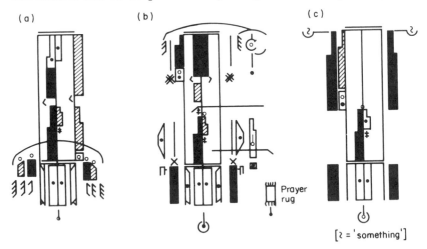

Fig. 2   (a) Genuflection; (b) Muslim "raka"; (c) woman in garden.

an immediate indication of semasiological trouble. Kinologically,[11] the actions appear to be the same: the general posture of "kneeling" is involved in all three actions, but the gross physical move by itself (like the repetitions of raw sounds in the words "tottered" and "rotted") do not themselves explain the semantic variations. Nor, I think, can we imagine that to invoke the term "context" is enough — useful though the term may be.

With reference to the three texts of "kneeling" for a start, the act of kneeling is, to most Muslims and Christians, a religious act. Kneeling in a garden is not, although it might be. Perhaps one kneels in that context to pull weeds, to gather melons or berries or to retrieve a dropped tool. Even in a religious context, kneeling has been part of the Muslim ritual since *ca* 610 A.D. The genuflection in Roman Catholicism was a sixteenth century innovation. Standing, not kneeling, was the posture of prayer before that, and standing is still the posture of faith in Orthodox Christianity.

Is "kneeling", therefore, a functional act, a religious act, or an act that connotes subservience, humiliation, or (as when someone is knighted) a posture that is assumed where a singular social honour is bestowed? Then, too, there are the vast differences that exist between an ethological and a semasiological view that must, I think, also be considered here: the question is often asked "what is the connection between, say, 'submission gestures' of primates or wolves and human liturgical actions such as genuflections?" Semasiologists would answer "none" to that, but there are a variety of unresolved philosophical and theoretical issues at stake here.

Crick rightly insists that we use the term "person category" and that we include the notion of "personhood" in our conceptions of status, rank and social class (1976: 115-118). He argues the case with reference to witches, but the fact remains that in the human domain, no category of person exists in isolation from others. To identify human actions like "genuflection" with the "submission behaviour" of animals thus invites an insidious form of deterministic thinking into our discourse via an almost un-noticed series of reductions; from "status" to "person" and from "person" to "animal". The meta-theoretical implications of this point of view have been ably spelled out in Varela (1982), in a critique of the phenomenological point of view regarding human movement (see Sheets 1981).

This kind of conceptual confusion is intolerable in semasiology and raises a point that is generally overlooked: in some way we seem to disambiguate the signals of animals *for them* in their systems of behaviours, but we do this *reflexively for ourselves*. That is, we seem to assume that animals are transparent, whilst we are opaque. We do not assume that we are transparent for the good reason that we are language-users, hence what we *see* of others (or ourselves) is not by any means obvious, nor can meanings of human actions always be inferred from observable acts.

After all, for a human being, doing nothing at all can be a semantic act, as is apparent in published research on an Anglo-Saxon counting system (Williams 1977). In that system, as in many others, body members which are not moved are often of equal significance as are those that *do* move. The point is that the epistemology of human actions and animal behaviours is entirely different. We disambiguate animals' signals for them precisely because our own reflexivity is based upon orders of logical complexity and an hierarchy of powers.

There are several arguments that can be invoked (see Williams 1975: iii-ix; Crick 1976: 100-108), but one would want to say, briefly, that repetitive gestures in the Dominican (or any other) religious rite are not "natural repetitions", as one could fairly assume that so-called "submission behaviour" among primates is "natural", i.e. biologically triggered. One can make these assertions with confidence because "submission", like "authority", "genuflection" and such, are human, linguistically-based concepts that are connected with ideologies and *conceptions of* actions. Thus, it is false to say that "people genuflecting" or "people kneeling" is somehow ethological, but that *why* they kneel or *how* they kneel is linguistic. Being a social anthropologist, I cannot favour an argument for lexicon as against system, just as I cannot separate the linguistic from the social. The facts of how it is that liturgical actions, gestures, and the like are named make such arbitrary separations spurious in my view. The additional problem (more serious than is credited) that certain components of primate behaviour have been named "submission gestures" by human investigators render these expressions in the animal context to a realm of rather woolly metaphor.

Spatial Referents

It will be useful now to turn to another triad of actions, shown in Fig. 3. These actions would all be classified in English as "bows". The stretch written for the T'ai Chi Master occurs at the beginning of the short form of the exercise. The stretch written for the Catholic celebrant is *inclinatio profunda sacerdote et ministris* from the Dominican liturgy. The third stretch is a move made by the Red Knight in the ballet Checkmate. The very spaces in which these three agents manifest (or exteriorize) their long, complicated sequences of actions is not the same. The spaces in which these three agents operate are discrete spaces; in other words, there exists a conceptually organized spatial orientation (a "p-structure"[12]) that is paradigmatic to the empirically perceivable movements in each, and we must be explicit about this.

In Fig. 3 it is critical that the T'ai Chi Master's system of spatial

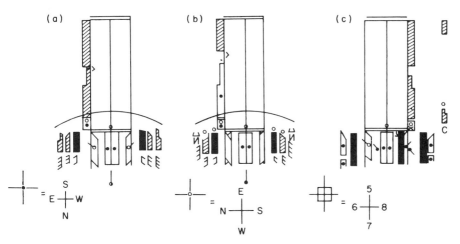

Fig. 3 (a) T'ai Chi; (b) Missa Major; (c) Checkmate

referents is designated (-ϙ-) (the spatial "key" sign), which tells us that it is a *standard* frame of referents, because the celebrant's, (-ϙ-), is a *fixed* point frame, whilst the dancer's is a *constant* frame of referents, i.e. (⊕) (see Durr & Farnell for a thorough explanation of these spatial constructs). The canonical coordinate space of T'ai Chi Ch'uan is based on the fact that "All directions in this system, whether they apply to the body instrument space or to the displacement space in which the body moves are given in terms of the directions of a compass . . . thus, (-ϙ-) corresponds in original Chinese usage to the (geographical directions of south = front (in front of), west = right (to the right of), north = behind (in back of) and east = left (to the left of) . . ." (Williams 1975: 112, Vol. II).

There is a different arrangement of spatial elements in the Dominican rite, where the liturgical space is "embedded" in the geographical space and is orientated towards the high altar, such that the direction "east" (corresponding to the high altar) is a fixed focal point. "West" is opposite to the altar, and right and left correspond to the Gospel and Epistle sides of the altar respectively (see Williams 1978 for a thorough discussion).

The Dominican Mass is based on two axes of oppositions of front/back and right/left in the semantic space, in contrast to the Chinese system, which is based on a clockwise movement *around* the perimeter of the directions, as on a compass. The ballet dancer's space is neither directly associated with the directions of the compass, nor is it based on an hierarchical set of directions: the canonical directional set in this case is determined by a schema that originated with the Maestro Cecchetti a little before the turn of the century (see Beaumont & Idzikowski 1922/1940: 220) and has been used by ballet dancers since then whether on stage or in classrooms.

Clearly, the semantic differences or similarities in the examples so far given relate to specific *kinesemes* of movement[13] : to the structures of the *whole body* gestures or postures and their combinations. There are different kinds of problems involved in longer kinesemic stretches. For example, relations that may seem to involve the same movements, but that convey different metaphorical or metonymic emphases, or whether the agent is *acting* or being *acted upon*, whether the referential features of the moves are personal or extrapersonal and so on.[14] Should there remain any doubts about the intricacies − or the crucial semantic characteristics − of spatial referents in human structured systems of actions, the reader is referred to Puri (1981) for a discussion of polsemy and homonymy with reference to body language.

Ardener's distinction between a "programme" and a syntagmatic stretch of manifest actions is surely apposite to the relation between the conceptual space(s) of agent(s) and their observable movements. From the evidence so far presented, it can be seen that the kinesemes of "bows" written in Fig. 3 are not synonymous: they neither "paraphrase" one another, nor do they "have the same meanings" as do the pair of gestures in Fig. 1. The difficulty is, of course, that where we presuppose a *real* level of "language" with regard to speaking, we do *not* tend to presuppose a level of "language" or anything remotely resembling that with regard to dancing, signing, the martial arts, liturgies or the great variety of ordinary structured systems of non-vocalized meaning to be found in the world.

No Concept of Language

There are many forms of dancing throughout the world that are roughly equivalent to what in our culture we call "social" or "ballroom" dancing. These have countless times been explained in terms of the function of "mate-hunting". Fair enough. But semasiologists would want to point out that there are many forms of *spoken* languages that are also used for the purposes of "mate-hunting". In either case, the notion of "mate-hunting" is merely *a minor and specific use of the medium of movement* − or the medium of sound, as the case may be. No one, of course, would attempt to characterize the whole of, say, the English language in terms of its minor and specific usages for "mate-hunting", yet over and over again, we encounter examples of body languages characterized in terms of minor and specific usages of the medium of movement.

The whole area of movement studies and, indeed, any concept of human action in any of its aspects is simply vitiated; rendered meaningless by generalizations that stem from comparatively limited notions about specific and minor usages of the medium of human movement. Worse yet, in this domain of human action, we are usually somewhat less than conscious victims of our own categories, definitions and models of the role of movement in human societies. We divide bodily actions (but not speech actions) into "symbolic" and "instrumental" categories (Ardener 1973). In particular we are betrayed by our received ideas of what a "scientific" or "sociological" explanation of what human actions consist.

David Best (1978) summarizes the rather depressing picture very well:[15]

reflexivity, intentionality, agency, language, meaning, semantics, teleology

---

causation, stimulus-response theory, behaviourism, "objectivity", value-free scientific explanation

If we let "X" stand for all that is above the double line, and "Y" stand for all that is below the lines, then we seem to expect that we will find "causes" for X in the realm of Y, with the result that all human actions are collapsed into gross physical movements and treated as if they were the same. Semasiology rejects this, or any similar view, on the grounds that traditionally acceptable paradigms of scientific method and explanation are conceptually and logically inadequate to handle the semantics of human spaces. We believe that ". . . no adequate scientific account of human action in its various spatial frameworks can ignore its profoundly semantic qualities" (Crick 1976: 101).

The actions of the human semasiological body are value-laden; meanings are arbitrary and culturally assigned. Human beings are not only the passive receptors of "role-takeovers"; they are *role-takers*, and it may be of significance to note in passing that so far, semasiologists are highly accomplished dancers — or they are professionally trained in signing, the martial arts or other forms of non-vocalized forms of communication. They bring to social anthropology the kinds of developed notions of body languages about which I have tried to speak because there is a sense in which they are "native informants" in these areas who are becoming anthropologists. Would it not be unusual if they did not protest at ethological and/or sociological explanations of their lives and activities as undifferentiated "behaviours" of some kind?

They are offered the banalities of "submission behaviour",

"smiling", "work movements", "greeting gestures" and the like, if not wider generalizations such as "birth", "death", "pleasure", "pain" — all of which involve sets of gestures or stretches of "behaviour" that are loosely tied together simply because there are features of the human anatomy that are "species specific" and therefore *must* be the "same".

They seem to be asked by other theoretical approaches to the study of human movement to ignore spatial designata and the features of human agency to which attention has been drawn here, with the result that the mysteries (or mystifications) of the world's religions, the complexities of the world's dances and body languages and much else belonging to the realm of human action is transferred to the commonplaces of nature, sans Philosophy, sans History, sans Mathematics, and above all — sans Language — and the irrevocable connections that body languages have with the human faculty for language-use.

The "facts of nature" are universal, but if the facts of language-use and the facts of human spatio-linguistic fields are removed from the facts of nature in the human case, there remains very little of interest to be said about them. What can be said along these lines has been adequately treated in the fields of physiology, kinesiology, sociology, experimental psychology, sometimes with tedious repetition. There is very little of interest, to us at least, about human actions looked upon as "non-verbal" behaviour (see Note 8).

The Notion of "Rules" Again

It needs to be said that we do not claim to study something that other anthropologists have not thought of or that they have never been interested in: we simply offer new ways of reconstituting and interpreting data of this kind. We are interested in the constructs that are formed in accordance with systems of spatial and general "gestural" relevance, and we look upon "ethnographies" of these systems in terms of (1) the development of texts for body languages and (2) upon ethnography in general as a rather complicated process of theory-building that is carried out in co-operation with native informants, whether those informants are members of our own ethnicity or of another.

Human knowledge of the world comes to us through many channels and many mediums. Our first topographic knowledge of our many personalized worlds consists of a kind of spatial exploration of our own bodies and its limitations, then our immediate environment and its limitations. Gradually, we are introduced into the vernaculars of everyday body languages and their conventions. We learn to define ourselves and others as much through the syntactical structures and "grammars" of events as we do through speech, beginning with "standing", "walking", "sitting", "crawling" and all the rest. At the same time that we learn these and a mind-boggling variety of other actions, locations and spatial referents (referred to in semasiology as the deictic[16] categories and coordinates of our worlds), we learn the *local systems of relevances* that are typical of our language and cultural setting: we learn the orientational metaphors that organize whole systems of actions with respect to one another — and most of these have to do with spatial orientation. We learn the obligations, freedoms, choices and constraints that constitute our moral and semantic spaces.

As human children, from the moment of our births, we enter into a world of structured spaces, of linguistic and deictic categories, into concepts of legitimacy, illegitimacy, conceptual fields, ideologies and all the rest. The human child is both an actual and a potential player in an unbelievably intricate set of language games that involve both speech and actions — and both are learned. During this process, we learn that some kinds of rules can be meaningless, just as we learn that "mistakes", "prevarication", "mishaps" and such are a part of the human condition. All of this represents a certain level of rules, and these rules are important. However, semasiology postulates a level of meta-rules; those that outlive all events, and from this level we would want to say that whilst there can be meaningless rules in human semantic spaces "on the ground" so to speak, there can be no meaning (or meaninglessness) at all without rules.[17]

In this short paper, I have briefly illustrated through the concept of synonymy and through limited ethnographic evidence, some of the diversities and complexities involved in a few "emic" examples of human body language games. I have done little except to point to the ethnographic materials that I and my colleagues possess, but felt that it would be pointless to try to extend the "fieldwork" aspects of semasiological research any further here, preferring to answer some of the many challenges that have been thrown our way over the past three years with more general statements of the theoretical position from which our conception of human body language begins.

We provide equally powerful arguments for a different approach to the study of human movement in social anthropology — one that is designed to go beyond the limitations of traditional scientific approaches to the field. Semasiology will only fully justify its existence and meet the challenges of its rival theories, of course, by the growth of evidence presented by those who have understood and accepted the premises of its explanatory paradigm. However, even with the relatively small amount of work so far produced, we have not crumpled under the accumulated weight of many years of work that has been produced using different methods and different definitions of humanity.

Semasiology itself is, therefore, an example of an attempt to break certain kinds of rules and to aid in the establishment of a new and different consensus of what "rules" consist in our field of study. A major point that we would like our critics to remember as they reflect on our proposals is that the rules of human actions with which we are concerned are precisely "paradigmatic". Indeed, they are intrinsic to the human body instrument and to the displacement space in which it moves *as an integrated system* and we never lose sight of this. Thus, the transitive rules of the kind we deal with can only be changed — they cannot be "broken". And without the particular brand of rules that we call "intransitive structures", we would be obliged to move our researches to another planet — one without gravity, where creatures had Janus-like bodies and Cyclopean eyesight, perhaps?

Notes

1. In the literature of functional anthropology, ritual and the dance were conceived of as "special" forms of human actions. Furthermore, they have often been defined as systems of actions related to "mystical ideas and beliefs". Whether or not the dance and ritual actions should be classified as "special" or not is one problem. That they are irrevocably bound up with conceptual systems and ideologies is obvious. It would not be difficult to defend the proposition that the terms "dance", "ritual", "idea" and "belief" are synonomous in important ways, if (and only if) "dance" and "ritual" are thought of in human "person" terms. And they are not usually thought of in this way; metaphorical usages of both terms indicate the opposite. In the case of the alleged "dances" of birds, bees and primates, for example, the terms are employed to mean biologically rooted, organized animal behaviours of an instinctive, impulsive kind, when, for instance, the creatures are defending a territory, attracting a mate, and the like. If these organized behaviours are "performances" in a human sense, then why do they never take place out of season, and on what ideas and concepts are they based? Where are the creatures' accounts of them?

2. Additional discussion occurs in the *Journal for the Anthropological Study of Human Movement (JASHM)* at New York University. There are in existence so far five issues; the sixth is in preparation. The Journal is produced by members of the Society for the Anthropological Study of Human

Movement, also at New York University. The special issue referred to in the text is Vol. I, No. 4, Autumn, 1981.

3. The rather broad, ambiguous term "movement" is, for a start, separated into two fields, i.e. "behaviours" which are taken to imply mechanical, causal accounts of movements that are appropriate when agency is either absent, or in a human being, destroyed temporarily or permanently. "Actions" are, by contrast, taken to be movements or comprehensive sets of movements that *have* agency, that is, intentions, language-use, meanings, rules. Thus, there are organisms and/or animals that "behave" and there are animals which can monitor their behaviour on an elementary or first-order level in terms of their movements. However, human beings are conceived of here as *agents* whose actions reflect an hierarchy of powers. That is to say that human actions are couched in a system consisting of reflexivity, simply stated as people possessing the power to be conscious of being conscious of being conscious — and so on. From a semasiological point of view, then, we may say that animals "live" or "exist" but human beings *have conceptions of* living or existing and because of this they "act". They do not merely "behave". It follows that "to act" is to be able to have models of "behaving". For further discussion on the term "behaviour", see Ardener 1973. For differences between the sciences of ethology and anthropology, see Callan 1970.

4. These considerations lead to questions like "do human beings live, in reality, in continuous spaces and continuous times?" There are only a limited number of formal possibilities available (cf. Harré 1970: 184) (metrics); 1970: 246-7 (event and duration); 1970: 286-93 (continuity of time);

    a) continuous space/continuous time
    b) discrete space/discrete time
    c) continuous space/discrete time
    d) discrete space/continuous time

There are two separate questions involved here: one is a philosophical question which, although discussable, is far from anthropological or physical science concerns — that is the general question of whether space/time is *by nature* continuous or discontinuous. The anthropological question in hand is the more pragmatic problem of the association of numbers with length and duration — a problem immediately perceivable in the use of a transcription system for movement. "Time" in other words, is so often "spatialized" in a specious sense. Adequate discussion would require more space than is available, but it is important to note the profound level of issues that is being addressed.

5. See Williams 1975 and 1979 for definitive explanations of "action signs" and their relation to the concept of "linguistic signs".

6. The standard work on this system is Hutchinson (1970; second edn).

7. The major exponent of an "emic-etic" approach to the study of human movement and the dance is the American anthropologist, Adrienne Kaeppler. Only two of her many valuable contributions are listed here

(1972 and 1978) and it would be inappropriate to attempt a facile definition of the approach she uses. Suffice it to say that like a "semiotic
approach", the term "emic-etic" indicates a general linguistic-anthropolo-
gical school of thought regarding the study of culture not designed to
handle movement *per se*. Kaeppler is, however, a spokesman for the
American ethno-scientific approach to human movement studies and
"units" of movement in that context are explicitly handled in Kaeppler
(1972).

The "motif-morphology" of units of movement are thoroughly discussed
in Kurti (1980), as they exist in the Hungarian school of dance "folkloristics", in a system for dealing directly with movement that was originated
by Molnar (1947). Major contemporary exponents of this highly developed
east European school of thought are Martin & Pesovar (1961), who
propound a type of "structural analysis" that does not deal with the
semantic content of the dances. "On the whole, it is more akin to phonological analysis in linguistics and in fact can be seen to derive from
traditional descriptive linguistics . . ." (Kurti 1980: 45).

8.   The term "non-vocal" rather than "non-verbal" is used here for reasons that
are made more explicit later. Among some movement specialists, the term
"non-verbal" is now used as if it were semantically neutral, but we cannot
assent to this because of the many positivistic and behaviouralist overtones
that are suggested.

9.   Research in hand includes the transcription, into Labanotation, of American
Sign Language and an analysis of these composite signs compared with
written texts in finger-spelling, alphabet forms. Comparative textual analysis
of deaf-signing with the *hasta-mudra* system is in progress as is the development of a phrase-structure grammar for the idiom of ballet dancing. Some
interest exists in the general notion of the conversion of scripts and of the
morphology of action sign material that is implied in the usage of English
verbs.

10.   Semasiology's predecessors include (a) kinesics: Birdwhistell, 1970; (b)
proxemics: Hall, 1966a and b; (c) standard kinesiological approaches,
exemplified by Fitt (1979), Vaughn (1981), Vinje-Morpurgo (1979) and
Smith (1975); (d) standard behaviouristic approaches, exemplified by
Argyle (1970) and Argyle & Graham (1975); (e) ethological approaches,
exemplified by Hewes (1955) and Peng (1975); (f) statistical approaches,
exemplified by Lomas *et al*. criticized in Williams (1974). We have mentioned above the "emic-etic" style of analysis used by Kaeppler, and the
East European school of dance folkloristics and hold these, plus the work of
Stokoe (1980), Kurath (1960) and Keali'inohomoku (1972 and 1980) to
be of particular significance. Two exponents of "dance anthropology"
are Hanna (1979) and Royce (1977).

11.   Kinology, in our context refers to different kinds of analysis that are
done for different purposes, but a kinological study is so designated because
it always means one thing: it is semantically null. That is, for whatever
purposes, the *meanings* of movements can be disregarded temporarily for a
specific analytical purpose. An example of one kind of kinological approach

is that used by Myers (1981), where the meanings of moves are disregarded for the purpose of uncovering certain grammatical and syntactical features of the American Foxtrot.

12. It is difficult not to use one's technical terminology, especially when it has been designed to disambiguate methodological confusion. However, I have tried to exercise great restraint in this paper. Suffice it to say, therefore, that in semasiological analysis, we use a sophisticated array of "p-structural" and "P-structural" formulations that are essential to our analyses of highly complex material and that the usage of the term here merely points to, but in no way develops the concept. One usage is, however, outlined in Ardener 1980; that of p/s structural analysis.

13. A "kineseme" roughly corresponds to a "morpheme" as used in linguistics, and its denotative characteristics are no more strictly defined, or definable. The one criteria that must be met is that a kineseme can never be less than a whole body position. Expressions of bodily parts are called "kinemes". By no means a satisfactory explanation, for this short paper, the notion of parts/whole and kineme/kineseme may be associated.

14. See Williams 1980: 119-122 for elements of spatial deixis in the idiom of ballet French.

15. This particular formulation (somewhat expanded) was used by Best in a seminar for SASHM (The Society for the Anthropological Study of Human Movement) in January, 1981. His book *Philosophy and Human Movement* was reviewed in *Ethnomusicology* (Williams 1980), and is a distinct and positive influence on semasiological theory and practice, since the work stems from a general position of language philosophy.

16. "The notion of deixis (which is merely the Greek word for 'pointing' or 'indicating' — it has become a technical term of grammatical theory) is introduced to handle the 'orientational' features of language which are relative to time and place of utterance" (Lyons 1968: 275).

    The term seemed particularly apt for many specific elements of human body languages. In our context, the concept is used mainly for features of direction, location, orientation and force.

17. This is not to say, of course, that "knowing" simply consists of rule acquisition, but that in "learning" looked at as a process, rule-acquisition is built into the process insofar as human actions are concerned. It follows from our construal of human beings as members of a self-defining species, because of their semantic powers, that any discipline concerned with the study of human activity considered as inherently meaningful must be concerned with the rule-bound actions of persons in a shared moral (ethical or semantic) space. Although the point may seem obvious, because it is how we *really* think about people and interact with them, it seems that in many of the social sciences, there exist attempts to avoid the issue of meaning and there are many who try to steer clear of the problems involved. See Bhaskar 1975: 240ff for a discussion of reductionism and underdevelopment in the social sciences.

180   *Drid Williams*

References

Ardener, E. W. 1971. Introductory Essay in *Social Anthropology and Language.* London: Tavistock.
—— 1973. Behaviour: A Social Anthropological Ciriticism, *JASO* 4(3) 153-155.
Argyle, M. 1970. The communication of inferior and superior attitudes by verbal and non-verbal signals. *Br. J. Social Clinical Psychol.* 9, 222-231.
—— and Graham, J. A. 1975. A Cross-Cultural Study of the Communication of Extra-Verbal Meaning by Gestures. *J. Human Movement Studies* New York: 33-39.
Best, D. 1978. *Philosophy and Human Movement.* Allen & Unwin.
Beaumont, C. 1940. *A Manual of Classical Theatrical Dancing* (acc. to the method of Cav. Enrico Cecchetti). (with Idzikowski, I.) London: Beaumont.
Bhaskar, R. 1975. *A Realist Theory of Science.* Leeds Books.
Birdwhistell, R. 1970. *Kinesics and Context. Essays on Body Motion Communication.* Philadelphia: University of Pennsylvania Press.
Callan, H. 1970. *Ethology and Society: Towards an Anthropological View.* Oxford: Clarendon Press.
Chapman, M. 1983. " 'Semantics' and the 'Celt' ". In this volume.
Crick, M. 1976. *Towards A Semantic Anthropology. Explorations in Language and Meaning.* London: Malaby.
Durr, D. and Farnell, B. 1981. Spatial orientation and the notion of constant oppositions. *JASHM.* 11.
Fitt, S. 1979. The use of observation techniques for the identification of neuromuscular excitation techniques. Dance Research Annual X, pp. 157-172, *CORD,* N. Y. University.
Hall, E. T. 1966a. *The Silent Language.* Garden City: Doubleday & Co.
—— 1966b. *The Hidden Dimension.* Garden City: Doubleday & Co.
Hanna, J. 1979. *To Dance is Human: A Theory of Nonverbal Communication.* Austin, Texas: University of Texas Press.
Harré, R. 1970. *Principles of Scientific Thinking.* London: Macmillan.
Hewes, G. 1955. World distribution of certain postural habits. *American Anthropologist* 57, 231-244.
Kaeppler, A. 1972. Method and theory in analyzing dance structure with an analysis of Tongan dance. *Ethnomusicology* 16(2), 173-217.
—— 1978. Dance in anthropological perspective. *Ann. Rev. Anthrop.* 7, 31-49.
Keali'inohomoku, J. W. 1972. Dance culture as a microcosm of holistic culture. New Directions in Dance Research: Anthropology and Dance – The American Indian. *CORD Research Annual* 6, 245-60.
—— 1980. An anthropologist looks at ballet as a form of ethnic dance. *JASHM* 1 (2), 83-97, reprinted from *Impulse,* 1970.
Kurath, G. 1960. Panorama of dance ethnology. *Current Anthropology* 1(3), 233-54.
Kurti, L. 1980. The structure of hungarian dance: A linguistic approach. *JASHM* 1 (1) Spring Term, N.Y. University, pp. 45-62.

Martin, G. and Pesovar, E. 1961. Structural analysis of Hungarian folk dance. *Acta Ethnographica*, 1-40.

Molnar, I. 1947. *Magyar Tanchagyományok* (Hungarian Dance Traditions) Budapest: Magyar Elet.

Myers 1981. A phrase-structural analysis of the foxtrot, with transformational rules. *JASHM* 1 (4) N.Y. University.

Peng, F. C. C. (ed.) 1978. *Sign Language and Language Acquisition in Man and Ape*: New Dimensions in Comparative Pedo-Linguistics. (For AAAS.) Boulder, Colorado: Westview Press.

Pouwer, J. 1973. Signification and fieldwork. *J. Symbolic Anthrop.* (1) July. The Hague: Mouton.

Puri, R. 1981a. Review of Morris, Collett, *et al. Gestures: Their Origin and Distribution. JASHM* 1, (3) Spring Term, N. Y. University.

―――― 1981b. Polysemy and Homonymy, and the Mudra "Shikara": Multiple Meaning and the Use of Gesture. *JASHM* 1 (4) Autumn, N. Y. University.

Royce, A. 1977. *The Anthropology of Dance*. Bloomington: University of Indiana Press.

Sapir, E. 1949. Communication. In *Selected Writings of E. Sapir in Language, Culture and Personality* (ed.) Mandelbaum. Berkeley: University of California Press, pp. 533-543.

Schieffelin, E. L. 1976. *The Sorrow of the Lonely and the Burning of the Dancers*. New York: St Martins Press.

Sheets, M. 1981. Thinking in movement. *J. Aesthetics and Art Criticism* **39** (4), 399-407.

Stokoe, W. 1980. Sign language structure. *Ann. Rev. Anthrop.* **1**, 365-90.

Varela, C. 1982. Cartesianism revisited: the chost in the moving machine, Review of Sheets, M., cited above. *JASHM* 2 (2) Autumn, N. Y. University.

Vinje- Morpurgo, A. 1979. Towards a scientific explication of synesthetic phenomena through kinesthetic stimulation. *CORD Dance Research Annual* **10**, pp. 31-38. N. Y. University.

Williams, D. 1972. Signs, symptoms and symbols. *JASO* 3 (1).

―――― 1974. Review of Lomax, A. *et al., Choreometrics*, in *CORD* News 6(2) 25-29.

―――― 1975. The role of movement in selected symbolic systems. DPhil Thesis, Oxford University, 3 Vols.

―――― 1976. Deep structures of the dance. *J. Human Movement Studies* **2**, 123-44; **3**, 155-181 (Parts I and II).

―――― 1977. The arms and hands, with special reference to an anglo-saxon sign system. *Semiotica* **21**-1/2.

―――― 1978. Sacred spaces: a preliminary enquiry into the Dominican High Mass. Publication forthcoming by the Sumner Institute of Linguistics, University of Texas, Austin.

―――― 1979. The human action sign and semasiology. *Dance Research Annual* **10, CORD**, N. Y. University.

―――― 1980. Taxonomies of the body, with special reference to the ballet. *JASHM* **1**(1), continued in **1**(2).

―――― 1981. Introductory essay. In *JASHM* (Special Issue "On semasiology") **1**(4) Autumn, N. Y. University.

THE SICK WHO DO NOT SPEAK[1]

BASIL SANSOM

Amongst Aborigines of Darwin fringe camps and the camps of the city's hinterland, each episode of serious illness leaves behind its sign. One way of putting the matter is to say that each recovered patient has a permanent limp or its equivalent. There is ol Luke's hugely swollen belly, so incommoding that he can only sleep sideways on. Then Roger has a facial tic that is the souvenir of a knife wound to the abdomen. Roger also has a nervous propensity: he jerks the back of his hand across his nostrils in times of stress. The hand jerk came of pneumonia. Nancy's sign of illness past is a dietary prohibition – ever since the car accident in which her forearm was injured, she has been unable to eat either the potato chips or the pies supplied by fast food shops. Humphrey has no fingers on either hand due to the ravages of leprosy while Johnny has a limp which came of a buffalo charge. After suffering a fever, Petey, a small boy, was left with a stutter. An episode of adult illness left Maisie with a squint. Her venereal problems intensified problems with eye-focus that the campers admit to her suffering in milder form from childhood times. However, it was after the course of big injections that the swivelling of Maisie's right eye became almost uncontrollable. And so on through the camps of a region in which hardly an adult is innocent of some patent and permanent debility that his or her fellows trace to an episode of illness past.

I have written this paper to show why in Darwin and the Aboriginal hinterland, each sickness must leave its sign. My argument is that such signs are essential to the creation and perpetuation of relationships of long-term indebtedness amongst a community of people who have no property but rely instead on verbal warranties (called "the word") to carry indebtedness over from the past into the present and so to transform local fields or networks of social relationships by locating obligations of enduring indebtedness within them.

Dealing with the souvenirs of illness in Darwin fringe camps, I am led to consider the creation of value amongst people whose investments are neither in things nor in impersonal institutions, but contained in relationships with associates. Investment in relationships as such requires particular communicative work if debt is to be established, obligation recognized and if past favours are to be answered with due recompense. By such work the resources for registration of debt have to be created and then the cultural forms for the mobilization of resources must also be supplied. My task will then be to contextualize Aboriginal souvenirs of illness within a system of communication in which rules that govern talking about sick people frame processes by which debts that arise out of episodes of illness are endowed with relevancy in the long term.

The first rule that I address is a stricture on the representation of events. Expressed in Aboriginal English, this imperative dictates that "you caan tell about that time you bin sick". So the recovered patient is denied what most speakers of standard English treat as a pleasure – the opportunity to rejoice with friends in one's own recovery by telling what it was like to be in hospital and to be treated by Mr Smith that notable surgeon of the ever successful lobotomy. The "caan tell" rule of the camps has, however, further and positive consequences. As I shall show, it demands that the recovered patient yield up a slice of biographical life. The bit of historical self that is taken away becomes someone else's holding, the property of another. The "sickness story" as a bit of property can then serve its owner who by the fact of ownership is ceded a lien on the person of the one-time patient.

Tommy Atkins' Cough

I came fully to appreciate the force of the "caan tell" rule and the significance of the souvenirs that illness leaves behind after some three months of fieldwork in the camps. It took this much time to qualify myself for the experience. The point is that the rules that I discuss have no relevance for the outsider and the stranger. They belong to the world of inter-subjectivity that is constructed only by consociates and until one has become part of that world, the information purveyed or withheld in terms of its prevailing rules is simply no part of one's business. And people do not tell the rules as rules "for no reason", keeping them instead to necessary moments for their application.

In the progression of fieldwork, a new order of information was vouchsafed me after I had been around long enough to establish a firm and service proven relationship of "mateship" with Tommy Atkins who was to remain my sponsor and mentor in the camps. When it all happened, the time was a general time of trouble. Tommy Atkins faced legal proceedings and the early morning incident that I shall now recount occurred as I, in company with others, waited for Tommy Atkins to get up so that we could get on with the job of the day which was to straighten out Tommy's police business. Tommy Atkins emerged from his blanket and went over towards a stand pipe to wash. As he went he was racked by a graveyard cough and having thus described it to myself, I was impelled to remark it. I asked if Tommy had had the cough for long, whether he'd taken it to the doctor and whether my companions did not share with me in alarm. I was told "not to worry for that cough" but to worry instead for "that police business". Everyone knew that cough and everybody knew all about it too. However, neither Tommy Atkins nor anyone else in camp was free to tell me just why the cough needed no medical attention. However, Big Bill was said to be coming up to town. He'd been sent for because Tommy was in trouble and when he came Big Bill would be told off to give me that coughing story. When he did I'd understand. Meanwhile, not to worry.

Big Bill did not arrive in town till five further days had passed. During this interim I was told and told again in public that Big Bill would have something for me. There was, then, a good deal of witnessing and affirmation to the effect that everyone agreed that I would be taken into Big Bill's story. By round the group "telling round" — a procedure I have analysed elsewhere (Sansom 1980: 115-118) and labelled broadcasting — the camp was set up to anticipate a telling.

Before telling what I was told when Big Bill did come up, let me return to the morning of the coughing to note in passing how, while being promised one story at a future date, I was instantly given another. As if to fill the time of waiting, ol Luke said that it was about time that I got told about that River poisoning business. People agreed. Given licence thus, ol Luke related how five people had died down on the River after having mistaken a tin of strychnine for a tin of flour. He went on to point the significance of the story noting that I knew that River mob and also knew that he (ol Luke) had run with members of that mob and, for a time, had been married into it. Surely I must have wondered about that mob — not enough "ol fellas" and pensioners in it! Demography apart, the mob was

"funny" in other ways that maybe I'd noticed. A story was then un-
folded to show how present group anomalies make sense to those
who qualify to command the privileged information of accredited
local history. Such stories are given and told "for reason" to people
who have shown by consociate involvement that they reasonably
need to know them. Command of a privileged history puts one's
relationships with members of the River mob on a different footing.
Once given the tale one also finds people averting to it unabashedly
both in conversations conducted in one's hearing and in remarks
directed to one. With a proper sense of audience, one can also use
the tale, not telling it but referring to it and employing it as a
metaphor when making sense of current happenings and dispositions.
I asked about a cough and received a promise. Note also that
tangentially I was ceremoniously made party to the mob-poisoning
story. (Let me say, however, that a sickness story is not like a story
of mob disaster. The first belongs to a person's history, the second is
a legend of group destiny. The transmission and ownership of group
history is governed by one set of rules, the ownership and telling of
biography by another).

Big Bill finally arrived and at once wanted details of the police
business with which Tommy Atkins was dealing. He was told to
"wait for that detail" because there was something else more urgent
to attend to. "That Basil" had been waiting on a promise "for days
n days". Bill was told its terms and straight away he took me across
town to collect Drover Thomas for a witness. Returning to the home
camp, Big Bill, the Drover and I stopped at the camp edge to go into
a private huddle for the telling.

Tommy Atkins' cough said Bill, was due to strychnine. Years ago
down on the droving trail Big Bill, Tommy Atkins and four named
others set out to collect a mob of cattle to herd over towards
Tennant Creek. When night fell, they camped at a site near a billa-
bong. Other campers had been there before them and the previous
occupants had left behind some strong quart size tin cans, empty
and very shiny. Tommy Atkins said that was good. He twisted
fencing wire to give one of the tins a handle and so turn it into a
billycan. He set water to boil as did the others. On the fire the new
can kept company with five soot-encrusted billies. After drinking
his tea, Tommy was seized with convulsions. As Big Bill explained,
the tin had been used by men who were after the dingo bounty. It
had held poison for making dingo baits.

The remainder of this story is a consummately detailed accounting
of the rescue of Tommy Atkins. Everyone did the right thing — made
Tommy vomit, kept him warm, tied him to a horse, transported him

to the doctor – and he got to the doctor in time. The patient apart, Big Bill is the only one of the surviving actors in this piece who are still people relevant to the group of Countrymen for whom the Darwin hinterland is a stamping ground. The other men of the original droving party are either dead or living far away and beyond ken. Drover Thomas, however, was peripherally involved in the event. He was present at Adelaide River when Tommy Atkins was brought in to be given over into medical care. So the Drover saw the patient in his state of "very danger" and was a member of a local community of concern made up of people who "worried for" Tommy Atkins until he was declared to be not "really sick" any more – i.e. well along the road to recovery. When a recovered Tommy Atkins returned to the camps, people watched him. They sought to divine what change the ordeal had wrought in him. As Tommy Atkins moved about the countryside, watchers noted the early morning cough and pointedly remarked it in one encampment after another. They thus made *times*; "That time, mornin time, we bin see that Tommy coughin, coughin, coughin". When the story reached this point in the telling we broke out of our huddle. Big Bill led me and Drover Thomas round the camp in the business of "checkin up la detail". We canvassed a population made up of people in the camp who had been party to the aftermath of the Atkins ordeal, those who had known Tommy as a recently discharged patient. The task of each was to attest, circumstantially and with particulars about place and the composition of camps, to his or her historical registration of the cough. In this way, Big Bill re-enacted a business of remarking and telling round that, years back, had caused the cough to be added to the common store of officially recognized consociate knowledge. In that store, the cough together with its aetiology had the status of an agreed determination. The still prevailing consensus is that Tommy Atkins' cough is his souvenir of strychnine poisoning.

Stories about illness are thus stories told by heroes. As stories which only the heroes themselves can tell, they are to be regarded as properties. Their value is that they serve as warrants and, as warrants, are used to back claims to a special order of relationship. The one-time patient is indissolubly linked to that person or set of persons who helped him through his trouble. Grounded in shared experience of trouble, the relationship is asymmetrical, rooted in an act in which the helper rendered up the boon of life-saving service to a person passive and on the threshold between life and death. The link that joins Tommy Atkins to Big Bill belongs to a special order of irredeemable debt. As the countrymen explain, there are debts, even debts as serious as those incurred through homicide, that people can pay off to be declared "clear" of obligation. However, the debt between patient and caring helper lasts for as long as they both shall live. When mortuary rites are performed, there is a general clearing of those who in life were linked to the dead person and debts of illness are amongst those that in these rites are put to rest. Ideologically the Aborigines I know refer all debts between carers and patients to this final accounting when, as they say, "everythin bin finish up". Debts begotten of illness are imbued with meaning that comes of their origins. So let me attend to illness and the relationship between sick person and carer during the bracketed time of the patient's crisis.

To experience a sickness worth the name is, of course, to go through a passage: to progress out of health into the liminality of the sick bed and then, the powers permitting, to be incorporated into everyday living once again. The onset of sickness is marked by public recognition, a marking of the moment when the sick person becomes just that. Moving on from these firm platitudes of routine interpretation, I have now to characterize sickness as experienced in an Aboriginal encampment as sickness that is at once expropriated from the patient and wholly appropriated to a community made up of current camp inhabitants. While the status of the sick person is obviously transformed, the point I seek to emphasize is perhaps not quite so much a familiar of medical anthropology.

"Community of suffering" is Turner's (1970) phrase and was established by him to define the set of regular co-participants in rites of affliction amongst Ndembu in Central Africa. Borrowed and turned to my purpose, the phrase refers not in a lasting long-term sense to a community of neighbours who live together over years in a rural vicinage, but to the short-lived and time-bounded aggregation that is the current "mob" of an Aboriginal encampment. The mob of an encampment will become a community of suffering for as long as it has a sick person for its focus. So I am promoting the notion that as well as being a passage for the patient, the time of that patient's sickness is also a time of passage for a social aggregation − the members of a mob. For the time of the sickness on which a mob's attention becomes focussed, all those who were made party to the initial recognition of the sickness are constrained to enter a phase of existence defined by rules that prescribe the modes of conduct proper to emergencies. For the duration of the sickness, all members of a whole mob become party to the "trouble" that is "sickness business". The observer thus witnesses a transition in which the focal person becomes patient, while the grouping about that person is itself reconstituted to become for the requisite period a community of suffering. Put summarily, the time of a community of suffering is, for those who make it up, a time of constraints when:

1) a freeze is put on decamping moves unless a person can show that his/her continuing presence would be positively unhelpful, i.e. an actual hindrance;
2) all present are obliged to exhibit concern ("worry for sickfella") and are further obliged to offer up any goods or talents they command in service of the crisis;
3) all present are obliged to become "properly witness for" the sick person's progress and so share wholly in the registered "details" of the experience;
4) all present share the responsibility to work to call up appropriate others who (because they are "close up" in degree of relationship to the sick person) should be brought to the event;
5) Finally and overridingly, an obligation falls on the collectivity: proper treatment of the sick person is to be secured.

In the event of sickness, each member of the original community of suffering together with every close up person who arrives later to be added to it is on trial for the duration of the emergency. The business will be brought to a conclusion in a recounting. Out of the experience of the illness of a fellow, people emerge not only credited as heroic stars or helpful supporters whose acts of caring will be celebrated whenever stories of sickness are told and retold. There is also blame. The unhelpful who did not do enough, and the derelict who denied themselves to the event will be charged with either the mistaken action of unhelpfulness or the wrong of abrogation.

Because the recognition of sickness entails the formation of a community of suffering, an aggregation of people bound to the progress of an illness, there is in the camps a very clear divide between two kinds of physical disorder. In local conceptions, sickness is, so to speak, either "on" or "not on". There is no sliding scale for the assessment of degrees of seriousness when it comes to diagnosis. So the root word "sick" together with all its derivatives is reserved to the life-endangering state of morbidity in formulations such as : "This mob got very danger. That fella ol Bill he really sick". But to be somewhat afflicted is, in contrast, to be "a bit crook". And if someone heretofore adjudged to be "crook" shows signs of progressing towards that moment when life is verily endangered, the possibility of the person's shift is contemplated in a way that makes of such shifts the transition of an instant — a leap out of being "crook" and into "that very danger". One can confer about

someone who is "crook" and showing signs that, after all, his in-
disposition could be serious: "You think that fella gonna sick?"

I have now worked in two very different places in which comuni-
ties of suffering in my special time-bound sense of this phrase are
formed in response to illness. Among the Druze of Mount Lebanon
there is the same focussed commitment of a group of concern for
as long as a sickness lasts. And like the people of the Darwin camps,
Druze distinguish two orders of morbidity. For being truly sick
they use the standard category word of Arabic that non-Druze
Arabic-speakers use for all illness, mild or severe.

Merrith there applies only to the sicknesses of community
concern, while any lesser complaint is dismissingly relegated and
called *shey besiita* – which translates as "a little thing", an incon-
sequential. The similiarities go further. While on the side of true
sickness there is community concern, either Druze with *besiita*
problems or Northern Aborigines who declare themselves to be
"a bit crook" are compellingly constrained not to ask for public
sympathy when experiencing the discomfort of an illness that does
not take its victim into the extremity of danger. Communication of
facts about minor suffering belongs then only to confidential
exchanges between intimates. A required stoicism concerning minor
maladies and afflictions is the consequence of the total involvement
of consociate communities in events of sickness that truly deserve
attention and evoke the community of suffering or grouping of
concern.

The Sick Who do not Speak

I began this account by remarking souvenirs of illness, went on to
deal with the "caan tell" rule that gives a person's past sickness away
into the possession of a carer and then took time to define the
mob around a sick person as an aggregation that is wholly caught
up in a patient's trouble and so made over into a community of
suffering that endures for its time. My final bit of reporting has to
do again with a rule that governs utterance. This is the "sickfella
caan talkin" rule and it denies the person deemed to be truly sick
any capacity to yield up a volitional statement.

From time to time linguists use the contrast between patient and
agent to deal in comparative terms with relationships that in native
English grammar would be described in terms of subject and object.
In the North Australian camps, the "sickfella caan talkin" rule
finally objectifies the sufferer who has gone into "very danger".
Patients are snatched out of the world of inter-subjective under-

standings to become patients — that is, human beings who will have to endure objectification for the period of their suffering. This objectification begins with diagnosis. It is a relegation to impotence, based not on enunciated complaining, but grounded instead in the ability of unaffected third parties to read signs. Those who progress into sickness yield up behavioural items: "That fella doin something really different. He bin long time makin toilet". Or, "That ol Jenny she bin sleepin too much. Sleepin, sleepin, sleepin. We gotta worry for that pensioner. Maybe she gonna stay sleepin. When she gonna gettin up?" The remarking of untoward behavioural signs is the first step in the business of consigning a once-healthy person to a "sickfella" status. Putting cases of accident aside because, in accident, the transformation of actor into injured patient is obvious and immediate, further progress towards sickness in the medical rather than the surgical department involves an intensification in which the registration of queerness quickens in pace and becomes increasingly various in its symptomatology. The rigours of a long strain with diarrhoea are first noted then there is the struggling and deliberate, foot in front of foot pacing of the diarrhoetic who returns from painful evacuation. The next sign is the groan the emptied sufferer emits despite himself as he relaxes onto his blanket. A camper approaches the bed to touch the person whose distress seems to verge on the suffering of true sickness. He diagnoses fever. Announcement of fever brings a few of those people who are beginning to worry to the bed. The sufferer then speaks. This is dismissed as babbling. "That not Long Billy talkin. Thatta sickness talkin."[2] The announcement hangs over an assembled group awaiting further confirmation. Someone touches the patient, turns back an eyelid and reads a further sign: "This fella really sick, you lookim eye!" Members of the company about the bed all look into the eye, exchange glances with one-another and then the most prominent person amongst this grouping of concern sallies forth to announce to all fellow campers: "We got trouble. Really sick." An announcement of this order is a call and campers rally to it. People come up to register for themselves the palpable signs of sickness and to hear from those who witnessed their presentation the recited catalogue of signs whose manifestation preceded and led up to the general announcement. In a camp, people become socially sick when a camping population has been brought to the signs of their debility and when by voiced or indicated motions of assent those present agree in the primary diagnosis.

Here I do not intend to take you through the vicarious experience of any one of those sicknesses I saw diagnosed as such and treated accordingly. Instead, I return to the rules that govern reaction to such instances. Today in the camps, the first concern is to get the now socially accredited sick person to a doctor, whether by ambulance or by exploiting locally available means of transport. This done, obligation is not yet discharged. The camp has been reformed to the shape that is a community of suffering. Camp members will join in the regime that belongs to this formation either until the patient recovers or the camp is summoned to a funeral. For the duration of any period of worry when a truly sick patient is in hospital and not yet out of danger, the social tone in the camp is modulated daily to the bulletins of news that camp delegates bring back from the hospital. One waits with others for the general release, the message that the sick person is out of danger. When the good news comes, those people conjoined in the community of suffering may dissolve it and return to their everyday affairs.

Because patients are generally taken away and so not treated in camps, their times of liminal silence are normally short-lived. The measure of such times is often the interim between crucial diagnosis and the arrival of an ambulance. My own observations are not limited to such brief periods for I have been out-of-town and with mobs when people have been taken ill. Whether brief or more prolonged, the time for whose duration a sick person remains in mob-care is a time when the "sickfella caan talkin" rule is regnant. Any lucid, well-constructed sentence that may be uttered by the sick person is wholly discounted — "That not thatfella talkin, that that sickness talkin."

In the terms of analysis, sickness is for Aborigines an entity. It "grabs" the sufferer, imposing an alien will on the seized person who is unable to supervene to mediate as a volitional person in the competition between self and the entity that has invaded his person. My phrasing is not fanciful. Thus in response to the fevered double-talk of a patient: "Thatfella fightin that sickness. You bin hear: one time maybe ol Max talkin; nother time that sickness talkin." Given such switching between sources of utterance the rule is straightforward: if sick people do utter coherently, such utterances are to be distrusted. There are no developed criteria by which one can truly tell whether the mouthings of a sick person are his own or those of the sickness itself. In culturally prejudiced translation let me say that when they are sick, Aborigines of Northern Australia are possessed by entities that are now designated by English words that label specific maladies — pneumonia, that liver business, TB, malaria and so on. For as long as patients are in their charge, the assembled members of a mob constituted to form a community of suffering are people who disclaim ability to distinguish with certainty between the mouthings that come of sickness and statements that could actually belong to the sick person and "come through" despite possession of the subject's body by an illness. The consequence is that the sick are generally reduced to untalking acquiescence. The sounds that come from the mouths of the sick are all "noise". Nor is "noise" irrelevant for grunt or groan or crying or words or coughs can be discussed by carers. But they are sounds talked about as symptoms and not given the dignity or status of utterances.

Conclusion

Pursuing my main concern which is with issues of indebtedness and the signs of sickness past, I have put a range of things aside. I have neglected those questions that concern medical anthropologists. What illnesses, for instance, are recognized within the constraints of this system in which a symptomatology of crises determines who will be recognized as truly sick? It should be clear that signs of many chronic and possibly life-threatening complaints are censored from general perception by the rules I have described. Let me conclude a limited analysis by referring only to the silence enforced on patients in an encampment and to the "caan tell" rule which deprives a once-sick person of part of his or her biography.

The sick who cannot speak are persons who are defined objectively as individuals who experience the usurpation of the self. In this state, the sick become wholly reliant on concerned others who simply by being there at the time an illness is diagnosed are culturally constrained to work to rescue the victim. The rescue accomplished, the once-sick person enters again into a world of inter-subjective understandings but with a deficit. The recovered patient is perpetually indebted – a bondsman to those who "helped him through". Bondsmanship depends for its definition on the total objectification of the sufferer during sickness which is itself due to an involuntary surrender of will to a usurping entity. A "sickfella" can't help himself but has, instead, to be helped. And the helpers are distinguished after helping: they have in their possession the tale of the happening. Only they can recount how the sick person progressed through an illness to recovery; only they can take credit for enabling the progression out of morbidity and into heath. The "sickfella caan talkin" rule is a correlate of the "caan tell" rule that forbids personal accounts of suffering. There is consistency between the rules for, in the first instance, a sick person is disqualified from uttering because a sickness holds him in possession. In the second, the recovered patient is a person who has experienced an event that belongs to others because for the time of suffering the patient gave up the inter-subjective world, leaving it to helpers. And those helpers henceforth are to be recognized for what they were: the essential mediators who assumed burdens of responsibility and "saw" a person "through" the time of his or her removal into an incoherent world of inner conflict where self and illness vied. In the end, the end of sickness is the return of self. "Thatfella better, he bin come back".

This, then, is my gloss of the logic that underlies the two cited rules of denial. The final task is to account for the ineluctable signs of past suffering. My answer to this problem is straightforwardly expressed. The souvenirs of illness are necessary manifestations. They are held in consciousness not only as reminders of signal service rendered, but also as manifestations to provoke the telling of stories that have past sickness as their theme and the registration of long-lived obligation as their end. Countrymen of the Darwin hinterland live in a world where primacy is given not to prescriptive rules of formal social structure but to rules that govern the presentation and representation of those signal events that determine the constitution of sets of associates – those a person reckons as "close up" Countrymen. And people become "close up Countrymen" because they have shared in experience of things with one-another. The links between close up Countrymen, established and modified in and over time, constitute the structure of actually existing relationships in which each self is located and in terms of which personal identity is established. In this context, the signs of sickness have their analogue in the symbolic wounds of Aboriginal initiation that mark not so much a person's status (as adult or cult initiate) but signal obligation to that set of people who "grabbed" one into a *rite of passage* and saw one through its rigours for a religiously enjoined time of "very danger". In this vein, each cicatrice or scar of initiation has its own story of personalities behind it. It signifies those named others, recalled by their ritual names of ceremony and ceremonial participation, who made the novice party to their rite and gave him its songs to own. Thus people can trace the passage of sacred songs from licensed giver to recipient, X to Y to Z, persons who are then linked through life because they entered together into the forms that frame the stuff of life.

The Countrymen of the Darwin hinterland are people of labile social groupings, the interrupted association that goes with movement between camps and the formation and reformation of camp mobs. While mobs have immediate actuality, the set of close up Countrymen so relevant to each person could be insubstantial because privately conceived as "me real mates" by each individual on his own account and for himself. However, through symbolic wound, the souvenir of sickness and a further neat set of devices that provoke stories of the grounds of and for particular relationships, each person's set of close up Countrymen is substantiated. Their identities are publicized and made real for others in a world made up of the specific understandings that all Countrymen have of one-another. The complex of rules that governs treatment of the sick is thus integral to a social order in which people rely and are known to rely on those named Countrymen whose closeness to a "mate" is reckoned from and out of some remembered occasion — a "time" that was a time of need that was dire or of an obligation that had imperatively to be fulfilled. Stories of happenings about which minister and not magister has the right to tell are stories which came of an "owner's" trouble through which the "helper" saw him. They are the means for realizing as common property an image for each person as that man or woman haloed round by those non-present but reachable others who in defiance of their absence are still reckoned to be "close up". To get at meaning in all this one has to look to stories, to their rightful ownership, to the things that evoke their telling, to the structure of situations in which stories properly may be told and to the procedures that bring witnesses to the telling and so make the "giving" of a story a published fact.

Notes

1. The fieldwork on which this paper is based was carried out during my tenure of a Research Fellowship in the Australian Institute of Aboriginal Studies, Canberra. I would like to thank Dianne Sansom for her helpful comments on an earlier draft.
2. Both the silence of the sick in Aboriginal encampments and the logic by which people deny the sick the capacity to speak as human persons is paralleled amongst the Dinka. As Lienhardt reports, those Dinka patients whose sickness is attributed to a Power are possessed by that Power which is a subject of activity within the victim whose self is its object. "Hence, when a man is strongly possessed, it is held that 'it is no use speaking to *him*', as a human person, for that which is acting is not the man but the Power" (Lienhardt 1961: 148).

References

GETTING TO KNOW YOU

MARTHA B. KENDALL

In the cold season in Mali, when the rains stop and the roads are passable, people travel. They go to visit relatives and friends, to recharge themselves with the energy humans mutually generate after long separations. Or they go to play the games of economics or politics, where the current is both more powerful and more dangerous. Or they go to hunt, to prowl after the elusive. They go on pilgrimages. They move through markets, through cities and villages, through tall brush — alert, concentrating, watchful.

The event I describe here took place in the cold season of 1980, in the market at Kati. Charles Bird (my husband) and I were there with a very famous Maninka musician whom we had known for years. The man was a traditional griot or bard, a lute soloist whose name and musical signature are as familiar to most West Africans as their own national anthems. He was looking for calabashes to make into musical instruments, for this is what he did in the cold season. We were along for the drive. For the hunt.

Our hunt was for experiences, for we were living in Mali at the time, trying to understand its people and their forms of life. We had no notion that anything special would happen at Kati; our being there was simply a question of our friend needing a ride, of us being bored with our work and wanting diversion, and of the urge to travel which came upon us with the cold season. The fact that we did witness something unexpected in the market that day allowed us to reflect on the nature of the social relations in Mali. The fact that I am going to try here to describe the event and my reflections on it allows me to consider what it means to be a semantic anthropologist.

We have just arrived at the Kati market. We park our car at the periphery of the market and enter through the section where vegetables and dried fish are sold. Charles and I are strolling along, looking at piles of tomatoes and commenting to each other about how aesthetically they are arranged when we discover that our friend has abandoned us and is across the market greeting another Maninka elder. The greeting is elaborate and effusive and our friend is delivering it in a voice loud enough to attract attention. Market women are looking up from their produce; customers are turning toward the action, some holding vegetables as if caught in mid-transaction. Our friend seems conscious of the attention, and it appears to animate him further. More eyes are drawn to the scene; more bodies are oriented to the action. Charles and I also feel the magnetism and move to the edge of the collectivity that is forming. With sideways glances both griot and noble acknowledge that they feel the presence of Europeans. Our friend is up to something, and whatever it is, it appears to discomfort the elder being greeted. The man, though clearly embarassed, bears himself as a person of the nobility. He is courteous and graceful and soft-spoken. The griot begins to announce the man's illustrious geneology, reciting the names of his most notable ancestors, exposing him to the awe and the stares of the less well-born. The noble lowers his head, listens, nods, shuffles nervously. Eventually he takes a five hundred franc note (about $1 American) from his pocket and gives it to the griot. He hastens off and the spell is broken. Witnesses return to their buying and selling. Our friend rejoins us, all exicted, holding out the money he has received for us to see. He tells us that the man is from an important noble family whom his own family is profession-ally obligated to praise. (Noble families act as patrons to griot families. The latter are expected to commit the geneologies of the former to their memories, to act as brokers and go-betweens in their marriage arrangements, and to officiate at all the important ceremonies of their lives.) The griot is pleased that he has discovered this noble in the market. He is delighted that he has chanced upon the opportunity to praise him so well and so publicly. He beams proudly and tucks the gift the noble has given him into his pocket. He says that he has enlarged the man's reputation.

The whole episode could not have taken more than two or three minutes on the clock, but the minutes seemed to expand through their unexpectedness and their potential.

My initial reaction was that we had witnessed an example of the gross insincerity and crass exploitiveness of which West African griots are often accused. I had read that griots were manipulative and that they used greetings as a way of pandering to nobles for money. I had heard similar reports from Maninka nobles, and occasionally from Maninka blacksmiths. Up until this moment I cannot say that I had thought of our friend *as a griot*, an instance of a category, but once the category was relevant I began to search my memory for other evidence of "griot duplicity".

I could find nothing that I was willing to attribute specifically to our friend's being a griot. I had known him to gossip, but lots of people gossip. I had known him once to lie, so as to save face in a compromising situation. I have done such things myself. He had approached us for rides, for medicine and for small favours. So had a number of nobles. In short, it occurred to me that I did not understand why griots have the reputation they have, nor did I know what it meant to say that someone was or was not acting "like a griot." I was bound up in a confusion between ideology and practice.

In the most widespread version of West African ideology, the image of griots is remarkably negative. They are claimed to be parasites on the noble class because they siphon off real material wealth in exchange for words and music. They are said to be liers, sychophants, glad-handers. They are seen as cunning and untrustworthy. They are even claimed to have been buried (formerly) in trees so that the earth would not be contaminated with their corpses. Needless to say, this is not the griot's ideology about griots, and, needless to say, they are very sensitive about such characterizations. Still, their own ideology is one which emphasizes their distinctiveness from others.

Griots see themselves as *animators*, as people who fire things up, who ignite others, who inspire change. They call themselves Masters of Words, and the label is not strictly metaphorical. They see words as having *nyama* — translated best as "force" or "power" or "energy" — and they see this *nyama* as having the capacity to transform the universe. They talk of words and music as entering the people's hearts and heating them up. They talk of the ability of words and music to empassion. They see passion as leading to action. Praise-singing, music, reciting geneology are activities designed to re-arrange everyone's force fields. They are activities to jangle things up, to move things along, to bring about change. This is what griots see as distinctive about themselves.

In practice the sharp distinctions griots and non-griots make among themselves blur and fade. The nobles who claim that griots are grasping and manipulative do not seem to notice that real flesh-and-blood griots act no better and no worse than they themselves act in the mundane spheres of work-a-day life. The nobles who claim that a rigid social separation exists between griots and themselves ignore the fact that they have griot friends with whom they share work in their fields. They forget the bonds of affection and genuine good will that tie them to the specific griots they grew up with and so they think of griots in the abstract.

The griots who claim that the ability to control the power of words is theirs exclusively are not thinking of the times that a noble friend commanded their laughter with an impersonation, or captured their imagination with an anecdote, or enthralled them with a story. Griots and nobles in Mali forget their private experiences with one another when you ask them normative questions. They concentrate on the public and the stereotypic, and tell you less than they really know about themselves.

A distinction between public and private behaviour is not one which occurs immediately to Maninkas when you talk to them about their social forms. It is certainly relevant though for understanding how outsiders think about them. Because the episode in the market was a public transaction − or, more accurately, because our friend made it public by involving others in it − it was easy for me to *typify* my friends action as "griot behaviour," taking of course the nobles' perspective. I should point out here that it is very difficult *not* to take the nobles' perspective, because this perspective is the dominant one. In any case it is the one represented in Western scholarship on griots, a point I shall return to later.

To *typify* my friend's behaviour in the Kati market as "griot behaviour" is to understand it in some diminished sense. It is to label, to act as if naming a thing is equivalent to comprehending it. The issue lying behind the label, however, is the nature of the relationship between ideology and practice that gives rise to such typifications. Let me explore this with you by taking you back to the market in Kati once again.

The noble is walking through the market. It is a pleasant day and the market is lively. Suddenly there is a griot upon him − one he recognizes as a very famous musician and one whose family is linked to his own. The man is greeting him and he must of course return the greeting. The griot engages him in conversation, then boosts the volume, attracting a lot of attention. People are looking at them. Staring. The noble feels the eyes of others upon him. He *feels* them. He feels the eyes of that European couple as well. He knows he is trapped and that there is nothing he can do about it. He cannot walk away from the griot; he cannot push him away; he cannot call a policeman to keep the griot from molesting him, because any of these strategies will attract further attention. More stares. The eyes of anonymous strangers. White men.

Nobles are taught from birth to avoid attracting attention to themselves. They are told to dress humbly and behave decorously. They are told to avoid ostentation. They are trained through explicit maxim and through observable example to monitor their behaviour closely. They learn soon enough the practical reasons for this. They learn that the less well born may be envious of their privilege, and they learn that the better off they are — or the better off people *think* they are — the more responsibility for others will fall to them. In Mali, the more you have the more you must suffer others.

Nobles are taught from birth to experience the eyes of others upon them as *shame*. When noble children are scolded, for example, they are warned that other people, people who are not nobles, are watching them. Nobles have both an inchoate set of feelings about what the eyes of others mean (learned through the experience of punishment), and they have a set of practical experiences concerning their responsibilities toward others (learned through interactions with them). Both of these sets of experiences predispose them to want to avoid the public gaze. It goes against the grain. Against the *habitus*.

For the griot, on the other hand, the public gaze is bread-and-butter. Griots are trained from birth to bring the eyes of others to themselves, to use the eyes of others, to attract the public regard. I have seen great griots and griottes bring children and grandchildren with them onto the concert stage, letting the toddlers play there throughout their performance. There is training for life in the lime-light, which is where a griot earns his livelihood. There are solid practical reasons for griots to discourage diffidence in their children, and a number of them recognize this explicitly.

Reflecting on this, I came to understand what nobles mean when they say griots are "shameless." They mean that griots not only do *not* avoid the public gaze; they actually seek out opportunities to experience it. To nobles, whose whole ideology and whole public practice is set against attracting attention, griot public behaviour is indeed repugnant. It is grotesque. Shameless.

When griots do things that make nobles uncomfortable, part of the discomfort they arouse is deliberate and part of it is unintentional. Griots do have strategies that hinge on unsettling people and they frequently profit from doing this (in the sense that they are given gifts or money), but to suggest that they upset people *in order to profit* is to oversimplify. The relationship of griot to noble to gift is much more complex.

This complexity can be illustrated with another reference to our friend in the market. It is true that the griot shamed or embarrassed the noble into giving him a gift and it is true that the gift excited him. It is equally true that this present was quite paltry, considering that the griot could make eighty times that amount playing at a baptism or a wedding. (I mentioned earlier that this man was known well beyond the borders of Mali. He was also, consequently, fairly wealthy.) He did not really *need* five hundred francs.

His evident delight in the gift was not for the thing itself, but for its meaning. The gift meant (to the griot at any rate) that he had "reached" the noble. He had sent his words into the noble's heart and agitated him, in effect creating a state over which the noble had little control. He had fired him up.

Being fired up is dangerous. It is an inherently unsteady state, requiring either passionate action leading to change, or an antidote leading to resolution.

Nobles consider passionate behaviour unseemly for the most part,[2] although they venerate in ideology just those ancestors who acted passionately. The Mande kings and warriors. The men of heroic action. Here then is a source of conflict for real flesh-and-blood nobles. They feel on the one hand that they are supposed to act decorously and deliberately; yet they feel on the other they are supposed to emulate the Mande heroes. Griots deliberately play on such conflicts by reminding nobles that they come from the lineages of their society's great "movers and shakers," and that they have the resources to bring about change, all the while drawing the eyes of others to them, reminding them not to act in any way which could be considered "flashy." This mixed message ACT PASSION–ATELY/ACT CALMLY is the source of the instability inherent in being "fired up."

The traditional Maninka antidote for this empassionment is the phrase *ka nyama bɔ* "Let the energy depart" and a gift to the person who inspired it. The way this antidote is supposed to work is that as soon as the griot gets his gift he lets the energy depart, freeing the person in his thrall. In practice, the way it works is this: the minute a griot gets his gift he stops talking or playing and members of the audience lose interest. They stop staring and the feelings of conflict dissipate.

Griots have nothing to lose in playing on nobles' sense of conflict in this way. Either they receive gifts from the nobles, which is directly in their interests, or they encourage the nobles to promote social change, which may be indirectly in their interests. Thus if a noble chooses not to give a griot a gift but to act passionately instead – say, work harder at his business, or go off to war, or run for public office or stage a military coup – the griot can always come around to visit the noble when he succeeds (reminding him of his responsibilities to the less fortunate), or he can try to inspire the noble again if he fails (perhaps receiving a gift this time from his once-burned and, therefore, twice-shy patron).

Griots know that social evolution is in everybody's interests while maintaining the status quo is not. Griots know further that maintaining the status quo is not even in the interests of nobles, who are nominally on top of the social heap, because the nobles' putative privilege is often translated into soul-destroying obligation to others, and the only way out of this obligation is to change things, move away, or die. Griots feel they have to make nobles want change, however, so they set about it in two different ways. The first of these is to approach them through art: through words and music (where the appeal is couched in strictly ideological language). The other way griots can make nobles want change is to add their own voices to the periodic but inevitable clamor that nobles hear from the underprivileged, making their lives so unbearable that they will do something about it.

In Maninka society griots are formally excluded from the political process, which means that they cannot legislate change themselves. They must make their influences felt in other more subtle ways. The whole social situation griots participate in is riddled with conflict and tension: the conflicts engendered by different interests located in different segments of society; the conflicts created by different definitions of social situations; the conflicts arising out of asymmetrical distribution of power and authority; and the conflicts surrounding their own moral status.

The fact that nobles have more practical access to sources of legitimation for their point of view from outside Maninka society only adds to tension. Nobles use outsiders to promote their own particular construction of reality and their own moral position over the griots, which means that the negative image of griots in the scholarly literature on West Africa is planted there by nobles. It represents the nobles' point of view.

Why do scholars perpetuate it? One of the reasons is that they have considerably more opportunities to meet nobles than to meet griots. Nobles outnumber griots statistically in the first place, and custom dictates that nobles be responsible for hosting strangers in their communities in the second place. Nobles are responsible for hosting strangers for two reasons. The first is simply that they have more economic resources to do so; the second is that strangers are considered potentially dangerous. The noble class has to deal with strangers because their moral virtues make them less vulnerable to potential attack than other people, or so they say.

Actually, strangers are viewed much less suspiciously than nobles would have it, for if they are seen as dangerous, they are not seen so unqualifiedly. They are also viewed as bearers of enormous potential for benefit. They often bring wealth into the community, or they open up possibilities for travel and education. Or they offer escape. Or they provide diversion from everyday routine. Sometimes, I think, nobles claim responsibility for strangers just because they want first crack at them.

In the pull and tug of interest and politics in Mali the noble class has a certain long-term advantage which allows them differential access to potential privilege. This advantage is institutionalized in prescription and in custom which means that if non-nobles are to compete with them for social benefits they must strategize more elaborately.

On our final trip to the Mande heartland of the old Maninka Empire Charles and I became involved in a particularly complicated bit of griot strategy — another unexpected episode involving greetings and a noble, and a griot with whom we were closely associated. This time, however, no gift was involved.

Charles and I had a close relationship with a family of griots in a village in the Mande, southwest of Bamako near the Guinea border. We stayed in their compound when we were in the village and they visited us when we were in the capital. We all knew a number of each other's friends in both places.

On the first morning of our final stay in their compound we told our host that we were going to visit a blacksmith family of whom we were very fond, and he told us that he wanted to come along.

It is important to know for understanding what follows that our host had been out of the Mande for several months by this time and that we had in fact brought him back to his village from Bamako, where we had picked him up on his return from Guinea. (He had been in a part of Guinea where he could have crossed the border without returning first to Bamako, but he chose not to do so. He had to visit the mother of one of his wives in the capital first, he said.)

When we left Bamako we anticipated that the relatively short drive would be smooth and brief, but our host insisted that we stop in every village between the capital and his home (six in all). Naturally we came upon people eating meals along the way, and of course we were invited to eat. The journey's temporal duration expanded by a factor of three and we arrived late in the evening after most of the village people had retired. We had not gone out greeting people when we arrived, but people knew we were there because our car was parked outside the compound's walls.

In the morning as we left to greet our non-griot friends with our griot host, he suggested we visit the village chief first. Normal protocol, I thought, although Charles and I would not necessarily have put the chief first if our host had not been along. Still, we knew that the chief and our host were special friends, which meant that eventually the chief would have to visit us if we did not go to visit him, so we took the path to his house. Our host called the chief out. He greeted the chief; the chief greeted him. He brought greetings from the chief's family and friends in Guinea. The chief thanked him. He brought greetings from the chief's family and friends in Bamako; the chief thanked him. He brought greetings from the chief's family and friends in Kirina; the chief thanked him. He brought greetings from the chief's family and friends in Bancoummana; the chief thanked him. He brought greetings from the chief's family and friends in Kangaba, and the chief thanked him again. And so on. Each time the griot mentioned a village he named specific people and used their specific kinship or friendship relationship to the chief, something which appeared to make the chief visibly nervous. Like the elder in the market, he lowered his eyes and stared at the ground with an occasional sideways look at Charles and myself. (I had the distinct impression that he would not have been so ill at ease had we not been witness to this little social drama.) Finally the chief cut the griot off with an abrupt *a banna* "It is finished" and greeted me and Charles briefly. He turned to his house with a look of resignation on his face. Charles and I were astonished to have been party to this interchange and mystified as to its meaning, although we understood enough to know that the griot had tried to unsettle his friend, that he had chosen to do it in front of us, and that he had used the most benign of social forms (a greeting) to accomplish it.

We found out later that the message was political. It was about personal influences and about power alliances in rural Mali and Guinea, about that great web of relationships that bind people into each other's lives. Our friend was in effect claiming to know all the important people the chief knew, and claiming to be able to talk to them freely about the chief when he wanted to — an alarming proposition to anyone concerned about reputation in a country where griots are held to be gossips and liars. That he delivered this message accompanied by two Europeans added another dimension to his claim about personal influence; *he* was the man who brought the Europeans to the village and *he* was the man who hosted them. *He* was the man that could command rides in a private automobile and *he* was the man whose wives and sons and daughters might benefit from contact with these outsiders. The fact that the griot delivered this message with consummate artistry and aplomb, converting an act which is normally aimed at establishing solidarity into a rebuke of sorts, added an element of surprise. Before he even knew the griot's sword was drawn, the noble was standing in a pool of his own blood.

The griot was frustrated because he had asked the noble to commit the communal labour force to reparing a dilapidated house in his compound while he was away. He went off, hoping that his friendship with the chief would guarantee the success of his petition. In the meantime, however, other people presented their own projects to the chief as more pressing, and he had responded to this pressure rather than going ahead with the griot's request. The griot had got wind of this while in Guinea and had launched a campaign to show the chief that he had made a terrible mistake. The griot's whole point in returning to the village through Bamako — and eating all those meals and drinking all that tea — rather than walking directly across the border was to line up allies to impress upon his friend that he too was an important and influential man whose social prowess exceeded the chief's even though the chief's authority exceeded his. There were good practical reasons for doing this: authority is officially located at the top of the social hierarchy in Mali, but decisions are not in fact made autocratically. Chiefs must have the support of their people and they must have the support of their praise-singers. An unhappy griot in one's midst is something to worry about. The griot was reminding him of that.

In reporting my understandings of these events to you, I am aware that I slide back and forth between the kind of analysis that focuses on individual strategies and the kind that relies on normative statements. Furthermore I am aware of a certain asymmetry in the kinds of analytic statements I make, recognizing, for example, that I rely more heavily on normative statements when characterizing nobles than when accounting for griots. I know that this has something to do with how well I knew or did not know the people involved, with how much information I was able to elicit about the actors' motives from the actors themselves or from others, and with how puzzling their behaviour initially appeared to be. Knowing this, I cannot help but conclude that my ethnographic knowledge is only partial and contingent, and that the interpretations I make cannot therefore correspond to some underlying reality. Still, the problems I faced understanding people in Mali are not unrelated to the problems I face understanding my own countrymen, nor are they unrelated to the problems Malians face understanding each other. People everywhere must render others intelligible, and they must resort to both biographical-historical and stereotypic information to do so.

We know enough about the nature of human social relations now to say that all social systems incorporate uncertainties and indeterminacies. We recognize that no social practice is so narrowly institutionalized that it precludes variation. We also know that the symbols we use in communicating with each other are multiply ambiguous, and we know that people exploit these ambiguities for strategic ends. A stinging insult can come clothed in the guise of a friendly gesture. A gift can be challenge. Praise for what has been accomplished can carry the suggestion that what was accomplished was not actually praiseworthy.

Since all competent social actors learn this lesson in the course of acquiring social experience, it follows that people everywhere deal with others on the basis of their expectations about the sorts of intentions other people hold. The structure of expectations we hold about particular others arises out of our practical interactions with them. The structure of our expectations in fact constitute the medium in terms of which interaction takes place and the unintended consequence of interaction as well. The more I learn about you in interacting with you the more I rely on biographical and historical information to interpret your actions. The more we interact, the more my expectations are structured. They can never be fixed nor certain, of course, for social life is ongoing and dynamic.

If social experience is grounded in time and history, then a certain relativity colours the content of experience. I am trying to say here that it is not just the quality and quantity of my actual exchanges with you that allows me to form certain expectations concerning your intentions. My thought processes are, after all, the products of twentieth century and Western modes of thinking, rooted in the material and social conditions of contempory existence. This suggests that thoughts are not entirely private, but incorporate and express the collective representations of a certain time and a certain society.

If this proposition is true, then it has profound implications for ethnography. It means that we depend on several sorts of interpretive procedures in translating our unique experiences in the field into the public language of academic discourse: some growing out of biographical and personal interchanges; some reflecting the collective representations others offer of themselves; some arising out of historically situated Western modes of thought; and some which are peculiar to the contemporary discipline of anthropology. To put this another way, we make interpretations of our experiences, but neither the interpretations nor the experiences are given under conditions of our own choosing. There will always be blindspots and gaps in our knowledge because we cannot know all the forces conspiring to influence our thinking; succeeding generations will see things differently from us. And they will interact with the descendents of the people we interacted with, who will themselves see things differently from their ancestors. Such intellectual lacunae should not promote despair or frustration so much as they should promote celebration. The gaps in our knowledge guarantee that our search for self-understanding will continue. They guarantee that this very interesting game we are playing will go on.

Notes

1. The research upon which this paper is based was partially funded by the Social Science Research Council, and partially funded by Indiana University. In writing it, I have profited greatly from suggestions and comments by Charles S. Bird, James T. Brink, Anthony Giddens, Michael Herzfeld, and Ivan Karp. I have also learned much from our graduate students at Indiana: Bill Graves, Don Jordan, Stan Knick, Georgia McMillan, Bonnie Wright, Barbara Pitchford-Hoffman and Ann Bates. It should be obvious to all who read this paper that I am experimenting with the style. There are no academic citations in the text, although of course, I recognize my indebtedness to other scholars in the bibliography. I have also excluded – as much as I could – the traditional markers of "anthropologese". What I hope to accomplish in doing this is a more readable product.
2. James Brink points out that this is only an ideal, of course. Some nobles are fairly flamboyant, and some bards are very shy. Our griot friend, however, is scarcely a retiring sort, and the noble in question seemed to have interiorized the ideal for nobles rather thoroughly. The noble you will encounter in the last example could, and did, feel that occasionally a noble is justified in telling griots to "bugger off."

Bibliography

I relied directly, or indirectly, on the following works in constructing this paper.

Bird, Charles & Kendall, Martha B. 1980. The Mande hero: text and context. In *Explorations in African Systems of Thought* (eds.) Ivan Karp & Charles S. Bird. Bloomington, Indiana: Indiana University Press.
Bourdieu, Pierre 1977. *Outline of a Theory of Practice*. London: Cambridge.
Brink, James T. 1981. Speech, play and blasphemy: Managing power and shame in Bamana theatre. Paper presented at African Studies Association Meetings. October 1981. Bloomington, Indiana.

Crick, Malcolm 1976. *Explorations in Language and Meaning: Towards a Semantic Anthropology*. London: Malaby.
Giddens, Anthony 1976. *New Rules of Sociological Method*. London: Hutchison.
—— 1978. *Central Problems in Social Theory*. Berkeley: University of California Press.
—— 1982. Four lectures on social theory. Delivered orally at Indiana University. February 1982. Unpublished.
Irvine, Judith 1974. Strategies of status manipulation in Wolof greetings. In *Explorations in the Ethnography of Speaking* (eds) Richard Bauman & Joel Sherzer. Cambridge: University Press.
Karp, Ivan & Kendall, Martha B. 1982. Reflexivity in fieldwork. In *Explaining Social Behaviour* (ed.) Paul Secord. Los Angeles: Sage.
Kendall, Martha B. & Bird, Charles S. 1981. Good timing: the meaning of tempo in Maninka greetings. Paper presented to African Studies Seminar on African Systems of Time. Spring 1981, Bloomington, Indiana.
Parkin, David 1980. The creativity of abuse. *Man* 15(1), 45-64.
Wright, Bonita 1981. Do *griots* lie? Presentation to Lying, Ambiguity and Contradiction Seminar, Fall 1981. Indiana University.

PERSONAL NAMES AND SOCIAL CLASSIFICATION

R. B. BARNES

There is no doubt that, as Lévi-Strauss has written (1966: 218), proper names can serve as terms for a classification or that (p. 190) there is an imperceptible transition from names to titles, provided that a sufficiently broad idea of proper names is in use. Philosophers however often wish, for their purposes, to restrict the notion of proper names so that the passage to descriptions, like that from pointing to signification (p. 215), is discontinuous. Philosophers may be motivated in this respect by the artificial demands of formal systems. Confronted by the natural continuity of empirical languages, anthropologists have entertained the idea that true proper names may sometimes be lacking. Zuni names " are more of titles than of cognomens" (Cushing 1896: 371). For Goldenweiser (1913: 367) Iroquois names are not comparable to our personal names, but must be conceived as ceremonial designations and expressions of membership in a clan. For Fletcher (1884: 295) an Indian name displaying a man's affiliation "grades him so to speak," and Lévi-Strauss (1966: 182) argues that in naming, someone is always signified, either the namer or the named.

Even when dissenting from it, anthropologists have been influenced by the school of philosophical thought concerning names deriving from Mill and have neglected one philosopher who has adopted a broader attitude. One of Frege's most important contributions to modern semantics is his unorthodox doctrine that proper names have both reference (*Bedeutung*) and sense (*Sinn*). Although it cannot be said that he has persuaded the majority [see the many interpretations in Klemke (1968) and Dummett's discussion of his modern opponents (1978)], he has provoked many attempts at refutation, enough that is to prove that there is life yet in his proposition. Perhaps anthropologists would gain by paying attention.

Frege's starting point (1892a) was the epistemological quandry how it is that such statements as $a = b$ have different value from logical tautologies like $a = a$. The difference cannot lie in what the expressions a and b refer to, since a and b both have the same reference. Nor do the statements concern the signs a and b themselves, which are in any case arbitrary. The equations may be drawn only in respect of the meaning of the signs. This train of thought led Frege to distinguish the reference of a name from its sense, where sense is the rather vaguely described "mode of presentation". If $a = b$ is true, then a and b have the same reference, which nevertheless they present in different ways. Hence it is an empirical truth that "The Morning Star" equals "The Evening Star," not a logical truism.

Much philosophical discussion of Frege's sense and reference has gone astray because many philosophers seem to have thought that only one interpretation of "sense" could be correct (compare Dummett 1978: 129; Linsky 1967: 125), a misunderstanding for which Frege may himself have been most responsible. At any event Frege's purposes were narrowly limited to clarifying the logical basis of mathematics, a sphere in which expressions and issues are necessarily kept under a tighter rein than in common speech. *Sinn* seems to function partly as Frege's unavoidable concession to the looseness and the multiplicity of functions of ordinary language, of which naturally he was fully and explicitly aware.

Working with a less specialized perspective on language, anthropologists may recognize that there are really many interpretations which can be given the idea of the sense of names, each of which answers in its own way Frege's epistemological puzzle. Indeed much of the social anthropology of proper names is devoted to mapping out permutations within the range of Frege's sense.

It is well to begin with a distinction between the logical function of names in statements and the sociological properties of empirical examples. Mill (1843: 29) held that proper names were unmeaning marks, they have denotation, not connotation. Frege argued that all proper names had a sense as well as a reference. It is easy to mistake the grounds of disagreement between them. Both in fact accept that when a proper name occurs in the subject of an actual sentence, its grammatical (and logical) function is only to denote or to refer to an object.[1] Furthermore, Frege would necessarily accept that proper names lack connotation in the precise logical sense, which Frege made explicit by claiming that proper names cannot be used in the same way as concepts. Frege departs from Mill largely in holding that the question of the meaning of proper names does not end with denotation and connotation.

English philosophers have steadfastly defended Mill's position against Frege; most notably Strawson (1950) has done so by claiming that singular terms which appear to have meaning besides reference are really either modified titles or definite descriptions. Here a real difference in interpretation persists. It is not the case that (*pace* Linsky 1967: 129-130) Frege was really talking about definite descriptions.[2] Frege explicitly wrote that, in his chief example, "Morning Star" and "Evening Star" were proper names (*Eigenna-men*) (1891: 14). Frege however was also explicit that for him designations consisting of several words may (*der Kürze wegen*) be called proper names (1982a: 27).

The difference between Frege and the English-speaking tradition on this issue lies in the fact that Frege includes "definite descriptions" as proper names and accepts that all kinds of proper names have sense, while his opponents prefer the view that any singular expression which shows a hint of meaning is by definition not really a proper name. The issue presents itself to anthropologists somewhat differently, but in a way which is familiar enough to them in their attempts to cope with many other comparative categories. Anthropologists frequently find that when they look for personal names (naturally a kind of proper name) in another culture, what they come up with are expressions with complex meanings whose elucidation requires considerable time and which may make up a significant portion of a sociological analysis. In these cases, the question quickly arises whether the terms under consideration are really proper names at all.

If we begin a comparative study of personal names, we soon and by a familiar train of circumstances, come to ask whether the examples we bring together are actually comparable and whether indeed they have anything in common other than the fact that in each culture they are the items which come closest in the way they are used to our idea of personal names. The philosophical definitional dilemma reproduces itself for us in the course of our comparison. If we follow Mill in thinking that personal names have no meaning, and we nevertheless find apparent names with meanings, necessarily we must conclude they are not really proper names and therefore are not relevant to the comparison. We are then in a circle we have encountered often before, whenever we attempted global comparisons of institutions, whether they were law, marriage, religion, money, patrilineality and other such topics. So expressed the quandry shows its negative side. Positively viewed, the discovery that personal names are really like titles may turn out to be a crucial sociological insight; and it is not to be excluded in advance that our understanding of a particular set of usages may depend on realizing precisely that a culture lacks personal names as conventionally defined.

Philosophers are preponderantly concerned with propositions and declarative sentences. Consequently their discussions of proper names consider then only in reference, never in address, whereas sociologically at least personal names cannot be understood by neglecting one or the other kind of employment. Empirically personal names have multifarious uses: they are given, received, employed in address or reference, even traded, borrowed or bought. Each of these means of utilization can be suppressed. Naturally there are intricate relations therefore between personal names and other singular expressions, such as pronouns, relationship terms, titles and so on, to which names are always tied by rules of contrast or substitutability. Personal names may be possessed in order not to be used. Relationship terms may be used to avoid personal names[3]. Names may be used to avoid relationship terms.[4] Regulations on address may contrast with those on reference. Lévi-Strauss (1966: 176-177) has remarked on the analogy between name prohibitions and other regulations in a culture. All such connections and rules give names a wider band of significance than they would have if they were mere verbal marks.

It is grammatical function which sets the limiting standard of meaninglessness of names and perhaps helps in conjunction with other factors to draw them in that direction. A speaker does not need to know a name's meaning, even if it has one, in order to use it. Thus in Kroeber's example, cited by Lévi-Strauss (*Ibid.*: 175), Miwok names are susceptible to various interpretations, and although the bestower may announce its meaning when he gives it away, a Miwok from another district might not know quite what was intended (Kroeber 1925: 453-4). Mendi names, according to Ryan (1958: 111), begin as deliberate descriptions but are later corrupted into insignificant sounds. Nevertheless, it is uncommon for ethnographers to report that personal names are absolutely meaningless, as does Lowie (1924: 270) for the Moupa and Shivwits Paiute.

Most often American Indian names derive from a description or extended segment of a statement. Iroquois individual names usually consist of a verb with an incorporated noun, or of a noun followed by an adjective (Goldenweiser 1913: 367). A commonplace form of an Hidatsa or Omaha name is a sentence lacking the subject. Lévi-Strauss (1966: 150, 206) speaks in such cases of syntagmatic chains converted into paradigmatic sets. Such obvious meanings however are not the same thing as connotations strictly speaking or definitions of the names.

Lévi-Strauss misses this point when he asserts (*Ibid*.: 185) that, "John is a member of the class of Johns". Logicians of course deny that there exists a class of Johns because John cannot be predicated of anyone. As Frege (1892b: 200) says, "a proper name can never be a predicate expression", and we should not become confused when the language permits the same word to be used on one occasion as a proper name and on another as a concept term. "Trieste is no Vienna", but Vienna serves in this sentence as a concept term like "imperial capital", rather than as a name. "He is a John" is either linguistically inadmissible or is an elliptic form of a quite different statement like "He is named John". In Lévi-Strauss's example (*Ibid*.: 188) of a family with several persons named "John", what the family recognizes is not a class of Johns, but a class of *relatives named John*, which is a true predicable expression. "John" derives from Hebrew, via Greek and Latin, and means "God has been gracious". Someone might say, "God has been gracious, I therefore name this child 'John' " as part of a rite of performative nomination. If so, what is predicated is "has been gracious" and the subject of the predication is "God". Nothing has been predicated of John himself (Barnes 1980: 325-326; Lyons 1977: 219).

Lyons numbers among those who have denied that personal names have sense or in Searle's version of the same idea "descriptive backing".

> The principle that names have no sense is not invalidated by the fact that performative nomination, whether formal or informal, may be determined by certain culturally prescribed conditions of semantic appropriateness (Lyons 1977: 221).

He acknowledges without conceding his position that a language may have an institutionalized set of personal names assigned according to sex. He also accepts that names may have symbolic, etymological or translational meaning. "But they do not have sense, or some unique and special kind of meaning which distinguishes them as a class from common nouns" (*Ibid*.: 223). Surely there is no single correct interpretation of Frege's idea of the sense of names, but perhaps some of the kinds of meaning Lyons recognizes are valid examples of Frege's notion. They all certainly figure in the mode of presentation. A potential problem with this suggestion is that such meanings may lack unique, direct, logical connection with the bearer of the name.

The focus of interest then turns to the kinds of connection they may display. Even the claim that proper names identify their referents "by utilizating the unique and arbitrary association which holds between a name and its bearer" (Lyons 1977: 214) needs further explanation if it is to hold up in the face of the facts that many persons may have the same name, that some may have several names, and that names may pass from one person to another. The observation is correct as a comment on grammatical function in actual use. In order for this unique association to exist in a given utterance, an actual speaker, hearer and set of conventions are required. As Hampshire says (1959: 201) in criticizing Russell's theory of descriptions, the meaning of a referring expression cannot be isolated from the intention of a particular speaker or writer on a specific occasion. The intention and the conventions imply an empirical language and a social organization. It is acts and agreements among persons which establish, maintain and even break off the required associations between bearer and name.

Lévi-Strauss maintains (1966: 185) that names always signify membership of a class, which is that either of the person named or the person giving the name. Though this claim may not always be so obviously true of European names, examples that bear it out are familiar from anthropology. Iroquois and Omaha names are the most commonly cited cases, where personal names belong to clans and give information about membership in descent groups. Conversely Hopi names have reference to the clan totem of the name giver, never that of the bearer (Voth 1905: 68).

The Hidatsa lack sets of personal names assigned to each of the clans and used only by their members, thus a Hidatsa name never provides a clue to descent group affiliation. Hidatsa names may be freely invented, rather than selected from a permanent stock, but the names still express a relationship for the person who receives it. It associates him with his father's matrilineal clan or that of his mother's father. These names have descriptive content relating either to the mythical figure of the Bear, to the sacred bundles of the name-giver, or to some member of the father's or mother's father's matrilineal clan. Since the Hidatsa do not prohibit the use of a dead person's name, names are kept in circulation once established. A man may give his own name or the name of a clan member to a son or brother's son. Because transmission follows agnatic lines, rather than names remaining within the clan, they pass from descent group to descent group. Hidatsa names identify the social position of both giver and receiver, but they do more than this in that they frequently indirectly refer to or describe a third person, neither bearer nor namer. Hidatsa rules on giving names accompany an elaborate system of rules nuanced by social relationship restricting the use of names and other kinds of social interaction (Barnes 1980; Lowie 1917; Bowers 1965). This background means that the names at least by implication express the social relations within which the bearer finds himself and thereby fix, if only temporarily, the tie between name and reference.

The personal names of a range of patrilineally organized Siouan tribes frequently refer to an animal species associated with the clan, and each clan has its own set of personal names for men. Ramos (1974: 176) interestingly remarks that Sanumá exclude a number of animal names from the repertoire of personal names in certain descent groups, a practice which is in some respects the inverse of Osage and Omaha patterns. Lowie remarks (1919: 42) concerning Siouan peoples, regardless of clan organization, they "uniformly recognize the existence of bilateral relationship by an appropriate nomenclature", and they assign duties and privileges to both sides of the family. Just as the matrilineal Hidatsa receive names from their father's clan-mates, the patronymic tribes assign special functions to the mother's brother. Some, such as the Oto (Whitman 1937: 67) and the Iowa (Skinner 1926: 249) permit a nephew or niece to receive additional names from the mother's brother, thereby imperfectly paralleling the matrilineal pattern whereby one clan acts as name giver to a segment of another. Among the bilaterally organized Assiniboin, names apparently could be taken from either side of the family (Lowie 1910: 38). The African Nuer exhibit an intermediate pattern, wherein the personal name eventually becomes a point in the lineage structure. Nuer men or women receive names from their own patrilineal clan and from that of their mother. Their paternal or maternal kin address them by the appropriate name, thereby marking the nature of the tie (Evans-Pritchard 1948).[5]

Lévi-Strauss (1966: 201) claims that proper names have close affinities with species names, a position confirmed among the Omaha by the great redundancy of deer and elk names in the Elk clan. The Omaha exhibit only very imperfectly Lévi-Strauss's model (*Ibid.*: 115) of a "pure totemic structure" in which the differences between species are homologous to the differences between groups. Omaha descent groups blur the clarity of this structure by sharing the same animal among more than one descent group, and on the other hand by compounding species differences with distinctions not at all on the same plane. While a species (e.g. the Elk) may represent one clan, part of an animal of a given species (e.g. Black Shoulder of Buffalo, Buffalo Tail) or the bodily discharges of a species (e.g. Red Dung of a Buffalo Calf) may represent another. Other clans are distinguished not as animals but by human attributes (Ancestral Leader), position in the tribal circle (Left Side), mythical function (Earth Makers) or natural phenomena (Flashing Eyes, implying lightning). For each such procedure an abstract model could be constructed which could in principle be used exclusively and systematically by a culture. Empirically the systems are jumbled together. Whether this confusion truly results from demographic changes alone is an open question. Possibly the multiplicity of competing means of classifying groups imperfectly carried through is the natural situation where classifications correspond to diverse needs and are propounded by many persons or groups, rather than by a single individual or centralized authority.

The clan-associated personal names compound this superfluity of redundant principles. Dorsey's somewhat naive attempt to classify personal names of Siouan tribes (1890: 267-268) shows at least how these multivalent procedures carry across a variety of forms of social organization. Dorsey distinguishes names in which colours are mentioned, iron names, whirlwind names, thunderbeing names, and composite animal names. His classification of course is not the only way of discriminating kinds of names even at the concrete level at which he is working. Not all Omaha personal names refer to species. Other Elk clan names mention for example thunder, a mystical being, paint used in ceremonies, the moon, bravery and so on. In other Omaha clans, besides animal names, there are appellations derived from such disparate sources as traditional offices, clouds, tent flaps, ceremonial paraphernalia, knives, dwellings, the sound of drums, personal qualities such as wisdom, activities like cooking, or achievements like victory.

Like those of the Osage, Omaha clan names and personal names exemplify in many cases the disintegration of a species of animal into the constituent parts, activities or attitudes proper to an individual representative of the species – a process to which Lévi-Strauss has given the name detotalization (1966: 146-148, 175). Strathern (1970: 61) has questioned the application of the idea of detotalization in these circumstances.

> Unless there is a finite set of names or a finite set of specific rules about how names can be created, it is perhaps difficult to speak of detotalization, at least if we mean by this a process of systematically "dividing" an animal into a number of parts which, taken together, would reconstitute the animal as a whole.

The problem raised here has to do with the empirical realization of such abstractions. Clan and personal names often seize upon a part of a greater whole, suggesting the possibility of retotalization in various ways, making names up for example by reference either to the corresponding part of different animals or to a complete inventory of the parts of a single animal. Detotalization in Lévi-Strauss's sense does of course take place, even though it is only one among many procedures and the Omaha never realize its full potential.

Goldenweiser (1913: 368) remarked that most Iroquois tribes create practically no new names, whereas the Mohawk at Grand River, lacking clan sets of names, constantly invent new ones. Mauss (1938: 266) infers that American Indian clans possess a predetermined number of names, defining the exact role of each member. In a similar vein, Lévi-Strauss writes (1966: 197) that, "Any system which treats individuation as classification (and I have tried to show that this is always so) risks having its structure called into question every time a new member is admitted". The Hidatsa, who do not hoard personal appellations as private or corporate property, invent new names freely and consequently do not run such risks. The Omaha have a sequence of names given to infants which indicate the sequence of their births. Dorsey (1884: 228) speculates that the other names in a descent group may have been resorted to at a time when the birth names were already appropriated. Whatever truth there may be in this suggestion, Omaha practice deviates in a variety of ways from the presumption of a set of terms derived from a specific order of classification with resulting styles fixed at a number which might fall short of the population requiring them. Birth order names certainly pose this problem, but then these names are soon replaced, and therefore quickly available again for another child. Omaha genealogies suggest too that families within one descent group did not pay much attention to whether another family within the same group were using the same birth name. Otherwise the Omaha have side-stepped the problem of a fixed list of names by permitting the invention of names and allowing alternative procedures for coining names – though whether these alternatives are the consequence of indifference or are responses to the pressure of the dilemma so defined remains open to argument.

Whereas Omaha male personal names often refer to rites and ceremonial paraphernalia, according to Fletcher and La Flesche (1911: 200, 255), those for women generally refer to natural phenomena. Occasionally two or more living Omaha men might bear the same name, despite the rule against such practice. There are signs in unpublished records suggesting that women may occasionally, like the men, have changed their names too. Nevertheless, there is a very striking contrast in Omaha culture between males and females regarding access to and the distinctiveness of appellations. Women did rarely or never have more than one name; by contrast the total of available female names is relatively small, so that there were always many women bearing the same names. Dorsey's unpublished monograph on Omaha and Ponca names shows just how disproportionate the relation between male and female names was, for he gathered over six hundred names for boys and men and a mere seventy-seven for women, though in neither respect is his record complete. Omaha men might easily have followed their rule of only one man per name at a given time; and for the most part they did, though since they frequently dropped, picked up and transferred names, it was easy for two men to share a name at different times in their lives. Women's names were not linked to descent groups, and there were as many as twenty-two women or girls, scattered among several clans, sharing a single name.

With regard then to the stated rules and preponderant practice, the names of Omaha males provide men with distinctive individuality, while also linking each unmistakeably to a recognized collectivity. The possibility of acquiring multiple names in adulthood enhances individual prominence for men. Such additional names sometimes reflect the activities or characteristics of the bearer. In the case of bravery or valour names, they undoubtedly establish a claim on public esteem, as in the example of one name which an Omaha chose for himself when underway with a war party, "Not Afraid of Pawnee." In constrast to the effects of male names, those of women barely rescue them from a general anonymity, neither conferring uniqueness nor indicating group membership.

Omaha names and the procedures for making them up are finite in the trivial sense that at a given period the number of names in currency is small enough to be manageable in human terms. Nevertheless, the conservative Omaha policy of regularly retaining and reusing names should not be confused with rigidity. Omaha names were not immutable, and there evidently was never any prohibition on inventing new names. Early documents reveal many individual names which subsequently fell into disuse and became forgotten. New names were brought into use from time to time, as is shown by the many Omaha buffalo names, which pertain to the environment which the tribe encountered after it moved from the woodlands to the plains. These permit us to infer that the gradual replacement of names as well as the adjustment of descent group associations took place in earlier times, just as they did more recently when "modern names" began to be invented.

Like the Omaha, the matrilineal Iroquois assign sets of names to descent groups, but the names generally make no reference to the descent group or associated mascot (Goldenweiser 1913). In this respect they are like Hidatsa names and those numerous Omaha designations which have so often appeared to commentators to lack classification or otherwise deviate from the established Omaha type. While they do not result from the detotalization of a clan animal, Lévi-Strauss maintains (1966: 178) that, "they do suggest a detotalization of those aspects of social life and the physical world which the system of clan appellations has not already caught in the mesh of its net." Strathern (1970: 62) comments that Mohawk names often refer to something which has happened to a person, so that whereas Osage names refer to a system or structure, Mohawk names refer to history or events. The various contrasts which might be established by such comparisons actually occur in one way or another *within* the collection of Omaha naming practices. Radin (1915: 21) has proposed that the historical pattern of Winnebago names has been to reinterpret names, sometimes converting one describing an event or aspect of the bearer into one connected with the origin of the clan.

When translating Siouan names in English, ethnographers often distort their syntactic shape in order to give them an acceptable name-like appearance. For example Dorsey often provides parenthetically the implied subject, as in "(Snake) Sheds its Skin" or "(Thunder That) Walks After Others, At the Close of a Storm" – the Omaha original corresponding only to the words outside the parentheses (Dorsey n.d.). Such names therefore contain verbs, adverbs and adjectives, and the grammatical structure always implies the third person. Dorsey never found a name in the first or second person (Dorsey 1890: 265).

When such a phrase appears in the subject position in a sentence it creates what seems to speakers of European languages a grammatical scandal, namely a predicate expression acting as though it were a referring one, giving the impression of a predicate within a predicate. When used in a sentence, these names do refer to or denote their bearer in an ordinary way, and their logical position can be explained in the same way that Frege accounted for the uses of Vienna either as a subject or as part of a predicate. However the elliptical shape of such names does not merely leave a space for a subject – in which respect they are like one place mathematical functions, Frege's model for concepts in general (1891) – they also imply what that subject is. Almost always Omaha names involve a sharing of reference between the bearer of the name and the animal or thing which could be the subject of an ordinary sentence made up by using the name as a predicate. Omaha names establish a meta-phorical relationship between the bearer and the nominal subject; and they can be said to be relationship terms in a different sense than terms of "kinship". They lay claim to a symbolic but not real identity between a person and an object, natural process or animal. Only in the exceptional cases of valour names and derisive names is the actual and implied subject one and the same. The question of reference in Indian names is quite complex. They arrive at personal names by means of truncated descriptive sentences, at the expense of the syntactic structure which made the names sentences in the first place, that is by suppressing their subjects. This end is achieved by a reversal of grammatical value from predicate to subject, and a substitution of a hypothetical but grammatically acceptable subject by one which, although it actually exists, is only metaphorically appropriate.

Some Omaha names, like White Buffalo or Big Elk, contain the species explicitly. Very rarely do the Omaha trim such predicates back to leave the species name standing by itself, as in Elk. Even in extreme cases like the last, the personal name Elk does not function like elk the concept. The relation between Omaha personal names and classification therefore is not a consequence of their gram-matical functions in sentences. In fact the names have not a single, but multiple ties to classification. Clan-owned names allow persons to associate the bearer to specific groups because people already know the tie between the name and the group. This connection exists regardless of whether or not the name is one of those which accept either explicitly or implicitly the animal of the appropriate species as the subject. Persons in the tribe may be expected to know in advance, and therefore to draw the appropriate conclusions about the bearer, whether a name belongs to the Omaha or the Ponca tribe, whether it is suited for males or for females, whether it is a baby name or an adult name, whether it is an old name or recently invented.

Perhaps the most extreme effort to interpret naming as classifica-tion was that by Cushing (1896: 372). In his understanding Zuni clans possess sets of names bestowed on children, relating to the parts and functions of the clan animal, and these functions them-selves correspond to a six-fold classification of the world. Lévi-Strauss's conception of classification is too imprecise to establish that personal names really classify (cf. Barnes 1980: 325-328; Tonkin 1980: 658-660). Rather names, at least Omaha personal names, because they have meaning, often derive from established classifications and therefore permit Omaha to situate persons, on the basis of the information their names provide and in view of accumulated experiences, within those classifications. By giving a name, an Omaha does convey information about himself or the named or both, but such an act of nomination does not in and of itself constitute an act of classification. Nor does such an act take place on subsequent uses of the name. Omaha names in other words do significantly bear on processes of classification, but that bearing is not as Lévi-Strauss often implies direct. Furthermore Omaha names distribute themselves through different stages which Lévi-Strauss indicates (1966: 181) exist between identifying marks on the one hand which indicate that a person is a member of a preordained class like a social group and on the other hand products of free creation.

Judged as titles, Omaha names give varying results. Some, such as Chief, directly derive from offices. Valour names figure in the Omaha system of status, wherein successful warriors may hope to advance in public position. The pattern of ascribed status conventionally indicated by personal names could among the Omaha be supplemented by designations signalling positions achieved through initiative and prowess. In this way the preordained structure was able to accommodate the individual ambitions of capable men, though it made no such concessions to women. Valour names however were coined for the occasions and in this respect were less like titles than the reusable, standardized names owned by clans. The latter however did not normally indicate occupation of a public trust or of an hereditary social position, other than descent group membership. There is no uniform respect therefore in which Omaha personal names are analogous to titles except in contrast to an ideal definition of proper names, that is they all have meaning. Even the analogies relate to their make-up, rather than use. Their function is similar to our use of names rather than our use of titles. For example, in reference they would not require, when rendered into English, the definite article we apply to the President, the priest, the mayor.

There is no need for a definite decision that American Indian personal names do or do not conform to the logicians' definition of true proper names (cf. Lévi-Strauss 1966: 188). This ideal and that of titles are alternative standards which help only by providing analogies to be exploited in analysis. Between Mill, who holds that names are only marks, and Lévi-Strauss, who assimilates them to classification, Frege recognizes an aspect of meaning in the way names present themselves, which differs from the workings of concepts. Frege left his idea of a name's sense undeveloped. The difference between reference and sense may be illuminated, very generally, by the difference between speech and society. The grammatical function of a name (so far as it concerned Frege) is to refer, when properly joined with a predicate in a sentence; it may assist in conveying information about the empirical world by the additional factor of its sense. Outside of ideal languages, sentences are human products.

As Dummett (1978: 122) writes, "to give an account of the sense of an expression is . . . to give a partial account of what a speaker knows when he understands that expression". Frege distinguished carefully (1918: 67-68) between senses, which are objective and can be shared, and private individual representations, which cannot, though he admitted (1892a: 28) that there may be disagreements about the sense of a name. Dummett prefers to interpret sense as semantic content. Plainly Frege's idea of sense pertains, as Dummett says (1978: 130), to features of language, as well as to collective aspects of thought and action. Indeed Bloor (1976) has noted the strong parallel between Frege's philosophy and Durkheim's sociologism. The anthropologist is freer to exploit the non-logical, therefore social, background of meaning than was Frege.[6] Much of the social anthropology of names devotes itself to exploring the range marked out by Frege's phrase "mode of presentation". What we commonly find is that names implicitly present their bearers by indirect reference to social relationship and systems of classification.

Notes

1. The distinction Lyons (1977: 176) draws between Mill's "denotation" and Frege's "reference" probably is clearest when speaking about concepts. Reference is utterance-dependent all right, but there can be no reference without the background of shared understandings implied by Lyons's description of denotation.
2. "It is, indeed, essential to Frege's view that a name *can* have the same sense as a definite description; but to think that a name can have no other kind of sense is seriously to misinterpret Frege" (Dummett 1978: 129).
3. For the Omaha of Nebraska, "the custom of never addressing anyone – man, woman, or child – by his personal name or of using a person's name when speaking of him, if he chanced to be present, made the use of kinship terms a practical necessity" (Fletcher & La Flesche 1911: 313).
4. Polak reports of the Indonesian Sasak of Lombok that as the result of a FBD marriage, a man and his wife found themselves required to reverse the terms they had previously used and therefore called each other only by personal names (Polak 1978: 34).
5. Bamberger (1974) describes an ideal of the Kayapó of Brazil, whereby male personal names are transmitted from MB to ZS and female personal names

from FZ to BD. Her model of the rule (*Ibid.*: 375) might be regarded as a variation on parallel descent or as an additional variety (see Needham 1971: 10). A similar manipulation of alternating descent would produce yet another rule, whereby transmission is from FZ to BS and from MB to ZD.
6. Kendall (1980) is an interesting and instructive example of a linguist moving toward a social anthropological treatment of names.

References

Bamberger, Joan 1974. Naming and the transmission of status in a Central Brazilian society. *Ethnology* **13** (4), 363-378.

Barnes, R. H. 1980. Hidatsa personal names: an interpretation. *Plains Anthropologist* **25**, 311-331.

Bloor, David 1976. *Knowledge and social imagery*. London: Routledge & Kegan Paul.

Bowers, Alfred 1965. *Hidatsa social and ceremonial organization*. Bulletin 194. Bureau of American Ethnology. Washington: Government Printing Office.

Cushing, Frank Hamilton 1896. *Outlines of Zuni creation myths*. A.R.B.A.E. (1891-92), Vol. 13. Washington: Government Printing Office.

Dorsey, James Owen n.d. Omaha and Ponca personal names [typescript]. National Anthropological Archives, Washington, D. C.

—— 1884. *Omaha sociology*. A.R.B.A.E. (1881-82), Vol. 3. Washington: Government Printing Office.

—— 1886. Indian personal names. *Proceedings of the American Association for the Advancement of Science* **34**, 393-399.

—— 1890. Indian personal names. *American Anthropologist* **3**, 263-268.

Dummett, Michael 1978. Frege's distinction between sense and reference. In *Truth and other enigmas*. London: Duckworth.

Evans-Pritchard, E. E. 1948. Nuer modes of address. *Uganda Journal* **12**, 2: 166-171. Reprinted (1963) in *The position of women in primitive societies*.

Fletcher, Alice C. The religious ceremony of the four winds or quarters. *Report of the Peabody Museum*, Vol. 3 (1881-87) No. 19, pp. 289-295.

—— & La Flesche, Francis 1911. *The Omaha tribe*. A.R.B.A.E. (1905-06). Vol. 27. Washington: Government Printing Office.

Frege, Gottlob 1891. Funktion und Begriff. Vortrag, gehalten in der Sitzung vom 9. Januar 1891 der Jenaischen Gesellschaft fur Medizin und Naturwissenschaft. H. Pohle, Jena, II, 31 pp.

—— 1892a. Uber Sinn und Bedeutung. *Zeitschr. f. Philos. u. philos. Kritik, N.F.* **100**, 25-50.

—— 1892b. Uber Begriff und Gegenstand. *Vierteljahrschr. f. wiss. Philosophie* **16**, 192-205.

—— 1918. Der Gedanke. Eine logische Untersuchung. *Beitr. zur Philos. des deutschen Idealismus* **1** (1918-1919), 58-77.

Goldenweiser, Alexander A. 1913. On Iroquois work. *Summary Reports of the Geological Survey of Canada* pp. 365-372.

226   *R. B. Barnes*

Hampshire, Stuart 1959. *Thought and action*. London: Chatto & Windus.
Kendall, Martha B. 1980. Exegesis and translation: Northern Yuman names as texts. *Journal of Anthropological Research* 36: (3), 261-273.
Klemke, E. W. (ed.) 1968. *Essays on Frege*. Urbana: University of Illinois Press.
Kroeber, A. L. 1925. *Handbook of the Indians of California*. Bulletin 78, Bureau of American Ethnology. Washington: Government Printing Office.
Lévi-Strauss, Claude 1966. *The savage mind*. London: Weidenfeld & Nicolson.
Linsky, Leonard 1967. *Referring*. London: Routledge & Kegan Paul.
Lowie, Robert 1910. The Assiniboine. *Anthropological Papers of the American Museum of Natural History*, Vol. 14.
——— 1917. Notes on the social organization and customs of the Mandan, Hidatsa, and Crow Indians. *Anthropological Papers of the American Museum of Natural History*, Vol. 21.
——— 1919. The matrilineal complex. *University of California Publications in American Archaeology and Ethnology*, Vol. 16.
——— 1924. Notes on Shoshonean ethnography. *Anthropological Papers of the American Museum of Natural History*, Vol. 22.
Lyons, John 1977. *Semantics*. 2 Vols., Cambridge: University Press.
Mauss, Marcel 1938. Une Catégorie de l'esprit humain: la notion de personne, celle de "moi". *J.R.A.I.* 68, 263-281.
Mill, John Stuart 1843. *System of logic*. London: Parker.
Needham, Rodney 1971. Remarks on the analysis of kinship and marriage. In *Rethinking Kinship and Marriage* (ed.) R. Needham (Ass. social Anthrop. Monogr. 11). London: Tavistock.
Polak, Albert 1978. *Traditie en tweespalt in een Sasakse boerengemeenschap (Lombok, Indonesie)*. Amsterdam: Koninklijk Instituut voor de Tropen.
Radin, P. 1915. The social organization of the Winnebago Indians. *Canada Geological Survey Museum Bulletin* No. 10.
Ramos, A. 1974. How the Sanumá acquire their names. *Ethnology* 13, 171-185.
Ryan, D'Arcy 1958. Names and naming in Mendi. *Oceania* 28, 109-16.
Searle, John R. 1969. *Speech acts: an essay in the philosophy of language*. Cambridge: University Press.
Skinner, Alanson 1926. Ethnology of the Ioway Indians. *Bul. Pub. Mus. City Milwaukee*, 5(4), 181-354.
Strathern, Andrew 1970. Wiru penthonyms. *Bijdragen tot de Taal-, Land- en Volkenkunde* 126(1), 59-74.
Strawson, P. F. 1950. On referring. *Mind* 59, 320-44.
Tonkin, Elizabeth 1980. Jealousy names, civilised names: anthroponomy of the Jlao Kru of Liberia. *Man* (N.S.) 15(4), 653-664.
Voth, H. R. 1905. Hopi proper names. *Field Columbian Museum, Publ.* 84. *Anthropological Series* Vol. 6, No. 3.
Whitman, William 1937. *The Oto*. Columbia University Contributions to Anthropology, Vol. 28. New York: Columbia University Press.

ON A MENTAL SAUSAGE MACHINE AND OTHER NOMINAL PROBLEMS

ROY WILLIS

As a hardcore secondary ethnocentrist, I find it virtually impossible to write anthropology without speaking of the Fipa of south-west Tanzania. And this paper is no exception. Basing myself on this adopted central standpoint, I shall attempt to move the earth. The theories of Western philosophers deserve the respect accordable to all indigenous models: no more and no less.

The doctrine that proper names are meaningless marks set upon things and persons to distinguish them one from another, though intuitively nonsensical, becomes comprehensible as the logical consequence of a basic cultural presupposition: the atomicity and uniqueness of the individual.[1] Small wonder that we find this doctrine, first formulated by the Utilitarian J. S. Mill (1868) being substantially endorsed by A. H. Gardiner (Gardiner 1940: 9) and more recently being accepted, albeit with signs of unease, by the linguist John Lyons (Lyons 1977: 219). Gottlob Frege's dissenting opinion that names convey both reference (*Bedeutung*) and sense (*Sinn*) has, as R. H. Barnes has noted, been ignored by anthropologists (Barnes 1980: 311).

Anthropology has indeed contributed remarkably little to the general theory of names and naming, with the exception of Claude Lévi-Strauss' interpretation in *La Pensée sauvage,* according to which proper names always have a classificatory purpose (Lévi-Strauss 1962: 200-216). But his claim that their taxonomic function exhausts the significance of names has been convincingly challenged by Barnes in the case of Hidatsa personal names, and, by implication, generally (Barnes, *op. cit.*). Ward H. Goodenough asserts on the basis of a comparison between naming systems on Truk and Lakalai that the systems appear to counterbalance the effect that the workings of the wider social system "tend otherwise to give to people's images of themselves and others" (Goodenough 1965: 275), but it is not clear whether this soundly functionalist conclusion is intended to have general application. Compared with the masses of data and theorizing on kinship systems, the topic of names and naming has Cinderella status in anthropology.

The situation is no better as regards the culture region from which my ethnographic material is drawn. T. O. Beidelman has observed that information on naming is poor for East Africa, as well as for Africa as a whole, and he concludes that "only when many more . . . ethnographic reports are available from culturally related peoples, along with the related sociological data, can we proceed to try to understand the broader social and psychological principles behind naming in African societies" (Beidelman 1974: 281). This conclusion could well be extended to non-African societies.

Let us now turn to the ethnographic substance of this paper. With respect to the matrilineal Kaguru of eastern Tanzania, Beidelman avers:

> . . . if we consider an individual Kaguru as a person, that is, as a complex aggregation of social statuses, then each possesses a number of names whose use depends upon a particular social situation. Names change with time, as an individual passes from the status of child to adult and sometimes to that of a distinguished personage. Furthermore, the name used for a person reflects the relation between the speaker and the one with whom he speaks. *One might describe a person as a social field of concentric circles with the most intimate (and dangerous) access to the person represented by the innermost circle and the most formal and neutral relationship at the periphery.* (Beidelman 1974: 282, my emphasis)

Beidelman's image of personal names as forming a structure of concentric circles is congenial to my purpose, since it fits the model of the person proposed by Fipa cosmology (Willis 1972, 1974, 1978, 1981). The most fundamental concepts in this cosmology, related in complementary opposition, are those of "being established", associated with centrality and authority, and of "coming in" or strangerhood, associated with movement and externality. At the microcosmic levels of descent organization and personality structure, this overarching binary opposition takes the form of the complementary opposition of "head" (*unntwe*) and "loins" (*unnsana*).

The "innermost" and most quintessentially "personal" Fipa name, following this schema, is the name, *isiina*, conferred on an infant almost immediately after birth. More exactly, as Fipa see it, the infant itself selects its name from a number recited to it by its mother in its father's presence, or *vice versa*. These names are those of the infant's best known cognatic ancestors, it being held that the spirit (*unnsimu*) of one of these is incarnate in the newborn, who acknowledges its name by ceasing to cry and accepting the mother's breast. According to *Père* Robert, this name may be discovered by divination during the mother's pregnancy, but it also has to be confirmed after birth by the procedure just described (Robert 1949: 46, 51-3; and statements by R. Ntwenya). Once a mother begins nursing her child it is said that "the ancestral spirit has returned", "*Unnsimu waaweela*", but the name of this spirit, which is the ancestral name of the child, is supposed to be a secret known only to the mother and father and eventually to the child itself, who receives it from one or other of its parents early in life and takes care not to reveal it to anyone else. My informant Mr Ntwenya refused to tell me what his ancestral name was, or to tell me those of his children. But there is an expectation that among the legitimate offspring of any couple, roughly half will reincarnate paternal ancestors (described as of the "head" side) and half maternal ancestors (the "loins" side).[2]

If the ancestral name occupies the innermost, most "private" position in the structure of concentric circles composing the Fipa personality, the outermost, most "public" domain belongs to names connoting either Christian or Islamic religious affiliation. Similar to these names are surnames unilaterally adopted by prominent and ambitious men during the early Colonial period and transmitted patrilineally in the European mode. These adopted surnames are usually words of Swahili, the prestigious trade, missionary and official language, and often denote innovations associated with European civilization. Examples of such adopted patronyms are *Baruti*, "Gunpowder", *Rupia*, "Rupee", the principal unit of currency in German East Africa, *Barabara*, "Road", and *Malimao*, "Limes"; an old Fipa friend and informant had long adopted the Swahili surname *Tayari*, "Ready".

Three other kinds of name belonging to the public domain of the Fipa personality should be mentioned. People who are both socially prominent and notable for some personal idiosyncrasy often come to be known by names connoting such characteristics. A well known female householder in my own community was generally known as *Waakalipa*, "the Fierce One", because of her fiery temper. A lone and long established European settler, Mrs. Hilda Damm, was called *Nakatuuce*, "the Thin One", because of what was considered to be her excessively slim figure. Two other common names of this kind are *Nakataale*, used of an unusually tall woman, and *Umwipi*,

"Shorty". These names resemble English "nicknames". A similar but much commoner custom is that by which the old woman, entitled *Nakalaale*, who acts as senior midwife at a birth (there are normally at least two such female attendants, drawn from the category of senior women, *amaloombwe*) has the right to bestow a satirical name on the child. Such names typically criticise the behaviour of one or more other persons in the village, and do not usually refer to the child's parents. Examples of such names are *Waansakiloole*, meaning "a woman who is good to look at but is otherwise useless and idle", *Watuwindwake*, meaning "parents who are so busy with other things that they neglect their own children", *Nalwaambo*, "a scrounging woman", and *Iwaasakiya*, "a wife who has no respect for her husband, who is meek and humble before her". These names which refer to a third person, or persons, rather than to the giver or receiver of the name, resemble in this respect the Hidatsa names described by Barnes (1980) and the Jlao names described by Tonkin (1981). The names seem intrinsically ephemeral. A third type of common Fipa adult and public name is that usually called the "teknonym" in the literature, the custom whereby a parent is known as "Father (or "Mother") of So-and-So" (the child's name). This custom, which may have been an innovation adopted from Swahili culture in the nineteenth century, is commonly observed in public, including spouses when addressing one another or referring to the marital partner in the presence of others.

The names ascribed in virtue of a person's descent constitute a nominal system of remarkable complexity and the main topic of this paper. These "descent names", as I call them, are divided by Fipa into two categories: patrilineal (and patrilateral) names, called *amasiina ya unntwe*, "names of the head"; and names transmitted from alternate ascendant to descendant generations through opposite-sex links in the intermediate generation and called *amasiina ya unnsana*, "names of the loins". Both subcategories of name apply to sibling groups without distinction of sex. Every Fipa has one "head" name and two "loins" names. Of the two "loins" names one is shared with the father and the father's mother. I call this the "personal" or "kindred" name because Fipa use equivalent terms to these (*unntu* and *uluko*) when referring to this name.[3] The other "loins" name I call the "genealogical" name and is normally prefaced by Fipa with the word *Mwaana* (pl., *Aana, Yaana, Ayaana*), "Child", and the siblings share it with their mother (whose personal name it is). Males transmit their genealogical "loins" names (those they share with and receive from their mothers) to their own children, and these names become the personal or kindred names of the children.

I would emphasize that the distinction between the two kinds of "loins" names is made by the Fipa themselves. Men, who are customarily more concerned than women with the public domain, memorize a standard form of reciting their descent names: such recitations were required when presenting evidence to an indigenous court, or when acting as representative of a kinsman in marriage negotiations. A man with the patronym ("head" name) of *Unndeenje*, the personal "loins" name of *Cifuunda* and the genealogical "loins" name of *Cipeta* recites them according to the following formula:

1)	*Ineene*	*Mwaana*	*Cipeta,*	*imbwa*	*Unndeenje*
	I (am)	Child (of)	Cipeta	I-am-made	Unndeenje

2)	*n'uluko*	*ineene*	*unntu*	*wa*	*Cifuunda*
	and kindred	I (am)	a-person	of	Cifuunda

3)	*infyaala*	*Yaana*	*Cipeta*	*yane*
	I-generate	Children (of)	Cipeta	mine

This brief recitation condenses a considerable amount of information. (1) It gives priority in defining the male speaker's public *persona* to the genealogical "loins" name, and with this "maternal" name is coupled its "paternal" complement, the patronym Unndeenje. The verb *imbwa*, the first person, present tense, and passive voice of *ukuwa,* "to be", is appropriate to the "head" name, which is cosmologically associated with ideas of centrality, fixity and continuance. (2) This statement makes a further distinction, between the "loins" name that signifies the speaker's personal identity within his kindred *(uluko)* and where he is "a person of Cifuunda", and the genealogical name "Child of Cipeta".[4] (3) The final statement establishes the speaker's status as begetter of children who derive their personal identities from their place within the naming system. An infant receives its personal name from its father soon after birth. The midwives, who have established themselves in the parents' hut, order the father to bring a log for the hut fire, so the infant may be warmed. Returning with his load, he drops it with a thud outside the hut door, saying (in the case of the present example): "I have cut firewood, I, Child of Cipeta" (*"Natiya, ineene Mwaana Cipeta"*). This "performative utterance" confers the name of Cipeta on the infant.[5]

The accompanying diagram (see Fig. 1) shows how "head" and "loins" names are transmitted. It is apparent that the naming system

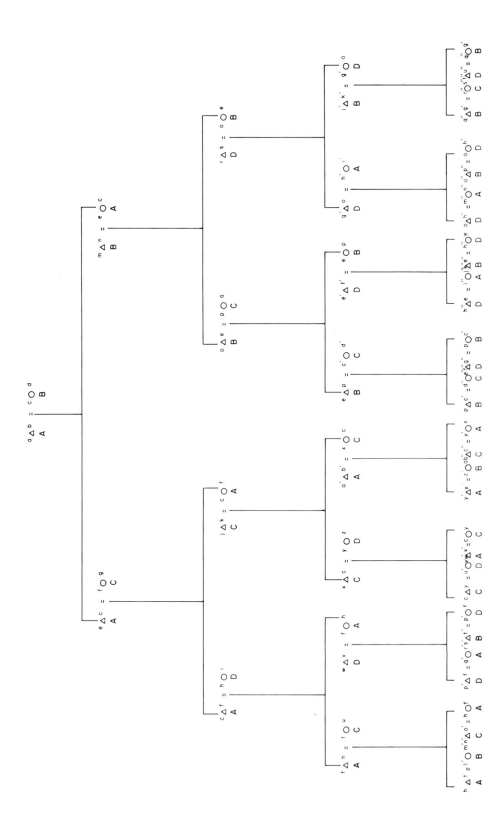

is an intricate conceptual braid that binds together cognates and affines, established households and strangers, males and females, senior and junior generations. But why this extraordinary complexity? We shall see that it is possible to "understand" the system, but only by going well beyond the limits of synchronic functionalism. In turn this "explanation", the answer to the question "Why?" confronts the anthropologists with the question of "How?", which has truly mindbending implications.

But first some necessary ethnography. The Fipa are a Bantu-speaking people numbering about 100,000 most of whom live on a high plateau and adjacent valleys near the south end of Lake Tanganyika in south-west Tanzania.[6] Their country is part of a natural "corridor" linking the savannah and southern tropical forest region of Central Africa with the East African plateau and has received immigrants, mainly from the south and west, for centuries. In pre-colonial times its people participated successfully in the transcontinental trade in ivory, slaves and petty commodities. The Fipa economy was and, to a large extent still is, based on a peculiar technique of compost mounding and finger millet (*Eleusine corocana*) cultivation that supported relatively large and effectively sedentary village communities. There was an indigenous state system that facilitated individual enterprise and social mobility (Willis 1981).

Kinship organization in late precolonial Ufipa, a time of remarkable social stability and prosperity, cohered around successful householders who were the elective heads of cognatic kindreds, a system that persists to this day. These kindreds are fluidly constituted interest groups that closely resemble the Melanesian "nodal kindreds" of the Lakalai of New Britain (Goodenough 1962: 10 and Willis 1981: xx, 272). Their functional importance as organizers of labour (on behalf of wealthy, dominant householders) and regulators of marriage and reproduction, is easily understood without reference to descent names (Willis 1981: 129-137). The anthropologist's initial problem with the system of names is that it is apparently devoid of social function: the four "head" names and twenty-six "loins" names denote only categories of persons and have no institutional referents. Although there are some half-whimsical notions and beliefs associated with descent names, to which I return below, the names as such have no exogamic significance. Persons with the same "head" and "loins" names may and do marry one another, and eligibility or otherwise to marry, in relation to possible incest, is determined by genealogical knowledge.

But when we look at Fipa cosmology the complexity of the

descent naming system begins to yield sense. For this cosmology not only, as any good cosmology should, orders society and the universe as a multidimensional totality, but also contains a theory of history. Even at the microcosmic level of personality structure, with its polar opposition of "head" and "loins", the diachronic aspect is represented: normal persons are born head first, endowing that symbolic pole of the person with its appropriate seniority over the lower and junior symbolic pole, the "loins". The "head" pole of the person is also symbolically male, established and central, whereas the "loins" are symbolically female, the source of energy and movement, and peripheral (Willis 1967, 1972).

The combination and opposition of the categories of "head" and "loins" in the system of descent names makes the social identity of the person, as signified in his or her descent names, consonant with the cosmological model of the person as a polar unity of opposed and interacting forces and principles (cf. Willis 1967, 1972, 1978, 1981: 187-193). The Fipa concept of personal reincarnation within the kindred also intersects with the naming system. An alternative form of asking someone for his personal (kindred) name, *"Uluko wako uwiini?"*, is to ask "Who is your ancestral spirit?" *("Unnsimu wako uwiini?")*, the expected answer being the respondant's personal "loins" name.[7]

Transactional relations between kindreds also appear to be reflected in the descent naming system. Fipa marriage is virilocal and the transfer of a woman from her father's household to that of her husband is legitimated by a public ceremony that includes the presentation of bridewealth by the kin of the wifetaking family and kindred. In late pre-colonial Ufipa, as now, the obligation to give bridewealth was divided almost equally between the paternal and maternal kin of the groom: in pre-colonial times the father was liable to produce 2½ exchangeable iron units (*ifyuuma*), the mother's brother 2 units. This production and transfer of wealth can be seen as a joint but competitive investment by two kindreds in the new marriage. The joint and separate interest is recognized by the eventual ascription of descent names to the children of the paternally and maternally sponsored marriage: the children receive both their father's "head" name (which is also the name of their father's father and his agnates and collateral kin) and his genealogical "loins" name (which is also the personal "loins" name of their father's mother and her siblings). The names represent opposed claims, registering past transactions and continuing economic interests (cf. Willis 1981: 143-145; and Fig. 2). One is reminded of the name conferred on a newly born infant by the senior midwife, a right which

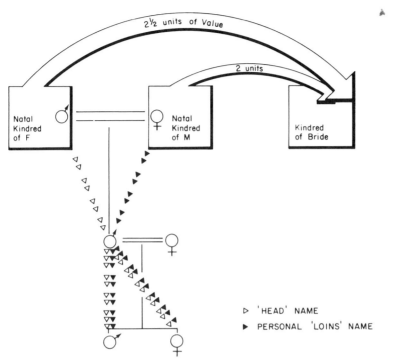

Fig. 2   Bilateral investment of bridewealth and ascription of "head" and "loins" names.

can also be seen as arising from the midwives' contribution of work and expertise during the infant's delivery.

At the level of state structure the symbolic union in opposition of "head" and "loins" can be shown to be analogous to that between the senior Fipa kingship of Milansi, associated with ideas of maleness, centrality and control, and the royal line of the Twa, associated with femaleness, strangerhood and movement (cf. Willis 1967, 1981). This concordance is perceptible to the Fipa, one of whom volunteered the comment, in the context of descent naming, that "We (i.e., Fipa men) generate on the 'loins' side because the Twa women entered the country peaceably".[8]

But it is at the widest level of intersocietal relations that the ideological significance of the Fipa system of descent names becomes most apparent, and also most problematic.

Both subcategories of descent name, "head" and "loins", couple the name itself with an associated "avoidance" (*umwiiko*; pl., *imiiko*), apparently reflecting a well-known feature of descent organization in the wider East-Central African culture region, whereby unilineal descent groups are associated with "totemic" objects that are usually, as they also are in the Fipa case, animals or vegetables. Thus of the four Fipa "head" names, *Unnsi* (pl. *Ayannsi*) is coupled with the earth or ground, *insi; Unndeenje* (pl., *Aleenje*) with the domestic dog, *ịsiimbwa; Unnkwaai* (pl., *Akwaai*) with the cow, *ịnyoolwa*: and *Umwiicisi* (pl., *Ayiicisi*) with the wild fig tree (*Ficus capensis*), *unnku*.[9]

Of the twenty-six "loins" names, eighteen have animals (including one insect, the locust) as their associated avoidances; four have vegetable avoidances; two (*Cileengwi* and *Luice*) have the "human being" or "person", *unntu*, as their avoidance, one (*Ingao*) has the human or animal ear, and one (*Cooma*) has both the human or animal nose and the fishhook as its avoidances.[10] Also associated with the coupling of descent names and avoidances are seemingly lighthearted beliefs suggestive of "totemism". It is said that a person with the "loins" name *Inkana* will be of a "fierce" disposition because that name has the leopard, *ingwi*, as its avoidance; and that someone with the "loins" name *Suumpi* will have knees that project backwards because that name has the chicken, *inkhoko*, as its avoidance. Conversely, it is said that all chickens are children of Suumpi and that the pied crow, *Corvus albicollis*, is a Child of Cipeta because that name-category has the crow as its avoidance; that all cows are Akwaai, all goats Pangaala, and so on. There are similar half-serious notions associated with descent names in the contexts of marriage and inheritance. In the case of the name-category *Insia*, one of the most common "loins" names, it is said that formerly people of that name could not marry one another. It is also said that a man who wishes to marry a woman with one or more descent names in common with him has to produce an extra item of bridewealth, such as a hoe or goat. After a man's death, an unrelated man who has the same personal "loins" name may claim to inherit the dead man's wooden stool, *icisuumbi*.

All these ideas, like the regular association of descent name and avoidance, are of course reminiscent to an anthropologist of the ideas and customs commonly associated with unilineal descent groups. This is hardly surprising, given that Ufipa has been substantially populated by immigrants from peoples to the south, southwest and west with unilineal descent organization, exogamic clans and associated "totems": the patrilineal Mambwe, Lungu and Nyamwanga, and the matrilineal Tabwa, Bisa, Lala and Bemba. Moreover, evidence from oral tradition and comparative ethnography suggests rather strongly that kinship organization at an earlier, pre-state stage of Fipa society was based on a unilineal principle (Willis 1981). In this perspective, the Fipa system of descent naming appears like a mental sausage machine, taking in unilineal group solidarity and descent at one end and producing at the other a continuous series of persons with homologous and complexly structured nominal identities, lacking intrinsic descent group allegiance, apt for participation in the individually mobile and production- and market-oriented society of late pre-colonial Ufipa.

It hardly makes sense to think of such a conceptual artifice as taking form in the unconscious way we anthropologists attribute to the convenient harmonics of social function. Someone must have thought it up, some unsung Planck or Einstein of the Fipa plateau, who might well have been female. There are similar problems with kinship systems and natural languages, but here the matter seems less pressing because of the vastly greater timescales involved. In the case of Fipa descent names, we are considering a system that could have come into existence as recently as the early or middle nineteenth century, and hardly earlier than the late eighteenth century. But having been conceived, how did such a strange and intricate system of naming come to be generally adopted in a non-literate society.[11] That is the second question I would put to myself, and to my esteemed colleagues.

In this paper I have surveyed the diverse ways in which Fipa personal names are acquired, adopted, conferred, and transmitted. As with the Kaguru (Beidelman 1974), Fipa personal names entitle different aspects of a person's social identity, this identity being structured as a set of concentric circles with the "innermost" name entitling the most private zone of the self and the "outermost" name or names referring to the owner's public *persona*. In this context Fipa descent names, the main topic of this paper, belong to the inner and private area of personhood, and are consequently used with circumspection and only in an appropriately private and intimate setting.[12]

Fipa descent names do appear to classify persons, but only in a peculiarly vacuous fashion, since the name-categories they denote have no social referents outside the sibling group. Contrary to the implications of Lévi-Strauss' well-known discussion of proper names in *La Pensée Sauvage,* which now appears like a variant of the dominant view in Western philosophy that such names have no meaning, the Fipa system of descent names appears to resonate with meaning derived from this people's perception of history as a cosmological process. This argument resembles Barnes' contention that Hidatsa names "encode events and thereby relate the person to the structure of his community and to its history" (Barnes 1980: 328). I have tried to show how, in the Fipa case, this nominal encoding of events occurs at a number of different levels of personal and social structure and how these various levels are reflected in the system of descent names and naming.

Notes

1. Lévi-Strauss' version of this axiom sees the individual of Western culture as equivalent to a species: "Tout se passe comme si, dans notre civilisation, chaque individu avait sa propre personnalité pour totem" (1962: 284-5).
2. Mr Ntwenya expressed this idea guardedly, saying that "If I have four children, two might have ancestral names from the 'head' side and two from the 'loins' side". In fact Mr Ntwenya had nine living offspring of his marriage.
3. Fipa use the term *uluko* to denote both the concrete group of cognates, the kindred, and the personal "loins" name-category to which a kindred member is affiliated. Raymond Firth has pointed out that my use of the word "personal" here is open to criticism, since it designates not just one but a collective of individuals. Nevertheless I retain the term here, *faute de mieux*. Sir Raymond's observation, for which I am grateful, was made in the course of discussion on this paper at the Durham conference of the ASA. Other interventions from which I also profited included those by Andrew Strathern and David Parkin.
4. Some Fipa also used the word *imbwa*. "I am made (or created)" to introduce their personal "loins" name. Thus Mr Ntwenya said:

1) *Ineene*	*Mwaana*	*Sinu,*	*imbwa*	*Unndeenje*
I (am)	Child (of)	Sinu,	I-am-made	Unndeenje

2) *uluko*	*imbwa*	*unntu*	*Insia*	
kindred	I-am-made	person (of)	Insia	

3) *nfiile*	*Aana*	*Insia*	*yane*	
I-begot	Children (of)	Insia	mine	

5. Cf. Robert 1930: 32, 1949: 52. In the 1930 manuscript Robert somewhat misleadingly calls this name "le nom patronymique".
6. Field research in Ufipa was conducted over 22 months in 1962-4 and 1966. The first and longer period was financed by the Emslie Horniman Anthropological Scholarship Fund and a three-month return visit was made possible by a grant from the Wenner-Gren Foundation for Anthropological Research. I am deeply grateful to both these bodies for their support.
7. Stefaniszyn, discussing the concept of "reincarnation" in the context of a cluster of northern Zambian peoples who are culturally cognate with the Fipa, has concluded that "the natives do not believe in reincarnation but in simple naming, conferring the name of an ancestor, dead or alive, on a child. This may be termed 'nominal reincarnation' ". (Stefaniszyn 1954: 131). This conclusion is too simple to meet the case of the Fipa, whose ideas embrace both "nominal reincarnation" (in Stefaniszyn's useful sense) and

notions of a dead person's spirit spending time in an "underworld" before being reborn among his or her descendants (cf. Robert 1949: 25-29).
8. Statement by Mr Rafaeli Rupia, Ntendo village, 5.9.1966.
9. Cf. Willis 1981: 137.
10. For a full list of Fipa "loins" names see Willis 1981: 138. The listing order is not significant.
11. I found that recent immigrants from the patrilineal Mambwe and Nyamwanga groups tended to adopt Fipa patrilineal ("head") and "loins" names, transmitting both patrilineally, in the same manner as their "traditional" clan name. There was an apparent tendency for the latter name to be dropped, or remembered only as the name of an ancestor. In about half of the 29 cases recorded, these recent immigrants alternated two Fipa "loins" names in the patriline so that, in a typical instance, a man's father and children were called Mimaansi while the man called himself (Mwaana) Cisi. This man and his father were of Nyamwanga descent. These adaptations of Fipa naming practices by immigrants can perhaps be seen as intermediate forms between "lineal simplicity" and the full complexity of the developed Fipa system.
12. "Loins" names are not used outside the context of a naming rite or, according to scattered examples in Robert (1930, 1949) in connection with religious or magical operations. "Head" names were occasionally used in ordinary social intercourse, according to my observations. Their use connotated friendly intimacy with the person referred to or addressed.

References

Barnes, R. H. 1980. Hidatsa personal names: an interpretation. *Plains Anthropologist (Journal of the Plains Conference)* **25-90**, 311-31.

Beidelman, T. O. 1974. Kaguru names and naming. *Journal of Anthropological Research* **30**, 281-93.

Gardiner, A. H. 1940. *The theory of proper names: a controversial essay*. London: Oxford University Press.

Goodenough, Ward H. 1962. Kindred and hamlet in Lakalai, New Britain. *Ethnology* **1**, 5-12.

—— 1965. Personal names and modes of address in two Oceanic societies. In *Context and Meaning in Cultural Anthropology* (ed.) Melford E. Spiro. New York: Free Press. pp. 265-276.

Lévi-Strauss, C. 1962. *La Pensée Sauvage*. Paris: Plon.

Lyons, John. 1977. *Semantics*. Cambridge: University Press. 2 vols.

Mill, J. S. 1868. *A System of Logic, raticinative and inductive, etc.* London: Longmans, Green, Reader & Dyer. 2 vols.

Robert, J. M. (*Père*) 1930. *Coutumes des Wafipa*. Kate Mission, Ufipa: mimeographed manuscript. (White Fathers' Archives, Rome, No. 803.11.)

—— 1949. *Croyances et coutumes magico-religieuses des Wafipa paiens*. Tabora: Tanganyika Mission Press.

Stefaniszyn, B. 1954. African reincarnation re-examined. *African Studies* **13** (3-4), 131-146.

Tonkin, E. 1981. Jealousy names, civilized names: anthroponomy of the Jlao Kru of Liberia. *Man* (N.S.) **15**(4), 653-664.

Willis, R. G. 1967. The head and the loins: Lévi-Strauss and beyond. *Man* (N.S.) **2**(4), 519-534.

——— 1972. Pollution and paradigms. *Man* (N.S.) **7**(3), 369-378.

——— 1974. *Man and Beast*. London: Basic Books.

——— 1978. Magic and "medicine" in Ufipa. In *Culture and Curing* (eds) Peter Morley & Roy Wallis. London: Peter Owen.

——— 1981. *A state in the making: myth, history and social transformation in pre-colonial Ufipa*. Bloomington: Indiana University Press.

THE CREATION OF IDENTITY IN SPIRIT MEDIUMSHIP AND POSSESSION

JUDITH T. IRVINE

In a vast number of societies around the world, including some sectors of our own, it is thought possible for a supernatural being to come into such close control of a human individual as to determine that person's speech and other behaviour in intimate detail. This condition − possession or mediumship − is considered unusual or abnormal, in the sense of being distinct from the condition that might be imputed to the medium's human social self. No matter how long possession lasts, or how regularly (or remuneratively) it occurs, it implicitly contrasts with some merely human, unpossessed state. But by what signs, if any, are these contrasting states displayed? How do people who witness or hear about particular behavioural events come to interpret them as instances of possession or spirit mediumship? Is it the behaviour of the medium or possessed person that creates, for an audience, the "meaning" of being derived from a supernatural agent residing in or speaking through the human medium, rather than from that human being's own social persona? Many works on possession (e.g., Oesterreich 1974; Beattie and Middleton 1969) seem to assume that the behaviour attributed to a supernatural agent is always *clearly distinct* from the behaviour characteristics of the human medium's everyday social self, just as the meanings, possessed and unpossessed, contrast. We shall see, however, that this is not always so.

Dominating much of the considerable anthropological literature on spirit possession are two issues: the psychology of possession, as subjective experience and as the expression or result of tensions in the possessed person's life (see, e.g., papers in Crapanzano and Garrison 1977); and the societal functions of possession, for example as an avenue of acceptable protest for the downtrodden (see Lewis

1971: 32). Although I do not dispute the importance of these aspects of possession my concern in this paper is more sociolinguistic and communicational: how a speaker's social identity, and the identity of a message source, are established through speech and other communicative behaviour. The creation of identity in spirit possession is thus merely a specific example of a more general question. It is a question for which the psychological state of the possessed person is less pertinent than the interpretive frameworks of the native observer. In fact, the native observer's interpretive process, and the complexity of factors entering into it, are my real subject matter.

The topics to be explored are the following:

1) The relationship between communicative form and "occult" meaning. The starting point here is the cultural repertoire of communicative codes. For a given society, communicative forms attributable to spirit sources may be compared with those attributable to human sources. Is the connection between some particular form and the occult source a *necessary* connection, within a particular cultural system? Cross-culturally? Does intelligibility play a role?

2) The relationship between spirit communication and its context, in the social situation in which it occurs. To what extent do interpretations of behaviour as mediumship or possession depend upon some special setting? In what ways do interpretations depend upon the audience's motives and interests?

3) The place of the possession/mediumship episode in a historical trajectory. How does that trajectory impinge on the interpretation of a communicative event as an instance of possession?

Although most of these questions could be fruitfully explored within a single ethnographic case, I shall take a comparative approach, in the hope that it will facilitate some general understanding of relationships between behavioural forms, cultural systems, contexts of situation, personal interests, temporal dimensions, and the "meanings" that these factors jointly create. The comparison is intended to show that the question of how people make an interpretation of the behaviour they observe can only have a very complex answer, because any one generalization about what the interpretive process rests upon will always find exceptions.

The Form of Spirit Communications

Let us start with code repertoires and their cultural matrix. Why is a spirit thought to communicate in a particular way, and how does this code compare with codes the medium or possessed person might otherwise use? In each cultural system, cultural ideas about what the supernatural being is like, and what its relation to human society might be, provide a basis for the symbolic forms the spirit will use and how spirit communication is organized. In other words, underlying each code repertoire is a conceptual system that organizes the ways of speaking (and other behaviour) considered appropriate conduct for supernatural and human actors.

In illustration of this matter, consider some descriptions, dating from the 1930s, of spirit possession among the Flathead Indians of Montana (Ray 1937; Turney-High 1933, 1937). During the Flatheads' annual midwinter ceremony there is an event called the Bluejay Dance, in which a group of shamans who have Bluejay as their guardian spirit become possessed by him. According to Ray (1937: 595), the shaman's transformation into Bluejay during the ceremony re-creates a mythical state when guardian spirit and man were a single being. The power to return to the original unified condition belongs specially to persons having Bluejay guardians.

As the Bluejay dance progresses, the shamans' transformation is reflected in changes in their behaviour, which becomes increasingly different from the speech and movements of ordinary social life. By the end of the second night of the ceremony the shamans begin to be possessed by Bluejay. In the words of Turney-High's description (1937: 39), they "talk backwards, in gibberish" and then start making bluejay sounds: "Chirping and cawing, they ascend the lodgepoles and run about the rafters with remarkable agility, perching and twittering in bird fashion." At this point they have actually become Bluejay. On the third night the shamans, restored to their human condition, hold a curing session which is supposed to be especially effective because the shamans have just been merged with the Bluejay spirit from whom their curing power derives.

Obviously, the behaviour attributed here to the possessing spirit is consonant with Flathead cultural ideas about who the spirit is: the spirit is Bluejay, so the possessed person makes bird-like sounds and movements. Bluejay's utterances are not intelligible to the audience and need not be translated for them, because the purpose of the shamans' possession is not to relay some particular message from Bluejay but to enhance their own curing powers through temporary identification with him. Here we have a case, then, where the behaviour attributed to the spirit is (a) widely different from any "human" code, (b) specifically iconic with respect to its supposed spirit source, and (c) unintelligible (i.e., lacking referential specificity). But while it is evident that all these matters are accounted for in the Flathead cultural system, how consistent are they, and how generalizable to other ethnographic examples?

Intelligibility, it turns out, is not a yes-or-no matter even in the Flathead case. Although the Bluejay sounds are modelled on animal noises and not on any human language, nevertheless the Flathead apparently do consider that animal noises can have some linguistic significance. Accordingly, some listeners hope to decipher the shamans' bluejay sounds and use them for prophecy (Turney-High 1937: 39).[1] Presumably, other Flathead listeners would agree that *someone* might be able to decipher the animal sounds, even though they themselves cannot. The intelligibility of spirit communications, therefore, is not a property of the spirit's code *per se*, but a negotiable matter involving participation by members of the audience. Even in a community where cultural ideas about spirit possession are relatively homogeneous, members of the audience may still differ in the degree to which they attribute referential specificity to the spirit's code, and the degree to which they are personally implicated as message recipients.

This quesiton of intelligibility also illustrates the difficulty of making any clearcut distinction between spirit possession and spirit mediumship, as some authors have proposed (e.g., Firth 1967; Beattie and Middleton 1969), on the basis of whether the spirit communicates to the audience. Indeed — as these authors recognize — a spirit identified as such by an audience always communicates *something* to them, if only its presence. But whether there are additional messages with more specific (and referential) content, how intelligible they are and to whom, and what portion of the audience finds them relevant or makes an effort to decipher them, are matters that admit many variations.

Some of this range of possibilities can be seen in another ethnographic example: American Pentecostalist sects where church members moved by the Holy Ghost "speak in tongues". Most Pentecostalists maintain that their glossolalic utterances are not gibberish, but are made in a language unknown to the speaker. That the speaker finds himself or herself able to command an unknown language is considered miraculous (and therefore evidence of the Holy Ghost's influence); moreover, the fact that the language is unknown is thought to show that God has touched the speaker's spiritual and emotional self, rather than the rational self, which is associated with known languages and considered antithetical to the deepest religious experience. As the evangelist Oral Roberts writes (1964: 22, quoted in Samarin 1972: 155), "If one prays through his intellect his mind creates the speech patterns and words. When one prays through his spirit, it is his spirit in cooperation with the Holy Spirit that forms the words of a new language".

Although all glossolalic speech forms are unfamiliar, some glossolalia nevertheless is thought to have specific message content. The "new language" encodes messages just as other languages do; the question is whether anyone can understand them. Sometimes it is the speaker who perceives, either immediately or after some lapse of time, what message has been conveyed and is able to offer an interpretation or summary of it (see Samarin 1972: 92, 171). Alternatively, the interpretation may be offered by a member of the audience, either someone who more or less regularly serves in this capacity or someone who suddenly and "miraculously" understands the message. For some Pentecostalists, only the presence of an interpreter distinguishes glossolalia that bears a message for the congregation from glossolalia that merely manifests the presence of the Spirit (although they may give the two types of glossolalia separate labels). The form of the glossolalic behaviour itself will not suffice to show which communicational function the Spirit intends, or to predict what the members of the audience will under-stand (see Willis 1966: 264-265). In other words, the form does not fully determine, or even signal, the communicative function, which depends as well on active participation by an audience that collaborates in attributing meaning to the speaker's behaviour.

In the two ethnographic examples so far discussed, Flathead Indians and US Pentecostalists, the speech attributed to a spirit source differs radically from any familiar human linguistic code; and both cultural systems provide a rationale for the unfamiliarity of spirit utterances. Of course, the cultural explanations are quite different, and so are the behavioural particulars of the spirit com-munications. Glossolalia, though far from uniform, cannot usually be described as "chirping and cawing". Indeed, it is quite difficult to make any cross-cultural generalizations about the behavioural form spirit communications will take. For example, in some societies the presence of a spirit persona in a human medium is signalled by the use of a verbal code much less different from everyday speech than in the Flathead and Pentecostalist examples. Thus the speech of some of the Haitian *loa* spirits differs from human speech in its specially "nasal tone" (Métraux 1959: 132-133), but apparently not in other aspects of linguistic form. In other societies, the spirit voice may be indicated by instrumental music. Among the Dan of Ivory Coast, for instance, certain spirit masks "speak" with a *mirliton* (a membranophone instrument) attached as a mouthpiece to the mask; and among the Bedik of south-eastern Senegal, the voice of one type of spirit is rendered by a flautist who stands behind the dancer wearing the spirit's mask.[2] In still other societies a spirit's behavioural "code" can consist in immobility and silence.

My next example, which comes from fieldwork in a rural Wolof village in Senegal, illustrates this last possibility – where a spirit communicates via zero-forms, as it were.[3] For these rural Wolof, one of the most important kinds of spirits that might possess a human being are the family spirits known as the "great *rab*" (distinguished from lesser *rab* who are not associated with particular families). These great *rab* are localized spirits who live in natural mounds of earth, or in the trees growing on those mounds. They are said to have associated themselves with the founding ancestor of a Wolof lineage and to watch over that ancestor's descendants and their dependants. If one of those persons should violate the rules of behaviour appropriate for his/her family and rank, or if he or she should neglect to make offerings to the *rab* and inform it of family affairs, the spirit may "catch" (*japp*) and perhaps even possess the offender.

Although the person who has offended a great *rab* may be agitated, feverish, or even convulsed as the spirit approaches, actual possession is marked by symptoms such as paralysis or rigidity and silence. Immobility and silence are considered appropriate behaviour for an earth spirit, and they also "correct" the human being's offense, should the offense have consisted in unbridled action. At least, this is the folk view taken in the village where I worked. Village informants drew a strong connection between the great *rab*, the earth, and the moral values involving stability, sobriety, and restraint (including restraint in movements and talk). Clearly, the Wolof spirit's silence is iconically accounted for within its cultural matrix, even though the zero-forms that constitute this "code" differ from the forms of spirit behaviour we have so far described for other cultural systems.

Now, what relation do these zero-forms have to Wolof notions of ordinary human behaviour? Apparently the spirit's behaviour – that is, the behaviour of the person fully possessed by the great *rab* – is thought to contrast with ordinary human behaviour, but only in degree, not in kind. Some degree of silence and restraint is considered appropriate for human beings too, especially those descended from the village's founding ancestor. Since the human version of restraint would not amount to total rigidity, a contrast with the ordinary is preserved. Yet, the contrast depends on an exaggeration of human signs, not a departure from them.

Thus there is no universal requirement that nonhuman agency

can only be signalled in nonhuman signs. Even for the other ethnographic cases discussed so far, any such proposition would be difficult to maintain. For instance, although glossolalic utterances of Pentecostalists can be shown, when recorded and subjected to linguistic analysis, to be significantly different from natural languages (see Samarin 1972), many members of the congregation suppose that some particular foreign language is being spoken, such as Hebrew, Spanish, Chinese, etc.[4] Apparently it is not the speech forms themselves that are necessarily thought to be supernatural, but their utterance by a particular speaker who can be assumed never to have acquired knowledge of them in the ordinary course of life. The contrast that is significant to the audience is the contrast with the speaker's own ordinary behaviour, not with human behaviour in general. Of course, this has implications about the audience's notions of what the ordinary behaviour of that speaker should be.

To examine this contrast further, let us return to the Wolof example. The great *rab* are not the only type of spirit which, in the Wolof view, might possess a human being. Lesser *rab* can also "catch" a person and alter his or her behaviour, as can some other categories of spirits, such as *jinni* and *saitaan*. Unlike the great *rab*, who mark their presence by paralysis and silence, these lesser spirits may speak through the person they have caught – at least in certain contexts, such as the public possession rites called *ndëp*, performed for the curing of illness.[5] The communicative forms used by these spirits parallel the human communicative repertoire, just as the social organization of the Wolof spirit world mirrors human society in certain respects. *Rab* may have ethnic, religious, and occupational identities just as human beings do, and these identities are variously displayed in the behaviour of the possessed. For example, a spirit displays Fulbe ethnicity by using some Pulaar vocabulary and phrases; a *sëriñ* (Muslim cleric) spirit recites verses from the Koran; a *griot* (praise-singer) spirit declaims the praises of persons in the audience and demands money from them; and so on (see Zempléni 1966: 403-404).

Apparently, the persons possessed by these spirits are usually (always?) individuals who would not use those forms of speech in everyday life – that is, they are not Fulbe, clerics, griots, etc. Indeed, in the Wolof folk view, a medium under the spirit's influence can speak a foreign language that he or she has never learned. Or, the medium might speak Wolof but in a manner contrasting with his or her everyday performance. If a noble, for example, is possessed by a *griot* spirit, and under this influence launches into the special declamatory style, and the begging and flattery, characteristic of praise-singers, then the spirit persona's behaviour contrasts sharply with the laconic, matter-of-fact style more appropriate to the medium's own social status as a noble.[6] But whether such behaviour might serve as *diagnostic* of a spirit presence — whether it will signal a change in identity — depends on the audience's assuming that the speaker would *not* otherwise be speaking Pulaar, or begging, or whatever. This may be problematic, particularly if the behaviour to be attributed to spirit agency is something that would otherwise be considered shameful or punishable (as many writers on spirit possession have pointed out).

I shall return to the matter of diagnosis later. For now, the point is that to identify certain modes of behaviour as deriving from a spirit persona is also to identify what behaviour is attributable to the medium's human persona. Where these definitions involve a contrast, they can be creatively played off against each other, so that when some type of behaviour is attributed to a spirit, neither the medium personally nor members of the medium's social category are implicated as engaging in it. But note that the effectiveness of any such playing-off depends on the degree of consensus in the audience as to (a) what social roles and categories there are and what behaviours are attributable to each, and (b) the personal history and category membership of the medium. How well members of the audience are personally acquainted with the medium and know to what social category the medium belongs must influence the expectations they hold about the medium's ordinary behaviour, and (in turn) influence their interpretation of the possession episode. (In this regard the *scale* of the community of witnesses — the social unit from which the audiences of possession episodes are drawn — becomes as relevant to the interpretive process as is the degree of cultural homogeneity within the unit.)

Now, all the ethnographic cases discussed so far do involve some contrast between possessed and unpossessed behaviour. That is, the presence of a spirit as message source is displayed when the human speaker behaves in a manner unusual for his or her everyday self. Some writers on possession and mediumship seem to assume that possession must always be contrastively marked — indeed, that all "religious language" must somehow contrast with secular forms. Yet, my next example of the ways spirits can communicate is a case in which the speech attributable to a spiritual source must be *identical* to the human medium's ordinary speech, in order to qualify as coming from the spirit. This apparent paradox obtains in a Quaker community in Maryland that I observed in the 1960s.[7] There, the speaker who uses unusual forms of speech or gesture during a meeting for worship risks being considered "crazy" or fraudulent, rather than one who speaks from divine inspiration.

It may seem a little odd to group Quaker "inspired speech" together with spirit possession, since the term "possession" suggests that the spirit enters the human medium from outside (and leaves again afterwards). For the Quakers the spirit is not intrusive; it is the "inner light," "that of God in every man" – something permanently present though usually masked by a person's worldly self.[8] But whether the spirit comes and goes, or is masked and unmasked, does not matter for our purposes here. What is important is that the Quakers' "inspired speech" is considered to come from God, who is inside the human being and moves him or her to speak as the spirit dictates.

Although "speaking from the light" is supposed to be spontaneous, divinely inspired, and free from any concerns of outward form, in fact there are definite rules about what it should be like and when it should occur. I derive these rules not only from Quaker writings but, more especially, from community gossip about members of the meeting, and from the informal instructions elders give the young about how to recognize divine inspiration in oneself. The elders said that God does not usually move people to speak very often or for very long; and in fact if someone spoke at three or more meetings in a row, or spoke twice in one meeting, or spoke for longer than about five minutes, other people made unfavourable (though private) comments afterwards. Also, divinely-inspired speech should be plain and unadorned speech. Adornments, such as fancy rhetoric or singsong voice, can only come from the earthly personality. Two people who spoke during meetings in a slightly high-pitched, quavering style, with frequent references to the Bible and Jesus, were considered "a little senile" and "a little crazy" respectively by their fellows. The speech of other adults in the meeting did not differ in style or content from their speech in serious discussion outside the meeting. Yet, the meeting speech was considered divinely inspired and the social speech was not.

Although "plain speaking" and its association with the spiritual have been part of Quaker doctrine since the sect's seventeenth-century beginnings, the modern Quaker's display of inspiration seems to have altered somewhat from seventeenth-century usage as described by Bauman (1972, 1974). In the early days of Quakerism, trance states, trembling, quaking speech, and loud declamatory speech were apparently not thought incompatible with the divine presence, and indeed might even signal that a spiritual conversion was imminent. Incoherent speech could be a sign of spontaneity and therefore of spiritual genuineness; biblical exhortation (provided it was unrehearsed) could be an instrument for converting the worldly. It appears, therefore, that certain forms of speech and behaviour now thought deviant might have been among those most favoured by early Quakers, although the principle of "plain speaking" has not itself changed. For early Quakers, spontaneity and the avoidance of forms associated with the worldly life (and with non-Quakers and the established Church) were the hallmarks of plain speaking; for modern Quakers, less concerned with proselytizing and less subject to hostility from the outside world, plain speaking comes to mean something more like everyday speaking.[9]

How, then, do the modern Maryland Quakers distinguish the utterances attributable to the spiritual source from those that come from the speaker's human persona? The answer lies in the context of the code rather than in the code itself. Inspired speech uses the same code as everyday speech, but it is differentiated from the everyday by its setting in the meeting for worship, which occurs at a regular time and place and contains a regular sequence of events. At 11:00 on Sunday (First Day, in Quaker parlance) the elders of the meeting lead the assembled members into the meeting room. After everyone is seated, there follows a silence of at least ten minutes. There are also silences between turns at talk, and silence at the end of the meeting, from 11:55 (or before) until 12 noon. At noon, after the final boundary-marking silence, the elders rise and lead the members out of the meeting room, across the corridor, and into a social room that occupies the opposite half of the building. Here people chat informally, eating cookies and drinking tea. Here is the everyday social self, bounded off from the inspired self by space, time, and silences, but not differing in verbal code. Ironically, while the Quakers disparage ritual and concern for outward form, they have come to depend on a special organization of behavioural sequences — that is to say, on a ritual form — in order to identify spiritual communication as such.

With Quaker "inspired speech" we have moved far away from the initial ethnographic case, the Flathead, where spiritual communication was marked by radically non-human behavioural forms. The Quakers present a virtual opposite; and we have seen various other possibilities in between. To summarize the cases considered in this section, they have illustrated the following points:

a) There is no cross-cultural regularity about the form of spirit communications, even as to whether they contrast with the communicative forms of everyday life, as long as there is some other means to identify which is which.

b) Although there is always some cultural rationale that relates communicative forms to their meanings, those meanings remain quite underdeterminative of the forms that convey them. Among the Quakers, the concepts of plain speaking and the inner light (as contrasting with outward form) "explain" the forms of speech used in the Quaker meeting; yet, the concept of plain speaking as inspired speaking does not predict whether a quivering voice is to be considered simplicity or adornment.

c) Many aspects of interpretation, such as the (referential) intelligibility of spirit utterances, and the organization of a ritual sequence, crucially involve active participation — one might even say collusion — by the audience.

Setting, History and Interests

The preceding section was principally concerned with questions about the *form* of spirit communications — their code — in relation to a matrix of cultural ideas. I have argued, however, that even in a community where such ideas might be relatively homogenous they would not fully account for the interpretive process, by which members of an audience interpret someone's behaviour as deriving from a spirit persona. Some of the other factors impinging on the process of interpretation should now be considered more closely (although they have already been at least mentioned). They concern the relationship of the interpreted behaviour to its context of situation, particularly including setting, past history, and audience interests.

To begin, it will be instructive to compare the Quaker case with some of the others, such as the Pentecostalists. We have seen that among some modern Quakers inspired speech is identical in form with everyday social speech, but it is distinguishable by its setting. That is, it is identifiable not by form but by its time and place. In contrast, Pentecostalist glossolalia, conspicuously different from everyday speech, can erupt quite suddenly and in any setting — at least, according to glossolalists. One of Felicitas Goodman's informants, a woman member of an Apostolic congregation in Mexico City, reported:

> As for me, I kneel to pray, I feel contact, and I speak in tongues. I may be washing the dishes, and the Lord may be telling me to speak in tongues, whether I am alone or with others. It may happen to me on the market, or walking down a road, wherever it may be. It doesn't matter, for it is the same benediction that the Lord also gives me here in the church. (Goodman 1972: 37)

This report is not unusual among Pentecostalists, nor among some other mediumistic groups. A woman Spiritualist medium practising in Connecticut told June Macklin this about an early mediumistic experience (Macklin 1977: 52):

> I lived near my mother and I used to go up there and help her do her work every day. I went up on a Monday and didn't feel good. I had just had a rotten day. She was a great tea drinker, and we sat down and had a cup of tea . . . She told me that we were talking about average things when all of a sudden my eyes closed; I slumped; my voice changed, and she said I started to talk. I told her things relative to her people that she didn't even know about herself. She took a special trip to Vermont to find out if they were accurate. I looked at her and said, "Ma, you mean that that's all there is to it? I never felt anything, going or coming." It was because of the change in my voice that she knew *I* wasn't talking to her.

In Haiti, too, possession by a *loa* spirit may occur during the course of a ceremony *or* in ordinary daily life (Métraux 1959: 131). From Métraux's descriptions, it seems as if the examples from daily life have a specially nasal voice quality, not necessarily found in the ceremonies.

What these examples suggest is that there is an inverse relationship between the symbolic forms and their setting, such that if the one is marked or special, the other may be unmarked or ordinary. "Ritual," that is to say some special, conventional organization of behavioural sequences, is most required in just those cases where spirits use the speech of everyday life. Where spirits use a different code, a ritual context does not seem to be required, although it may occur.

If this is true it is an important matter, because it concerns our ideas about ritual forms in general. Many writers tend to assume that social activities, and the behavioural forms that occur in them, can be lined up on a one-dimensional scale as they become progressively marked and "ritualized" — ranging from the informal, ordinary, and unstructured on the one hand to the formal, special, and rigidified on the other. But the materials I have examined here (concerning code and context in spirit possession) suggest a more complex, nonlinear relationship among behavioural forms. Code does not merely reflect context, but (instead) interacts with it.[10]

Now, although I think this point generally holds true, the matter is actually even a bit more complicated. For example, the contrast between Quakers and Pentecostalists may seem somewhat less compelling when we discover that many Quakers might also *claim* that inspired speech can occur at any time.[11] In reality, however, the only modern day examples of truly inspired speech that community members were willing to identify occurred during meetings for worship. Can the contrast (between spirit-inspired speech as occurring any time, and spirit-inspired speech as occurring only in special settings) be reduced to a difference between what people claim they do and what they actually do? Not quite. The Quaker claim that inspired speech can occur outside the meeting apparently remains an abstract claim, at least for modern times — rather lacking in specific examples, unlike the Pentecostalist statements; and the contexts in which Samarin (1972) and others report Pentecostalist glossolalia occurring seem to be a broader set than in the Quaker case. Nevertheless, the argument made above about the relationship between code and context needs to be reframed, focused more on the interpretive process than on code and context *per se*.

This brings us back to the question that started this paper: how an interpretation is created. In other words — for spirit possession and mediumship — how an audience comes to interpret particular behavioural events as instances of a supernatural agent speaking through, or residing in, a human medium. The critical issue, then, is diagnosis. What criteria, if any, identify the spirit presence? What does the audience itself contribute?

The Quaker case indicates that a change in verbal code on the part of the medium is not universally either a necessary or a sufficient criterion identifying spiritual communication; other aspects of the situation, such as spatial and temporal setting, can take on this semantic load. There still remain some other questions to be answered, however. First of all, part of what is accomplished by regularities of setting (as with the regulation of time and space in the Quaker meeting) is to establish a set of expectations on the part of the audience, expectations which are perhaps the more powerful to the degree that the audience has already been actively participating in the activities that establish them. But are there not other factors, extending beyond the bounds of a particular social occasion, that influence such expectations? A history of past interactions and personal reputations is obviously important too.

Thus for the Quakers (for example), it makes a difference whether a speaker has spoken in meetings before, including whether these contributions have been frequent or lengthy. And, in the case of a young person essaying inspired speech in the meeting for the first time, it is considered difficult for either the audience or the speaker to assess whether the speech is truly inspired or not. Personal histories then become especially relevant. In one or two instances where I heard elders discussing the utterances of particular teenagers, attention was focused on the reputation for sincerity and probity which these teenagers had established, or failed to establish, in the recent past.

As another example, let us look again at Macklin's Connecticut medium, quoted above. The medium attributes her mother's identification of the spirit persona to her (the medium's) altered speech: "It was because of the change in my voice that she knew *I* wasn't talking to her." Yet, it seems that the change of voice was not actually sufficient evidence. The medium goes on to say (Macklin 1977: 52): "And it was proof enough to her that I was under control, because I told her things about her family that she herself did not know. She tested me regularly because she wasn't convinced of the reality of it at first." It is not only the change of voice, therefore, but also the content of the statements and, especially, the establishment of a pattern over time that seem to be crucial. Conceivably, now that the informant has a firm reputation as a medium it might be sufficient for her merely to alter her voice in order to signal a spirit's presence, at least for an audience of believers. But this was not so in her first possession episodes.

The doubts that attended the Connecticut medium's first signs of possession are not just the product of a Western skepticism. I have already touched on this point with reference to the Wolof; let me return to it in more detail. What I mentioned earlier was that whether a particular form of behaviour can serve as diagnostic of a spirit presence – signalling change of identity – depends on the audience's assuming that the medium would not otherwise behave in quite this way; and where the behaviour at issue is something shameful or punishable, interpretation becomes problematic. For example, in a Senegalese radio play broadcast in the village where I worked, a male character claimed that his violent, undisciplined behaviour, in the course of which he had raped his stepdaughter, was due to possession by a *saitaan* (fire spirit). The village audience, commenting on the play, found this account less than fully convincing. Although they did not doubt the *possibility* of possession by *saitaan*, they doubted its relevance to the particular case.

In fact, despite widespread agreement among Wolof villagers as to how, in principle, persons possessed by various sorts of spirits are likely to behave, the interpretation of actual cases is rarely clearcut. It is not only that there is a variety of spirits, such as great *rab*, lesser *rab, saitaan*, etc., that might be implicated, but that possession by a spirit is not the only meaning that can be attributed to unusual behaviour. Other possibilities include organic causes (e.g., disharmony of the bodily fluids); attacks by witchcraft or sorcery; and counterattacks by anti-witchcraft forces, that cause a person to reveal his or her witchhood. Although each of these causes or agencies has some resulting state or behaviour typical of it, the differences are not sharply defined, only probabilistic. For instance, since witches usually harm people by poisoning them, digestive troubles are a likely sign of witch attacks; but they are not the only possible sign. Witches might do "anything" to their victims. So when someone becomes ill or behaves in a peculiar way, it is often quite unclear what might have caused the condition. Divination by experts does not really solve the problem, because no diviner on the local scene has unquestioned authority or is free from suspicion as to his own interests in the diagnosis.

A particular case will illustrate this ambiguity. In 1971, "Kumba Samb" (not her real name) was a middle-aged woman whose life had not, so far as I know, been marked by any strikingly unusual behaviour until, early one morning, she sat down in the middle of her household courtyard and began to rock back and forth, shaking and crying out loudly. This went on for several hours. Her husband sent for her mother and older sister; they consulted a diviner, who gave them a medicinal potion that calmed her. Apparently no further episodes occurred, although it is hard to be sure because the family kept her out of sight.

Kumba Samb's family claimed that she was possessed by a *rab* (perhaps not the local great *rab*, but some lesser spirit), because she sat down, because she shook, and because the diviner said so and his medicine worked. Some other villagers thought, however, that if she were possessed at all it was most likely, for genealogical reasons, to be by the great *rab*; and her agitation and shouting did not suggest the great rab's presence. Instead, they argued, she was probably a witch confessing her identity. For, if a witch attacks someone who is well protected by holy amulets, in the confrontation of forces the witch may break down and confess (*jifuur*) – babbling in the witches' secret language and naming his/her evil acts and confederates. The evidence of this in Kumba Samb's case was her agitation and shouting, and especially a particular phrase she used: *man rakkajju naa*, "I have *rakkajju*'d." Since nobody knew what the word *rakkajju* meant, it sounded like secret language. The morphology and syntax of the utterance (the use of perfective aspect plus the topicalized redundant pronoun *man* "I") also suggested confession.

The people I spoke to about this case were careful to point out that they "did not know enough about such matters" to be *sure* whether Kumba Samb was a witch or possessed – they only thought she *probably* was whichever one they opted for. There were not active reprisals against Kumba Samb or her family, nor any public accusation, and the family never had to back down from their position. But whether because of the witchcraft rumors or because of a wish to conceal some continuing eccentricity on Kumba's part, later that year the family sold their property and moved out of town.

That this case was never definitively resolved is not only because the behaviour in question was ambiguous to begin with. Efforts to clarify its meaning through ritual manipulations (divination) failed as well, since they could not escape the charge of conflict of interest, and conflicting interests were probably at the root of the disagreement in the first place. For the implications of the two diagnoses are quite different. If Kumba Samb is to be considered a witch then the rest of her family probably should be considered witches too, and avoided, because witchcraft is a family trait. But if she is merely possessed by a spirit, then the family is not implicated (at least, not to the same extent). That the family has a vested interest in someone's not being considered a witch was pointed out by those villagers who discounted the family's arguments. On the other hand, other villages stood to gain by a witchcraft diagnosis, either by acquiring a convenient scapegoat for their own ills, or by acquiring the family's property at a low price (since a family that has to leave town in a hurry will have to sell at a loss).

This case is not particularly unusual, among the Wolof or else-where. It is a case in which the cultural frameworks for interpreting a person's behaviour as possession or as something else provide no unambiguous answer, in spite of divination and apparent cure, and in spite of the fact that the villagers did not dispute the observable evidence or disagree as to the typical characteristics of spirits and witches. The point, of course, is that the members of a community may have conflicting interests as to how someone's behaviour is interpreted. When this is so, the conceptual framework for inter-pretation will not prevent the behavioural evidence from being used in support of competing arguments. The behavioural evidence is ambiguous, and the principles of interpretation are flexible. Although Wolof maintain that ritual manipulations (such as divina-tion or the *ndëp,* public expression rites) can sometimes clarify the meanings of ambiguous behaviour, there is no guarantee that this imposition of special settings and behavioural contexts will actually put an end to the debate, if the interests at stake are sufficiently strong. Rather, the ritual occasion may simply provide new material for discussion.

Once again, then, we have seen that the process by which people who witness or hear about particular behavioural events and come to interpret them as instances of spiritual agency does not depend on properties of communicative code alone, even if that code is well-grounded in a cultural system of meanings and fully agreed-upon by all parties. Rather, the emergence of an interpretation will also depend on contexts of situation; it will depend on the observers' knowledge of participants' past histories; and it will depend on the motives and interests of the various observers who interpret what is going on. In other words, interpretation is a creative process, incorporating a historical trajectory, and involving active collusion among participants. The strictly semantic relation placing a behavioural form in a system of cultural meaning is not the full picture.

Conclusion

This paper has examined the process of interpretation by which witnesses come to attribute supernatural agency to human actions. The principal argument is two-fold: that the interpretive process is very complex; and that it is a creative process, not merely residing in the symbolic forms taken by the interpreted behaviour itself — important as those forms and their cultural matrix are — but also drawing upon the witnesses' own motives, and their knowledge of setting, personal histories, and surrounding events.

There is no reason to suppose that these arguments apply only to cases of spirit mediumship and possession. Although those have furnished my ethnographic materials other communicative phenomena might have done as well. For example, one could look at other types of spokesmanship — message-bearing, interpreting, quoting, and so forth — in all of which cases the audience must suppose that the speaker's message has some source external to himself or herself. Another possibility would be cases of role-switching. In spirit mediumship the roles taken by the medium are particularly divergent (associated with spirit and human identities), but less drastic sorts of role-switching also suggest an audience who concur that the switcher is now acting in some different capacity. Yet another example would be the attribution of insanity, especially in the insanity defense, where juries must decide whether defendants are personally responsible for their actions. In some societies, of course, the attribution of insanity overlaps with spirit possession, which may be invoked as its explanation.

What all these examples have in common concerns the allocation of responsibility to a person acting in some particular capacity.

Perhaps putting the matter this way can make it more apparent that the audience's decision as to whether, or in what way, a person is responsible for his or her acts is itself a moral act as well.

This is not the place to explore these other kinds of examples further, however. My point, rather, is that all the considerations this discussion has brought to bear upon spirit mediumship should apply to these other communicative phenomena also: the relation of communicative forms to a cultural rationale; the interaction of behavioural form, context of situation, motive, and historical trajectory; and the collusion between performer and audience. It cannot be assumed, therefore, that code-switching – some shift in behavioural forms – will be necessary or sufficient to effect a shift in attributed roles or identities without any other factors being relevant. No simple correlation can capture the richness of the process by which interpretations are reached.

Notes

1. Whether Flathead ever attempt (or attempted) to decipher specific messages from sounds made by actual animals is somewhat unclear in the literature. The importance of animals in the vision quest (as the form in which a guardian spirit appears and communicates with the seeker), and the use of animal noises as sources for songs, are suggestive of this point but not conclusive. See Merriam 1967: 3-8.
2. This case illustrates the difficulty of distinguishing between the *representation* of a spirit voice and possession/mediumship, where the spirit "actually" communicates directly. I observed these Bedik masks on a brief visit to a Bedik village in May 1971. Thanks are due to Marie-Paule Ferry for facilitating my entrée.
3. My fieldwork among rural Wolof was carried out in 1970-71, 1975, and 1977, mostly in a village in the Préfecture de Tivaouane. I am grateful to the National Institute of Mental Health, the National Science Foundation, and Brandeis University for financial support of that research, and to the Institut Fondamental d'Afrique Noire and the Centre de Linguistique Appliquée de Dakar for institutional sponsorship.
4. Pentecostalists differ as to whether they distinguish glossolalia from xenolalia (speaking an unlearned foreign tongue); see Horton 1966.
5. For extensive descriptions of *ndëp* possession rites, see Zempléni 1966, 1977.
6. See Irvine 1975 for a fuller description of these speech styles.
7. Modern Quakerism is actually quite diverse. My comments about modern Quakers in this paper, therefore, must be taken as applying only to the community I observed and any others which may resemble it; they are not generalizable to all Quaker communities.
8. For these reasons Quakers do not use the word "possession" to describe the

presence or activity of the spirit, nor shall I apply it here to Quaker "speaking from the light." Nevertheless, the distinction between a divinely-influenced self and an ordinary worldly self brings this case into the same sociolinguistic rubric — where one may ask how these selves, or personas, are behaviourally manifested and how they are identified — as in the cases of possession and mediumship considered elsewhere in this paper. It is important to recognize that these questions do not pertain only to non-Western societies or to what some people think of as the lunatic fringe.

9. Although modern Quakers retain a few special usages, such as the pronominal forms *thee* and *thy*, which distinguish Quakers from non-Quakers, these usages vary only with the identity of the addresses (Quaker/non-Quaker), not with the shift from social discussion to meeting for worship.
10. For discussion of a similar point, see Irvine 1979.
11. Indeed, many Quakers would maintain that inspired speech ought not to be restricted to the meeting for worship. Ideally, one would bring the spirit so fully to bear upon one's everyday life that social speech and inspired speech would effectively merge.

References

Bauman, Richard 1972. Quakers, seventeenth century. In *Prolegomena to Typologies of Speech Use.* (eds) R. Darnell & J. Sherzer. *Texas Working Papers in Sociolinguistics*, special number, March 1972.

—— 1974. Speaking in the light: The role of the Quaker minister. In *Explorations in the Ethnography of Speaking* (eds) R. Bauman & J. Sherzer. London and New York: Cambridge University Press. pp. 144-160.

Beattie, John & Middleton, John (eds) 1969. *Spirit Mediumship and Society in Africa.* New York: Africana.

Crapanzano, Vincent & Garrison, V. (eds) 1977. *Case Studies in Spirit Possession.* New York: John Wiley.

Firth, Raymond 1967. *Tikopia Ritual and Belief.* Boston: Beacon Press.

Goodman, Felicitas 1972. *Speaking in Tongues.* Chicago: University of Chicago Press.

Horton, Wade H. (ed.) 1966. *The Glossolalia Phenomenon.* Cleveland, Tennessee: The Pathway Press (Church of God).

Irvine, Judith T. 1975. Wolof Speech Styles and Social Status. *Working Papers in Sociolinguistics* No. 23.

—— 1979. Formality and informality in communicative events. *American Anthropologist* **81**, 773-790.

Lewis, Ioan 1971. *Ecstatic Religion.* Baltimore: Penguin.

Macklin, June 1977. A Connecticut Yankee in Summer Land. In *Case Studies in Spirit Possession* (eds) V. Crapzano & V. Garrison. New York: John Wiley. pp. 41-86.

Merriam, Alan P. 1967. *Ethnomusicology of the Flathead Indians.* New York: Wenner-Gren Foundation. Viking Fund Publications in Anthropology No. 44.

Métraux, Alfred 1959. *Voodoo in Haiti*. (trans.) H. Charteris. New York: Schocken.

Oesterreich, T. K. 1974. *Possession and Exorcism*. (trans.) D. Ibberson. New York: Causeway Books. (First Published 1921.)

Ray, Verne 1937. The Bluejay character in the Plateau spirit dance. *American Anthropologist* **39**, 593-601.

Roberts, Oral 1964. *The Baptism with the Holy Spirit and the Value of Speaking in Tongues Today*. Tulsa, Oklahoma: Published by the author.

Samarin, William 1972. *Tongues of Men and of Angels*. New York: Macmillan.

Turney-High, Harry 1933. The Bluejay Dance. *American Anthropologist* **35**, 103-107.

—— 1937. *The Flathead Indians of Montana*. Menasha, Wis.: American Anthropological Association. AAA Memoir No. 48.

Willis, Lewis J. 1966. Glossolalia in perspective. In *The Glossolalia Phenomenon* (ed.) Wade Horton. Cleveland, Tennessee: The Pathway Press (Church of God). pp. 245-284.

Zempléni, Andras. 1966. La dimension thérapeutique du culte des rab. Ndöp, tuuru et Samp. Rites de possession chez les lébou et les wolof. *Psychopathologie Africaine* **2**, 295-440.

—— 1977. From symptom to sacrifice: The story of Khady Fall. In *Case Studies in Spirit Possession* (eds) V. Crapanzano & V. Garrison. New York: John Wiley. pp. 87-140.

MEANING AND CONTEXT: THE INTERPRETATION OF GREETINGS IN KASIGAU

KAY MILTON

It is a basic assumption in anthropological studies of meaning that the meaning of a cultural phenomenon is derived from the context in which that phenomenon is placed. The central argument of this paper follows from this assumption. If meaning depends on context then the analyst's ability to infer meaning depends on his identification of the appropriate context.

I further assume that the concept of meaning necessarily implies the existence of a cognizing subject, i.e. that meaning has to be meaning *for* someone, it has to be part of someone's cognitive world. I shall also assume that we are interested in discovering the meanings of cultural phenomena for the people of whose culture they form a part.

I acknowledge that this latter assumption runs contrary to the claims made by some anthropologists who have held that cultural phenomena can have meanings of which the actors are unaware (e.g. Evans-Pritchard 1956: 232; Willis 1974: 10; Turner 1967: 25). This view seems to me to be particularly obstructive to the continuation of discussion on how we might best infer and describe meanings, and on how far specific techniques have been successful in the accomplishment of this task. If the meaning is held not to lie in the actors' minds, the only possible conclusion is that it lies in the analyst's mind, and that the analyst therefore has the final say on what that meaning is and on how it can best be inferred from the data, in which case there is little to discuss. If, on the other hand, the meaning is assumed to lie in the minds of the actors, then any inferences we make can be tested against the actors' verbal statements and actions. This assumption lies behind much of the work done in the field of cognitive anthropology and is often made explicit (Frake 1964; Hanson 1975: 65; see also Holy and Stuchlik 1981: 24-5).

Since we are trying to infer the actors' meanings, it follows that the relevant contexts, those from which we derive the meanings, should be defined by the actors; they should be the contexts in which the phenomena concerned are meaningful to them. This stipulation has generally not been followed in anthropological studies of meaning. More often than not, the meaning of a cultural pheno- menon has been seen as lying in its relations with other phenomena present in the culture; the culture is seen as a system and the meaning of any particular item as deriving from its place in that system. This conceptualization of meaning allows the analyst to draw what he sees as relevant connections out of the mass of cultural items with which he is faced, without recourse to the actors' state- ments and actions. For example, Willis infers the meaning of the Fipa sovereignty myth from the relations he perceives between the ideas contained within it, and other ideas prevalent in Fipa culture (Willis 1967). Because it is the analyst who defines the relevant connections, the meanings derived are meanings for him and not for the actors, as is often admitted (e.g. Leach 1976: 27; Burridge 1969: 199).

This style of analysis has a further disadvantage. Even given that the connections drawn by the analyst might be the appropriate ones (i.e. those the actors themselves might draw in making their interpre- tations), in restricting his analysis to the cultural or conceptual level of phenomena, he is ignoring an important part of the context on which, it can be argued, the meanings of things depend. In deriving meaning solely from the relations obtaining among phenomena at the cultural level, the analyst concentrates on the "syntactic" context at the expense of the "situational" context (Keesing 1972: 18); i.e. he implicitly assumes that the meanings of cultural phenomena can be understood independently of their invocation in action.

There are, I think, sound empirical reasons for arguing that the context from which the meaning of a phenomenon is derived, should always include the actions in which that phenomenon is invoked. People do not simply hold cultural phenomena in their heads along- side, and in structured relations with, other such phenomena; cultural items are used, referred to, invoked in social interaction, and it is only in the context of such interaction that their inter- pretation by the actors is made socially (and therefore sociologically) available. To argue that the meaning of a term or a symbol can be understood independently of this context, is to ignore the fact that meanings allocated to things in everyday life generally form a basis for action (Tyler 1978: 27). Communicative acts are generally performed in expectation of a response, and for meaningful communication to continue, the appropriate response must be given. To quote an example used by Tyler (1978: 31), on hearing the word "Fire!", we need to know whether to duck, pull the trigger, or run for the nearest exit, and performing the appropriate action will depend on consideration of the word's situational context; who says it, to whom, in what precise circumstances, etc.

It can be argued, of course, that the meaning of a term exists in people's minds prior to any instance of its invocation; it is only because we already know what the term means that we can make sense of its use in any given instance. However, it is only through their being brought to bear on actions that cultural items acquire their known meanings, and these meanings are by no means constant, but are modified (reinforced or changed) according to the contexts in which the items are invoked. The meaning of the term "father", for example, depends on to whom it refers (one's pater, genitor, God, a priest) and the manner in which it is spoken; jokingly, angrily, with deference, with scorn, etc. (cf. Keesing 1972: 19).

The point to be made here is that the relations existing among phenomena at the cultural or conceptual level, while they certainly form an important part of the context from which an interpreter (actor or analyst) might derive the meanings of specific items, do not have a static existence but are created through social interaction. Through being invoked in action, cultural items are juxtaposed, placed in opposition to each other, identified with each other, etc.; diverse items of knowledge are brought into relation with each other by being made relevant to the same action or set of actions. I shall return to this point later.

I would suggest, then, that anthropologists should infer the meanings of cultural phenomena from *both* their conceptual (cultural) context, *and* their processual (situational) context. I also insist that, since we are interested in the meanings cultural items have for the people of whose culture they form a part, the relevant context at both levels, conceptual and processual, should be defined by the actors and not by the analyst.

The remainder of this paper is devoted to an analysis of the manner in which the inhabitants of Kasigau, in southern Kenya, ascribe meaning to specific types of greeting. I shall show that, although the types of greeting can be said to have a general meaning, which is defined by the rule held by the actors to govern their use, they also have more specific meanings which depend on the context within which they are used.

In Kasigau, the verb *"kuroghua"* ("to greet")[1] describes an event in which people, on coming together, shake hands and exchange words. People greet each other whenever they meet, and the same individuals may exchange greetings several times a day. The words exchanged vary according to several factors: the time of day, the formality of the relationship or of the occasion, and the religious affiliations of the participants. Here I shall be concerned only with variations that depend upon religious affiliation.

As a result of certain historical developments (see Milton 1981: 141-143) the Wakasigau (people of Kasigau) see their society as divided, on the basis of religious affiliation, into a number of categories. The entire population is regarded as Christian. About 90 per cent of the adult population claim to belong to the Anglican Church, which is referred to as "CMS" (Church Missionary Society). Some of these people claim to be "saved" (*kukiriwa*) and belong to two separate fellowships: "Tendereza" (a Luganda word occurring in the song sung by members), and "Dina ya Kupaa" (a Swahili expression meaning "the religion of going upward" or "ascending"), whose members seceded from Tendereza in 1976. Outside the Anglican Church are a further three fellowships whose members claim to be saved: "Gospel" (which resulted from the influence of American missionaries in the 1950s), "Ilago" (meaning "The Word"; its members seceded from Gospel in 1976), and "Neno" (Swahili, meaning "The Word"; its members seceded from Ilago in 1978). There are thus five fellowships whose members regard themselves as saved, and who are collectively designated as "saved" by unsaved members of the community. The total adult membership of these fellowships is about 100; the individual membership varies from 30 or 40 in the case of Tendereza or Ilago, to 4 or 5 in the case of Dini ya Kupaa or Neno.

The members of different fellowships uphold different standards of behaviour, and the members of each regard their own standards as complying with God's will and, therefore, as setting them on the surest path to Heaven. Standards of fellowships other than one's own are generally seen as falling short of God's ideals. In order to have his or her claim to saved status accepted by others, an individual must become a member of one of the saved fellowships. An individual joins a fellowship by testifying before its members that he/she has decided to lead a life free from sin and to follow God's will. Thereafter he is accepted as a member and treated as such by other members as long as he shows himself able to keep to the standards of behaviour upheld by them. If he fails to do this he will be branded

as a backslider and expelled, and only allowed to rejoin the fellowship if he repents his sin. Both acquisition and loss of membership
are frequent occurrences in the community, and the membership
of each fellowship is constantly changing. Acceptance into and
expulsion from a fellowship rests in the hands of its members who
indicate, through their actions, whether or not they regard a
particular individual as one of them. Greetings constitute the
principal medium through which such perceptions of religious
status are communicated.

Unsaved people greet each other by saying "*wawuka*?" (or, to
more than one person, "*mwawuka*?"; literally, "have you woken
(well)?") or "*wasinda*?" (or "*mwasinda*?"; "have you spent the day
(well)?"), depending on whether it is morning or afternoon. The
correct replies are, respectively, "*nawuka*" (or "*dawuka*"; "I/we have
woken (well)") and "*nasinda*" (or "*dasinda*"; "I/we have spent the
day (well)"). Saved people, though they use these greetings with
unsaved people, greet each other by saying "*Bwana okaso*" ("Praise '
the Lord"). Each fellowship has its own variation of the greeting;
for example, members of Gospel and Ilago often add "Halelujah!"
and "Amen" (see below, Cases 3 and 6).

That saved people greet each other "*Bwana okaso*" was stated
several times by both saved and unsaved, and I feel justified in
treating it as general rule, which is seen by the Wakasigau as
governing their behaviour. That it is perceived in this manner was
made most explicit when the loss of saved status by particular
individuals was discussed. The loss of status was often expressed
in terms of the use of the greeting: "He is no longer our brother (in
Christ), we have stopped greeting him *Bwana okaso*". On several
occasions, individuals who knew their own behaviour to have fallen
below the standards required of the members of their fellowships,
voluntarily stopped using the greeting.

In view of the presence in Kasigau society of a number of fellowships, each of whose members regard themselves as saved, the
statement "saved people greet each other "*Bwana okaso*" requires
some qualification. As mentioned above, the members of different
fellowships uphold different standards of conduct. Since, for the
members of each, "being saved" is defined in terms of the standards
they uphold, it is reasonable to expect that the members of each
fellowship will regard only themselves and each other as truly saved,
while members of other fellowships, who uphold different standards,
will not be so regarded. If this were the case we could expect the
Bwana okaso greeting to be used only within fellowships and not
across fellowship boundaries. The situation is complicated, however,

by the fact that people do not always judge each others' claims to saved status on the basis of fellowship membership alone, but sometimes on the basis of their knowledge of each other as individuals. Thus, while some saved people regard only their own fellowship members as truly saved, others will include in this category specific members of other fellowships, whose lives they know intimately enough to judge as meeting the necessary standards. Still others accept as saved all people who make the claim, regardless of fellowship membership.

These differing opinions are reflected in the use of the *Bwana okaso* greeting. Some saved people use the greeting with all others who claim to be saved, some only with members of their own fellowship, and some with their own fellowship members plus selected individuals from other fellowships. These variations in no way affect the applicability of the rule that saved people greet each other *Bwana okaso*. This rule is consistently applied and the variations are derived from the fact that people hold differing opinions about who is and who is not really saved.

The rule "saved people greet each other *Bwana okaso*" (and, conversely, that when one or both of the parties to the greeting is not saved, the ordinary form will be used) defines, in general terms, the meanings of both kinds of greeting. Any greeting performed in accordance with the rule can be assumed to be saying something about the relative religious statuses of the participants. A *Bwana okaso* greeting will be taken to mean that "we are both saved", while an ordinary greeting (*wawuka, wasinda*) will be taken to mean, "one (or both) of us is not saved". Once these meanings have been stated, however, we have not described in full the actors' ability to understand their greetings. By using greetings to say, "We are both saved" or, "One (or both) of us is not saved", the actors make more specific statements about their own and each others' religious statuses. Thus:

1) One can claim saved status for oneself by greeting a saved person *Bwana okaso*.
2) One can deny saved status to oneself by greeting a saved person *wawuka* or *wasinda*.
3) A saved person can claim saved status for another by greeting him *Bwana okaso*.
4) A saved person can deny saved status to another by greeting him *wasuka* or *wasinda*.

These more specific meanings depend on the situational context of the greeting: who says it, to whom, in what circumstances, etc.

Depending on this context, a *Bwana okaso* greeting can either be a simple statement of a situation acknowledged by both parties, or it can mean that the speaker is claiming saved status for himself, or that he is claiming it for the person spoken to. The *wawuka/wasinda* greeting similarly varies in meaning according to its situational context. By considering the context in which a greeting is used, the actors are able to distinguish these variations in meaning. If we are to document fully the process through which they understand their greetings, then we must be able to specify the grounds on which they make these distinctions. This can only be done through an examination of the way in which specific greetings are interpreted.

I shall assume that, in the ascription of meaning to specific greetings, knowledge of the rule that saved people greet each other *Bwana okaso* is a constant factor. I received no evidence to suggest that this is not the case; the rule is universally known and expected to be adhered to. If knowledge of the rule is constant, other relevant knowledge is variable; specifically, knowledge of people's religious affiliations and of their opinions regarding each others' religious statuses. Knowledge of these things is frequently exchanged in gossip and at any one time people hold in their minds specific ideas about each others' religious affiliations, against which observed greetings can be measured and judged as appropriate or inappropriate. This knowledge is variable because religious affiliations frequently change and knowledge of these changes takes time to become distributed throughout the community: A might have left Tendereza but B doesn't know it yet and therefore assumes him still to be a member. In such a situation, greetings are a means through which the knowledge is brought back into step with the reality. B will come to know of A's having left Tendereza through, among other things, hearing him greet Tendereza members *wawuka* or *wasinda* instead of *Bwana okaso*. Conversely, it will become known that someone has been saved when he is heard to greet other saved people *Bwana okaso*. Opinions of people's religious statuses can change without changes in fellowship membership necessarily taking place, and these changes of opinion are also communicated through greetings. Undoubtedly, the vast majority of greetings are non-problematically understood as appropriate statements about religious affiliations, and such greetings invariably pass without comment. However, where people are puzzled or surprised by a greeting, or learn something new from it, they tend spontaneously to make explicit their interpretations of it, and so offer the analyst the best opportunity for describing the knowledge

on whose basis specific meanings are ascribed. The following eight
instances were selected for analysis on the grounds that they contain
such spontaneous interpretations on the part of the actors.

Case 1

In January 1978 Joshua (Ilago) visited Damaris (Tendereza). He
greeted her *"Bwana okaso"*, but she said *"Wasinda"*. He then asked
her, "Why can't you say *'Bwana okaso'*?" Damaris smiled but
said nothing. Joshua later said to me, "Anyone who says he is
saved is my brother in Christ, but those people criticize us; they
don't consider me saved."

What concerns us here is Joshua's interpretation of the manner
in which Damaris greeted him. He greeted her *Bwana okaso* because
he regarded them both as saved. Assuming that she was also con-
forming to the rule, he could have interpreted her response in three
ways: a) Damaris did not consider herself saved, b) she did not
consider Joshua saved, c) she did not consider either of them saved.
Interpretations a) and c) were ruled out by Joshua's certain
knowledge that Damaris did consider herself saved. She was well
respected in the village as being "truly" saved, and he had received
no indication that her status had changed. Moreover, he knew that
Tendereza members had criticized his own fellowship, and therefore
had reason to suppose that Damaris might not consider him saved.
Her statement of this opinion probably appeared all the more
forceful to Joshua because it was he who spoke first. He stated his
opinion of their relative religious statuses by greeting her *Bwana
okaso* and she, in replying as she did, contradicted his opinion.

Case 2

Shortly after the split between Ilago and Neno, Kinusa (Neno)
visited Paulo (Ilago), and greeted him *"Wasinda"*. Paulo replied,
"Nasinda, ndugu" (*ndugu*, the Swahili term for "brother" is used
between people who consider themselves brothers in Christ, i.e.
who regard each other as saved). Paulo used the term *"ndugu"*
several times during the subsequent conversation, but Kinusa did not
once reciprocate. After Kinusa had left, Paulo said, "He does not
say *Bwana okaso*, he no longer considers me a brother (in Christ).
If that's what he wants, okay."

As co-members of Ilago, Paulo and Kinusa had always greeted
each other *Bwana okaso*. As far as I know, this was their first
meeting after the split. In terms of the rule, Paulo could have

interpreted Kinusa's greeting by concluding, either that Kinusa no longer considered himself saved, or that he no longer considered Paulo saved, or that he no longer considered either of them saved. Again, the second interpretation makes the most sense in terms of Paulo's knowledge. Kinusa had just left Paulo's fellowship (Ilago) and started up a separate one (Neno). There was, therefore, no question of Kinusa no longer considering himself saved. Rather, Paulo knew that Kinusa had left Ilago because he had been dissatisfied with Ilago standards of conduct. It was therefore quite reasonable that he should cease to consider Ilago members saved. Obviously, Paulo could not have been surprised at Kinusa's greeting, but until this meeting there had remained for Paulo the question of whether Kinusa would continue to greet him *Bwana okaso* in spite of their now belonging to separate fellowships. Paulo was left in no doubt of Kinusa's intentions, not only by the greeting itself, but also by his failure to reciprocate Paulo's use of the term *"ndugu"*. Paulo's own status as saved depended, of course, not on Kinusa's opinion, but on his confirmed acceptance by his fellow Ilago members, and was therefore not affected by this exchange.

Case 3

Ade (CMS) was feeling ill and so went to an Ilago meeting at the house of her neighbour Paulo (Ilago), and asked to be prayed for. When they had finished their prayers, the Ilago members told her, "Now you must say *'Bwana okaso'* ", and went to their homes claiming that they had got a new "sister". The following morning, Avua (Ilago) visited Ade and they exchanged the following greeting: Avua: "How are you, sister?" Ade: "Sister" Avua: *"Bwana okaso"* Ade: *"Bwana okaso"* Avua: "Hallelujah!" Ade: "Come and eat meat with the Lord". Shortly afterwards, Paulo, who overheard the exchange, commented to me, "She (Ade) does not want to say *'Bwana okaso'*." Ade herself later admitted, in the absence of Paulo and Avua, that she had not wanted to be saved, merely to get some relief, through prayer, for her illness.

The interpretation that concerns us here is again made by Paulo. To most people, the exchange between Ade and Avua would probably have seemed like a normal greeting between two members of Ilago, but Paulo took it as a sign that Ade did not really want to belong to the fellowship. The rule in terms of which Paulo interpreted the greeting was not simply that saved people greet each other *Bwana okaso*, but the more narrowly defined rule governing greetings within the Ilago fellowship: that members of Ilago greet each other in a specific way. Instead of entering enthusiastically into the customary Ilago greeting, as a new member might be expected to do, Ade cut it short by failing to return Avua's "Halelujah!", and diverting her attention by inviting her to eat. In adding "with the Lord", she maintained the habitual Ilago manner of speaking and thus avoided an outright denial of Avua's definition of her religious status, which would have been impolite and highly embarrassing in view of the fact that Avua thought she had just acquired a new sister in Christ. Ade's failure to use the complete greeting could, of course, have been interpreted as a reluctance to accept Avua as a member of Ilago. But Avua's membership was well established and widely known, so Paulo had no reason to suspect that this might be the case. On the other hand, Ade's membership resulted only from the events of the previous evening when she had expressed a wish, not to join the fellowship, but simply to be prayed for.[2] Paulo therefore had sound reasons for suspecting that Ade might not have intended to become a member. That he interpreted her greeting to Avua in this way is indicated by the fact that, before Avua's arrival, he had himself greeted Ade *"Bwana okaso"*, and yet later the same day was heard to greet her *"Wasinda"*.

Case 4

Akora had been saved (Gospel) late in 1978. In May 1979 I was sitting with Manga (Gospel) in her house when Akora walked passed and called, *"Wasinda?"*, to which Manga replied, *"Nasinda"*. After Akora had passed on her way, Manga said, "She used to greet us *Bwana okaso* but now it is just *wasinda*. If she doesn't want to be saved, that's up to her."

I do not know whether this was the first greeting between the two women following Akora's loss of saved status, but Manga made clear, in her comment, that it was a change from what formerly had been done. Assuming that Akora was acting in accordance with the rule, Manga could have interpreted her greeting in one of three ways: either Akora no longer considered herself saved, or she no longer considered Manga saved, or she no longer considered either of them saved. Manga opted for the first conclusion on the basis of other knowledge she possessed. Rumours had been circulating in the village that Akora had behaved in ways inappropriate for a saved person, while Manga knew of no such lapses in her own behaviour which would have led Akora into thinking that she was no longer saved.

All the greetings in these four cases were ultimately interpreted as appropriate statements about religious statuses in accordance with the rule that saved people greet each other *Bwana okaso* (or, in Case 3, the rule stating that Ilago members use a specific elaboration of this greeting). In other words, the actors had no difficulty in reconciling what they observed people doing with the knowledge they held about these people's religious affiliations, and their known or assumed opinions of others' religious statuses.

Since three of the cases (1, 2 and 4) involve an ordinary greeting rather than a *Bwana okaso* greeting, and since in Case 3 the *Bwana okaso* greeting was rather less enthusiastic and elaborate than expected, the inevitable conclusion in each case was that saved status was being denied to someone. The question of whether this person was the speaker or the person spoken to was settled by recourse to specific knowledge held about the participants. Joshua and Paulo both knew, beyond doubt, that Damaris and Kinusa respectively considered themselves saved (Cases 1 and 2), and that, as members of fellowships other than Ilago, they might both be expected to consider Ilago members unworthy of saved status, while Paulo and Manga (Cases 3 and 4) both had reason to suspect that Ade and Akora respectively might wish to deny themselves saved status.

Not in every case can greetings be so easily made meaningful in terms of knowledge already held. In the following case, the speaker's religious status was rather more uncertain.

Case 5

Mshai (Ilago) called at Anton's house and greeted his daughter Sulivia (Tendereza) as she usually did by saying, "*Bwana okaso*". Anton then came out of the house, shook Mshai by the hand and said, "*Bwana okaso*". She did not reply, and later asked me whether Anton had been saved. I assured her that he had not.

I assume that, after I had told Mshai that Anton was not saved, then her inevitable conclusion was that he had broken the rule in greeting her *Bwana okaso*. What interests me, however, is her initial interpretation of the greeting. Clearly, she was not expecting it; her failure to reply indicates this. When she had last seen Anton, the previous day, he had been unsaved; she therefore expected him to say, "*Wawuka*". When he said "*Bwana okaso*", she did not know what to reply, and remained silent; his greeting had made her uncertain of his religious status. This uncertainty was based on her knowledge that Anton had been saved several times before, and in view of this the possibility of his having become so again, literally overnight, could not be discounted. Anton had also been known, however, to practise a certain amount of deceit. Mshai therefore had to consider two possibilities: a) Anton could genuinely have been saved since their last meeting, and b) Anton could have been pretending to be saved. Having insufficient knowledge to choose between these possibilities, Mshai did not answer his greeting. To have replied, "*wawuka*" would have been unequivocally to have denied Anton's saved status, and to have replied, "*Bwana okaso*" would have been to acknowledge it. She chose to suspend her opinion until she could confirm one possibility or the other.

The following cases were treated unambiguously as "mistakes", i.e. as violations of the rule that saved people greet each other (and only each other) *Bwana okaso*.

Case 6

While I was sitting with Manga in her house, Johane (Gospel) walked past and they exchanged the following greeting: Manga: "*Bwana okaso*" Johane: "*Bwana okaso*" Manga: "Halelujah" Johane: "Halelujah". Johane went on his way. He later said to me, "She is not saved. She has no right to say '*Bwana okaso*'." When asked why he had returned her greeting, he said, "I was surprised, so I just answered".

Manga had once been a fully accepted member of Gospel, but her behaviour had fallen below the standards expected of members and she had been expelled. She did not accept her expulsion, however, and, as in this instance, occasionally made efforts to assert her claim to membership. The greeting she used is a typical one between Gospel members, though this was the first time since her expulsion that I had heard her use it to Johane (hence his surprise), and I suspect that she did so on this occasion to impress upon me her claim to Gospel membership. Johane, as an accepted member of Gospel, was one of the people whose judgement of her behaviour had brought about her expulsion. His interpretation of her greeting was simply that she had broken the rule and done so knowingly: she had "no right" to say "*Bwana okaso*". Had she had reason genuinely to consider herself saved, then she would presumably have had a right to say it.

Case 7

Damaris (Tendereza) and I, while walking through the village, met Helen (Gospel), who greeted Damaris as she usually did by saying "*Wasinda*?". Damaris replied in like fashion. Helen then turned to me and said, "*Bwana okaso*", to which I replied, "*Bwana okaso*". After Helen had gone on her way, Damaris commented, "Everyone wants the *mzungu* (European) to join their fellowship".

Helen's greeting to me, an unsaved person, was a breach of the rule that saved people greet only each other *Bwana okaso*. In fact, Helen's greeting was based on an agreed suspension of the rule between her and myself. At a Gospel meeting the previous day, I had been reluctant to say "*Bwana okaso*" for fear of misrepresenting my own religious affiliations. Helen had said to me, "You don't have to be saved to say '*Bwana okaso*'. If you say it, you will feel it in your heart to be saved." Helen thus established new conditions under which she and I might interact, and the greeting described above appeared to me as a light-hearted reference to the incident of the previous day. Damaris, however, knew nothing of this incident. As far as she was concerned, Helen had simply used the *Bwana okaso* greeting to someone whom they both knew was unsaved, and she had to make sense of it in these terms. Since Helen's own saved status was well established, her use of the greeting could only be interpreted as a claiming of saved status for myself. Since I was not saved, however, and since Damaris knew that Helen was aware of this, it seemed unlikely that this claim was made as a statement of an existing situation. Instead, Damaris saw it as a statement of what Helen would like to be the case, i.e. as an invitation to me to be saved and join Gospel. This interpretation was no doubt based partly on the fact that there had been some speculation in the village about which fellowship the "*mzungu*" would join.

Case 8

Mwashuma (Unsaved) visited the house of Paulo (Ilago). While he was there, Alfonsi (Ilago) arrived for the regular Ilago service held every Sunday at Paulo's house. Paulo greeted Alfonsi in their usual fashion (*Bwana okaso*, Halelujah, Amen). Mwashuma then shook Alfonsi's hand and said, "*Bwana okaso*", at which all of them laughed.

Again, Mwashuma's greeting was a breach of the rule. In saying "*Bwana okaso*" to someone whose saved status was beyond doubt, his action could only be interpreted as a claim to saved status for himself. Since he was unsaved, this claim was illegitimate. However, Mwashuma's greeting was not interpreted simply as an inappropriate action; Paulo and Alfonsi took it as a joke, and its meaning as a joke depended on other knowledge they held about Mwashuma's character. Mwashuma was well known as an habitual drunkard who cared little for religion. For him to say "*Bwana okaso*", therefore, was absurd; far more so than it would have been for some other unsaved, but more virtuous person to say it. His joke was an act of self-mockery. He drew attention to what they all knew to be true, that he was an irreverent drunkard, by stating, or pretending to state, the opposite. By pretending to behave as a saved person would, Mwashuma drew attention to the fact that he is actually the antithesis of what a saved person is expected to be. In order to be appreicated as a joke, as it was by Paulo and Alfonsi, Mwashuma's greeting had to be understood on two levels at once. At one level it meant, "I am saved", and at another level it meant, "I am the opposite of saved". It could not be understood at the second level without being understood at the first.

What is interesting about these last three cases is that, although they were all interpreted as breaches of the rule, they were ascribed different meanings. By examining the knowledge on which the interpretations were based, it is possible to see why this was the case.

Manga's greeting (Case 6) was simply a "wrong" or inappropriate action, an attempt to claim a status to which she had no right. Mwashuma's greeting (Case 8) was, in some ways, similar; an unsaved person claiming saved status by greeting a saved person *Bwana okaso*. Why, then, did Manga's greeting incur a reproach while Mwashuma's was appreciated as a joke? While Manga was seen as making a serious attempt to claim something to which she was not entitled, Mwashuma was seen as making a non-serious, and therefore acceptable, attempt, and in so doing actually acknowledged that he had no claim. This difference in interpretation is in turn based on further knowledge: Mwashuma had never made any serious attempt to claim saved status, whereas Manga had been a member of Gospel and was known by Johane to have resented her expulsion from the fellowship.

Case 8 is in some respects similar to Case 5. Since it is possible, and apparently acceptable, for an unsaved person to claim saved status as a joke, then why did Mshai not see Anton's greeting as a joke when he was, to the best of her knowledge, unsaved? The difference between these two cases lies in the fact that Mshai was unable to tell whether or not Anton's greeting was intended as a serious attempt to claim saved status; and the reason for this inability was her knowledge that he had made serious claims to saved status in the past and might therefore do so again. Mwashuma, on the other hand, was known to be content with his irreverence and had never had any aspirations to saved status.

Case 7 is similar to these others in that an apparently illegitimate claim to saved status is made; but in this instance Helen's greeting was not interpreted purely and simply as an inappropriate action, nor was it seen as a joke. Unlike Manga, Helen was not claiming saved status for herself, but for another. Because saved status is desirable, it makes sense that someone should claim it for him or herself, as Manga and Anton did (Cases 6 and 5), but there are no obvious reasons why one should want to claim it for someone else. Damaris therefore assumed that Helen's greeting was not simply an illegitimate claim. It made sense to her as an invitation to me to join the fellowship. There was always a certain amount of argument among members of different fellowships over what standards of behaviour constituted the surest path to Heaven, and my joining any one fellowship could have been seen as a kind of stamp of approval for that fellowship from outside the community; indeed, from Europe, the known source of Christian missions to Africa. Damaris therefore saw Helen as having good reason, not to claim that I was saved, but to encourage me to join Gospel rather than any other fellowship.

Apart from the fact that Helen's greeting made sense in other terms, there are specific reasons why it would probably not be interpreted as a joke. Firstly, it is one thing to joke about one's own shortcomings, as Mwashuma did, but quite another to joke to their face about someone else's. Secondly, I assume that the possibility of my being saved would not, in any case, have appeared amusing, since I did not indulge in the kind of behaviour for which Mwashuma was renowned!

I shall now return to the argument made earlier in the paper, in which I suggested that the meaning of a cultural item is derived from both its conceptual context and its processual context. This suggestion is fully borne out by the examination of greetings in Kasigau. The two types of greeting discussed (*Bwana okaso* and *wawuka/wasinda*) have generally accepted meanings which are based on their relations with other cultural items; namely, concepts of "saved" and "unsaved" and the rule that saved people greet each other *Bwana okaso*. These meanings always form part of the knowledge on whose basis a specific greeting is interpreted. In none of the cases discussed, however, do these general meanings provide the actors with sufficient knowledge satisfactorily to understand the specific greetings. The general meanings are always narrowed down through recourse to other knowledge which is derived from the processual context; i.e. the identities of the participants, their personal attributes, their membership of specific fellowships, their known past behaviour, and so on.

Having examined the data, I am now in a better position to argue the point made above (p. 263), that the relevant relations between cultural items, those that give these items their meaning, are created through action rather than existing independently of it. There is nothing in Kasigau culture to state that the *wasinda* greeting must be understood in terms of the differences between Tendereza and Ilago, or between Ilago and Neno, for instance. The rules governing its use allow for the possibility that these differences might be relevant, but they are not so *per se*. Rather, they are made relevant, in Cases 1 and 2, through the actions of Damaris and Kinusa respectively.

Case 3 is particularly interesting in this respect. Paulo understood Ade's greeting, not simply in terms of the rule that governs greetings between Ilago members, but also with reference to the events of the previous evening, and ultimately in terms of a distinction, which he was able to make, between being prayed for and being saved. Again, there is nothing in Kasigau culture which states that this distinction is necessarily relevant to the meaning of the type of greeting Ade used; it was made relevant by the specific circumstances of the case. Many people who get prayed for at Ilago meetings get saved at the same time, and it was in terms of their knowledge that this often happens that Avua and the other Ilago members assumed Ade to be their sister in Christ. Had Paulo not been able to make a distinction between being prayed for and being saved, then Ade's greeting would presumably have been understood by him in some other way. As it was, he was able to conclude that she acted as she did because, the previous evening, she had only wanted to be prayed for and not to be saved (as Ade herself admitted).

Although it would be impossible to reconstruct the historical process involved, I would want to say that the *Bwana okaso* and *wawuka/wasinda* greetings acquired their general meanings in the same way. The greetings are meaningful to the actors in relation to the recognized distinction between saved and unsaved, and this relation is now an established part of Kasigau culture. I would assume that it came to be established through being repeatedly created and recreated in action; through being made the object of repeated acts of interpretation of the kind described above. The interpretations of Paulo and Joshua represent a small part of the process through which cultural phenomena generally come to have the meanings people ascribe to them.

Notes

1. The language spoken in Kasigau is Kitaita. Vernacular terms given are in this language unless otherwise stated.
2. "Being prayed for" involves having evil spirits, held to be responsible for illness, cast out of one's body through a laying on of hands. This is the manner in which members of Gospel, Ilago and Neno usually deal with sickness, and it is treated, even by some non-members, as an alternative form of medical service to those offered by traditional curers and the local dispensary.

Acknowledgements

My thanks are due to the following for their comments on earlier drafts of this paper: John Blacking, Hastings Donnan, Ladislav Holy, Graham McFarlane, and the members of the social anthropology departmental seminar at Queen's University, Belfast.

Fieldwork in Kasigau, which was carried out from 1977 to 1979, was financed by a project grant from the Social Science Research Council.

References

Burridge, K. 1969. *Tangu Traditions*. Oxford: Clarendon.

Evans-Pritchard, E. E. 1956. *Nuer Religion*. Oxford: Clarendon.

Frake, C. O. 1964. Further Discussion of Burling. *American Anthropologist* **66**, 119.

Hanson, F. A. 1975. *Meaning in Culture*. London: Routledge & Kegan Paul.

Holy, L. & Stuchlik, M. 1981. The structure of folk models. In *The Structure of Folk Models* (eds) Holy, L. & Stuchlik, M. (Ass. social Anthrop. Monogr. **20**). London: Academic Press.

Keesing, R. M. 1972. Simple models of complexity: the lure of kinship. In *Kinship Studies in the Morgan Centennial Year* (ed.) Reining, P. The Anthropological Society of Washington.

Leach, E. 1976. *Culture and Communication*. Cambridge: Cambridge University Press.

Milton, K. 1981. On the inference of folk models: discussion and demonstration. In *The Structure of Folk Models* (eds) Holy, L. & Stuchlik, M. (Ass. social Anthrop. Monogr. **20**). London: Academic Press.

Turner, V. W. 1967. *The Forest of Symbols*. London: Cornell University Press.

Tyler, S. 1978. *The Said and the Unsaid*. London: Academic Press.

Willis, R. 1967. The head and the loins: Lévi-Strauss and beyond. *Man* **II**, 519-34.

—— 1974. *Man and Beast*. St. Albans: Paladin.

THE ALTERNATIVE MEANINGS OF NUMBER AND COUNTING

THOMAS CRUMP

The understanding of number, and the mathematical theory of numbers, according to the tradition of the Western world, represents, in its present form, a self-contained logical system or remarkable purity. Russell and Whitehead's *Principia Mathematica*, first published in 1913, which was intended to be a complete formal presentation of the logical basis of pure mathematics, did not in the end succeed in being entirely self-consistent, although it was not until 1931 that Gödel[1] proved that such success was unattainable in any formal system. If, however, in the Western world, the question still remains open as to whether mathematics, to be significant, must depend upon concepts capable of being constructed by the human mind[2], there is no doubt that the "individual confronts mathematics as a body of truth which must be mastered" in the firm conviction that "all cultures develop the same mathematics, [and] . . . that there is no such thing as an alternative mathematics" (Bloor 1976: 75). This, of course, is a position which almost any anthropologist would instinctively reject, and Russell himself, in a short popular introduction to his work (1920: 3), acknowledged that it was the product of a high stage of civilization. The present chapter has the same cognitive basis as Russell (1920: 2) in the unclouded pre-Gödelian age ascribed "to the average educated person of the present day", that is, the series of whole numbers,

$$1, 2, 3, 4, \ldots \text{etc.}$$

noting, in agreement with Russell, that

> It must have required many ages to discover that a brace of pheasants and a couple of days were both instances of the number 2: the degree of abstraction involved is far from easy. And the discovery that 1 is a number

must have been difficult[3]. As for 0, it is a very recent addition; the Greeks and Romans had no such digit . . .[4]

Russell's statement (1920: 3) that "the natural numbers seem to represent what is easiest and most familiar in mathematics" is true in a sense which extends far beyond our own civilization. It is in the accepted meaning of the natural numbers, whether standing alone or in combination with each other in some form of *mathematical* statement, that the anthropologist will expect to find substantial variations among different cultures. Although this defines the general approach in the present case, it is still necessary to adopt some definite scheme for the purposes of exploration and analysis: for this reason the number 7^5 has been chosen as a sort of catalyst, which will be used to reveal a number of different ways of understanding numbers in general. The procedure adopted will be to start with an essentially modern, logical approach, and then to take into account, in increasing measure, the connotations of the number 7 in our own as much as in other traditional cultures[6]. The use of this procedure will then lead to a number of general, theoretical conclusions.

According to the formal symbolic system of typographical number theory, 7 is defined as SSSSSSSO, where "S" has the meaning "successor to" and "O" means simply "zero"[7]. At first sight this says little more than that logically the existence of the number 7 is implicit in that of its predecessor, 6, the existence of 6 in that of 5, and so on until zero is reached[8]. In fact this way of expressing the matter turns the logical procedure, by which all natural numbers are defined by reference to the terms "O" and "successor", on its head (Russell 1920: 20).

More important, even this elementary level of mathematical induction plays no part in any number of numerical systems to be found in pre-literate cultures. It is not only, as Gerschel (1962: 695) notes, that the spoken languages in which such numbers must be expressed have no word for any number above a certain low limit – which may be no higher than 2 – but also that such numbers as may exist, such as the Thonga 1, 2, 3, 4, 5, 10 and 100 (Junod 1027: 167), do not necessarily occur as an unbroken sequence of natural numbers. This deficiency, moreover, does not necessarily preclude the counting of large quantities, such as of the hoes which the Thonga use as bride-wealth[9]. In practice, even such spoken languages as do provide the means for the unrestricted expression of the unbroken series of natural numbers tend to be lexically chaotic at least up to the level of a hundred (Crump 1978: 304), although the degree of chaos varies widely between different languages[10]. In most such languages in current use the disorder is made tolerable by the fact that beyond a certain level numbers are communicated, visually, in a more or less well-ordered written form — a point which will be returned to later.

Even in purely logical terms the process of induction can be extremely misleading when it comes to quite elementary arithmetical properties of different numbers. The number 7 illustrates this point as well as any other. Its predecessors can all be expressed as the sum of at least three squares — which might suggest, intuitively, that this is a property of all numbers. The proof that 7, and all other numbers of the form $4^k(8n-1)$ cannot be so expressed is quite elementary (Hardy and Wright 1945: 311) in modern number theory, but the significant point is that it establishes 7 as the first term in a discontinuous series of natural numbers, all of which have the property that they can be expressed as the sum of four[11], but not of any fewer squares[12]. If modern number theory generates any number of such series, they are not unknown in earlier traditions. An example of this is the series defined by

$$n_k = \tfrac{1}{2}k(k+1)$$

which is in fact the sum of all the whole numbers up to and including k. This series, if relatively uninteresting in any modern theory, represents in many traditional systems of arithmetic the first stage in constructing triangular numbers, for reasons which Fig. 1 makes

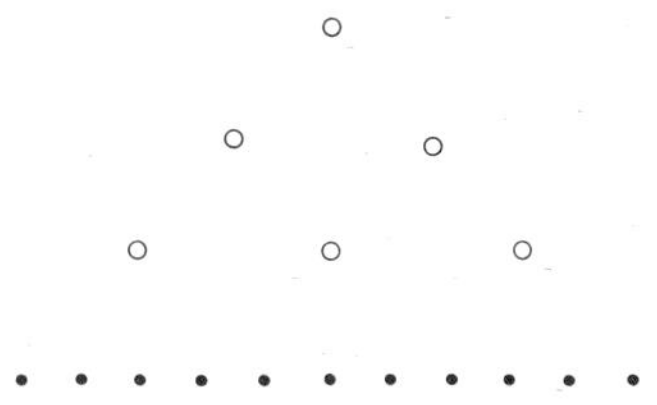

Fig.1

immediately clear. Is it, for instance, purely coincidental, that two of the few relatively large numbers mentioned in the Bible, 153, being the number of fish caught by Simon Peter in the last chapter of St John's gospel (xxi:11) and 666, the number of the last of the beasts engaged in the war in heaven in the Book of Revelations (xiii:18), are both of this form.

Returning to the number 7, and taking it to represent the abstract property common to all possible groups of 7 things, what sort of problems can this lead to in numerical systems other than those familiar to us in the western tradition? Plainly any system of

numeration, such as that of the Aranda (Gerschel 1962: 695) or the
Thonga, which does not even allow for this number to be
represented, excludes any form of deeper analysis. Assuming,
however, that the existence of 7 is acknowledged, what sort of
further difficulties can then arise? The first question to ask is
whether the rules of cognition, in whatever culture, must necessarily
allow all possible groups of 7 "things" to be lumped together into
one single category defined by the common property of "7-ness".
Linguistic considerations, which must be paramount in any
discussion of this kind[13], strongly suggest that this is not necessarily so. The point is obscured for native speakers of Indo-European
languages, where numerals tend to be invariant in form and are
hardly governed by special rules of syntax[14]. There are, however,
language families as wide-ranging as the Sino-Tibetan, the Bantu and
the Mayan, in which the form and syntax of numerals are governed
by the classification of the nouns which they qualify: Japanese
presents a particularly complicated variation of this pattern, so that,
for instance, the numerical element common to 7 days and 7 minutes
is not immediately apparent in the spoken language, although the
same ideograph   occurs in both, the basic system of cardinal
numbers − borrowed originally from China − being remarkably
simple (Crump 1982: 4). Numerical forms are not always
immediately obvious, even in Indo-European languages. In English,
for example, Wednesday and April both import the idea of 4, or
better its ordinal form, 4th, in a context in which the same idea is
quite explicit in both written and spoken Chinese, where April is
quite literally "4-month" (*sì-yuè* or 四月) and Wednesday "day-4"
(*xīngcī-sì* 星期四)[15]. In China (and equally in Japan) this allows
for date such as July 7, that is the 7th day of the 7th month to relate
directly to the special properties of 7 in the traditional number
mysticism.

   The number 7 happens also to play a significant role in what is
known in development psychology as "subitizing" (Kaufman *et al.*
1949: 521), which means no more than the process whereby the
number of objects present in a set is correctly grasped at the moment
of perception (Crump 1982: 2). To see at a glance that there are
six eggs in a basket provides an obvious example of how this works.
With low numbers, then, subitizing takes the place of counting, but
the question is, at what number does the limit to the process occur?
The result of research, usefully summed up by Miller (1956), is that
the number 7 is the critical threshold. Beyond this threshold, the
process of counting requires "pairing successively each object in the
group with a numeral from a numerical series, beginning of course

with the first numeral in the series" (Kaufman *et al.* 1949: 522). Not surprisingly, in a study based on experiments conducted in the United States, the implications of this process for cognitive domains in which the series of numerals is discontinuous are hardly considered[16].

It is significant also that all the experimental work directed towards discovering how a child learns to count, takes for granted that the objects to be counted can not only be seen, but in the *literal* sense of the word, manipulated. That is, in the process of counting, the objects counted are moved from one place to another[17]. But how, then, does one apply such a procedure to counting, say, the number of days to Christmas? Hopi numerals cannot in fact be used for counting days (Hickerson 1980: 109), and the Japanese numerals used for this purpose fall into a category all of their own. But where tangible movable objects are counted, the process requires a quantitative correspondence to be established between two groups of perceptions, one, that of the "counters", generally consisting of an ordered set of arbitrary symbols, retained by the memory and which we know as "numbers", and the other of the objects to be counted. The end of this process is characterized by "correspondence freed from perceptual or spatial limitations, and persisting in spite of the elements" (Piaget 1952: 82). The child who has reached this stage has come to realize that however a group of objects is counted, the number reached at the end of the process is independent not only of the way in which they are arranged but also of the order in which they are counted. Moreover the actual identity of the objects has no effect on the final result. There is, to adapt a phrase used by Keynes (1936: 231) in relation to money, "an elasticity of substitution equal to zero". The end result is for the child paradoxical. For Piaget establishes that ". . . number is essentially a synthesis of two logical entities, class and asymmetric relation. Enumeration effaces distinction between objects . . . but for counting objects must be ordered, [so that it is] a relation operation . . . [or] set of relation operations . . . based on different ordinal position. The psychological basis of numerals . . . is therefore very broad. It follows also that 'classes, relations and numbers are cognitive domains which develop sunchronically in a tightly intertwined mutually dependent way' " (Flavell 1963: 311-12).

This is all very well, but what about Japanese, in which the numerals used for counting are not the same as those used for stating the number of objects present in a class. A Japanese child, therefore, counting aloud the 7 oak trees in a copse, would be heard to say, "hitotsu, futatsu, mittsu, yottsu, itsutsu, muttsu, nanatsu", knowing that wherever he stopped, the number reached — at least if it were not greater than ten — could *not* be used for actually expressing "7 oaks" — or 7 of anything else for that matter. In the correct form, *nanahon-no-nara* (七本の楢), the word *nanahon* for seven is that appropriate for the noun class defined by trees.[18]

But if the class of trees is theoretically unlimited, what about classes which, by definition, are closed, such as the 7 notes in a musical scale or the 7 days in a week. English, perhaps significantly, uses the first 7 letters of the alphabet to label the notes in the scale, which recalls the general practice adopted in Greek and Hebrew for expressing numbers in written form. There is, however, the important difference that the notes in the musical scale, A, B, . . . G are only *ordinal* numbers, as are the actual names of the days of the week. The musical scale is interesting also for introducing two alternative numerical systems. The first, which it shares in common with the days of the week, is the *cyclic* system in which a defined closed sequence of natural numbers repeats itself almost indefinitely. The number 7 of Saturday, the 7th day of the week, will recur indefinitely, at least for so long as the earth continues to turn on its axis, and day follows night[19]. In the musical scale, however, physical factors prevent the indefinite recurrence of the 7th note G in successively higher octaves[20]. The problem is that every successive octave doubles the frequency of the note, G, so that it quite soon reaches a point beyond the frequency response of the human ear — making it useless for any musical purposes. The key point here is that the succession of octaves establishes a second *exponential* system of numeration, based upon a sequence of powers of 2, . . . 2^5, 2^6, 2^7 . . . and so on. This may be quite a recent scientific discovery, but its implications in the field of cognition were established at a much earlier stage. More generally it is to be noted that the Chinese numerical system is built up of two independent component series, one consisting simply of the numbers from 1 to 9 (which standing alone, but with the incorporation of a zero can be taken to constitute a cyclic system), and the other of numbers representing successive powers of 10[21]. Elements from the two systems can always be chosen to combine to form any natural number — at least up to the limit of the highest power in the exponential series[22]. Since one is concerned here with Chinese, this is as true as much of the written as of the spoken language[23]. It is true that the "place value" system[24] of the so-called Arabic numerals can theoretically be extended to express a natural number of any size, but this is exclusively a *written* system used in language domains where the spoken forms are highly disordered[25], and unrelated to it.

The combined use of two or more discrete cyclic systems in the calendar allows for new cycles of increasingly longer duration to be built up. The classic instance of this process is provided by the Maya calendar round, which by combining two cycles, one of 365 and the other of 260 days, established a long cycle of 52 years duration[26] (Crump 1978: 511f). In this case, also, the 260-day cycle was itself formed in the same way. The process is, however, more conveniently illustrated by a simpler case from China, in which two systems, one based on the 10 "celestial stems" (tian kan 天干), and the other on the 12 "earthly branches" (ti chi 地支), combine to make a cycle of 60. The members of each class, whose order is invariable, while plainly homologous to the sequence of natural numbers, have, at the same time, their own cultural or mystical connotations. From at least the fourteenth century BC the system has been used to denote cycles of 60 years, 60 months and 60 days, but in any such use the mystical significance of any particular year, month or day, as the case may be, is determined by its "kan" and its "chi" − a principle of Chinese numerology which is familiar even at popular level in the west.

This principle of connotation as opposed to denotation lies at the heart of the distinction between traditional and modern systems. The point was made clear by a Chinese philosopher a long time ago:

> If one follows the numbers then one can know their beginnings, if one traces them backwards then one can know how it is that they came to an end. Numbers and things are not two separate entities, and beginnings and endings are not two separate points. If one knows the numbers, then one knows the things, and if one knows the beginnings, then one knows the endings. Numbers and things continue endlessly − how can one say what is a beginning and what is an ending. (Sung Yuan Hsueh, Ch. 67, p. 15a cited Needham 1956: 273)

Survivals of this principle are still to be found in any modern culture, in songs, stock phrases, proverbs, folklore, place-names and religious tradition. If one looks at "Green grow the rushes, O"[27], the connotation of 7, the "seven stars in the sky" refers not only to the constellation variously known as the Plough, the Big Dipper or the Great Bear, but also to a host of astrological implications, none of which relate to the classes enumerated by the other eleven numbers occurring in the song. The origin of the stock phrase "at sixes and sevens" can be variously explained, but the numbers have quantitatively no significance, and it is not surprising that the Dutch equivalent "vijven en zessen" is based on 5 and 6. The same point is made by any number of proverbs incorporating numbers. The English "A bird in the hand is worth two in the bush" becomes, in Dutch, "Een vogel in de hand is beter dan tien in de lucht", that is ". . . better than *ten* in the air". If one divides the English version by 2, the connotations are quite different, so that "Half a loaf is better than no bread" − or in Dutch, "Een half ei is beter dan een lege dop", or "half an egg is better than an empty shell". The numbers only matter in so far as they stand in an ordered relation to each other: it is significant that both 2 and 10 are greater than 1. Indeed, the proverb, in its different versions, is no more than a shorthand form of Aesop's familiar fable about the dog and the bone. The principle could be made intelligible even to the Aranda and the Thonga. In many parts of the world, for reasons which the specialist in this field could no doubt readily supply, 7 is a "lucky number"[28]. In a place-name, such as Sevenoaks[29], it is now no more than a name, but a local historian could no doubt discover the existence, some hundreds of years ago, of some mystical grove of 7 oaks in that part of Kent. In our own religious tradition the Oxford Dictionary of the Christian Church lists 14 entries under the rubric "seven", some of biblical origin[30] and others relating only to the Church of England. More significant, in this connection, are the connotations of the word "sabbath", which in Hebrew connotes not only "rest"[31] (שָׁבַת) but also "seventh" (שְׁבִיעִי)[32]. Then, according to Christian theology, the coming of Jesus, as Messiah, completed the work already begun by God at the beginning of time − as recorded in the opening chapters of the Book of Genesis − on the *eighth* day, so that Sunday then became the "sabbath"[33]. But Sunday is also the first day, so that the first cycle comes to an end, and a new one begins. This explains such sayings as those recorded in the Book of Revelation (xxi: 6) as "It is done! I am the Alpha and the Omega, the beginning and the end".

This is but one case of what Gerschel (1962: 696) calls "Le nombre marginal" which he defines as "un nombre *qui n'existe pas*, puisqu'il surpasse d'une unite le dernier nombre réel, mais qui, en vertu des lois de la fiction, gagne en extension ce qu'il perd en compréhension". Such numbers occur as much at a trivial as at a cosmic level, as witness "the 19th hole" on any golf course[34]. They are, however, particularly significant when they exceed by one a power of 2, perfectly formed by the process of binary multiplication[35]. This analysis makes the number 32 particularly significant for Gerschel (1962: 706), for with this number the limit attainable with four equal blocks of eight is reached, so that 33 becomes "un nombre marginal", at least for Indo-Europeans. One notes, for example, that Jesus lived for 33 years[36], but the number may be equally significant for Buddhism. It occurs in the name of the famous Kyoto temple, San-ju-san-gen-do (三十三間堂) where, in each of the 33 bays, there are 33 statues of the Kanon Buddha. This sort of analysis is capable of almost indefinite extension, but the time has come to present the conclusions following from the above discussion.

The fundamental discovery is that there is a definite line of cultural evolution established by the development of number, counting and arithmetic from the most elementary primordial level to that of the complex logical system which now forms the basis of pure mathematics. The starting point, as noted by Hallpike (1979: 236) is that

> . . . number can be constructed at the pre-operatory level . . . the existence of verbal numerals among primitive peoples does not of itself *prove* that the members of such societies conceive numbers as a system of logical classes.

The understanding of seriation and induction, followed by the use of arithmetical processes of addition, multiplication etc., occur at later stages[37], and require, sooner or later, not only the development of visual, and more specifically written forms[38], but also of mechanical aids to calculation such as the abacus. At every stage, the whole cognitive system, however simple or complex, is conceived of in terms not only of its internal logical consistency, but also of its application to external phenomena. As to the differences between traditional and modern thought, it is not so much that the former is concerned with application, and the latter with internal consistency, but rather that there is, as between traditional and modern cultures, a pronounced preference for metaphysical[39] as opposes to physical applications. The metaphysical aspect is well-explained by Needham (1956: 281) in relation to Chinese thought:

> Things behaved in particular ways . . . because their position in the ever-moving cyclical universe was such that they were endowed with intrinsic natures which made that behaviour inevitable for them. If they did not behave in those particular ways they would lose their relational positions in the whole (which made them what they were), and turn into something other than themselves. They were thus parts in existential dependence upon the whole world organism. And they reacted upon one another not so much by mechanical impulsion or causation as by a kind of mysterious resonance. Nothing was uncaused, but nothing was caused mechanically. The organic system in the prompter's book governed the whole.

The modern tradition (whose roots in the Near East are in fact quite ancient) has a pre-occupation with law, expressed in terms of a search for the meaning of the will of a supernatural law-giver, and introducing a *progressive* element into the evolutionary scheme. This led to a spectacular change of direction with the Copernican revolution, the application of the logical system then being turned to natural phenomena[40] with far-reaching consequences for its own further development. But if, in the modern world, the metaphysical focus is almost completely eclipsed, it still provides the key to any anthropological understanding of number and counting.

Notes

1. Hofstadter (1980) is a fascinating explanation and interpretation of Gödel's theorem for the non-specialist.
2. The key modern work is Bishop (1967), whose significance is explained, in non-technical language, in Calder (1979).
3. The Greeks did not accept 1 as a number, for reasons given in Bloor (1976: 98ff).
4. 0 can be used as a digit, but not as a true zero, as the Chinese numeral system illustrates. The first true zero was that of the Mayas.
5. "7" will be generally used in preference to "seven" if only to emphasize that one is concerned with 7 as a cultural universal.
6. "Traditional culture" is perhaps a pleonasm, but the choice of this phrase is deliberate.
7. This notation is adopted from Hofstadter (1980: Ch. 3) "Typographical Number Theory".
8. This is also Russell's (1920: 3) starting-point.
9. Richards (1939: 204), in relation to the Bemba, points out that they have no reason for using high numbers, in contrast to Bantu herdsmen.
10. The different versions for 91 in such diverse languages as French, Danish and Yoruba, well illustrate the point. The French "quatre-vingt-onze" is particularly intractable. At this level the most logical system is almost certainly the Japanese, where 九十一 simply means 9 × 10 + 1.
11. A proof of the theorem that all natural numbers can be expressed as the sum of at most four squares is to be found in Hardy and Wright (1945, chapter 20) "The representation of a number by two or four squares".
12. In geometry 7 is the lowest number of sides of a regular polygon which cannot be constructed with ruler and compasses.
13. This point is discussed in greater detail in Crump (1981).
14. The syntactical rules relating to numbers in the Slavonic languages are extremely complex, particularly where the final digit is 1, 2, 3 or 4. One is sceptical, however, about Gerschel's (1962: 700) claim that in proto-Indo-European 1, 2, 3, 4 were adjectives, 5 a sort of adverb, and 8, a noun. The morphology of numerals appears to be a field largely neglected by

linguists, but note Gay and Cole's study of the linguistic problem confronting the Kpelle of Liberia in dealing with modern arithmetic (1967: 31ff.).

15. Here, somewhat paradoxically, the distinctive names for the days of the week in Japanese are based on the sun, the moon, and the five basic elements of Chinese science (fire, water, wood, metal and earth).

16. The only exhaustive study of the problems which arise in teaching "modern" mathematics in a traditional society is Gay and Cole (1967)

17. For an intriguing example of the use of counting for ritual purposes, see the counting of the coins by the Zinacantan religious officials, as described in Vogt (1976: 128).

18. The counting numerals can however be used in what is essentially a predicative form, so that "There are seven oak trees" is best translated as "Nara wa nanatsu arimasu", lit. "The oak trees are seven". In this case "7" is written ' 七 つ ', the kana form つ "tsu" indicating the use of the counting form of the numeral. At the same time a Japanese, who is asked to count up to say, "7", but *without* reference to any objects to be counted, will not use the counting numerals, but the general form of cardinal numbers.

19. In the famous Scopes trial, which took place in Dayton, Tennessee in 1925, Clarence Darrow, attorney for the defendant, having pointed out to a *soi-disant* expert on the Bible — who was none other than William Jennings Bryan — that, according to the Book of Genesis, God made the sun on the *fourth* day, asked,

> They had evening and morning for four periods without the sun, do you think?

to which Bryan replied,

> I believe in creation as there told, and if I am not able to explain it, I will accept it. Then you can explain it to suit yourself (Weinberg 1957: 225).

Tennessee in 1925 was undoubtedly still a traditional society, and the position has not necessarily changed since then.

20. The root of the word "octave" of course means 8, but the 8th note is the same as the 1st, just as in Christology the last day is the same as the first.

21. The Japanese have a special word "keta" (桁) for the classes comprised between successive powers of 10. The sequence of *keta* plays a notable part in number mysticism at popular level.

22. The different exponential series are given in Needham (1959: 87).

23. There are of course many different versions of spoken Chinese, but the statement made is true of any of them.

24. The *local* or *place* value system is that in which its place in a numeral establishes the value of every digit as a multiple of a power of 10 (Cajori 1974: 47ff).

25. Cf. Crump (1978: 504). Note also how the Japanese have adopted the use

of their *kanji* numerals from 1 to 9, together with a digit for 0, to express telephone numbers according to an Arabic-type place value system. The Chinese now do the same in expressing years according to the Western calendar.

26. 52 years, expressed in days, is the lowest common multiple of 365 and 260.

27. "The twelve days of Christmas" would be an equally good alternative here.

28. See also Barnes' (1982: 16-7) interesting discussion of the place of 7, and of odd numbers generally in Kédang culture.

29. Sevenoaks is inevitably conceived of as a single word, which is how it is written. This type of naming is extremely common in China and Japan. Of the four main Japanese islands, for isntance, Kyushu (九州) means "9 regions" and Shikoku (四国), "4 districts".

30. The succession of the 7 years of plenty, followed by 7 years of famine, and the related symbolism, as recorded in Genesis xli, is well known. Note also that the words for 7 in the different Indo-European languages may be cognate to the Hebrew *sheba* (Gerschel 1962: 700).

31. Note that the two forms for "rest" and "seven" are not quite identical.

32. The semantic relationship between "rest" and "the seventh" day is first established in Genesis ii: 2, as the original Hebrew makes clear.

33. In the nineteenth century this doctrine was explicitly rejected by the sect now known as the "Seventh Day Adventists".

34. This explains also the significance of the 1001 nights: Sheherazade was saved because she succeeded in surviving one night longer than the number of nights which could be counted (Gerschel 1962: 697).

35. See Needham's (1956: 312ff.) discussion of *trigrams* and *hexagrams* (which are no more than numerals expressed according to a binary system) in Part II of the Book of Changes.

36. A bell tolling 33 times summons the religious of the orthodox churches to an hour's silent prayer before the beginning of the morning office.

37. It is these processes which allow low numbers to be "operatory" beyond the limit of their being expressible as words. Note the example given of the arithmetical skill required of the Thonga for counting hoes for bridewealth (Junod 1927: 168).

38. Schmandt-Besserat finds the origins of writing in Mesopotamia in the use of tokens, expressing numbers, for keeping accounts.

39. The point is made by Bloor (1976: 76):

> The unique compelling character of mathematics is part of the pheno-menology of that subject . . . a notable characteristic of some philo-sophies of mathematics [is] that they uncritically take over the phenomenological data and turn them into a metaphysics.

cf. Goody (1977: 122):

> Mathematics is international because its language is independent of phonetic systems; its concepts are inter-cultural because they are not phrased in a particular vernacular.

This rather over-states the case in the light of the conclusions reached in the present article.
40. To the end of his life Sir Isaac Newton also remained pre-occupied by supernatural phenomena.

References

Barnes, R. H. 1982. Number and number use in Kédang, Indonesia. *Man* (N.S.) **17**, 1-22

Bishop, E. 1967. *The Foundations of Constructive Mathematics.* New York: Mc Graw Hill Book Company

Bloor, D. 1976. *Knowledge and Social Imagery.* London: Routledge & Kegan Paul

Cajori, R. 1974. *A History of Mathematical Notations.* La Salle, Ill.: Open Court Publishing Co.

Calder, A. 1979. Constructive Mathematics. *Scientific American*, October, 134-143

Crump, S. T. 1978. Money and number: the Trojan horse of language. *Man* (N.S.) **13**, 503-18

—— 1981. Le problème linguistique du nombre. Colloque de l'Association Francaise des Anthropologues, Sèvres. To be published by Editions de Lacito.

—— 1982. The Computer and the Abacus: the Problem of Large Numbers in China and Japan. Amsterdam: VAZZOA working paper.

Flavell, J. H. 1963. *The developmental psychology of Jean Piaget.* New York: Van Nostrand, Reinhold.

Gay, J. and Cole, M. 1967. *The New Mathematics in an Old Culture.* New York: Holt, Rinehart and Winston.

Gerschel, L. 1962. La conquête du nombre: des modalités du compte aux structures de la pensée. *Annales E.S.C.* **17**(4), 691-714.

Goody, J. R. 1977. The Domestication of the Savage Mind. Cambridge University Press.

Hallpike, C. R. 1979. *The Foundations of Primitive Thought.* Oxford: The Clarendon Press

Hardy, G. H. and Wright, E. M. 1945. *Pure Mathematics.* Oxford: University Press.

Hickerson, N. P. 1980. *Linguistic Anthropology.* New York: Holt, Rinehart and Winston

Hofstadter, D. R. 1980. *Gödel, Escher, Bach.* New York: Vintage Books.

Junod, H. A. 1927. *The Life of a South African Tribe.* London.

Kaufman, E. L., Lord, M. W., Reese, T. W. & Volkmann, J. 1949. The discrimination of visual number. *American Journal of Psychology* **62**, 498-525.

Keynes, J. M. 1936. *The General Theory of Employment, Interest and Money.* London: Macmillan.

Miller, G. A. 1956. The magical number seven, plus or minus two: some limits on our capacity for processing information. *Psychological Review* **63**, 81-97.

Needham, J. 1956. *Science and Civilization in China.* Vol. 2. *History of Scientific Thought.* Cambridge: University Press.

———— 1959. *Science and Civilization in China.* Vol. 3. *Mathematics and Astronomy.* Cambridge: University Press.

Piaget, J. 1952. *The Child's Conception of Number.* London: Routledge & Kegan Paul.

Richards, A. I. 1939. *Land, Labour and Diet in Northern Rhodesia.* Oxford: University Press.

Russell, B. 1920. *An Introduction to Mathematical Philosophy.* London: George Allen & Unwin.

Russell, B. & Whitehead, A. N. 1913. *Principia Mathematica* (3 Vols). Cambridge: University Press.

Schmandt-Besserat, D. 1979. The earliest precursor of writing. *Scientific American,* June, 38-47.

Vogt, E. Z. 1976. *Tortillas for the Gods.* Cambridge, Mass.: Harvard University Press.

Weinberg, A. 1957. *Attorney for the Damned.* New York: Simon & Schuster.

NOTES ON CONTRIBUTORS

Edwin ARDENER
  Born 1927, Great Britain. University Lecturer in Social Anthropology, Fellow of St John's College, Oxford. Read Anthropology, University of London; Oppenheimer Student, University of Oxford (B.A. Lond., M.A.). Malinowski Lecturer 1971. Chairman, Oxford University Institute of Social Anthropology 1977-82. Chairman, Association of Social Anthropologists 1981-present. Ethnographic areas: West Africa, European minorities. Publications in various theoretical and applied fields.

R. H. BARNES
  Born 1944, USA. Lecturer in Social Anthropology, University of Oxford. Educated Reed College (B.A. 1966), University of Oxford (Dip. Soc. Anth. 1967; B. Litt. 1969; D. Phil. 1972). Field research in Eastern Indonesia (Kédang, Lembata). Many publications on alliance theory, collective representations, personal naming systems and numerology.

Malcolm Kenneth CHAPMAN
  Born 1951, Bradford, England. Studied at New College, Oxford (M.A. (Human Sciences); Dip. Soc. Anth. 1975; B. Litt. Soc. Anth. 1978). Research worker, Institute of Social Anthropology, Oxford, 1979-80. Currently Junior Research Fellow, Balliol College, Oxford. Fieldwork in Scotland and Brittany. Editor of the *Journal of the Anthropological Society of Oxford* 1976-78. Author of *The Gaelic Vision in Scottish Culture* 1978.

Malcolm Ronald CRICK
  Born 1948, England. Lecturer in School of Social Sciences, Deakin University, Australia. Educated University of Sussex (B.A. Hons Soc. Anth. 1969), Oxford University (Dip. Soc. Anth. 1970;

D. Phil. Soc. Anth. 1974). Author of *Explorations in Language and Meaning. Towards a Semantic Anthropology* 1976.

Thomas CRUMP

Born 1929, London, England. Senior Lecturer in Anthropology in the University of Amsterdam. Educated Trinity College, Cambridge (M.A. 1956), University of Michigan Law School (Ll. M. 1954) and University College, London (Ph. D. 1976). Called to the bar (England) 1956, in practice in London 1958-66. Teaching in Holland since 1972.

Author of numerous books and papers in law and anthropology, among which see: *The Law for Everyman* 1963; *Man and his Kind* 1973 and *The Phenomenon of Money* 1981.

Stephen F. GUDEMAN

Born 1939, USA. Professor of Anthropology, University of Minnesota, Minneapolis, Minnesota, USA. Educated at Harvard (A.B. Social Relations 1961; M.B.A. 1965), Cambridge (M.A. Soc. Anth. 1963; Ph.D. 1970). Taught at University of Minnesota 1969-present, Carleton College 1981. Institute for Advanced Study, Princeton, New Jersey 1978-79. Author of various articles on kinship, ritual kinship and economics. See also *Relationships, Residence and the Individual* 1976; *The Demise of a Rural Economy* 1978.

Kirsten HASTRUP

Born 1948, Denmark. Lecturer in social anthropology, Aarhus University, Denmark. Educated at University of Copenhagen (B.A. Anth. 1970; Mag. Scient. Soc. Anth. 1973), and Oxford University (D.Phil. Soc. Anth. 1980). Taught at University of Copenhagen 1970-1974, and at Aarhus University since 1976. Author of a number of papers on post-structuralist anthropology, on the (historical) anthropology of medieval Iceland, and of the following books: *Culture and history in Medieval Iceland. An anthropological analysis of structure and change* (in press); (with Jan Ovesen) *Etnografisk Grundbog* 1980; (with others) *Den ny Antropologi* 1975.

Mark HOBART

Born 1946, England. Lecturer in Anthropology with reference to South East Asia, at the School of Oriental and African Studies, University of London. Educated Trinity College, Cambridge (B.A. Soc. Anth. 1967); S.O.A.S. (Ph.D. Anthropology 1979). Taught at University of Singapore 1967-68, at Universitas Udayana,

Indonesia 1970-72; S.O.A.S. 1972-present. Author of various articles on political and symbolic anthropology including: "Orators and Patrons: Two Types of Political Leader in Balinese Village Society" in M. Bloch (ed.) *Political Language and Oratory in Traditional Society*; "The Path of the Soul: The Legitimacy of Nature in Balinese Conceptions of Space" and "Padi, Puns and the Attribution of Responsibility" both in G. Milner (ed.) *Natural Symbols in South East Asia* S.O.A.S. Press 1978.

Judith Temkin IRVINE
Born 1945, USA. Associate Professor of Anthropology at Brandeis University. Educated Harvard University (Radcliffe College) (B.A. 1966); Ecole Pratique des Hautes Etudes; University of Pennsylvania (Ph.D. Anth. 1973). Faculty positions at Brandeis University 1972-present. University of Texas-Austin 1979. Australian National University, Research Fellow 1981, 1982. Author of various papers in linguistic anthropology, including: "Formality and informality in communicative events", *American Anthropologist* 81 (1979); "How not to ask a favor in Wolof", *Papers in Linguistics* 13 (1980); "When is genealogy history? Wolof genealogies in comparative perspective", *American Ethnologist* 5 (1978).

Martha B. KENDALL
Born 1943, Virginia USA. Associate Professor of Anthropology, Indiana University. Educated College of William and Mary (B.A. 1965) and Indiana University (M.A. 1970; Ph.D. 1972). Taught as Vassar College 1971-77 and Indiana University 1977-present.
Author of various books and papers in linguistic anthropology and linguistics, among which see *Coyote Stories V.II* 1980; *Soninke Grammar* 1980; and *Soninke Culture and Communication Handbook* 1980. Also co-editor of the journal *Anthropological Linguistics*.

Kay MILTON
Born 1951, London, England. Lecturer in social anthropology at the Queen's University of Belfast since 1974. Educated Durham University (B.A. Anthropology 1972) and the Queen's University of Belfast (Ph.D. Soc. Anth. 1981).
Author of several articles including: "Male Bias in Anthropology" *Man* (1979); "On the inference of folk models: discussion and demonstration", in Holy, L. and Stuchlik, M. (eds) *The Structure of Folk Models* (1981) ASA Monograph 20.

David John PARKIN
Born 1940, England. Professor of Anthropology School of Oriental and African Studies, University of London. Educated London University (B.A. 1962; Ph.D. 1965). Research in Kenya and Uganda. Author of *Neighbours and Nationals in an African City Ward* 1969; *Palms, Wine and Witnesses* 1972; *Town and Country in Central and Eastern Africa* (ed.) 1975; *The Cultural Definition of Political Response* 1978; and numerous papers, latterly on cross-cultural semantics and language use.

Mischa PENN
Born 1934. Currently Associate Professor at the University of Minnesota. Principal interests are problems of explanation in anthropology, with specific emphasis upon the nature and role of models. Papers include "The mere notion of a model" 1980; "Robert Koch and two visions of micro-biology" 1978; and others.

Anne SALMOND
Born 1945, New Zealand. Senior Lecturer in Anthropology at the University of Auckland. Educated University of Auckland (M.A. 1968), University of Pennsylvania (Ph.D. 1972). Author of papers on sociolinguistics and semantics, and books on Maori ethnography, among which see *Hui : A Study of Maori Ceremonial Gatherings* 1975, *Amiria : The Life Story of a Maori Woman* 1976 and *Eruera : The Teachings of a Maori Elder* 1980.

Basil SANSOM
Born 1938, South Africa. Professor of Anthropology (Urban Studies) in the University of Western Australia. Educated Johannesburg University of the Witwatersrand (B.A. 1959; B.A. Hons. 1960); Victoria University of Manchester (Ph.D. 1970). Taught at Rhodes University Grahamstown 1962; Manchester, 1963-1974; U.W.A. 1977-present. Research Fellow Australian Institute of Aboriginal Studies 1974-1977. Author of essays on social change either in Africa or Australia and a book on Australian Aborigines: *The Camp at Wallaby Cross* 1981.

Elizabeth TONKIN
Born 1934, England. Studied at Oxford University (B.A. 1955; M.A. 1961; D.Phil. 1971). Home Civil Service 1955-1958; Education Officer (Kenya) 1958-1963; Lecturer in English, Ahmadu Bello University, Nigeria, 1963-1966; Lecturer in Social

Anthropology, Centre of West African Studies, Birmingham University, 1970; Senior Lecturer, 1981. Author of Some Coastal Pidgins of West Africa", in E. Ardener (ed.) *Social Anthropology and Language* (1971) ASA Monograph **10**; "Model and Ideology: Dimensions of Being Civilized in Liberia" in L. Holy and M. Stuchlik (eds) *The Structure of Folk Models* (1981) ASA Monograph **20**; and other articles.

Drid WILLIAMS
Born 1928, Baker, Oregon, USA. Completed Diploma, B.Litt. and Doctoral degrees at Oxford University, June 1976. Member of St Hugh's College. Area specialization: human movement studies. Originator of theory of movement analysis, "semasiology". Presently director of a graduate program of the Anthropology of Human Movement at New York University and Faculty Editor for the *Journal for the Anthropological Study of Human Movement (JASHM)* at New York University. Author of numerous articles on liturgy, manual counting systems, the dance, etc., among which see: "The Arms and Hands, With Special Reference to an Anglo-Saxon Sign System". *Semiotica* **21** (1/2) (1977) and "Introductory Essay" in special issue of *JASHM* 1(4), entitled "On Semasiology". Also Associate Editor for *Human Movement Sciences*, Free University, Amsterdam.

Roy Geoffrey WILLIS
Born 1927, London, England. Research Fellow in Social Anthropology and African Studies, Edinburgh University. (Educated Oxford University Dip. Soc. Anth. 1961; B. Litt., 1962; D. Phil., 1966). Field research in Ufipa, Tanzania, 1962-6 and 1966. Has taught at University College London and Edinburgh University. Author of *Man and Beast*, 1974; *There was a Certain Man: spoken art of the Fipa* 1978; *A State in the Making* 1981; and a number of papers.

AUTHOR INDEX

SUBJECT INDEX